MW00466168

# Cuban-Jewish Journeys

# Cuban-Jewish Journeys

## Searching for Identity, Home, and History in Miami

Caroline Bettinger-López

With a Foreword by Ruth Behar

The University of Tennessee Press / Knoxville

Copyright © 2000 by The University of Tennessee Press,
Knoxville, Tennessee.
All Rights Reserved.
Manufactured in the United States of America.

First Edition.

The paper used in this book meets the minimum
requirements of ANSI/NISO Z39.48-1992 (R 1997)
(Permanence of Paper). The binding materials have been
chosen for strength and durability.

Library of Congress Cataloging-in-Publication Data

Bettinger-López, Caroline.
Cuban-Jewish journeys : searching for identity, home, and
history in Miami / Caroline Bettinger-López; foreword
by Ruth Behar.— 1st ed.
        p. cm.
Includes bibliographical references and index.
ISBN 1-57233-097-X (cl.: alk. paper)
ISBN 1-57233-098-8 (pbk.: alk. paper)
1. Jews—Florida—Miami—History—20th century.
2. Jews, Cuban—Florida—Miami—History—20th
century. 3. Miami (Fla.)—Ethnic relations. 4. Jews—
Cuba—Migrations. I. Title.
F319.M6 B48 2000
975.9'38100492407291—dc21

00-008613

In memory of
Sharon Stephens
and Lisa Strongson
and for
my Great-Uncle Aaron

# Contents

## Part I.
## The Past in the Present: A History of the Cuban-Jewish Community in Miami

## Part II. Explorations

# Illustrations

## Figures

## Maps

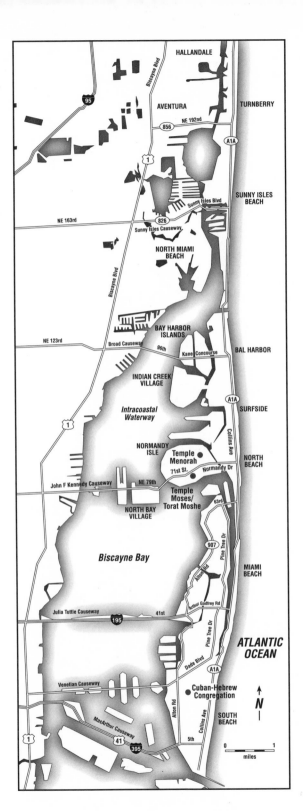

*The Beaches Today.*

ix

*South Beach Today.*

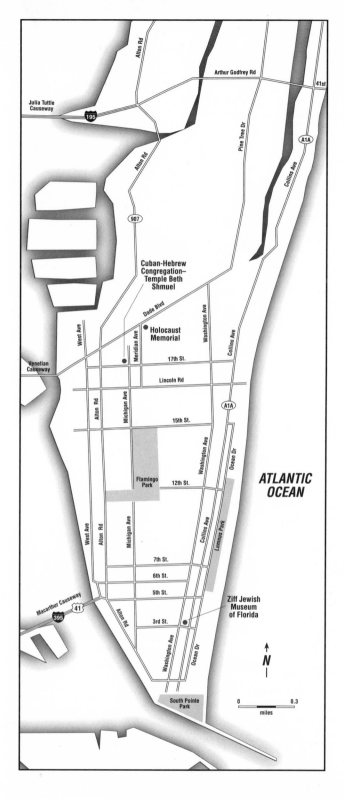

# Foreword

## Ruth Behar

First things first: Reader, I want you to know that this is the first time that I have written a foreword for a book by one of my students. I'm trying not to feel more than just a little old. I'm also trying not to feel more than just a little jealous. I'm a Jewish-Cuban professor of anthropology, and it's about time I wrote my own book about Jewish Cubans. But you know what? My book will get written. And I couldn't have written this book. So I sure am glad that Caroline Bettinger-López did.

It's not often that a student publishes a book that had its humble origins in a senior thesis written for an undergraduate degree. I was encouraged to publish my own senior thesis by my advisor when I was a student, but I didn't take his encouragement seriously. My thesis ended up languishing on a shelf, and now I no longer have the energy or desire to return to subjects that so passionately interested me twenty years ago. I wasn't sure if Carrie would take me up on my suggestion that she publish her thesis, but I hoped she would. Her work was so highly esteemed at the University of Michigan that it won her both Highest Honors in Anthropology and the Virginia Voss Memorial Writing Award given by the Honors Program. However, Carrie never rests on her laurels, and she put another two years of reflection and revision into this book before letting it go.

Her book proves that original, engaged, and rigorous research can be accomplished by young fresh-off-the-boat anthropologists, such as Carrie, who bring fresh eyes, caring eyes, and critical eyes to realities that are close to home and yet foreign. During the year that she researched and wrote the first draft of this book, she came to see me every week during my office hours to talk about her work as it emerged. The level of Carrie's dedication to her research was such that she would go jogging to the beat of her conversations with Jewish Cubans, tapes of which she played on her Walkman. The words and stories of her informants, myself included, got into Carrie's head.

She had to write this book so she could jog to music again.

✽

A few months ago my mother's cousin in Miami Beach sent an email message to the "realcubans," which is the unique internet name of my mother and father in New

York. The subject of the message was "How can you tell if you're a Latin Jew?" Among the nineteen answers included in the list were: "You have a relative named Moises (Moishe)"; "You were raised on Goya and Manischewitz products"; and "You dance merengue and salsa at Bar Mitzvahs."

Although lighthearted, this summary accurately portrays the distinct cultural mixing, or *mestizaje*, that is a way of life for Jews of Latin American origin currently living in the United States. "Latin Jews," if Cuban, buy Goya brand black beans and guava paste for everyday feasts, but for Passover we turn to Manischewitz for our matzo. And yes, in our families there's always a relative named after the beloved Moses of our ten commandments, but the name is Latinized to Moises, as happens with the patriarch Abraham, who in the Latin Jewish milieu becomes Alberto. A Bar Mitzvah without merengue and salsa dancing is inconceivable. And among Jewish Cubans, there is always a conga line. Indeed, for my son Gabriel's Bar Mitzvah this past summer in Ann Arbor, my parents schlepped four *faroles* from New York. These tall lantern poles decorated with streamers are carried by those leading the conga line, following a tradition that stems from Afrocuban carnivals.

Until recently, to say you were both Jewish and "Latin" in this country produced a shock effect. But now, at the dawn of the new century, multiculturalism and diversity rather than the "melting pot" are being recognized as the key building blocks of American society. A hybrid identity like "Latin Jew" should no longer need to be explained and justified at every turn. And yet this unexpected fusion of identities continues to seem exotic.

How is it possible, ask the uninitiated, for a group of "Jewish people" to be fluent Spanish-speakers and move their hips like natives of those islands and chaotic cities south of the border? Why do a group of "Latin people" claim so fierce a connection to Jewish traditions? More frequently, the uninitiated don't even realize that there are such hybrid people in their midst. "Latin Jews" are often an invisible community who blend, depending on the context, into either the larger Jewish or Latino community. Carrie herself admits that for her this community was "uncharted territory." She wonders how she "could grow up Jewish in South Miami and not know about a community numbering ten to fifteen thousand centered in Miami Beach?" And she concludes, "In truth, I had never considered the possibility of Cubans belonging to my ethno-religious group."

Categories of identity in the United States are reduced to little boxes on the census that hardly allow for such an unexpected convergence of cultures and allegiances. The Jew of popular American representations is the neurotic post-Yiddish New Yorker made popular in the novels of Philip Roth and the films of Woody Allen. The Latino of popular American representations is to be found in the figures of Ricky Ricardo and Ricky Martin. The image of the Jewish-American woman swings between the feminist Gloria Steinem and the ultra-Orthodox Hassidic mother of eight in Brooklyn. The image of the Latina swings between the Brazilian Carmen Miranda, tropical fruits arranged voluptuously on her head, and the devotee of the Virgen María who makes pilgrimages to the shrine of the Blessed Mother on bleeding knees.

"Latin Jews," by conforming neither to the typical image of the Jew nor the typical image of the Latina and the Latino, scramble, confuse, challenge, and overturn these stereotypical representations. They also embody a complex and disturbing history surrounding ideas of race and immigration in the United States. The reason that Jews found their way to Latin America and the Caribbean, particularly in the inter-war years, was subtle anti-Semitic quotas limiting their entrance to this country. Only later, as natives of the other America across the border, did they find their way to this side.

No longer is it unusual to find Jews from Venezuela, Chile, Argentina, Mexico, Puerto Rico, and Cuba living in this country who are committed to maintaining both their Latinness and their Jewishness in equal parts. It is a Jewish Latino by the name of Don Francisco who hosts the popular Spanish-language program "Sábado Gigante" on Saturday nights, but on Saturday mornings he can often be spotted attending services at his synagogue in Miami Beach. In turn, writers like Marjorie Agosín, a Chilean Jew, Aurora Levins-Morales, a Puerto Rican Jew, and Ilan Stavans, a Mexican Jew, are among the key voices helping to expand public discourse in the United States to make it more inclusive of the multiculturalism embedded both in Latina/Latino and Jewish identities and diasporas.

*

But there is no question that, among the wide range of "Latin Jews" in this country, Jewish Cubans, or "Jewbans," as this community sometimes refers to itself, attract most of the touristic and scholarly attention, especially among Jewish-American observers. Carrie is no exception to this rule. She is drawn, as others are, to these Jews who came to the United States from Cuba because they personify a crossroads of exile positions, as members of both the Jewish diaspora and the Cuban diaspora. Not surprisingly, the Jewish sense of exile is a concept that has come to strongly mark the Cuban sense of exile. "Next Year in Havana" is a toast among Cuban immigrants in Miami, and the connection to the Jewish diaspora has grown more apt as Fidel Castro and his regime linger on and the possibility of return to Cuba, for all Cubans living outside the island, is continually postponed. For Jewish Cubans, their exilic consciousness echoes with resonances of the Torah, memory, and lived experience.

Caught, like their Cubans compatriots, in the crucible of the Cuban revolution of 1959 which brought Fidel Castro to power, Jewish Cubans had to make the excruciating decision between staying in Cuba and living under socialism, or abandoning forever what to many had become their tropical promised land and emigrating to the United States to remake their families and community within the great power to the north, which years earlier had closed its doors to them. Doubly displaced, from Europe to Cuba, and from Cuba to the United States, Jewish Cubans faced not only the economic challenge of rebuilding their livelihood but the cultural challenge of weaving a coherent identity out of a bicultural and often tricultural heritage that includes an Ashkenazi background in Yiddish or a Sephardic background in Ladino. Indeed, in the widely circulating email about "How can you tell if you're a Latin Jew," the first item is "You are either a 'Polaco' or a 'Turco,'" a reference to the two terms that were used in Cuba to describe the Jews: those from Eastern Europe were "Polacks" and those from Turkey and the Mediterranean were "Turks." The list is obviously the creation of a "Polaco," and captures especially well the linguistic inventiveness of people caught between Yiddish and Spanish: "You say crazy things like 'Me cago en el shmendrik ese'" (literally: *I shit on that dumb fool*) and "You say things like 'Pu, Pu, Pu,' and 'toca madera'" (the Yiddish and Spanish ways of saying *knock on wood*).

The Jewish community in Cuba was a young community, barely thirty-five to fifty years old, when Fidel Castro took Havana. The majority of the Jews arrived after the passage of the 1924 Immigration and Nationality Act that limited their access to the United States, and it was they and their Cuban-born offspring, most just beginning to raise families of their own, who confronted the difficult decision of whether to stay or leave after the revolution. Jews on the island had risen from peddlers to merchants while maintaining their identity through a closed social system of Jewish schools and institutions. It was a community made up primarily of people who were small shopowners, both in Old Havana and in scattered towns and villages around the island. That is why you can also tell if you're a "Latin Jew" if "Your parents or grandparents had a tienda (a store)" and "You have someone in your immediate family that sells shmates (rags)."

By the eve of the revolution, the Jews of Cuba had attained prosperity and a sense of security, which was reflected in the construction in the 1950s of two prominent synagogues, El Patronato and El Centro Hebreo Sefardí, in the elegant Vedado neighborhood of Havana. Little did the Jews of Cuba imagine that these synagogues would become monuments to their flight from the island just a few short years later. After the revolution, properties and businesses were nationalized by the state and the community disbanded, with the Jews of Cuba forming part of the general exodus of the white upper and middle classes to the United States. The community of the pre-revolutionary island, numbering about fifteen thousand, froze prematurely in time and had to remake itself in the diaspora. Left behind were those few Jews who chose to form part of the revolutionary project, or who, through intermarriage and acculturation, entered into the creation of the new Cuban national consciousness, where Cubans were Cubans above all else.

✳

With only a handful of intellectuals, writers, and artists in the community who might have articulated a coherent vision of Jewish Cuban identity, it fell to the social circles and synagogues that took form in the aftermath of exile in Miami to create that vision. Here exactly is where Carrie's book makes a hugely important and unique contribution. With care and dedication, Carrie documents the historical process by which Jewish Cubans in Miami created the social institutions they needed in order to be able to maintain the complexity of their identity and reproduce the tightly knit community of the island.

Rebuffed upon arrival by the Jewish-American community that just barely lent a helping hand, the Jewish Cubans marked their presence in Miami with characteristic Cuban audacity. They established two of their own synagogues, the Cuban-Hebrew Congregation and Temple Moses, as well as a social circle at Temple Menorah, following the island model of keeping separate Ashkenazi and Sephardic houses of worship. The synagogues offered Jewish education, parties, beauty pageants, religious services, and burial societies. In their newsletters and bulletins, they created a forum for the community to describe itself to itself. And of greatest importance, they kept alive the network of social bonds and collective memory formed in Cuba between the 1920s and the 1950s, as well as the nostalgia people felt for their all-too-brief but happy existence on the island.

As Carrie daringly suggests, the particular idea of the "new Jewban" that took root in Miami was based on the ideals and aspirations of those Jewish Cubans who were part of the first wave of immigration to the United States. It has been difficult for the original Jewish Cuban community in Miami to incorporate more recent Jewish Cuban immigrants, who have arrived since the 1970s, with the Mariel boatlift of 1980, or more recently in the 1990s. The newest immigrants, whose voices are heard in print for the first time in Carrie's book, bring a wholly different set of life experiences, forged from having lived through the turbulent economic and political changes brought about by the Cuban revolution. These "other Cuban Jews," as Carrie notes, do not share the same longstanding bonds of friendship and business partnership of the original "Jewbans." They have not automatically felt at home in the social circles and synagogues built by "Jewbans," who as a community are now more prosperous than they were in Cuba.

The new Jewish Cuban immigrants, although still few in number, form a counterpoint and quiet challenge to the self-concept of the original Jewish Cuban immigrants. While the newer immigrants are just beginning to find their way in the United States, the older immigrants have come to feel quite settled in this country, and increasingly their children, grandchildren, and great-grandchildren are becoming more grounded in their American identity. To be sure, the most dramatic counterpoint in the Jewish Cuban community is between the generations, between those who came of age in Cuba and those who came of age in the United States and are now raising their own families here.

Can the idea of "Jubanidad" stretch far enough to include the growing diversity in the community? Is it perhaps the tension of such a stretch that is leading to the elaboration of a more inclusive identity, like "Latin Jew," that can accommodate a broader range of immigrant experiences and translations of self in the United States? Indeed, as English becomes the dominant language among Jewish Cubans and the ideal of returning to Cuba is postponed ever farther into the indefinite future, for how much longer will there be a community that can accurately be called Jewish Cuban?

The possibility that the Jewish Cuban community in Miami will one day cease to exist is a scenario pondered by Carrie and her informants. And yet I think we need to be careful not to forecast a doomsday prophecy too soon. It is a well-known fact that anthropologists always arrive on the scene just when communities are on the verge of transforming themselves and appearing to disappear. The ethnographies we write are often cast as works of salvage, efforts to inscribe what won't be around much longer, but which the anthropologist, by a stroke of good fortune, got to see and record for posterity.

Fortunately, Carrie keeps resisting the temptation to write salvage ethnography by placing her reflections on her encounters and interactions with Jewish Cubans at the center of her account. Carrie's fieldwork stories capture the vitality of present-day contradictions and the definitions of self that emerge as Jewish Cubans act out their identity, both when they think they're not being watched and when they're trying to find ways to reach out to their young, beautiful, and earnest anthropologist. Telling some of those fieldwork stories makes Carrie uncomfortable. This happens most dramatically when she recounts how some highly esteemed informants showed their appreciation for her by attempting to match her up with their son. But it is precisely through Carrie's discomfort with how she is being engendered by Jewish Cubans that we gain the most vivid sense of the particular idiosyncrasies of identity and history that inform how Jewish Cubans perceive the roles of women and men in the world.

Similarly, in what I think is a stunning moment of revelation, the community comes alive before our eyes and jumps out of the pages of her book when Carrie expresses her disappointment with the bad manners of her Jewish-Cuban natives. At the installation of their own Isaac Zelcer to the presidency of the Greater Miami Jewish Federation, what do they do but walk out of the event before it has barely begun, once there is nothing more on the agenda celebrating them and their community. What an act of supreme self-centeredness, right? I think to myself, *Ay, my people, my people!* And yet I cannot blame them. I too would have walked out at the first opportunity and gone in search of a café cubano. Let's not forget: We Jubans didn't come all the way from Cuba to listen to long speeches.

✼

And so it is that Carrie returns home to Miami to carry out fieldwork among the Jewish Cubans and discovers a home she didn't know was there in the city she grew up in. I, in turn, reading her book now as it goes to press, see the way in which anthropology comes home for me as I alternately serve as Carrie's professor and native informant, an object of anthropological interest and an intellectual guide on her journey to understand "my people."

Teachers lose their ability to teach when their students only take and do not return the gift of their learning. I first got to know Carrie when she was a student in my class on "Cuba and Its Diaspora," a course I teach regularly at the University of Michigan. She is the star graduate of that class, and with the publication of this book her name will now be included in the syllabus for my course.

I taught Carrie something of what I know about cultural anthropology and something of what I know about Jewish Cubans. In this book she returns the gift of her learning and multiplies it a hundredfold.

Ann Arbor<br>December 1999

# Preface

"Cuba was a country with a soul," Betty Heisler-Samuels told me. It was with this in mind that I set out to discover how the Cuban-Jewish community recaptured this soul in Miami. Initially I contacted the Cuban-Hebrew Congregation, the Sephardic Congregation of Florida—Torat Moshe, and several social service agencies dealing with issues of immigration, Cuban affairs, and Jewish affairs. From 1996 through 1997, and again in 1999, I researched Miami's Cuban-Jewish community—centered in Miami Beach—by attending synagogue services and community functions, and by conducting family and individual interviews. Through these contacts, I met many people who discussed with me their experiences as "diasporics"—people who have experienced one or more migrations in their lifetimes.

What temporal, spatial, and physical factors allow today's Cuban-Jewish community in Miami to remain so unique? How do the different generations (in terms of both age and wave of migration) represented within this community understand the notion of homeland, as well as their own identities? What factors influence this understanding? How does memory function for individuals, families, and the community at large? How are gender roles defined in the Cuban-Jewish community, and what relationship do these have to traditional Cuban and Jewish gender roles? What is the relationship between Cuban Sephardim and Ashkenazim? These were some of the questions I posed time and again, both to myself and to my interlocutors.

An *interlocutor* is a person taking part in a conversation or dialogue. I use this term rather than *interviewee* to emphasize the two-way exchange between myself and those whom I interviewed as part of my research. I see these interviews as conversations, not as "question-and-answer sessions" based on checklists or other predetermined formats.

In this book I have recounted individual stories that shed light on these issues. My work is neither a comprehensive history nor an objective demographic study. While it incorporates elements of these genres, it focuses primarily on the subjective and the particular—on the ways in which my interlocutors understand their own positions in their families, communities, city, nation, and world. Additionally, this book depicts my own position in my research—as an anthropology student, a feminist, and a Miamian fascinated by my own (non-Cuban) Jewish roots and the diasporic history of my city. This book thus is my own subjective exploration, influenced by my own position. I share ethnographic stories and examine issues that interest me personally and intellectually. Many of these issues have not been considered by other researchers or community members studying the Cuban-Jewish community's history.

I have chosen to present snapshots in time: family portraits and ethnographic moments which capture, for me, Cuban-Jewish experience(s). My writing merges ethnography, oral history, and autobiographical narrative to create an open and flexible forum for dialogue. In doing this, I have come to understand better the fluid nature of history and identity, whether focused along national, religious, gender, or ethnic lines.

The primary research for this book was conducted in 1996 and 1997 for my senior thesis in anthropology at the University of Michigan. Unless otherwise noted, the interviews, events, and discussions presented in these chapters take place during this period.

I received a sincere welcome from most people I encountered in the Cuban-Jewish community, particularly after I got to know a few prominent community members who introduced me to others. My research strategy was to interview a broad range of people from this community and its surrounding environment: young and old; women and men; Sephardic and Ashkenazic; rich and poor; American-born, Cuban-born, Eastern European-born, Mediterranean-born; active community members and those who do not participate in community functions; and people arriving as émigrés in the United States at various times since 1959.

Overall, I interviewed approximately fifty people from the Cuban-Jewish community and dozens of people outside it. Most of our conversations took place in my interlocutors' homes and offices and in the Cuban synagogues in Miami Beach. These conversations ranged in duration from brief encounters to extended discussions and repeat visits lasting several hours each. I recorded most of my interviews on audiotape and have included the parts which I think best reflect the characters of my interlocutors.

Generally, the ages of my interlocutors ranged from late teens to late sixties. I was unable to interview as many European- and Asian-born elders as I would have liked, due mostly to language barriers between us and health problems they were experiencing as eighty- and ninety-year-olds. Yet I was able to converse with some community members of this older generation who provided fascinating insights into the issues of diaspora and homeland.

It was also difficult to connect with Cuban-Jews who did not attend the "Cuban" synagogues and participate in the community, since synagogue office workers and members of boards of directors put me in contact with those whom they felt best represented the community—generally the most active community members. Yet I was able to locate several people who were disconnected from the community. Their feedback proved invaluable in helping me understand issues of community identity and collective memory.

Another obstacle I encountered related to gender roles. Many times, a couple or family preferred to be interviewed together; but, once we began, the eldest man would dominate the conversation. In several of these cases, I would direct a question to the eldest woman, and her husband would answer it. Time and again, the women would go off to other rooms and let their husbands finish the interviews. When I beckoned them to return, they responded that their husbands knew more about the questions I was asking than they did. Similar gender roles often applied to children, with male children having more voice than their sisters and, sometimes, more than their mothers. Some of my most illuminating interviews with women took place in the absence of their husbands and children.

Some of my most interesting interviews were with young Cuban-Jews my age. Although at times we seemed to be worlds apart, many of us shared experiences of growing up Jewish in Miami which allowed us to establish a common ground. This was particularly important for me personally, for it stimulated me to expand my own sense of Jewish identity and worldview.

I think my "Jewishness" gave me access to the Cuban-Jewish community that a Gentile might not have had. My interlocutors expressed a sentiment I have heard my entire life: they trusted me to enter their lives primarily because I was a Jew. Indeed, our Jewish heritage, among other things, allowed us to relate to each other on many levels, even if there were points on which we disagreed. On the flip side of this was my marital engagement to a Catholic American of Irish–Puerto Rican heritage. I intentionally emphasized Sean's Latino heritage when asked about my personal life, so as to establish another point of connection with my interlocutors. Sometimes this approach helped me build rapport, but often his Latino heritage was set aside as I answered uncomfortable questions about our interreligious union. In many ways, I welcomed these role reversals, in which my interlocutors became the anthropologists and I the subject of inquiry. This allowed me to develop a more empathic approach to fieldwork and to understand better my own subjectivity in my research.

Since one of my goals is to reveal the subjective nature of ethnography, in many cases I contextualize my interviews by placing myself and the setting within the text. Whenever reasonable, I retain entire quotations rather than presenting fragments of discussions, to provide richer portraits of individuals and families. When I quote material from oral interviews, I simply list the person's name with the quotation. When I quote material from published sources, I use a citation format commonly employed in the natural and social sciences (e.g., Bettinger-López 2000: 10). When I quote material from personal correspondences, I use a similar citation format (e.g. [person's name] to Caroline Bettinger-López, [date]).

Many of my interviews took place in English, my native language, but the second (sometimes third or fourth) language of the majority of my interlocutors. Thus, while I could feel linguistically secure, my interlocutors often could not. Throughout, I include the original transcripts of our conversations, correcting only major grammatical and spelling errors, in order to show the complications involved in reaching a common understanding in a language not equally accessible to all participants. Putting original transcripts in the text also leaves them open to multiple interpretations.

Any texts and conversations in Spanish are included in their original forms, along with translations. This serves to show when and how I used Spanish, how I translated it, and when synagogues and community members used Spanish in their publications rather than English, Hebrew, or, for the *Ashkenazim* (Jews with Eastern European heritage), Yiddish.

I gave my interlocutors the choice of having a pseudonym used in place of their real names. About half of those quoted in this book requested this option; the other half chose to use their real names, so as to leave a record of their family histories for future generations. Those interviewed individually generally preferred that I use their real names, and those interviewed within a family setting often preferred to be identified by pseudonyms. A list of real names and pseudonyms can be found in the Acknowledgments section.

Generally I refer to my interlocutors by their first names, to indicate the informal nature of most of my interviews and to personalize my interlocutors' stories. In chapters 1, 2, and 4, where the tone is more formal and detached, I use their last names.

The history I present in this book follows the histories narrated to me in interviews and published in community newsletters and bulletins as *historias,* brief community histories. It is thus a history of memory, recounting the events which stand out most vividly in community members' minds. It is also an institutional and cultural history of what is not remembered, either by choice or simply through forgetfulness. This history is necessarily partial and incomplete. While it is *a* history, it is not—nor could it ever be—*the* history of Miami's Cuban-Jewish community. I doubt that any historical text can fully capture a community's past.

Even so, certain historical events are remembered in a common way, resulting in a "collective memory" that has been passed down through the community and that often translates into a collective understanding of Cuban-Jewish history. As I spoke with community members, different people repeatedly told "the story of the Cuban-Jews," using similar chronologies to highlight events which shaped the community's development. In my history, I reconstruct the ways in which they told their stories by taking the reader on a journey that jumps back and forth through time and among Cuba, Russia, Turkey, New York, Poland, and Miami. I find this to be the best way to tell the history I have learned.

While following this format, I have attempted to fill gaps in the community's "collective memory" with outside interviews and research, in order to avoid the trap of writing a panegyric. The product is a history specific to those who remember it, though interpreted by myself.

In chapters 1 and 2, I consider the wide range of terminology Miami's Cuban-Jewish community has used, orally and textually, to define itself since its beginnings four decades ago. This terminology includes *Jewish Cubans, Jewish-Cubans, Cuban Jews, Cuban-Jews, Jew-Bans, Jewbans,* and *Jubans.* Throughout the book, I attempt to use the term most appropriate for the context in which I am writing. I use the term *Jewish Cubans* (usually unhyphenated) to refer to the Jews who, on the basis of their Cuban identity, arrived in Miami from Cuba in the 1960s. I use *Cuban Jews* to describe the emphasis placed on their foreign nationality by the established American Jewish community in Miami Beach. *Cuban-Jews* I use to describe the hyphenated identity that emerged as their *cubanidad* and Jewishness became linked in Miami. Finally, I use *Jew-Bans, Jewbans,* and *Jubans* to reflect the evolving identities and growing rootedness of Cuban-Jews in their new home.

Because of the confusion inherent in switching among so many designations, I primarily use *Cuban-Jews,* since this was the term most widely employed by those with whom I spoke. Many also used the term *Cuban Jews* interchangeably with *Jewish Cubans;* in community publications, these terms sometimes were hyphenated and sometimes were not.

The Cuban-Jewish community does not necessarily use these terms in the same way I analyze them theoretically. I think it is more important to consider the qualitative ways people discuss their identity than the specific terminology they use to define it. Many of my interlocutors, I think, would have felt uncomfortable constantly using the term *Jewban* to describe themselves to an "outsider" such as myself. For someone from outside the community, *Cuban-Jew* is a term much more readily understood than *Jewban.* Most important is that many people with whom I spoke identified with the model of the *Jewban/Juban* presented in this book, even if they did not explicitly refer to themselves as such (in fact, many did refer to themselves as *Jewbans*).

In several instances, I juxtapose Cuban-Jews with the previously established Jewish community in Miami Beach during the 1960s. I refer to the latter community as the "American Jewish community in Miami Beach" and to those who composed it as "American Jews." I use this language to highlight the differences between these

Jews, who (often) had lived in the United States for two or more generations, and Jewish émigrés who had recently arrived from Cuba. This admittedly inadequate language should not be taken to mean that the Cuban-Jews do not consider themselves Americans; rather, it reflects the ways in which Miami's preestablished Jewish community perceived them as "foreigners" and how they, in turn, came to perceive themselves as "Cuban-Jews" who also might be "American" by citizenship or inclination.

Two final notes about terminology. First, the phrases *Metropolitan Miami, Dade County,* and *Greater Miami* generally are recognized as synonymous (Boswell and Skop 1995: 1). I often use *Miami* as a synonym for these phrases. *South Florida* generally refers to the tri-county area of Miami-Dade, Broward, and Palm Beach counties. I use this designation when referring to a broader spread of people across these areas, although usually I mean specifically the Greater Miami area.

Second, most of my interlocutors know me by my nickname, Carrie. I therefore have written my name this way in the text.

Scholarship on the Jewish communities of Cuba can be found in various articles, theses, film documentaries, and other works: Kahn (1981), Levine and Szuchman (1985), Bejarano (1985, 1986, 1988, 1990a, 1990b, 1991, 1993, 1996a), Asís (1989), Burt (1994, 1995), Behar (1995a, 1995b), Paull (1995), and Levine (1996). Three major works have been published on the subject: *The Jewish Community of Cuba: Settlement and Growth,* by Boris Sapir (1948); *Tropical Diaspora: The Jewish Experience in Cuba,* by Robert Levine (1993); and *La Comunidad Hebrea de Cuba: La Memoria y la Historia,* by Margalit Bejarano (1996b). Two short pieces and one master's thesis focus on the transplanted Cuban-Jewish community in Miami: Liebman (1977), Bejarano (1994), and Epstein (1981). My book specifically addresses the evolution of Miami's Cuban-Jewish community since the early 1960s. Therefore, it is not a comprehensive account of the history and culture of this community but rather a contribution to extant scholarship.

This book is the product of eighteen months of research and writing. Because I had only a short time to complete it, I focused on issues emphasized by my interlocutors and issues that interested me personally and intellectually. Framing many of these issues were the Cuban-Jewish community's development in Miami Beach and its relationship to the established American Jewish community from the 1960s to the present.

Many issues surrounding Cuban-Jews and their relationship with Miami's larger Cuban community merit further development than can be found in this book. My hope is that future scholars will explore the following areas in greater depth: the Cuban-Jewish community's relationship with the larger Roman Catholic and Santería communities of Cuban exiles in South Florida; the alliance of some Cuban-Jews in

Miami with many hard-line anti-Castro groups in Florida led by Cuban Gentiles; the increasing tendency for Cuban-Jews to visit Cuba for humanitarian, scholarly, and nostalgic reasons; the question of Cuban-Jewish political tendencies in the American political system; professional and economic status of Sephardic and Ashkenazic Cuban-Jews in South Florida; anti-Semitism associated with American Jewish employers' exploitation of new Cuban arrivals in Miami in the 1960s; culinary traditions in the Cuban-Jewish community; the choice of schooling for children; the choice of languages to speak at home and in public; and views on race, race relations, and cultural diversity in the Cuban-Jewish community.

Because I was completely unfamiliar with the Cuban-Jewish community before I started my research, I entered my fieldwork with few preconceived notions of what it represented. How was it, I wondered, that I could grow up Jewish in South Miami and not know about a community numbering ten to fifteen thousand and centered in Miami Beach? In truth, I never had considered the possibility that Cubans might belong to my ethnoreligious group.

I learned that I was not alone in this thinking when I talked about my research with friends and colleagues who repeatedly asked, "There are *Cuban* Jews?" This book answers that question with a resounding "Yes!" by exploring the dimensions of Cuban-Jewish history and identity in Miami since 1959.

In this book I chose to take chances that I knew would not be received enthusiastically by all readers. As Ruth Behar writes in *The Vulnerable Observer*, anthropologists who place themselves within the situations they document automatically make themselves vulnerable to the uncertainty inherent in those situations. Yet, Behar asks, is it possible to write a truthful ethnography—the medium of the anthropologist—without exposing our own positions in our ethnographic encounters? Is there a strict boundary between ethnography and autobiography? How, I have continually asked myself, will I be received in writing a community history that is self-reflective?

"As I wrote," Behar recalls, "the ethnographer in me wanted to know: Who is this woman writing about others, making others vulnerable? What does she want from others? What do the others want from her? The feminist in me wanted to know: What kind of fulfillment does she get—or not get—from the power she has?" (1996: 19–20). At the same time, Behar asks, how is the self-reflective ethnographer—the vulnerable observer—personally affected by the stories she hears? As a writer, when is it her responsibility to act, and when is it her privilege to observe?

I have chosen to make myself vulnerable in this book. I do this knowing that such vulnerability will generate discussion, perhaps disagreement, among the very people I wish it could wholly please: the Cuban-Jews. Indeed, this issue has been very difficult for me personally to grapple with, and I have asked myself continually how I should write this story. I have tried to balance honesty with fairness, and personal values with historicity. My hope is that such a subjective and yet balanced approach will demonstrate the complexities of any interaction, especially an ethnographic interaction. Furthermore, I hope this book inspires my readers to record their own individual and family histories for future generations.

# Acknowledgments

Ethnographies are always produced jointly. While I take full responsibility for the final product that is this book, I would like to acknowledge those who have assisted in my process of thinking and writing.

This book began in a small seminar room in the Titiev Library at the University of Michigan. Through Sharon Stephens and her illuminating course on postmodern anthropology, I became increasingly interested in the concept of identity in the "borderlands" between ethnic groups—specifically, the borderlands in Miami, my hometown.

I would like to thank the following people for helping me develop my ideas about the Cuban, Jewish, and Cuban-Jewish communities in Miami in the early stages of my writing: Juan Clark at Miami Dade Community College; Max Castro at the University of Miami North/South Center; and Holly Ackerman, Enrique Baloyra, Thomas Boswell, Juan Carlos Espinosa, Robert Levine, and Ira Sheskin at the University of Miami. Special thanks go to Henry Green at the University of Miami's Judaic Studies Program, who provided rich and detailed insight and references on Jewish history and culture. His intimate knowledge of Miami's Cuban-Jewish community helped me approach many issues with a new perspective.

This book would not have been possible without the assistance of many wonderful people and the archives they maintain. Librarians in the Miami-Dade Public Library's Florida Room provided generous assistance in locating newspaper articles on Miami's Cuban-Jewish community. Remko Jansonius, Ginger Young, Marcia Zerivitz, and others at the Ziff Jewish Museum of Florida in Miami Beach offered great enthusiasm for, and assistance with, my research, allowing me time and again to comb through that museum's fascinating archives. Sharon Yudowitz at the National Council of Jewish Women (NCJW) in Miami Beach assisted me greatly in locating NCJW bulletins from the 1960s. Betty Heisler-Samuels, editor of *Entre Nosotros*, furnished me with numerous back issues of her magazine, along with fascinating insights into the Cuban-Jewish community. The University of Michigan's Harlan Hatcher Graduate Library was another important resource. Ines Kleiman, Estrella Behar, and others at Torat Moshe generously supplied synagogue bulletins, magazines, historical documents, and wholehearted support for my research. Ofelia Ruder at the Cuban-Hebrew Congregation was a constant source of illumination in this book's development; she provided abundant archival material concerning the Cuban-Jewish community's past and meticulously recounted historical events as if they had happened yesterday. She is a constant reminder of the value of preserving history for future generations.

Two long-time Miamians offered their valuable perspectives on Miami's development and the Cuban-Jewish experience. Thanks to Rabbi Mayer Abramowitz, who spoke candidly of Cuban-Jewish history in Miami and of his role in the community's development; and to Myra Farr, who discussed the changing face of Miami Beach throughout this century and NCJW's role in Cuban Jewish affairs since the 1920s. Also offering generous assistance were Sunny Map Corporation and the Miami Beach Community Development Corporation. Their detailed maps of Greater Miami and the Beaches helped me better understand and visualize the areas about which I write in this book.

For information regarding contemporary Jewish life in Cuba, I turned to Paul Margolis of the Jewish Communication Network, June Safran of the Cuba-America Jewish Mission, and Gary Monroe of DeLand Community College, all of whom thoughtfully shared anecdotes, impressions, and experiences with me. Margalit Bejarano at the Hebrew University of Jerusalem and Ruth Behar at the University of Michigan generously shared their extensive research on Cuban-Jewish communities in Cuba and Miami.

Gary Monroe's refreshing insight on the Jewish communities of Cuba and Miami Beach helped me to better contextualize my research. His vivid photographs capture, for me, the essence of Jewish Miami Beach in the 1970s and 1980s.

Although I speak Spanish, I am not a native speaker; nor am I entirely fluent in the language. Although I read Hebrew, I have little knowledge of the meanings of Hebrew words. I therefore needed assistance with Spanish and Hebrew translations at several points in my research. Ruth Behar, María Capote, Ileana Díaz, Viviana Quintero, and Ofelia Ruder generously commented on my Spanish translations and offered valuable interpretations of my work. Naomi Brenner and Henry Green provided detailed translations from Hebrew, as well as essential background information on Jewish customs. Oftentimes there were several possible translations for a particular set of words. I chose the reading that made the most sense contextually, so any mistakes are my responsibility entirely.

As this book took shape in Ann Arbor, I received generous assistance from a number of people at the University of Michigan. Zvi Gitelman not only allowed me to sit in on his engaging course on Eastern European Jewry, but also answered all my questions on the subject, always with a smile. Judith Elkin's vast library was extremely helpful for my archival work, and our lively discussions of Latin American Jewry helped me contextualize much of Cuban-Jewish history. Erica Lehrer and Viviana Quintero provided encouragement and guidance in my consideration of Jewish and Latino identity issues. The Honors Program at the University of Michigan provided funding to help cover the costs of my travel and research.

Two people at the University of Michigan deserve special thanks. Ruth Behar's hours of patient listening, refreshing insights, and critical commentary truly enhanced my thinking about the Cuban-Jewish community and the larger issues surrounding anthropological methods and ethnographic writing. As both my advisor and an "insider" in the community, she never failed to augment my "outsider" perspective, guiding me on new and exciting paths previously hidden from view. As I discuss in the text, I was greatly influenced by her theoretical views concerning the importance of merging personal experience with ethnographic research. Erik Mueggler's constant support kept me going when writing seemed an insurmountable task. Providing keen insight into my research, he gave me both practical and theoretical direction.

I am deeply grateful to the wonderful people from Miami's Cuban-Jewish community whom I have been privileged to get to know over the past several years. The following people generously shared their personal and community histories with me: Alina Becker, Estrella Behar, Bernardo Benes, Moreno Habif, Betty Heisler-Samuels, David Hochman, Moisés Jrade, Arón Kelton, Lucía Kelton, Marcos Kerbel, Bernie Kremen, Isaac Motola, Pincho Papir, Ofelia Ruder, and the people identified by the following pseudonyms in the text: Benjamín Cohen, Susana Hamla, Jacob Lajapo, Luisa Lajapo, Becky Levy, Raul Levy, Rosa Levy, Vicky Levy, Damien Losger, Elena Losger, Rafael Losger, Nelly Peres, Albert Ralvey, Alberto Ralvey, Esther Ralvey, Berta Samopla, Miriam Shalper, Eva Simazi, Marisa Tanan, Enrique Tirani, and Luis Tirani. These people never failed to encourage me in my research, providing me with the stories upon which this book is based. Always with smiles, they welcomed me into their homes and offices, sharing personal information with a total stranger. Their trust and openness allowed this book to materialize.

I am also grateful to Joyce Harrison and Stan Ivester of the University of Tennessee Press for their enthusiasm and faith. Lisandro Pérez at Florida International University and Jack Kugelmass at Arizona State University brought to their readings of my initial manuscript deep knowledge of issues concerning Cuban and Jewish identity. Mavis Bryant's editorial suggestions helped the flow and substance of my writing.

I cannot thank my family and friends enough for their kind patience and encouragement throughout my writing process. This has been of utmost importance to me, allowing me to retain a sense of balance in my life and my writing. I am deeply grateful to Ruth Bettinger, who served as my alter ego in Miami, conducting mini-interviews, taking photographs, proofreading manuscript drafts, and faithfully clipping newspaper articles on Cuban and Jewish affairs. I am also indebted to Kathy López for her thoughtful commentary on the substance and form of my work. She maintained a sensitive approach while applying the highest standards of intellectual rigor. The result was a nuanced, invaluable reading. Thanks also to Jeanne Haffner and Cecily Czapanskiy for going through this project with me every step of the way. Of course, thanks to Phish, Lap, Tiger, Tammi, and Toonces for their loving support.

The faith, determination, and candor of my husband, Sean Bettinger-López, always amazes me. Sean never failed to provide detailed critical commentaries on my writing, while exploring new ideas and avenues of expression. With his keen sense of language, he helped sharpen my arguments and clarify abstruse passages. Perhaps most important, he remained flexible, supportive, and empathic throughout this consuming project.

I write this book in memory of two people who changed my life. Sharon Stephens's talent and devotion as a teacher inspired me to study anthropology. I cannot convey adequately what her encouragement and compassion have meant to me and to countless others whose lives she touched.

Lisa Strongson always symbolized for me independence and freedom of thought. She flew where her delicate heart led her, as she dodged life's obstacles with vision and wit. Her idealism allowed her to achieve her dream just years after graduating college, a feat so few people ever achieve in their lifetimes. Her fierce spirit lives on in those of us who are also dreamers.

My great-uncle, Aaron Emert, has been a true inspiration in my life. For me, Aaron is the paragon of a *mensh,* always thinking of the global village before he considers his individual household. He is a constant source of energy and vitality, qualities he derives from his unceasing passion for life. I dedicate this book to him, for he has taught me perhaps the most important lesson in life: that I must listen in order to understand.

# Introduction

*Una vez cada siglo*
*nace un astro . . .*

*Del fondo de la noche*
*surge la luz pura de un astro.*
*La palabra que esperan muchos hombres.*
*El héroe que soñamos. . . .*

*¡Oh, poeta, Martí! Tuyo es el tiempo,*
*tuya la eternidad desde la rosa,*
*tuyo el destino de tu Patria—Cuba—*
*donde mi corazón halló paloma . . . !*

*Una vez cada siglo*
*nace un astro*

*Tu figura de Apóstol se agiganta*
*por las tierras de América.*
*Tu nombre todos lo dicen con amor*
*y los niños te besan.*

*Cuba será feliz algún día,*
*tus enseñanzas serán nuestras.*

*Yo que aprendí de ti a amar la tierra,*
*a ver al hombre como a igual,*
*sin odios ni vergüenzas;*
*a amar la libertad*
*—la libertad que es nuestra—*
*te estoy amando desde mis raíces*
*porque tú también amaste a la proscrita raza de Judea.*

*Once each century*
*a star is born . . .*

*From the depths of the night*
*arises the pure light of a star.*
*The word that many men hope for.*
*The hero we dream of. . . .*

*Oh, poet, Martí! Yours is the time,*
*yours the eternity of the rose,*
*yours the destiny of your native land—Cuba—*
*where my heart found peace . . . !*

*Once each century*
*a star is born*

*Your Apostle image enlarges*
*through the lands of America.*
*Your name everyone says with love*
*and the children adore you.*

*Cuba will be happy one day,*
*your teachings will be ours.*

*I who learned from you to love the land,*
*to see my fellow man as an equal,*
*without hate or shame;*
*to love liberty*
*—the liberty that is ours—*
*I am loving you from my roots*
*because you yourself also loved the exiled Jewish people.*

*—Abraham Vainstein, "De Cara al Sol" ("Facing the Sun")*

In 1953, Cuba was celebrating the centennial birthday of its national hero, José Martí (1853–1895). Martí's relentless advocacy for Cuban independence from Spain in the nineteenth century made him an icon of freedom in the Cuban collective memory. Born to Spanish immigrant parents, Martí, through his experiences as lawyer, writer, politician, and military leader, was credited with spearheading the island's victory in the Cuban War of Independence in 1898.

Among those celebrating Martí's birthday were Cuba's Jews. Although most could date their settlement in Cuba back a maximum of fifty years, they identified with Martí's democratic ideology and his dedication to his—and their—*patria*. The interest Martí, a non-Jew, expressed in Jewish culture and the Hebrew language brought him even closer to the island's Jews, who found numerous avenues through which they could relate to this "Cuban Apostle" who advocated "Comprensión Humana, sin distinción de credo o color" ("Human Understanding, without distinction of creed or color") (Gambach 1990: 7).

Martí represented, for Cuba's Jews, a paragon of *cubanidad*. For many, his acceptance of and support for religious, racial, and ethnic diversity in Cuba epitomized the reasons why they enthusiastically embraced the tropical island as their home. "The Cuban Apostle," wrote the Cuban Rabbi Nesim Gambach, "was not Catholic, nor did he belong to another organized religion. . . . Martí was 'religious without Religion'" and was a friend to all peoples, including the Jews (Gambach 1990: 7; translation mine).

Abraham Vainstein's poignant poem, "De Cara al Sol" ("Facing the Sun"), reveals the Cuban Jews' profound attachment to their nation and national hero. A poet and essayist, the German-born Vainstein originally wrote the poem in Yiddish, his native language and the language of the Eastern European Jews. Through using this "foreign" Jewish language to celebrate Cuban history, Vainstein links his native Yiddish culture with Martí's native Cuban land, where Vainstein's "heart found peace." Indeed, Vainstein writes, "I am loving you from my roots"; his connection with Cuba and its Apostle is deeper than he knows and so has become a part of his very being.

"De Cara al Sol" forms part of a larger collection of poems and essays entitled *Martí Visto por Hebreos (Martí Seen by Jews)*, edited by Abraham Matterin and published in 1954 by the Cuban-Jewish Cultural Association of Havana. This group of young Jewish intellectuals, formed under Matterin's direction, sought to construct a bridge between the two elements of their Cuban-Jewish identity by uniting the Jewish colony and the Cuban people in artistic and cultural activities. During this time, Cuba's Jews published several other commemorative works, including Marco Pitchón's *José Martí y la comprensión humana* (1953), a gift to the Cuban nation from the Jewish community of Cuba. These works all pay homage to Martí as a martyr who died in the name of justice and liberty, who loved humanity, and who supported the Jewish people through his study of the Bible, the Talmud, and the Hebrew language. They also document Jewish participation in the Cuban War of Independence (Matterin 1953: 7–8; Bejarano 1996b: 200).

"De Cara al Sol," Abraham Matterin writes, is "Nuestro Homenaje a Martí en Yiddish" ("Our Homage to Martí in Yiddish"). As such, it bridges two worlds—the old world of Eastern Europe and the new world of the Americas—and affirms the permanence of the Jewish settlement in Cuba.

This Jewish settlement, however, was comprised of more than Eastern European Jews. It also included thousands of Mediterranean and smaller numbers of Syrian and Lebanese Jews who had come to Cuba in search of tranquillity and acceptance. Known in Cuba as *polacos*, the Eastern European Jews identified themselves as *Ashkenazim*, a Hebrew word referring to Jews born in what is now Poland, Russia, Germany, and other areas of Eastern Europe, and their descendants. First-generation *polacos* in Cuba spoke Yiddish, a thousand-year-old vernacular language which uses letters of the Hebrew alphabet phonetically to spell vocabulary words from Germanic, Slavic, and Hebrew languages.

The Cuban Ashkenazim's Mediterranean and Syrio-Lebanese coreligionists were known as *turcos*. Cuba's *turcos* identified themselves as *Sephardim*, from the Hebrew name for Spain—*Sepharad*—where Jewish culture flourished until 1492, when King Ferdinand and Queen Isabella expelled the Jews from their country during the infamous Spanish Inquisition. Those Sephardim who did not convert to Christianity or become Crypto-Jews (practicing their religion secretly) migrated to the Mediterranean—particularly to the areas now known as Turkey, Greece, and North Africa. With them they took their vernacular *Ladino* language, also called *Judezmo* or *Judeo-Spanish*, a form of fifteenth-century Castilian Spanish sprinkled with Hebrew (and later Arabic, Turkish, and Greek) and written in Rashi letters, a variant of Hebrew characters (Rosten 1968: 19–20, 203, 314–15, 435–37; Levine 1993: 20).

While both are written in Hebrew script, Ladino and Yiddish are completely distinct languages which have developed out of distinct cultures—cultures which many argue share little more than a Jewish religious foundation (Rosten 1968: ibid. (Rosten 1968: 19–20, 203, 314–15, 435–37).[1]

American Ashkenazim were the first practicing Jews to settle in Cuba. Many served in the United States military during both the 1898 Cuban War of Indepen-

*Jewish community members gather in Havana's Parque Central in January for the annual parade of Jewish schoolchildren, celebrating José Martí's birthday. Circa 1940s. Photo courtesy of Ziff Jewish Museum of Florida.*

dence—also known as the Spanish-American War—and the subsequent United States occupation of the island from 1902 to 1909. Decrees of religious freedom brought Jewish religious services to Cuba as early as 1904; in 1906, eleven American Jews established the United Hebrew Congregation. While they learned enough Spanish to communicate with others on the island, their community effectively remained a United States enclave (Levine 1993: 3, 5).

It was not long before the first waves of Jewish immigrants began arriving in Cuba from across the Atlantic Ocean. Sephardim arrived first, and Ashkenazim followed; both brought languages and customs largely unfamiliar to the tropical island. Yet, as Meir Matzliah Melarmed, the second rabbi of Miami Beach's Cuban Sephardic Hebrew Congregation, notes, Jewish culture was not entirely foreign to turn-of-the-century Cuba. In fact, the island's beginnings are intimately linked with Jewish history.[2]

## The Star of David in Cuban Jewish History

On the cover of Rabbi Meir Matzliah Melarmed's *Breve Historia de los Judíos de Cuba y de la Comunidad Sefaradita de Miami* (*Brief History of the Jews of Cuba and of the Sephardic Community of Miami*) is a map, a visual documentation of the many "homes" of the Cuban Sephardim. It includes the original Sephardic home, Spain, as well as the post-Inquisition Sephardic homes: Morocco, Turkey, Greece, Cuba, and the United States. Linking these seemingly distant places is a disproportionate Star of David. Four of its six points fall into these homes, so they become part of a larger system, a Jewish world order.

If one inspects Melarmed's map more closely, however, something seems wrong. From a United States perspective, Spain lies roughly in Michigan, and Turkey and Greece just off the shore of New York. No other land appears on the map but these countries: they are surrounded by emptiness, white space. They are, in a sense, "everywhere," composing the fundamental elements of the Sephardic world.

Nowhere in his history does Melarmed explicitly refer to his curious map. Yet his account of the Cuban Sephardim's history wholly contextualizes it. He begins this history with the legendary story of the first Spaniard to set foot in Cuba. "According to the diary of Columbus's first voyage," Melarmed writes,

> el primer español que pisó la tierra de San Salvador (el 12 de octubre de 1492) y luego la de Cuba (el 2 de noviembre de 1492), fue Luis de Torres, enviado por Colón para traerle informes acerca de los habitantes de la mencionada isla. Luis de Torres, que era "marrano" (término despectivo de los españoles al referirse a los cripto-judíos),

servía de intérprete de la expedición y conocía, según se dice, además
del español, los idiomas hebreo, arameo y árabe.

(the first Spaniard to set foot on the land of San Salvador [October
12, 1492] and then Cuba [November 2, 1492], was Luis de Torres,
sent by Columbus to collect information about the inhabitants of
the island. Luis de Torres, who was a "marrano" [the pejorative term
that the Spaniards used to describe the Crypto-Jews], served as an
interpreter for the expedition. It is said that, besides Spanish, he
knew Hebrew, Aramaic, and Arabic. (198?: 2)

Melarmed traces the subsequent arrival of hundreds of Sephardim in Cuba in
the wake of the Spanish Inquisition of 1492. Because the island was a Spanish
colony, however, Jews were prohibited from practicing their religion in Cuba. As a
result, Jewish religious life—except for that of the Crypto-Jews—was absent from
the island until after Cuba's liberation in the 1898 War of Independence.

Melarmed shifts his discussion from Cuba to the eastern Mediterranean, the region to
which the majority of Sephardic Jews fled in the fifteenth and sixteenth centuries. Almost
immediately, though, he lands them—four centuries into the future—thousands of miles
across the Atlantic Ocean, returning once again to the mythical tropical island of Cuba.

Sephardim, Melarmed notes, were not the only Jews arriving in Cuba in the early
twentieth century. By the 1920s, Eastern European Jews also were landing on Cuban
shores *en masse.* These Ashkenazim left their home countries for markedly different
reasons than their Sephardic coreligionists. While the former fled a legacy of
pogroms, economic persecution, and the rising Lenin regime in Russia, the latter fled
what had been a hospitable and accommodating homeland until 1918, when the
collapse of the Ottoman and Hapsburg empires and a subsequent upsurge of
nationalist ideologies increasingly threatened the comfortable life Jews knew. Arriving
in Cuba, most Jews—particularly Ashkenazim—sought, in Melarmed's words, "to
use the island as a trampoline to jump to the United States" (198?: 3; translation
mine). Indeed, many Yiddish speakers called the island *Ashsanie Kuba* (Hotel Cuba),
considering it a temporary refuge until they could enter the *goldene medine* (golden
country) ninety miles to the north (Levine 1993: 33). Many thought that the United
States, as a "land of immigrants," would open its arms to Jews.

During the height of Jewish migration to Cuba, in 1924, the United States
Congress passed the United States Immigration and Naturalization Act, effectively
stopping the seemingly endless migration of Europeans and others that had been
permitted for three decades. With this xenophobic act, the island which began as a

"hotel" for thousands of Jews became, of necessity, a home. This was not difficult for the Jews to accept, however. Comparing the treatment they received in their adopted home with the anti-Semitism they had suffered in their countries of origin, most had only high praise for Cuban hospitality (Bejarano 1996b: 199).[3] With the passage in the 1930s of a law permitting Jewish immigrants to become Cuban citizens, Jews increasingly came to feel Cuban. As Ruth Behar writes, "By the late 1930s, the goal of gaining entrance to the America across the border became less and less urgent for the many Jews who had made tropical lives for themselves, after awakening to the realization that Cuba was to be their America" (Behar 1995b: 156).

Many Jews initially worked as peddlers and factory workers in Cuba, earning barely enough to feed and clothe their families. As many Jews achieved increasing social and economic stability by mid-century, however, some vibrant and prosperous Jewish communities developed throughout the island, most notably in Havana. These were a far cry from the ghettos of Eastern Europe, which nearly two-thirds of the island's Jewish population had left behind. Cuba's warm and friendly atmosphere allowed the Jews to develop tightly-knit Jewish communities while maintaining ties with Cubans from all walks of life and with the island nation itself. Thus, for many Jews, the Jewish identity which emerged existed within a Cuban framework. Vainstein's "De Cara al Sol" and Melarmed's Star of David map pay tribute to this fact. For these writers and the communities they represented, Jewishness was rooted firmly in the island. By the 1940s and especially by the 1950s, Cuba had become a place where many Jews settled happily, rather than a place Jews hesitantly settled for.

The 1950s saw unprecedented prosperity for many Jewish Cubans. As the community stabilized after experiencing an influx of German refugees in the wake of World War II, it solidified its institutional structures and community organization. The children of immigrants who had arrived in the pre-World War II years were becoming businesspeople, managers, and, to a lesser extent, professionals. Jews living in the United States offered assistance to their Cuban coreligionists, advising them on how best to unite Cuba's Jewish communities, particularly those in Havana, Camagüey, and Matanzas. These efforts were realized in 1953 in the creation of the *Patronato de la Casa de la Comunidad Hebrea de Cuba*, a large synagogue and social center for both Sephardim and Ashkenazim, built in the wealthy Vedado district of Havana. The *Patronato* functioned as the center of Jewish life on the island, hosting events which brought Jews together socially and religiously. Many Jewish social events also took place at private clubs throughout Havana, resulting in an unproblematic commingling of Jews and Gentiles.[4]

This lifestyle was to change abruptly six years later. The year 1959 marked the overthrow of Fulgencio Batista's government, loyally supported by many Jews throughout Cuba. Fidel Castro quickly assumed power as revolutionary Cuba's new leader. His socialist leanings and antipathy toward both Batista supporters and the United States (the two, in fact, were intimately linked) effected the political exile of thousands of Jewish and Gentile Cubans ninety miles across the Florida Straits to the United States, which opened its arms to these "temporary refugees from Communism." While many relocated to New York, Puerto Rico, and other parts of the United States and Latin America, most chose South Florida as the site of their temporary settlement. Within two years, Miami became the largest Cuban exile center in the world, a place where tens of thousands of Cubans waited to return to their homeland.

Within this group of Cuban exiles in Miami were approximately 3,500 Jewish Cubans (Liebman 1977: 300).[5] Cuba now was home to these Jewish Cubans, and exile was an unwelcome reality. While they, too, initially conceived of exile as temporary, by 1961 many sought to take their lives "off hold." They did so largely through the establishment in Miami Beach of the *Círculo Cubano-Hebreo*, the Cuban-Hebrew Social Circle, modeled on the beloved *Patronato*. Sephardim and Ashkenazim alike became Círculo members; by the mid-1960s, the organization was a vital social and religious establishment. In 1968, many Cuban Sephardim branched off from the Círculo, forming the Cuban Sephardic Hebrew Congregation, modeled on Havana's foremost Sephardic congregation, Chevet Ahim.[6]

The United States now was the home of most Jewish Cubans. Ironically, these people entered the Land of Opportunity—the land which thirty-five years before had slammed its doors in their foreign faces—on the basis of their *cubanidad*, their Cubanness (Behar 1995b: 157). The original homeland imagined by so many Ashkenazim and some Sephardim had become a reality for the Jews from Cuba. By the early 1960s, though, the equation had been reversed: Cuba now had become the yearned-for homeland of its Jewish exiles, who in the preceding decades had "made their America in Cuba," as a common Yiddish saying went (Levine 1993: 20). Arón Kelton, a former president of the Cuban-Hebrew Congregation, put it this way: "Look how things turn out. Our fathers stayed in Cuba because it was the country closest to the United States. We came to the United States because it was the country closest to Cuba" (quoted in Fernández 1986b: 12).

Castro's unanticipated forty-one-year reign in Cuba has prompted the emigration of over 90 percent of the island's pre-revolutionary Jews, most of whom left in the early 1960s. Centered in Miami, New York, and San Juan, Puerto Rico, Cuban-Jewish communities today maintain traditions and friendships begun in pre-revolutionary Cuba. While allowing for continuity, this situation also requires a flexible approach to new cultural influences stemming from American society. Indeed, four decades after the Cuban Revolution, many Cuban-Jews feel a great attachment to their new *patria*, which opened its doors to them when they were Cuban exiles. Alina Becker, program director of the Miami-based Cuban American National Council and an Ashkenazic Cuban-Jew, emphasized the multifaceted identity which has emerged for her in exile: "People are always amazed to find out that my background is both Cuban and Jewish, as though I couldn't be both at the same time. But you know what? I'm really proud to call myself a Cuban-Floridian-American-Jew" (quoted in Sanford L. Ziff Jewish Museum of Florida 1997).

## Cuban-Jews in Miami

This book traces the development of the Cuban-Jewish community in Miami and then uses this development as a framework to explore issues of identity facing both the community at large and its individual members. The community today traces its development not only through the past four decades in Miami, nor only through the previous half-century in Cuba. Like Rabbi Melarmed, the community—both Sephardim and Ashkenazim—sees its Miami location as one point on a larger Jewish star. Other points, as Melarmed shows, may include Turkey, Greece, and Cuba, as well as Poland, Russia, Lithuania, Belarus, and Israel.

Displacement and migration characterize much of the Cuban-Jewish experience for the community. Unlike most other Jewish communities in the United States, this

*The Freedom Tower, through which all Cuban émigrés were processed upon arriving in Miami in the 1960s. This became a powerful symbol of democracy for Cuban-Americans in the years following the mass exodus effected by Fidel Castro's 1959 Revolution. Photo taken in 1999 by Caroline Bettinger-López.*

community includes Cuban-Jews of three, or sometimes even four, generations, each with a different place of birth and a different native language. Most older members were born in "pre-Cuba" locales—generally Eastern Europe or the Mediterranean (primarily Turkey)—and thus often speak Yiddish or Ladino as their primary language.[7] Their children were born in Cuba, and thus speak Spanish as their native language. Their grandchildren generally have been born in the United States and speak English as their first language, although a significant number are part of what Gustavo Pérez Firmat calls the "one-and-a-half generation," that group of Cubans "who were born on the island and came to the United States as children or adolescents" (1995: I).[8] Although members of the youngest generation personally may have experienced only the United States, their connection with the Jewish Diaspora often is maintained through their contact with parents, grandparents, and great-grandparents born in distant lands. As they listen to their elders' stories of places called Cuba, Poland, Russia, Turkey, and Syria, as Jews they gain a familiarity with these lands.

This familiarity, however, is placed within a well-defined context. Be they of Polish, Russian, Turkish, or Syrian heritage, the members of the younger generation are *American Cuban-Jews* in Miami. For those of the older generations, who settled or were born in Cuba, nearly four decades of life in the United States certainly has had an "Americanizing" influence as well. Yet these people retain a Cuban-Jewish identity and pass this on to their American-born children and grandchildren.

Because most of Cuba's Jews left their island home immediately in the wake of the 1959 Cuban Revolution, today's Cuban-Jewish community in Miami, temporally (i.e., in terms of time of migration) and ideologically, is not representative of the much larger population of non-Jewish Cuban émigrés in the United States, which includes thousands of recent émigrés from the island. Miami's Cuban-Jewish community is composed primarily of those who consider themselves political exiles and assume a hard-line anti-Castro stance, in line with the powerful "exile community" of Miami. While Cuban-Jews and the larger Cuban community of Miami both encounter recent Cuban émigrés on a regular basis in Miami, the situation differs markedly when it comes to recent *Jewish* Cuban émigrés. The few Jewish Cubans (less than one thousand) who have arrived in Miami since 1970 are placed in an awkward position when they attempt to ally themselves with their religious brethren who left Cuba decades before. Since a part of the hard-line anti-Castro position entails labeling Cubans who have remained in revolutionary Cuba as Communists, Castro-lovers, and traitors to the "real" Cuba—the Cuba of the past—the Cuban-Jewish community views these recent Jewish-Cuban émigrés with ambivalence. On the one hand, it is believed, these are fellow Jews and thus should be welcomed into the community. On the other hand, however, these people often are assumed to be Communists—perhaps even infiltrators for the Castro government—and thus may not "belong" in a community which, as explicitly stated in its list of general provisions and objectives, is democratic in spirit and wholly allied with the United States against Fidel Castro. Although these recent arrivals eventually may become accepted members of the Cuban-Jewish community, they first must "prove" their hatred of the Castro regime and their nostalgia for pre-revolutionary Cuba.

While these recent arrivals may effect some reconfiguration of the Cuban-Jewish community, it remains remarkably stable. Much of its composition and leadership, in fact, dates back not only to the early 1960s in Miami, but also to pre-revolutionary Cuba. As these community leaders grow older, they look to the members of the next (American-born) generation to lead the community and to carry on the Cuban-Jewish tradition in the only home these young people know: Miami.

For the members of this younger generation, Cuba's meaning is subsumed within their parents' stories, their "Cuban" synagogues, and the "Cuban" reality in and of Miami. For them, Cuba is a place both distant and proximate. Although most of them have no direct contact with the *tierra* (land) itself, their family's connection with this mythical island has been perpetuated through both the family history which is passed on and the "extended family" (community) history which is recreated through the community structure itself.

For the younger generation, the Cuban-Jewish community often is not as much of a priority as it is for their parents and grandparents. While many have grown up with this community occupying a prominent position in their lives—attending synagogue services and social events on a regular basis, and spending large amounts of time with their parents' Cuban-Jewish friends—they also have grown up within a larger "American" society. Their friends often are a mix of American Jews, Gentiles of many nationalities, and Cuban-Jews; their preferred language generally is English; and their home is Miami. So, while their elders place the future of the Cuban-Jewish community in their hands, these young people often consider it impossible to perpetuate what was created under circumstances they never experienced and which differ dramatically from their own experiences growing up in the United States.

This book frames issues of identity, memory, and homeland for the members of Miami's Cuban-Jewish community within a historical context. Through ethnography, oral history, and personal reflection, I have tried to illustrate the many cultural, spiritual, and geographical spaces occupied by the Cuban-Jews, as members of a "transplanted" Cuban community in the United States. I consider these issues from the perspectives of age, wave of migration, gender, and sub-ethnic group (Sephardic and Ashkenazic Jews), invoking the past in order to reveal more about the present.

# Part I.

## The Past in the Present:
## A History of the Cuban-Jewish
## Community in Miami

The three "Cuban" synagogues extant in Greater Miami in 1999: (a) Temple Menorah, (b) Sephardic Congregation of Florida—Torat Moshe/Temple Moses, and (c) Temple Beth Shmuel—Cuban-Hebrew Congregation. All are located in Miami Beach. 1999. Photos by Caroline Bettinger-López.

(a) Temple Menorah

(b) Sephardic Congregation of Florida—Torat Moshe/ Temple Moses

(c) Temple Beth Shmuel— Cuban-Hebrew Congregation of Miami

# Chapter I

## From Jewish Cubans to Cuban-Jews: Arriving in Miami and Establishing a Community

Bernardo Benes, a founder of Miami's Cuban-Jewish community, tells a grim story of the arrival of thousands of Jewish Cubans in Miami in 1959 and the early 1960s:

> When we [the Jewish Cubans] arrived in Miami, the local Jewish community basically ignored us. The only person who did anything was Rabbi Abramowitz, who opened his doors to the Cuban Jews. That's why that congregation [Temple Menorah] today has more than fifty percent Cuban-Jews. . . . The situation was so bad that the National Federation of Conservative Judaism compiled statements I made and other Cuban Jews made: the title was "A Cold Day in Miami." They [the local American Jewish community] didn't give us a hand—no financial aid or moral support. We all had a very negative attitude. We were—quote —forced to create our own institutions. Three of us started the Cuban-Hebrew Congregation, which today is a very viable synagogue with a good organization, in a building we built some years ago.

Benes's statement is echoed by the rabbi, Mayer Abramowitz, to whom he refers:

> No one really welcomed the Cuban Jews, because the American Jewish community looked at Cuban Jews as wealthy, not in need of help. The Greater Miami Jewish Federation family didn't immediately help. So they all came to Temple Menorah. I gave them free temple membership, free Hebrew school, free everything. As a result, a decade later, eighty percent of the families who were our members were Cuban Jews. From their early arrival to Miami, Temple Menorah was the center of Cuban Jewish affairs: the social hall was a place for their social and political meetings, as well as religious services. The entire Cuban Jewish community ended up in my synagogue. In view of the heavy child enrollment in our Hebrew School, we changed the well-known Hebrew song to "Havana-gila."[1] Cuban teens began to join USY [United Synagogue Youth], and because of a language barrier, American teens dropped out soon after. So although we lost much of our American youth, the confirmation classes actually increased in size because of the Cuban Jewish teens.[2] (Mayer Abramowitz to Caroline Bettinger-López, May 1999).

Abramowitz elaborates on the Miami Beach Jewish community's reaction to the arrival of its Cuban coreligionists in Sue Fishkoff's article, "A Revolution of Faith."

> When the first Cuban Jewish refugees from Castro arrived in Miami in 1959 and 1960, they received a lukewarm welcome from the established American Jewish community.
>
> "The Jewish community [of Miami] did very little to absorb the fleeing Jews of Cuba," recalls Abramowitz. "First of all, we thought they were wealthy, and could manage. Second, the U.S. government had a program to absorb all Cuban refugees, so the [Greater Miami Jewish] Federation didn't get involved." The lack of interest was compounded, he adds, by a certain "anti-Latin sentiment" in the largely Ashkenazi American Jewish society (1993: 10).[3]

Jewish historian Seymour Liebman arrives at the same conclusion in his 1977 study, "Cuban Jewish Community in South Florida," in which he discusses Temple Menorah's role in the settlement of the Jewish Cuban exiles in Miami Beach and in the religious and social development of the Cuban-Jewish community:

> A strong inducement for many [Jewish] Cubans to settle on the North Beach [of Miami Beach] was that Temple Menorah (Conservative) in the area was the most hospitable of all Greater Miami congregations. It invited the newcomers to share, without charge, its services, including seats for the High Holy Days, and its Talmud Torah for the education of their children. It continued this practice for five years. Most other congregations, including the Sephardi Jewish Center on Miami Beach, requested nominal payment, thus antagonizing the Cuban Sephardim. . . . It was rather surprising that the Floridian Sephardim did not show more cordiality to the new arrivals, since many of them, like the Cubans, were of Turkish ancestry. (1977: 302)[4]

As Marisa Tanan, an elderly Ashkenazic Cuban, describes, South Florida's Jews seemed to forget their own immigrant roots in the face of the Cuban migration. Their sense of *Americana* struck her as particularly ironic: "When I first came to Miami, I had a very painful experience with the Jewish community here. I was standing in line at Thrifty [a local store] to go to the register. And a Jew turned to me and said, 'Why don't you go back to Cuba?' I thought to myself, 'Where did you and your family come from?'"

Even in the late 1960s, many Cuban-Jews continued to feel the pains of ethnic and linguistic discrimination from Miami Beach's local Jewish community. Alina Becker arrived in Miami's Opa Locka Airport with her parents and grandparents in

March 1966, through the American-sponsored Freedom Flights. Expecting to receive a warm welcome from the local Jewish community, she received just the opposite: "I felt rejected by the American Jewish community [when I arrived in 1966], and I still do. There are individuals that just can't get over the fact that we've continued to speak Spanish. Some people don't see bilingualism as an asset, but an insult.

I remember having an elderly Jewish neighbor [in Miami Beach] when I was fourteen or fifteen years old, and sometimes I'd turn on the Latin music on the radio. He was supposed to be deaf, quote unquote, and he'd always yell, 'turn that crap off!' It was because of the language, I think."

Félix Reyler, a founding member of the Cuban-Hebrew Congregation and its second president, describes similar difficulties faced by the organization in "Los Primeros Años del Círculo," his brief history of the Jewish Cubans' first years in Miami: "El primer año de vida social del Círculo fue difícil, por la poca cooperación que recibimos de nuestros vecinos" ("The first year of the social life of El Círculo was difficult, due to the small amount of cooperation we received from our neighbors") (1981: 9). Reyler is referring specifically to the establishment of El Círculo Cubano-Hebreo (Cuban-Hebrew Social Circle) in Miami Beach—a city which, in 1961, was overwhelmingly Jewish. The "neighbors" he refers to were the American Jews also residing in Miami Beach.[5]

Rafael Losger, an Ashkenazic Cuban who arrived in New York in 1960, discusses the reactions of these "neighbors" to their Cuban coreligionists: "When we [Jewish Cubans] came to Miami, we were not one hundred percent accepted by the American Jewish community, [who thought] 'you were foreign, you had an accent, you were not one of us.' We were sort of—I mean, I moved to New York, we had a smaller community. But I understand that the Cuban-Jewish community of Miami was sort of—a branch: it wasn't the main body of things, and it took a few years."

In his documentation of Jewish Miami Beach in the twentieth century, Jewish historian and sociologist Henry Green also describes this "branch" of Jewish Cubans who "lived on the Beach and had little contact with the established Jewish community. No concerted Federation effort was organized to integrate them into the community. With the exception of Rabbi Meyer [sic] Abramowitz's congregation, Temple Menorah, many synagogues . . . tended to open their doors to individuals, rather than extend their resources and facilities to the refugee Jewish-Cuban community as a whole" (1995: 131). And Margalit Bejarano, an Israeli historian of Cuban Jewry, writes of how her oral interviews with Cuban-Jews in Miami today, much like mine, "reflect the feeling of bitterness still felt towards their American coreligionists who had received them with coldness and indifference" (1994: 133).

5

Bernie Kremen and Eva Simazi both compare their positive experiences as Jewish Cuban émigrés in New York with the painful experiences of many of my other interviewees who arrived in Miami during the early 1960s. Kremen, an Ashkenazic Cuban, arrived in Manhattan in 1960. He discusses the effects on the Cuban Jews of the general hostility toward Cuban exiles in Miami in the 1960s, contrasting this negative experience with his own positive experience in New York: "Some Cuban Jews who lived in Miami after arriving from Cuba felt that Miami Beach's American Jews didn't differentiate much between Cuban Jews and Cuban Gentiles. . . . In New York, we [Cuban Jews] had support and warmth from American Jews. In New York, I would've had a much harder time being Cuban Christian than Cuban Jew because the only ethnic group for the Cuban Christians to connect with was the Puerto Ricans. I had the support of some Jewish people in New York; some other Jewish families welcomed us. At least I had some avenue to connect with. But the Cuban Christians had no one to immediately connect with."

Simazi, a Sephardic Cuban, arrived in Brooklyn in 1961. Her memories of her Sephardic family's settlement in the heavily Ashkenazic Canarsi section of Brooklyn in 1961 are equally moving.

> We [Sephardic Cubans in Canarsi] were looking out for each other. . . .
> I used to help them [those who arrived after I did] to go to HIAS-NYANA.
> HIAS helps you with immigration papers and whatever. NYANA helps you
> get a job. They used to help everyone get apartments, because there was—I
> would call it a little—[hesitant pause]—discrimination. We were Jews, but
> we didn't speak Yiddish, so we were not Jews. And every time that someone
> was trying to rent an apartment, and they could not communicate in
> Yiddish with the landlord or the landlady, they wouldn't rent. So they had
> to get someone that spoke Yiddish, and then come, "Look, these people are
> Jewish. They just came from Cuba," . . . and that was the only way. But then
> NYANA used to help us with that. They would give [the Cuban Jews]
> three months' rent, they would give them the money to buy groceries for
> about a month, until they got a job. And then you were supposed to pay
> them back. And we did.

Our South Florida vignettes all point to a highly prejudiced, anti-Jewish-Cuban (and, more generally, anti-Cuban) atmosphere in Miami, while Kremen's and Simazi's stories both point to a more welcoming environment in New York, where, as Simazi shows, prejudice that existed was felt in a different, and seemingly less hostile, form.

In contrast to these gloomy depictions of Jewish Miami's reception of the Jewish Cubans, historian Robert Levine paints a positive picture of the Jewish Cubans' arrival in Miami. In *Tropical Diaspora,* his history of the Jewish experience in Cuba, he writes "Some 30,000 Cuban refugees clustered in the Greater Miami area by late 1960. Of these, 2,500 were Jewish, one-fourth of the total Jewish community of Havana. Refugees came on tourist visas but were granted permanent residence by the United States on arrival. The Greater Miami Jewish Federation (GMJF) set up a reception center at the airport, as did other welfare agencies, including the Miami archdiocese's Catholic-Spanish Center. Jewish Cubans with destinations elsewhere were aided by local welfare organizations, generally coordinated by HIAS [Hebrew Immigrant Aid Society]" (1993: 246–47).[6] Levine depicts an American Jewish community well aware of the dire economic straits of many Jewish Cuban (and Gentile Cuban) refugees, as well as the precarious political situation in Cuba. He quotes the American Jewish Committee's description of the exodus of Jewish Cubans to Miami in 1960: "Most of the exiles are middle-class people who arrive here [in Miami] with a very small amount of money and almost no possessions. They crowd into households and make ends meet by doubling, tripling, and quadrupling the number of people normally housed in these facilities. There is constant local fighting between the Fidelistas, Miami's permanent Cuban population of about 45,000, and the anti-Castro exiles" (American Jewish Committee 1960, qtd. in Levine 1993: 247).

The *Federation Magazine of the Jewish Floridian,* published monthly in the *Jewish Floridian* by the GMJF, reflected upon the Cuban Jews' arrival in Miami in the early 1960s in a 1979 article, "Miami's Cuban Jews: 20 Years After the Revolution." Like Levine, this article depicts Miami as a hospitable haven, especially for the Cuban Jewish émigrés, who benefited both from the United States government's efforts to aid all Cuban refugees and from the support of the established Jewish community in Miami: "About 5,000 people settled in Miami—Miami because it was so close, in climate and geography similar to sub-tropical Cuba, because it had an already-existing Jewish community which welcomed them and lent financial support, and because it was the primary refugee center for all emigré Cubans" (*Jewish Floridian* 1979: 15).

Clearly these accounts of generous assistance and support provided by South Florida's Jewish community to the newly arrived Jewish Cubans conflict with the solemn accounts quoted earlier. In order to understand these discrepancies better, we must consider the conditions under which this mass migration of Cubans to the United States transpired.

# The Cuban Revolution and the Exile Generation

January 1, 1959, marked the beginning of the Cuban Revolution. After nearly two years of guerrilla fighting, Fidel Castro emerged as a revolutionary leader seeking to eradicate corruption in the Batista government and inequities among the island's people. Much of the revolution's initial idealism and optimism quickly faded, however, as middle- and upper-class Cubans realized the lasting impact that Castro's socialist ideals would have on their comfortable lives. Indeed, nearly all Cubans (including Jewish Cubans) immigrating to the United States in 1959 and the early 1960s belonged to Cuba's elite: businesspeople, entrepreneurs, professionals, managers, and their families. The revolution continued to receive unwavering support from the poor masses, for it promised not only national pride and hope, but also immediate access to food, health care, and education.

On the eve of the revolution, between eleven and fourteen thousand acknowledged Jews lived in Cuba, among more than six million Cubans. Three-quarters of these were *polacos* and one-quarter *turcos*, as Ashkenazim and Sephardim, respectively, were called. While the vast majority of Jews resided in Havana, approximately three thousand lived in the provinces (particularly in the eastern provinces of Oriente, Camagüey, and Las Villas). More *turcos* than *polacos* could be found in these outlying areas, due perhaps to their greater adaptability to tropical Cuban society, or to their discomfort with the fast-paced lifestyle of major urban centers (Levine 1993: 236). The mass migration to the United States in the immediate wake of the revolution included more Ashkenazim than Sephardim, due primarily to the higher economic status of the Ashkenazim, and secondarily to the fact that urban dwellers were more mobile than rural denizens.

Castro's revolutionary political views surfaced as early as 1953, in "History Will Absolve Me," his speech defending his assault on the Moncada Barracks under the Batista regime. In its call for a complete reconstruction of the political, economic, and social systems established by Batista and his predecessors, the speech glorifies "the vast unredeemed masses, those to whom everyone makes promises and [who] are deceived by all; . . . the people who yearn for a better, more dignified and more just nation; who are moved by ancestral aspirations for justice, for they have suffered injustice and mockery generation after generation" (qtd. in Brenner 1989: 31–32).[7] Invoking José Martí, Cuba's quintessential revolutionary hero, Castro maintains that these oppressed people can achieve liberation only if they follow him on "the path where duty lies, . . . because he who has looked back on the essential course of history and has seen flaming and bleeding peoples seethe in the cauldron of the ages, knows that, without a single exception, the future lies on the side of duty" (35). This path leads away from "the hands of foreigners" and certainly away from a lust for imported industrial goods (33). Although everyone agrees that Cuba needs to industrialize, Castro argues, "the capital- ists insist that the workers remain under the yoke" (33). Thus, he thinks, under a corrupt and fundamentally flawed system such as that seen under the Batista regime, the masses remain unredeemed, and society cannot progress.

By 1961, Castro celebrated the atmosphere of change in revolutionary Cuba, explicitly attributing it to the viability of socialist doctrines. The revolution, he said, had "exchanged the conception of pseudo-democracy for direct government by the people," thus changing Cuba into "a socialist regime." In November, Castro declared, "I am a Marxist-Leninist, and I shall be one until the last day of my life" (qtd. in Pérez 1995: 331).

Almost six years before the Cuban Revolution, then, we see the anticapitalist, antiforeign sentiment so characteristic of Castro's government, both in 1961 and today. Unlike today, however, Cuba (especially Havana) in 1959 was filled with elites, many of whom had achieved socioeconomic success through connections with the United States, ownership of large land tracts and private businesses in Cuba, and intimacy with the Batista regime. The revolutionary regime's initial goals thus posed imminent political and economic dangers for these elites. Their ties with capitalist America made them revolutionary targets, and their migration was spurred by the Castro government's nationalization of private businesses and American industry, its implementation of agrarian reform laws, and the United States government's increasingly strained political and economic ties with Cuba (Pedraza 1992: 237).

Many Jewish Cubans belonged to elite socioeconomic groups and later would come to be known as members of "the exile generation." According to Eva Simazi, "They were geared into business, and then, professionals: lawyers and doctors." The first part of Simazi's statement is more accurate than the latter part; a large percentage of Jews in Cuba were involved in business, largely because many did not have the means, the time, or the educational background to devote themselves to pre-professional studies. In Cuba in 1959, the Jewish sector dated back (at most) only sixty years, and most Jews had arrived much more recently. Most *polaco* and *turco* immigrants worked as merchants or peddlers, with the more successful ones opening small businesses. Thus, the Jewish businessman (this was a decidedly male profession) became a familiar figure in Cuba. In contrast, American Jews tended toward professions such as medicine, law, and teaching. Mendel Kochanski documents this phenomenon in his 1951 account of Havana's Jewish community: "There are few Jewish professionals in Cuba. Sons of prosperous merchants attend the University of Havana or study in the United States, but after graduation they enter their father's businesses or start their own with father's money" (27).

One result of the community's prosperity in the 1950s was increased contact with American Jewish businessmen living on the island. These wealthy Batista supporters numbered 6,500 before 1959, and their improved relationship with the Jewish Cubans prompted the latter to increasingly orient itself toward the United

States (Levine 1996: 799). Furthermore, many Cuban-Jews told me, Communism was an all-too-familiar and unwelcome reality for many from Eastern European countries, since Russia's socialist-inspired Bolshevik Revolution of 1917 had created an oppressive atmosphere which eventually pervaded these neighboring countries.

Dora Benes belongs to this group of Jewish Cubans. Born in Lithuania, she immigrated to Cuba in the 1920s and then moved again to the United States in the early 1960s. In a *Miami Herald* article, she describes her husband's overwhelming fear of Communism: "Boris grew up under Communism in Russia. He knew about oppression; he knew how bad things could get and he was afraid [of Castro's Communist tendencies]" (qtd. in Laughlin 1994: 11). In fact, most Cuban Jews in pre-revolutionary Cuba staunchly opposed Marxist-Leninist ideas and felt embarrassed by Jews who continued to support socialism in Cuba after Castro's rise to power (Levine 1996: 799).

Many Jews equated Castro's rise to power with the ascendancies of Adolph Hitler and Benito Mussolini thirty years earlier. Even though Castro did not specifically target Jews on the basis of their religion and ethnicity, Jewish Cubans argued that he unjustly sought to "cleanse" Cuba of religion and power, both of which challenged his ambitions as a Communist dictator. In the Cuban-Hebrew Congregation bulletin for November 1965, Félix Reyler made this comparison in "El Perfil Fascista de Castro" ("The Fascist Profile of Castro"):

> Igual que Hitler, [Castro] es un consumado autócrata y ególatra que no admite cortapisas ni frenos de hombres ni de Partidos. . . . Cuando Castro uniformado y bravucón habla al sufrido pueblo cubano concentrado el la plaza pública, repite exactamente lo que hacía Mussolini en la Plaza de Roma y Hitler en la de Nuremberg. (Like Hitler, [Castro] is a complete big-headed autocrat who allows no restrictions or restraints by the people or by Political Parties. . . . When the uniformed and swaggering Castro speaks to the suffering people of Cuba concentrated in the public square, he repeats exactly the actions of Mussolini in the Plaza of Rome and Hitler in the Plaza of Nuremberg.) (20–21)

Reyler speaks against Castro not simply as a Jew, but as a Jewish Cuban who has learned the lessons of hate from the Holocaust and has learned the pleasures of democracy from pre-revolutionary Cuba. Jews in revolutionary Cuba feared losing their social, political, economic, and religious freedoms, particularly when Castro repeated Hitler's haunting promise of a "New Order" (20–21). Castro's language and actions evoked memories of Jewish oppression and suffering in the twentieth century, and so provided greater impetus for many Jews to go into exile in the United States.

# The Ashkenazic Experience

By 1921, the question of what the Bolsheviks should do with Russia's Jewish population loomed over Lenin's government. While conceding that the Jews should have complete access to vocational and educational opportunities, the Bolsheviks sought to destroy traditional Jewish culture, which they thought perpetuated a reactionary mentality. Jews looked to the past, the Bolsheviks claimed; thus, they did not align well with Bolshevik ideology, which emphasized the future. Within this focus on a time yet to come was a framework for understanding the present, in which suffering was an inevitable fact of life. The Bolsheviks understood this pain as a necessary prerequisite to pleasure, which can be found only in a far-away time and place: the future. This philosophy could help soothe the apparent inequities of life, allowing the masses to be content with their faith in the future and the bounteous gifts it might hold. It also could serve to deny the Jews their history, making it illegal to look backward.

By 1923, the Bolshevik party and the Russian government had either disbanded or co-opted all pre-revolutionary political parties. Additionally, they had abolished all *kehillot*, the organized Jewish communities which had gained some degree of autonomy in pre-socialist Eastern Europe, and seized all assets owned by these communities. The secular and socialist pro-Bolshevik campaigns which began in 1917 gained force throughout the next decade. Religion, Zionism, and the Hebrew language increasingly came under attack, with proponents of these three enduring ostracism and reprimands at best, and exile and imprisonment at worst. The Bolsheviks promoted religious and ethnic intermarriage as "Soviet." As a result of all these efforts, Jewish affiliation declined, while assimilation into Soviet society increased.[8]

Not all Jews accepted this assimilation. March 1921 marked the beginning of a mass migration of Jews from Eastern Europe to Cuba. Between 1921 and 1930, nearly eighteen thousand Eastern European Jews migrated to the island (Bejarano 1993: 46). These Ashkenazim came for economic and political reasons and, to some extent, religious ones as well, "fleeing the legacy of the pogroms [in Eastern Europe] and the difficult economic conditions that arose in the aftermath of World War I" (Behar 1995b: 154). Additionally, many sought to reunite with family members who had migrated to Cuba previously (Levine 1993: 38).

The height of Sephardic migration to Cuba coincided with this exodus of Ashkenazim from Eastern Europe. The Sephardim, however, had arrived in Cuba steadily since the turn of the century. Between 1902 and 1920, nearly ten thousand Sephardim migrated to Cuba, compared with less than five hundred Ashkenazim (Bejarano 1993: 46). Thus the 1920s saw in Cuba an unprecedented mixing of these formerly unassociated sub-ethnic groups.

*Banquet in the Centro Israelita de Cuba, Havana, October 12, 1931. This social and cultural center later became the Centro Israelita School. Photo courtesy of Ziff Jewish Museum of Florida.*

These statistics do not take into account the vast numbers of Jews—particularly Ashkenazim—who used Cuba as a way station in traveling to their final destination, the United States. Indeed, many Eastern European Jewish immigrants proceeded to leave Cuba within weeks after arriving there, usually because they obtained visas to the United States. The number of Jews who pursued this route is astonishing. In 1924 alone, nearly twenty thousand Ashkenazim entered Cuba, and the vast majority quickly continued on to the giant neighbor ninety miles to the north (Sapir 1948: 22). In comparison, between 1921 and 1930, only eighteen thousand Ashkenazim settled in Cuba as immigrants (Bejarano 1993: 46).

Coming from Eastern Europe and Russia, most of these Jews were familiar with socialism, and some (though few) even embraced it. Although Bolshevik Socialism created a dangerous, oppressive atmosphere for Jews in Russia, this did not mean that, in its "pure" form, socialism could not work as an ideology. By 1925, a fundamental political split developed among the Ashkenazim in Cuba. Those who tended toward socialism formed *Kultur Farain–Unión Cultural Hebrea* (Cultural Association–Hebrew Cultural Union), a secular community group for Yiddish-speaking, leftist Jews, comprised mostly of workers. This group engaged in antireligious propaganda and functioned much like a

Communist party cell (Sapir 1948: 66; Levine 1993: 296). Those who leaned toward capitalism, on the other hand, formed Centro Israelita (Hebrew Cultural Center), composed of moderates (usually bourgeoisie) who tended to oppose any political creed (Sapir 1948: 63). The Centro sponsored *Oifgang* (*Exit*), a Yiddish-language Zionist journal published from 1927 to 1930 and from 1933 to 1935. *Oifgang* assumed an assimilationist editorial position and thus represented a significant shift in Ashkenazic attitudes toward the stay in Cuba (Levine 1993: 43).

When Castro's regime came to power thirty-four years later, both these groups recognized language and propaganda reminiscent of Communist Russia. On both sides, this development aroused suspicion and fear. Castro resembled all too closely the young Lenin who irreversibly had changed (and, in the opinion of many Cuban Jews, destroyed) the home country of millions of Jews. Four years after the Cuban Revolution's commencement, less than 20 percent of the pre-revolutionary Jewish population remained in Cuba (Levine 1993: 236, 245). Many of those who remained in Cuba had Communist leanings and wanted to support the revolution; others did not want to leave family members remaining on the island; and still others were drafted into compulsory military service. Among the émigrés was a small group of leftist Jews who were uncomfortable with the form of socialism they saw developing within revolutionary Cuba. Most of the émigrés, however, were more conservative Jews with an aversion to Communism—an attitude they brought from the "Old World."

Bernardo Benes describes his own family's immediate reaction to Castro: "In 1959, I identified clearly that the Revolution was Communist-inspired. My father saw it eight days after he [Castro] came to power. But we students were in the enthusiasm of the Revolution." Benes's story is echoed by many other Cuban-Jews. While those of the younger, Cuban-born generation saw infinite possibilities for reform and equality in the force of the Cuban Revolution, many of their parents viewed it as something far more sinister. Bernie Kremen describes a scenario similar to the one recounted by Benes: "My parents had the advantage. Their European Jewish experience that brought them to Cuba let them know better than Cubans: they recognized Communism early. . . . The European Jewish experience made it easier, intellectually, for them to move again, this time to the United States."

Dow Rozencwaig, a former rabbi of the Cuban-Hebrew Congregation, also attributes his quick decision to leave revolutionary Cuba to his personal experience with Communism in Eastern Europe at the turn of the century: "I saw what was coming in 1959. I took Castro for three months. Then I recognized what he was doing. I saw it as Russian Communism. I wanted to get out" (qtd. in Stuart 1973: 45). Rafael Losger, whose parents were born in Poland, describes the same situation: "My family left in 1961, one year after Castro. My father right away realized what the situation was, and he said, 'I gotta get out of here.'"

## The Sephardic Experience

Like the Ashkenazim, many Cuban Sephardim reacted to Castro's Communist rhetoric with alarm. Unlike their Eastern European coreligionists, however, the Sephardim were frightened by the very ideas of religious persecution and societal secularization, rather than by any direct experience with these threats to Jewish life. Eva Simazi, a Sephardic Jew, describes her Turkish father's knee-jerk reaction to the introduction of Communist rhetoric and ideology to the Cuban people by Castro's army:

> I was talking to a friend [while waiting on line], trying to get into Havana University. I always wanted to be in the diplomatic course. I think I'm good at public relations, and I wanted to get there. So I was trying to see if, with a permit, I could get in. So I'm talking to this girl, and I say, "God willing, I'm trying to get this and that."
>
> So there comes this guy, with his olive green uniform, and he says, "What is that 'God willing'?"
>
> I said, "Well, because God is the one who decides everything."
>
> He says, "Why do you believe in God?"
>
> I said, "I believe in God because I exist."
>
> He said, "No, you exist because of biological reasons. It's like, the Indians used to believe that the sun was God, because when the sun was out and they had good crops, it was the Sun God. But there is no such thing as God."[9]
>
> When I went home, and I told my father about this conversation— "Tomorrow we are leaving" [he said]. And that's when we started to get in touch with this guy [a family friend who had personal connections with the Hebrew Immigrant Aid Society]. My father said, "I have to take her out of the country."

Simazi's story highlights the unease many Sephardic Jews in Cuba felt with Communist rhetoric, even though most never had experienced Communist rule directly. Nationalist revolution, however, was a concept familiar to most Sephardim from the former Ottoman Empire. Reigning from 1300 to 1918 and spanning much of northeastern Africa, southwestern Asia, and northeastern Europe, this empire in 1908 suddenly was threatened with revolts by nationalist, secular Young Turks and by wars with Italy (1911–12) and the Balkan countries (1912–13). As a result, important Ottoman centers were seized by Greeks, Italians, Serbians, and Yugoslavs. As new nationalist regimes emerged from the ashes of the Ottoman Empire after World War I, Jews realized that no longer could they count on the good will the empire had bestowed upon them for four centuries, nor on the relative autonomy it had granted them. In particular, the 1923 triumph of the strong-willed revolutionary and ultranationalist Mustapha Kemal in Turkey signaled the beginning of difficult and painful adjustments for Asia Minor's minority groups (Papo 1987: xii). One of these adjustments, often cited as a key factor in Jewish emigration, was the new regime's introduction of compulsory military service. Also, Jews worried, political instability easily could wreak economic havoc, especially for groups on the margins of a newly formed nationalistic regime. Finally, the impact of modernization and Western education contributed to the large exodus of Jews from the Ottoman Empire region in the 1920s and their migration toward more developed Western countries, such as Cuba (Bejarano 1996a: 3). The first two adjustments are clearly articulated in Rabbi Meir Melarmed's *Breve Historia*:

> Los emigrantes sefaraditas que se aventuraron hacia los puertos cubanos, desde el inicio de este siglo hasta la Primera Guerra Mundial, fueron bastante limitados. En sus comunidades del Imperio Turco, de donde la mayoría de ellos procedían, vivían una vida tranquila, disfrutando de libertades sin sobresaltos y de bienestar económico, que aunque modesto, era suficiente para sus limitadas necesidades, no sintiendo, por lo tanto, ningún pronunciado impulso para emigrar. Fueron solamente los dotados de un espíritu aventurero, de la ambición de hacer fortuna en el Nuevo Mundo, y especialmente aquellos que querían evitar el servicio militar en las condiciones de discriminación impuestas a los no-musulmanes, los que se alejaron de su ambiente familiar para correr los riesgos de una vida diferente.
>
> La Primera Guerra Mundial, con la interrupción casi completa de las comunicaciones marítimas, representó un obstáculo para la corriente emigratoria de nuestros correligionarios del Mediterráneo Oriental, pero una vez terminadas los hostilidades en 1918, nuevas olas de emigrantes vinieron de la Tracia turca (de los pueblos de Silvirie, Kirkli-Hisar, Chorlu), así como de Istambul, Izmir y otras pequeñas localidades.

> (The Sephardic emigrants who ventured toward Cuban ports from the beginning of this century until the First World War were fairly few in number. In their communities in the Turkish Empire, from whence the majority came, they lived a tranquil life, enjoying undisturbed liberties and economic prosperity; those, although modest, were sufficient for their limited needs. Therefore they did not feel any strong impulse to emigrate. The only ones who went were those gifted with an adventurous spirit, those ambitious to make a fortune in the New World, and

especially those who wanted to avoid military service under the conditions of discrimination imposed on non-Muslims. Only these took leave of their familiar environment to run the risks of a different life.

The First World War, with its near-complete interruption of maritime communications, presented an obstacle to the ongoing emigration of our coreligionists from the Eastern Mediterranean; but, once hostilities terminated in 1918, new waves of emigrants came from Turkey [from the towns of Silvirie, Kirkli-Hisar, Chorlu], as much as from Istanbul, Izmir, and other small towns.) (2)

## Migration, Diaspora, and *Regreso*

Eva Simazi points out that Jews had migrated relatively recently to Cuba and that Jewish Cubans knew from past experience the dangerous implications of fiercely nationalist and/or Communist ideologies. For her, these are key reasons why Jewish Cubans, by and large, had an easier time immigrating to the United States than did Gentile Cubans. Simazi also emphasizes that Jews' familiarity with uprootedness and movement permeates their views on nationality and homeland, easing their migration experience: "I would say there is a difference between the Jewish people and the rest of the world. We are more able to detach ourselves from where we are and move on. . . . I mean, we are Cubans, but we were able to detach ourselves, and now we're here. And if we have to move from the States someplace else, we will do it [unlike Gentile Cubans]." The historical connection between Jews and migration, resulting in what commonly is known as the Jewish Diaspora, is illustrated once again in the case of revolutionary Cuba. Indeed, as Simazi and many others point out, this played a key role in the readiness of thousands of Jewish Cubans to emigrate from Castro's Cuba in the 1960s.

Some Sephardic and Ashkenazic Cubans of the exile generation immediately felt uncomfortable with the nationalist, Communist rhetoric that accompanied Castro's rise to power. In their minds, fervor such as this, especially when inspired by a political cause, was intimately connected with political, economic, and/or religious persecution, both in the former Ottoman Empire and in Eastern Europe and Russia. Indeed, by 1959, the economic success achieved by many Jews—and particularly Ashkenazim—in the preceding decade attracted the scrutiny of the revolutionary regime, which targeted them politically as members of the bourgeoisie.[10] Over the next five years, the revolutionary government appropriated the private property of these absentee elites. Simazi recalls the day the revolution "hit home" in her family: "My father was one of the ones, that on October eleventh, my father read the paper, and his business was confiscated. He never went back to his business. They never let him in. They just took it and that's it." Simazi's emphasis on both the spontaneity and the finality of this event is characteristic of many Cuban exiles of this generation (see García 1996; Pedraza 1992 and 1996; Pérez 1995; Pérez Firmat 1995). In exile, these people reflected in sheer disbelief on the abrupt, drastic changes in their lives after 1959; surely all they had worked for in Cuba could not be stolen overnight. Labeled *gusanos* (worms) by Castro, these exiles viewed their condition as a temporary phenomenon. Expecting the United States swiftly to topple Castro and restore Cuba to its previous state, they anticipated a prompt *regreso* (return) to their island home. The United States, in the meantime, would function as a safe haven until the revolution was reversed.

These expectations of *regreso* are expressed clearly in former President Félix Reyler's discussion of the circumstances under which El Círculo Cubano-Hebreo (the Cuban-Hebrew Social Circle) formed in Miami:

> Hace veinte años, tuvimos la feliz iniciativa de constituir una organización que agrupara a todos los cubanos hebreos, que estaban en Miami. Veíamos a nuestros amigos tratando de reunirse en distintos lugares para cambiar impresiones sobre la situación cubana, y el futuro incierto de la estancia en Miami. Todavía no se sabía si éramos turistas o exilados, pues, pensábamos que dentro de algunos meses regresáramos a nuestra amada Cuba, a nuestros hogares, negocios, profesiones y empleos, y que todo iba a recordarse como una dantesca pesadilla.

> (Twenty years ago, we happily undertook to establish an organization that would bring together all the Jewish Cubans in Miami. We saw our friends trying to meet in different places in order to exchange impressions of the Cuban situation and the uncertain future of the stay in Miami. It was not yet known whether we were tourists or exiles, and we thought that within a few months, we would return to our beloved Cuba, to our homes, businesses, careers, and jobs, and that all would be remembered as a nightmare out of Dante.) (1981: 7)

Reyler's emphasis on the distinction between tourists and exiles is telling, for it points to the Jewish Cubans' view of the United States as simultaneously a safe haven and a waiting room. Expecting *regreso* within weeks, the Jewish Cubans never imagined creating new lives for themselves across the Florida Straits, in a land which, ironically enough, many had seen as their destination earlier in the century, when they and their families first became exiles.

Throughout the Cuban-Hebrew Congregation's bulletin for November 1965 are countless examples of nostalgia for a lost land and the expectation of prompt return to "'our sweet and lovely Cuba' where life was milk and honey" (White 1965: 4). A

*Cuban passport of Elisa Gerskes, who immigrated from Poland to Cuba in 1917, and from Cuba to Miami in 1962. From Henry A. Green and Marcia K. Zerivitz, "Jewish Life in Florida: A Documentary Exhibit from 1763 to the Present" (Coral Gables, Florida: Mosaic, Inc., 1991), p. 49.*

list of future congregation projects includes developing in Miami Beach a blood bank, a synagogue and social building, a library, and youth organizations; and, most important (in capital letters), "VOLVER A CUBA" ("RETURN TO CUBA") (p. 19). The bulletin's editor, Isidoro Lerman, writes, "A Dios pedimos que esta separación sea breve y que ojalá podamos celebrar en Cuba en corto plazo el recobro de la libertad perdida.... Que vuelva a renacer la patria soñada a la sombra venturosa de la bandera mas linda del mundo . . . la bandera Cubana." ("To God we pray that this separation be brief and that we be able to celebrate in Cuba in the near future the recovery of our lost liberty.... May the dreamed-of homeland be reborn under the daring protection of the most beautiful flag in the world . . . the Cuban flag") (Lerman 1965: 5). Also included in the bulletin is a poem by seventeen-year-old Marina Esteva Cobian, entitled "Cuba: A Pearl in the Vast Blue Sea." This is a moving testimony to the impact of this "dreamed-of homeland" on Jewish Cuban youth. Cobian links her own journey across the Florida Straits with Cuba's position in the water, describing the island as a "pearl lost in the sea," much like herself in the unfamiliar whirlwind of exile:

> *Now, I look over the vast blue sea*
> *And the stillness of the waters makes me cry;*
> *My mind is full of shadows of the past*
> *And the only word my lips repeat is: Why?*
>
> *You see, my friend, this pearl is my country,*
> *The land I love with all my heart.*
> *I remember the day I left her . . .*
> *I almost died when I had to part!*

*Every night I dream of returning,*
*Of the sugar-cane's sweet smell . . .*
*My mind can't conceive that some traitors*
*Made, out of paradise this hell!*

*. . . Remember this story forever . . .*
*Remember that once my homeland was free . . . !*
*Don't be sorry for me or my people*
*But be sorry for the pearl we lost*
*In the vast, blue sea!!! (1965: 22–23)[11]*

An equally poignant example of the emotional cyclone experienced by so many Jewish (and Gentile) Cubans awaiting *regreso* is captured in "Estampas de un Refugiado" ("Images of a Refugee"), a short memoir by Izzy published in 1965:[12]

It has been several years since we left our Beautiful Cuba. First the fear of leaving. If we should tell our neighbors. If we should close our business or not. If we should leave an employee in charge or not. Finally, we make a decision and one fine day we show up at the airport with as many suitcases as we were able to find. The airplane is ready to depart. Then we hear our name. What's going on? Should we keep going or not? Our blood freezes, but the militiamen are gentle and they are only interested in our Canoe cologne and a tube of toothpaste. It is natural that they are only interested in toiletries. Finally the airplane lifts its silver-plated wings in swift flight. We are leaving behind the lights of the Paseo of the Malecon and the Morro Castle. We feel calm, as we finally embark on a much-anticipated flight. Our vacation is beginning. But what we will do in Miami is a question we ask ourselves over and over again. But it's not important. All the days will pass quickly and in an opening and in the blink of an eye, we will have returned. These are our thoughts as we cruise the famous ninety miles and soon we touch down in the city of Miami, cradle of tourists. And here we arrive, as new tourists awaiting our prompt return.

We look for a place where we can settle ourselves. Difficult? Going to Miami Beach has been our dream during every one of our summer vacations. To rent houses they require one-year contracts. They are crazy. Who is going to rent a house for one year when we will return within three months? The best is a hotel. Which? Any that suits us, the cheapest possible. How does the San Juan [Hotel] look? Perfect.

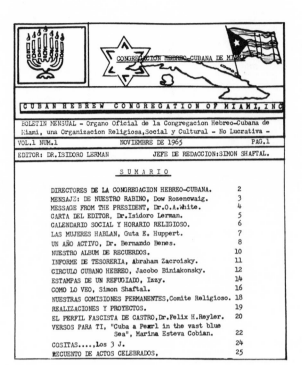

Two items published as part of the Boletín Mensual (Monthly Bulletin) of the Cuban-Hebrew Congregation of Miami, November 1965. Cover (top). Drawing (bottom) entitled "Cubita Bella . . . Volveremos!" ("Beautiful Cuba . . . We shall return!") accompanies Izzy's memoir, "Estampas de un Refugiado," pp. 14–15. Both show the Cuban-Jews' profound attachment to, and nostalgia for, their lost patria.

Estampas de un Refugiado...

La radio comunista se jacta del fracaso. Los Jefes de la invasion enmudecen y todo aquel torbellino de alegria y de ilusiones se - evapora como por obra de magia. Que hacer ahora. La cosa ha cam- biado. El regreso ya no nos parece tan facil. Las vacaciones se estan extendiendo. Los dolares se nos estan agotando. Los intere- ses no producen lo suficiente para cubrir los gastos. Tenemos que hacer algo. Que tal si buscaramos empleo. Magnifico. Pero que pa- sa ahora. Aqui quieren gente con "Experience" y que no pase de 35 años. Nuevamente los empleos estan limitados. Nada que como quiera que uno se ponga tiene que llorar.

Que salida nos queda. Pues que les parece un negocito. Si en - Cuba nos levantamos por que no podemos hacerlo aqui. Empezaremos en chiquito. Buscaremos un localcito barato y nos buscaremos un - socio para no pagar empleados. Asi vamos tirando. Poco a poco las ventas mejoran, los locales mejoran, los sueldecitos mejoran. Ya salimos a pasear mas a menudo. Ya no gastamos los 5 ni los 6 por 1. Ahora gastamos el 1 por 1. El que sudamos aqui al estilo yanqui con el Hamburger o el Hot Dog a la hora del almuerzo. La vida es - mas dura pero aprendemos a vivirla. Los automoviles van mejorando. Las casas alquiladas se van sustituyendo por casas compradas.

Ya tenemos nuestro Club. Ya jugamos poker. Ya hablamos de ahorrar en Income Tax y de cuando cogeremos la Ciudadania. Que lejos van quedando aquellos dias en que pensabamos en unas cortas vacaciones y en un pronto retorno. A decir verdad estas vacaciones ya nos van pareciendo demasiado largas, requetelargas. Como diriamos en argot beisbolero: La bola pica......y se extiende.

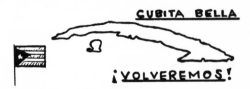

So the days go on and on. Many entertain themselves playing ball, others tuning into Cuba through their short-wave radios and listening to the rage of Castro ("the Bearded One") attacking day after day those who have not been hurt by his "nationalistic" policies. Hourly radio programs begin and every day the commentators cheer us up and comfort us with the news that tomorrow will be the day of return. Others, so as not to bore themselves, go to the stock exchange to put their precious money in one or other stock that indicates to us that it will rise in value. But, what of business? What of work? Nothing is spoken of these things. If we're going tomorrow, who is going to bother themselves with petty things during their vacation?

But so passes one month and another month. One day we get up early. The town is a party. Liberating forces have disembarked in Cuba. We run to hear the news. Everything is in confusion. The radio proclaims that we are winning. But the next day the result is sad. We have been defeated. Our men were captured. The Communist radio boasts about our failed attempt [in the Bay of Pigs invasion]. The leaders of the invasion say nothing and those whirlwinds of happiness and unfounded hopes disappear like in a magic trick. What do we do now? Things have changed. Return doesn't seem so easy anymore. Our vacations are extending. Our money is used up. Interest [on stocks] doesn't make enough to cover the costs. We have to do something. What if we look for employment? Perfect. But what will happen now? Here they want people with "experience" and not over 35 years old. Again the jobs are limited. No matter what we do, we have to cry.

What way out is left for us? It seems we should start a little business. If we were able to succeed in Cuba, why not here? We will begin small. We will look for a small cheap location, and we will look for a partner so we don't have to pay employees. We manage. Little by little sales improve, our locations improve, the little salaries improve. We can afford to go out more often. Now we don't spend 5 or 6 for 1. Now we spend 1 for every 1. We cough up money here in Yankee style with a Hamburger or Hot Dog at lunch. Life is harder, but we learn to live it. The cars are improving. The rented houses are being replaced by purchased houses.

Now we have our Club. Now we play poker. Now we speak of saving on the Income Tax and when we will acquire citizenship. How far away are those days when we thought of short vacations and a prompt return. To tell the truth, these vacations are already seeming too long, extremely long. Like we said in baseball slang: The ball hits the ground. . . . and it's extra bases.

Beautiful Cuba
We will return! (Izzy 1965: 14–15)

# Anti-Semitism in Cuba

Most scholarly research on Jewish life in Cuba documents an absence of any entrenched tradition of anti-Semitism on the island throughout the twentieth century, as well as an absence of systematic religious persecution within the Cuban Revolution (see Bejarano 1988; Bejarano 1991; Levine 1993; Sapir 1948). This was substantiated by all my interviewees.

While this picture is generally accurate, its details nevertheless bear scrutiny. Before Castro's rise to power, pro-Hitler followers and Falangists—a Fascist group founded in Spain in 1933 that supported Franco during the Spanish Civil War and advocated revolution through terrorism and violence—could be found in Cuba. The lack of anti-Semitism was due largely to a lack of knowledge about Jewish culture and to the fluidity of *mestizaje* in Cuban society (Ruth Behar to CB-L, July 27, 1999).

The work of Boris Sapir, a Jewish sociologist who fled Nazi Europe and sheltered in Cuba during the war years (Judith Elkin to CB-L, Mar. 3, 1999), illuminates the complexities inherent in trying to characterize the anti-Semitic presence in pre-revolutionary Cuba—particularly during World War II. While in Cuba, Sapir wrote *The Jewish Community of Cuba: Settlement and Growth* (1948), a foundation for all subsequent publications concerning the island's Jewish communities (especially since the rise of the Castro regime, which has severely limited foreign researchers' access to Cuban archives). While claiming that anti-Semitism "has never been firmly rooted in Cuba, and has never assumed the form of a mass movement," Sapir documents numerous incidents of anti-Semitism on the island: propaganda distributed by a "Jew-baiting" Cuban press, government curbs on Eastern European immigration and prohibition of Jewish meetings, and army-led attacks on Jewish stores and people (54, 57, 74–75). Sapir claims that the roots of anti-Semitic tendencies in Cuba lie not in discriminatory attitudes toward Jews from Europe, but "in the oversensitive national self-consciousness," the economic competition Jews posed to other merchants (particularly Spaniards), and the economic crises of the 1920s and 1930s (55). These issues, he contends, contributed to the call for protection of native labor and the implementation of the 1933 Cubanization Law, which required all businesses to employ at least 50 percent native Cubans. These anti-Semitic tendencies were seen in Cuba only after 1933, when Hitler assumed power and began to distribute his propaganda worldwide. After World War II broke out, Sapir stresses, anti-Semitism in Cuba waned, proving that Cubans were not anti-Semitic but merely influenced by Nazi propaganda like the rest of the world.

Margalit Bejarano, an Israeli historian of Cuban Jewry, also concludes that "Cuba lacks any tradition of religious anti-Semitism" (1991: 115). Similarly, historian Robert Levine contends that "anti-Semitism occurred sporadically in Cuba, although it never captured the mood of the larger population and was always the product of foreign instigators" (1993: 303). Like Sapir, Bejarano and Levine portray Jews as a group generally welcomed in Cuban society in the early twentieth century. They depict Cuba as one of the most welcoming host countries for Jews in the Western Hemisphere, and emphasize Cuba's rescue of Jewish refugees during the Holocaust and the wide support of all of its political parties in the late 1940s for the establishment of a Jewish State in the land of Israel (Levine 1993: 7; Bejarano 1991: 118).

Sapir, Bejarano, and Levine thus draw distinctions between "institutional" and "economically motivated" anti-Semitism; between nationalism and discrimination; and between international propaganda influence and domestic ideology. While Cuba often welcomed Jewish refugees, as these scholars stress, it still is important to recognize potential motivations behind this welcome. Was the friendly welcome extended to white Jewish refugees, and the unfriendly rejection handed to blacks from Haiti and Jamaica, a reflection of the Cuban government's attempts to whiten the island's population during the first half of the twentieth century? Furthermore, it is essential to recognize periods in Cuba's history when the island was not so accommodating to Jews and to investigate the motivations impelling this "unfriendliness." Bernardo Benes, for example, notes that Cuba's Jews were forced to attend a for-profit Beach Club in pre-revolutionary Havana, "because we weren't allowed in high society clubs." Did the fact that the Jews were "outsiders" make them more vulnerable to attack in Cuba with increased economic insecurity, the rise of nationalistic ideologies, and the looming threat of World War II?

## Another "Cuban Invasion"?

According to many sources, the Jews of Miami—both large organizations, such as the Greater Miami Jewish Federation, and individual synagogues—in the early 1960s ignored the influx of Jewish Cuban immigrants arriving daily in Miami Beach. Why? Information on this issue is sparse, and it is likely that Rabbi Abramowitz's reasoning—that the American Jews assumed that the Cuban Jews were wealthy and so did not need economic or social assistance—is largely correct. As Izzy suggests, some Jewish Cubans in Miami were fortunate enough to have small savings, though these quickly ran out.

Seymour Liebman discusses Miami Beach's familiarity with wealthy Cubans, who often vacationed there in the mid-1940s and the 1950s: "For many years since World War II, Cubans of all faiths came to Miami Beach during the summer, when hotel and restaurant rates, as well as prices in general, were much lower than in the winter season. This was particularly so before 1959. Local residents of Miami Beach called the summers the 'Cuban invasion.' Cubans were familiar with the streets, shops, and general area of Miami Beach. This familiarity and the proximity to the ocean contributed to their choice of this city for settlement" (1977: 301).

Most Cubans wealthy enough to travel to the States in the 1940s and 1950s were among Cuba's elite; indeed, by the 1950s, many Jews figured among this group. According to Liebman, they spent significant amounts of time and money in South Florida, visiting friends and relatives and investing in the area (300). In Miami, these Jewish Cubans, mostly nonreligious Ashkenazim, generally focused on vacationing rather than on associating with the city's Jewish community. A few even sent their children to summer camps and private schools in the United States before 1959. Thus, the masses of Cubans arriving in Greater Miami during the early 1960s did not seem as "foreign" as one initially might believe: as annual "invaders," they were familiar to many Miamians. It is likely, in fact, that Miami residents viewed the Cubans' *estancia* (stay) in Miami in much the same way that most Cuban exiles did: as "una estancia transitoria" ("a temporary stay"), much like the summer "invasions." Many Miamians did not grasp the grave distinction between the Cuban invasions before and after the revolution. This time around, these wealthy Cuban vacationers came with little or no money, baggage filled with family heirlooms, and passports stamped "Salida Definitiva" ("No Return").

By late 1960, forty thousand Cuban émigrés had arrived in the United States, with the majority remaining in Miami. Amid an economic recession and at the height of the winter tourist season, South Florida residents worried about the potential local consequences of this influx of unemployed, penniless Cubans. Letters poured in to the *Miami Herald* and the *Miami News,* grieving over the huge burden placed upon local governmental agencies and South Florida's residents. Simultaneously, much of the general population of the United States (often those far removed from major centers of immigration), the federal government, and the media celebrated the refugees' heroism and middle-class values (García 1996: 20). One 1961 *Newsweek* article, for instance, assured readers, "They're OK!" (qtd. on 20).

In 1961, President John F. Kennedy established the Cuban Refugee Program, which provided funds not only for resettlement but also for general relief, health care, job development and training, adult education, and surplus food distribution. National government funding also went to Dade County public schools to help them accommodate the more than 3,500 Cuban refugee children who had arrived by January 1961 (García 1996: 22–23).

Because the Castro government prohibited teachers and professionals from taking their diplomas out of Cuba, it was nearly impossible to verify their credentials in the United States. Private institutions reached out to these refugees, giving them Spanish-

and English-language training in their fields of specialization. In January 1961, for example, the University of Miami designed the Post-Graduate Medical Program for Cuban Refugees, a sixteen-week course taught in Spanish to Cuban doctors. In 1962, the same university sponsored the Cuban Teacher Training Program to prepare refugee teachers for the National Teachers Exam. Dade County public schools even established a teacher's-aide program specifically to enable Cuban teachers to assist in classes designed for Spanish-speaking children (García 1996: 26–27).

Cristina García's documentation of the initial years of Cuban post-revolutionary migration to Miami complements Robert Levine's description of the initial response to the refugees' arrival in Miami. Both portray a city, as well as local and national government and religious organizations, well aware of the political situation in Cuba and its implications for the United States. In fact, precisely this heightened awareness appears to have elicited the notably mixed reactions to the refugees. On the one hand, Miami's general public, which immediately felt the drastic socioeconomic effects of this mass migration, was quite aware of the economic situation of many Cuban émigrés in Miami. This public resented the extensive financial, occupational, and moral support the immigrants received from the United States government. Indeed, with increased federal assistance came increased local resentment, particularly as Cuban refugees began receiving more assistance than was available to United States citizens living in Florida (García 1996: 28–29). On the other hand, governmental and religious leaders, the media, and Americans sympathetic to the positive image of Cuban émigrés portrayed in the national media saw these refugees as heroes fleeing the horrors of Communism. Well aware of both the émigrés' precarious financial and political situation and the impact of the Cuban Revolution on Cold War politics, they reached out to support these people in their adjustment to the United States.

This ambivalence highlights the complex, multiple reactions of Americans to the rise of Communism ninety miles south of American soil and to the northward exodus of thousands of Cubans following the revolution. Was there, however, a "Jewish American reaction" to the Cuban exiles? In her book, Havana U.S.A., García briefly addresses this question by mentioning the Hebrew Immigrant Aid Society (HIAS) as a VOLAG (Voluntary Relief Agency) which, "in cooperation with the Greater Miami Jewish Federation, opened up offices to [financially] assist the [Jewish] refugees" (19). This claim is somewhat misleading, since the federation was only nominally involved in the refugee project, which was spearheaded by the National Council of Jewish Women (NCJW), Miami's HIAS representative, in cooperation with the United States government's Cuban Refugee Program. The federation did not extend its usual services directly to the Jewish Cubans.

García's claim challenges Rabbi Abramowitz's and Liebman's suggestions that the American Jews' failure to help Jewish Cubans was the result of the Americans' assumption that all these people were wealthy and had carried their fortunes with them to Miami in the early 1960s, as they had year after year in the 1940s and 1950s. Her words contrast starkly with the review of "The Cuban Refugee Situation" given by Arthur Rosichan, executive director of the Greater Miami Jewish Federation (GMJF), at a National Conference on Jewish Communal Service, held in Boston in May 1961. Of the approximately 30,000 Cuban refugees in Miami at that time, Rosichan estimated that "some 2000–3000 newcomers are Jews . . . nobody can tell exact statistics . . . Miami has borne the brunt . . . most came poised on one foot . . . ready to return . . . They have no money . . . We must try to persuade Cuban Jewish refugees that they have no future in Miami . . . resources of the Miami Jewish community have already been strained to the utmost . . . Miami as a port of entry is not the same thing as Miami as a permanent place in which to live" (Rosichan 1961: I, II; qtd. in Medin 1989: 15).

Rosichan's comments confirm the picture painted by many Cuban-Jews with whom I spoke: a well-established, prosperous American Jewish community in South Florida that frowned upon and in fact resented the arrival of Jewish Cubans there in the early 1960s. Perceiving these Cuban Jews as permanent, poor émigrés, Rosichan discouraged their settling in Miami, predicting deleterious consequences for both the Miamians already resident and the newly arrived refugees themselves if they did stay. Cuban Jews, who lacked both money and socioreligious roots in Miami, should search for these resources elsewhere, he said; they should refrain from considering their landing site to be their settlement site.

This GMJF does not appear to be the same organization portrayed by Levine, García, and the Jewish Floridian as bestowing generous assistance on the Jewish Cubans upon their arrival in South Florida. Instead, its very spokesperson voiced the anti-Cuban attitudes prevalent in Miami during this time (García 1996). Depicted by my interlocutors, as well as Bejarano, Fishkoff, Green, Liebman, and Reyler, as an institution which turned its back when faced with thousands of desperate Jewish Cuban refugees needing immediate financial assistance and religious guidance, the GMJF appears not only to have ignored the Jewish Cuban immigration crisis, but openly to have denied its ties to the Jewish Cubans.[13] Rosichan's and my interlocutors' statements contradict accounts which document extensive support by the federation for the newly arrived émigrés. Sentiments similar to this one by Eva Simazi often are heard today in Miami Beach's Cuban-Jewish community: "I don't think that Miamians, generally, discriminated against Cubans arriving in the 1960s. People do talk, but I don't think it's true. I think Miami has received the Cubans more than well. . . . As I told you, in the beginning we [the Jewish Cubans] did feel discrimination here [in Miami]. But it wasn't from the American [Gentile] community. It was from the American Jewish community. It's sad to say but it's true. Americans [i.e., Gentiles] never made us feel uncomfortable or unwelcome."[14]

As we compare personal testimonies, and especially Rosichan's 1961 paper, with García's and especially Levine's published historical narratives of the Jewish Cubans' experience in Miami in the 1960s, a huge discrepancy emerges. Those intimately involved in the migration experience of the Jewish Cubans—both Jewish Cubans themselves and those who witnessed this migration first hand—tell a story completely different from the one recounted by more detached scholars relying primarily on documentation from various relief agencies and the United States government, and relying only secondarily on personal recollection.

The Cuban-Hebrew Congregation's bulletin for November 1965 reprints an article from the newspaper, *Jewish Floridian*, which discusses the Rabbinical Association of Greater Miami's request for local Jewish community support for the Jewish Cuban refugees. The biblical principle "Love ye therefore the stranger" is invoked, as well as "the American tradition of being a haven for the oppressed." Yet, as Jacobo Biniakonsky highlights in a critique following the reprinted article, that which is written is not necessarily that which is practiced. Although the Rabbinical Association directed Jewish Cubans to local Jewish organizations, he writes, this did not guarantee that they would be received kindly by their coreligionists. Biniakonsky contrasts the United States government's generosity to the Cuban refugees with the South Florida Jewish community's cold reaction to the Jewish Cuban refugees:

> Es lamentable y doloroso[,] sin embargo, que los refugiados hebreos no hayan encontrado en Miami una acogida fraternal por parte de las Instituciones Hebreas ni sus componentes. Ninguna sintió la necesidad de interesarse por nuestros problemas, ni extendernos una mano en los momentos en que más lo necesitábamos, cuando acabábamos de llegar huyendo de un régimen de terror.
>
> Que distinta fue la Comunidad Hebrea de Cuba. Ella sí aportó su apoyo material y moral a los miles de refugiados que tocaron playas cubanas durante y después de la conflagración mundial.
>
> En Miami, los refugiados hebreos se dirigieron a las organizaciones hebreas locales en petición de un local para reunirse y sobre todo para que pudieran reunirse nuestras juventudes. Pero todas las peticiones nos fueron denegadas, con la excepción honrosa del

Washington Federal Saving and Loan Association of Miami Beach,
que nos ofreció su auditorium para reuniones sociales y para la
celebración de festividades religiosas.

    . . . El deber de todo hombre es contribuir para hacer un mundo
mejor en que vivir. . . . y la manera más práctica de contribuir es
comenzar por hacernos mejores nosotros mismos.

    (It's lamentable and painful, however, that the Jewish refugees didn't
    encounter in Miami a brotherly reception by the Jewish Institutions or
    their constituents. None felt the need to involve themselves in our
    problems, nor to extend a hand to us when we needed it, when we arrived
    fleeing a regime of terror.
    How different that was from the Jewish Community of Cuba, which
    contributed its material and moral support to the thousands of refugees
    who arrived on Cuban shores during and after World War II.
    In Miami, the Jewish refugees approached the local Jewish organiza-
    tions, seeking a place to meet and above all where our young people
    could meet. But all these requests were denied, with the honorable
    exception of the Washington Federal Saving and Loan Association of
    Miami Beach, which offered us its auditorium for social gatherings and
    for the celebration of religious holidays.
    . . . The duty of everyone is to contribute to making the world a
    better place to live. . . . And the most practical way to contribute is to
    begin by making ourselves better people.) (1965: 12–13)

Biniakonsky's account helps to reconcile the discrepancies between the aforementioned historical narratives and interviews. On paper, South Florida's Jews reached
out to their Cuban coreligionists. This became the documented historical "truth," as
it were. By considering unpublished counternarratives, however, we can discern the
limitations of these written organizational histories. Since the latter serve as public
records, their authors have a motivation to portray their respective organizations in
the best possible light.[15]

The questions raised about such "historical" documentation are complicated
further when we consider Jeffrey Kahn's discussion of the relative ease with which the
Jewish Cubans settled into Miami:

    Although most Jews left Cuba with only the clothing they wore, many
    had money waiting for them in the United States. Since World War II,
    Miami Beach had become a popular summer resort for Cubans of all

faiths. Through the years, many Jews had purchased vacation homes in South Florida and had deposited much of their savings in United States banks. Even Cuban Jews who had no previous ties with the United States found that they were able to redeem the Israel Bonds they had purchased in Cuba, and thus begin their lives again. As a result, only 808 resettled Cuban refugees required extensive financial assistance from Jewish communal organizations in the United States. (1981: 90)[16]

As we have seen, Liebman asserts that a familiar relationship existed between Miamians and Cubans, and in particular between Miamian and Cuban Jews. According to Kahn, not only were Miamians familiar with the Cuban "invasions" Liebman refers to, but also the Jewish Cuban "invasion" of Miami in the years immediately following the Cuban Revolution had much the same character (at least financially) as those in previous years. Thus, Kahn disputes the idea that desperate refugees were shunned *financially* by their fellow coreligionists in Miami.

Kahn's account is somewhat misleading, however. He gets the figure 808 from Ilya Dijour's article, "Jewish Immigration to the United States," written for the *American Jewish Yearbook* in 1962. Dijour's article examines Jewish immigration to the United States only for the fiscal year ending June 30, 1960, by which time only some of the estimated 2,500 to 3,500 Jewish Cubans who left Cuba in the early 1960s had arrived. Also, Dijour discusses only those Jewish Cubans who sought assistance from HIAS, not any other relief organization. Therefore, the "808 resettled Cuban refugees" whom Kahn describes as "requiring extensive financial assistance from *Jewish communal organizations in the United States*" (emphasis mine) arrived in the United States before 1960 and sought assistance from only *one organization*, HIAS. This figure, then, fails to take into account hundreds, perhaps thousands, of Jewish Cubans who arrived destitute in the United States after June 1960 and who requested assistance from non-Jewish groups or "Jewish communal organizations" other than HIAS.

## Cuban Ashkenazim and Sephardim in Miami

Kahn's more detailed discussion of the separate experiences of Cuban Sephardim and Ashkenazim in Miami in the 1960s brings his argument closer to those of the people I interviewed. "The only established South Florida congregation to actively welcome Cuban Ashkenazic Jews was the Conservative Temple Menorah on Miami Beach's North Beach," he writes, pointing to the failure of Miami's other established synagogues to welcome the Cuban Ashkenazim (1981: 91). Furthermore, he continues, "although they did not receive the warm welcome experienced by their Ashkenazic coreligionists, most Cuban

Sephardim joined the Sephardi Jewish Center in Miami Beach" (91). According to Rabbi Melarmed, this membership was extremely short-lived after the center reacted with outright hostility to the Cuban Sephardim:

> Antes de formar la sociedad llamada Cuban Sephardic Hebrew Congregation de Miami, los emigrantes sefaraditas llegados de Cuba pensaban juntarse a la ya existente Congregación Sefaradí de habla inglesa y ladino, situadada en la Avenida Collins, entre los calles seís y siete, la cual lleva el nombre de Sephardic Jewish Center. Entretanto, según lo que declararon dichos inmigrantes, éstos se vieron discriminados particularmente por el rabino Sadi Nahmías, de la mencionada congregación, y de cual se dice que es un jazán sefaradí. A raíz de esta supuesta discriminación, los nuevos inmigrantes sefaraditas cubanos rentaron un local en la Avenida Washington 715, en Miami Beach, convirtiéndolo en un pequeño templo y en un lugar para juntas, meldados (Yahrzeit), etc.

> (Before forming the society called Cuban Sephardic Hebrew Congregation of Miami, the Sephardic immigrants arriving from Cuba expected to join the extant Sephardic Congregation where English and Ladino were spoken, located on Collins Avenue, between Sixth Street and Seventh Street, and which bore the name Sephardic Jewish Center. Meanwhile, the immigrants saw themselves as discriminated against, particularly by Rabbi Sadi Nahmías of the aforementioned congregation, who, it is said, is a Sephardic cantor. As a result of this alleged discrimination, the new Cuban Sephardic immigrants rented a meeting place at 715 Washington Avenue, in Miami Beach, converting it into a small temple and a place for meetings, Yahrzeit [the Jewish death ritual], etc.) (198?: 9).[17]

Expecting to be welcomed by the Sephardic community, the newly arrived Cuban Sephardim looked to the Sephardic Jewish Center, the largest Sephardic congregation in Miami Beach, as a safe haven in which a common Jewish religion, common Sephardic customs, and a common Ladino (and for some, English) language would bring Sephardim of all nationalities together. According to Melarmed, these hopes were dashed. Even the rabbi of this congregation rejected the Cuban Sephardim, forcing them to form a separate community *as Cuban Sephardim,* a group seemingly ostracized by other Jews. Cuban Sephardim took this rejection seriously but attempted to reverse its negative implications by proudly maintaining their distinctive collective identity in the name of the congregation they built later in that decade, the Congregación Sefaradita Cubana de Miami (Cuban Sephardic Hebrew Congregation of Miami).[18] Unfortunately, Melarmed does not elaborate on the forms of, or possible reasons for, the original discrimination; nor does he discuss the relationship between specific events and the Cuban Sephardim's overall initial experience with Miami Beach's Jewish community. He also does not discuss the adjustment process for Cuban Ashkenazim who moved to Miami.

As we review various discussions of the arrival of Cuban Jews in Miami Beach, it becomes increasingly evident that historians and interviewees tend to document and remember the events of the 1960s in distinct ways. Benes and Abramowitz, in particular, examine certain religious and financial issues that arose upon the Jewish Cubans' arrival, and use these as the basis for a general notion of the way these émigrés were accepted by Miami Jews. In their descriptions, as well as in Levine's, the term "American Jews" becomes a code name for the Greater Miami Jewish Federation (GMJF) and for Miami Beach synagogues filled with "snowbirds" from the Northeast and other Jews whose families had lived in the United States for several generations. Kahn exposes some of the problems inherent in viewing the situation in this light. Different Cuban Jewish families undoubtedly had very different financial situations upon arriving in Miami in the 1960s; some already had substantial assets in the city. The social/religious situation seems to have been structured along different lines, however. These numerous accounts, taken together, suggest that few Miamians welcomed the Jewish Cubans *as Jews*. Although these émigrés may have received financial assistance from the Cuban Refugee Program, HIAS, or GMJF (as we have seen, this last claim is dubious), it does not appear that the new arrivals, as a group, received much social or religious support from Miami's Jews, aside from that provided by NCJW and Rabbi Abramowitz at Temple Menorah.

The situation becomes more complicated when we look at the differing receptions accorded Sephardim and Ashkenazim by Miami Beach synagogues, both socially and religiously. Kahn's account points to a separation between Sephardic and Ashkenazic Cuban communities immediately upon arrival in Miami, although he implies that this breach was the result of a voluntary choice on the part of these two communities, with the Ashkenazim choosing Temple Menorah and the Sephardim initially opting for the Sephardic Jewish Center. Susana Hamla, a Sephardic Cuban, offers an alternative story. She did not bother to mention the Sephardic Jewish Center in her discussion, she told me, because the Cuban Sephardim's experience there was so brief. Instead, she thinks, the Ashkenazic-Sephardic split was the result of Ashkenazic Temple Menorah's lack of familiarity, and discomfort, with the Cuban Sephardim.

> Yes, [Rabbi Abramowitz] was my rabbi, my children's rabbi. Let me tell you a story about Rabbi Abramowitz. When we first came from Cuba, the only place that opened its doors to us was Temple Menorah. And we were in the situation that we couldn't afford to pay for Hebrew School, so they let us in and let our kids [attend Hebrew School] and whatever we

could afford, we paid. And you know, years after, as the situation was improving, we paid more, and more and more, and even we belonged to that temple [as paying members]. So [my children] were Bar Mitzvahed there. [Yet,] even though we [Sephardim] are Jewish, many of them didn't believe we were Jewish because we didn't speak Yiddish. And we had, sometimes, a hard time. When my son was going to be Bar Mitzvahed, the rabbi asked me if whoever was going to come to the Torah, if they knew what they were going to say, or if they knew how to read Hebrew. And I said, "Of course, we are Jewish. Whoever is going to come to the Torah is Jewish and they know what to say in Hebrew."

Hamla calls attention to the discomfort felt by Cuban Sephardim in the unfamiliar Ashkenazic world in Miami. Even a welcoming Ashkenazic synagogue such as Menorah, which offered free membership and other services to Cuban Sephardim and Ashkenazim, was not perceived as completely hospitable to the Sephardic émigrés. Concerns about the Cuban Sephardim's "Jewishness," according to Hamla, loomed over Temple Menorah in the 1960s, most notably in questions surrounding the Cuban Sephardim's ability to read Hebrew and their knowledge of Jewish customs and liturgical practices.[19]

Questioning the "Jewishness" of Sephardim—particularly Cuban Sephardim—was not unique to Temple Menorah. It was (and still is) assumed by many American Ashkenazim that a lack of knowledge of Yiddish meant a lack of knowledge of Hebrew and a consequent loss of Jewish identity. For this Jewish majority, Yiddish language and customs had become inextricably linked with being Jewish; a foreign accent, Ashkenazim often assumed, was the mark of a Gentile. In her book examining Sephardic identity in the United States, Judith Mizrahi examines the "incongruity between Sephardic and American cultures, including the misinformation that leads to the confusion that 'Jewish' means only 'Ashkenaze'" (1993: 57). "When one hears 'Jewish'," she writes, " one thinks of the Ashkenaze Jews who emigrated from eastern or central Europe, and one thinks in terms of certain values, traditions, time of immigration, tastes in food, and of language—German and its derivative, Yiddish" (60).

Susana Hamla tells another painful story which illustrates this ignorance of Jewish diversity:

When we just got here [from Cuba], we were talking on a public bus once, and an elderly [Ashkenazic] woman asked us, "Where are you from?" We said, "We are from Cuba." And she said, "But you are not Jewish." I said, "Yes, we are." She said, "How come you don't talk Jewish or Hebrew?"[20] I said, "Hebrew is the Jewish language. But the language that you're talking [about] is Yiddish. Do you think that if I don't talk Yiddish I'm not Jewish?

This is the language from my country. So Jewish people don't only talk Yiddish. You are wrong. We are as Jew as you are. Even though we don't talk Yiddish, and we talk in Spanish and Ladino." She couldn't understand that I was Jewish but I didn't speak Yiddish. And I explained to her but I don't know if she understood. But many people found it hard to understand that we were Jewish but we didn't talk Yiddish.

Nelly Peres, a Sephardic Cuban, emphasizes that this tension did not exist solely between Cuban Sephardim and American Ashkenazim. Relations between Cuban and American Sephardim, particularly at the Sephardic Jewish Center, were extremely tense during the 1960s and resulted in the unexpected transfer of Cuban Sephardim to Temple Menorah:

[At least] Temple Menorah opened the door for us, because we asked the Sephardim on Collins and Seventh [Street]—we asked for help, to go there and worship, and they didn't care about us. They didn't open the doors for us. That's why they're not there anymore. They thought that they had God in their hands, and all those people—they were very wealthy people at that time. They never thought that their shul was going to close, because all the rich people who were there passed away, and they didn't have enough members, and they had to sell the place. They had to sell the property and everything. Now I think it's a discothèque. In the beginning, the first year, we asked them that we want to go for the high holy days, and they said if we don't pay, we cannot go. So we stayed home because we didn't have a place to go. So they got what they—you know. . . . At that time there were a lot of rich people that could've done something with that shul. But they didn't. And we could've been a strong community but they didn't want us [Cubans].[21]

Like Melarmed, Peres describes a fundamental tension between the members of the Sephardic Jewish Center and the Cuban Sephardim. She dolefully recounts this period of ultimate rejection of Cuban Sephardim by their American counterparts. Her story, as well as those of Hamla and Melarmed, document a sad chapter in history, when a group of people was continuously ostracized by those whom it assumed would be its greatest allies.

## A Hyphenated Identity

What can we discern about the nature of the Cuban Jewish community which emerged in Miami Beach in the 1960s? In my interviews, most Cuban-Jews—particularly Ashkenazim—recalled the establishment of the Círculo Cubano-Hebreo as a cultural necessity, due in part to the American Jewish community's rejection of them, but also due to their own need to congregate *as Cuban Jews,* to discuss events "back home," and to rekindle the warm familiarity of the community they had known in Cuba. This is reflected in Reyler's "Los Primeros Años del Círculo:" "En todos los lugares observábamos el ansia que había de comunicarse las ideas y comentar las opiniones sobre las últimas noticias internacionales. Parecía cumplirse aquel aforismo de que el dolor propio compartido en forma colectiva se sentía individualmente menos intenso." (Everywhere we observed the longing we had to communicate our ideas and to discuss our opinions about the latest international news. It seemed to fulfill the aphorism that, when one's own pain was shared in a collective form, it was felt less intensely by the individual) (1981: 7).

The Jewish Cubans belonged nowhere in Miami. Among other Cuban exiles, they became "Jews"—religious brothers and sisters of the many Jewish landlords and employers in Miami who treated these Cuban émigrés poorly upon their arrival. Marcos Kerbel, a past president of the Cuban-Hebrew Congregation and still an active member of the Cuban-Jewish community today, contrasts this negative attitude toward Jews held by many Cuban exiles in Miami with the positive inter-actions between Jews and Gentiles in pre-revolutionary Cuba: "In Cuba, they were not anti-Semitic, per se. . . . It was only when the Cubans came here that some anti-Semitic sentiments arose. Many of the landlords in Miami were Jewish; many of these landlords rejected renting to families with kids, which included many Cuban families. . . . Also, Jewish employers and bosses were in some cases inhumane in treating their Cuban employees. That created some animosity toward the Jewish employers from the people who were laid off or whose jobs were given [away] to [others] at lower wages."

Apart from this, Gentile and Jewish Cubans became further estranged, since Gentile exile communities began to develop in Little Havana (Southwest Eighth Street) and Coral Gables, while the Jewish community continued to develop in Miami Beach. Placing their religion above all else, the Jewish Cubans chose to settle with their coreligionists. While the Jewish Cubans found it difficult being separated from the familiar Cuban culture situated on Miami's mainland, the refusal of Miami Beach's established Jewish community to open its arms to its Cuban coreligionists was a much more painful experience.

The Jews from Cuba arrived in the United States as (Jewish) Cubans, viewing their religion as an afterthought, compared to their central national and political identity as Cuban exiles from Communism. Once in South Florida, however, they placed their religious identity above all else, reaching out to the Jewish community of Miami Beach. Yet their nationality prevented them from consummating this alliance. Whereas in Cuba they had stood out *as Jews,* in Miami Beach they stood out *as Cubans.* Those who had arrived on the shores of the United States as "Jewish Cubans" thus became "Cuban Jews" in Miami Beach.[22]

Once the Cuban Jews realized that their stay in Miami would not be temporary, their attitudes toward their new home changed drastically. Miami Beach's Jewish community had made its feelings toward its Cuban coreligionists abundantly clear. Temple Menorah, the exception to the rule, kindly had offered them temporary assistance and a chance to get their feet on the ground. Now it was time, many felt, to consolidate and attempt to reconstruct what had been left behind in the *patria* (homeland). Yet these émigrés understood that this was a new time, place, and atmosphere. While they could never transplant Jewish Cuba to Miami Beach, they could try to rebuild the most cherished aspects of their lost island home.

This consolidation, which resulted in the development of the Círculo Cubano-Hebreo (Cuban-Hebrew Social Circle), signified the entrance of the Cuban Jews into a new space—one where they would not be challenged as Cubans or as Jews. Within this space, these émigrés' identities changed, both as individuals and as members of a larger group; here they became the (intentionally hyphenated) "Cuban-Jews." The symbolic significance of this label was monumental, for it marked the passage of Jews from Cuba into a new phase—one in which they developed a new and unique group identity. No longer were they "Cubans," as the United States government and Miami Beach's Jewish community had classified them; nor were they simply "Jews," as they had been labeled in Cuba and as they had chosen to label themselves upon arrival in Miami Beach. As a hyphenated combination of the two, the Cuban-Jews defined an entirely new space in which they could grow as a distinct community. In that community, their Cuban and Jewish roots melded, shaping each other in intricate and indistinguishable ways.

# Chapter 2

## A Second Transformation: From Cuban-Jews to Jewbans

The Cuban-Jewish community of Miami Beach developed rapidly after the émigrés' initial period of adjustment to the area. In light of their rejection by the preexisting Ashkenazic and Sephardic congregations in Miami Beach, the Cuban-Jews—numbering approximately five thousand in Greater Miami by 1965—set out to construct their own congregation, which would simultaneously function as a social circle, a place of worship, and a place to carry forward Cuban-Jewish culture (see Jewish Floridian 1979: 15; Kaplan, Moncarz, and Steinberg 1990: 303; Levine 1996: 802; Liebman 1977: 300–301). Four Ashkenazic men founded the Círculo Cubano-Hebreo (Cuban-Hebrew Social Circle), whose membership immediately came to include both Sephardim and Ashkenazim.

Alberto Ralvey, a forty-three-year-old Sephardic Cuban-Jew, reflects upon the changing relationship between Ashkenazim and Sephardim:

> There was some difference in the beginning in Cuba, when the Ashkenazis went to Cuba. . . . Since they came from Eastern Europe, they didn't have too much contact with Sephardic Jews. In the Ashkenazis' eyes, the Jewish people first of all spoke Yiddish, second had light eyes and light skin and things like that, and ate pastrami [smiles]. And then in Cuba they found Sephardic Jews, that came from Turkey, that in many cases were dark, that were not too tall. . . . They loved to play cards and dominoes and drink tea and take life easier because they were living all the time between Arabs in Northern Europe and Turkey and everything, and it was a different system. And since the Arabs didn't discriminate against Jews the way the Russians and the Germans and the Polish did, the Sephardics didn't have the feeling against the Gentiles that these people from Eastern Europe had. And on top of that, they didn't speak Yiddish. So, for many years, when an Ashkenazi girl married or was going out with a Sephardic, it was like marrying or going out with a Gentile. And these people were more successful in business than the Sephardics, in general. They became rich faster than the Sephardics—through hard work and saving . . . and they didn't like the Sephardics. It's a very interesting phenomenon: in here [Miami], Ashkenazi and Sephardic Cubans mix perfectly well. It didn't happen like that in Cuba. Here it doesn't matter: you're a Sephardic, you're

a Jew. You're Ashkenazic, you're a Jew. It doesn't matter. . . . If you speak Yiddish or eat pastrami, it doesn't matter. . . .

The change took place here [in Miami]. It's an interesting phenom-enon that everything disappeared. The funny thing, my temple, Temple Moses, is a Sephardic temple.[1] We have Ashkenazics and Sephardics there. Menorah is another very populated-by-Cubans Ashkenazi temple here on Dickens Avenue, and there's a lot of Ashkenazics and some Sephardics there. And then there's the Cuban-Hebrew Congregation, that is the original *polaquitos* congregation, . . . that is mainly Ashkenazic but there are also Sephardics there, because of marriage.[2]

## El Círculo Cubano-Hebreo: Community Growth and Development

In *Círculo Cubano-Hebreo de Miami, 1961–1981: 20 Aniversario,* a booklet marking the twentieth anniversary of the Cuban-Hebrew Congregation, Arón Kelton, the congregation's president in 1979–81, discusses the conditions under which the community was formed:

Surge el Círculo de una necesidad muy lógica en aquellos tiempos: se necesitaba un lugar que sirviera de punto de reunión de los que llegaban de Cuba, de los que querían saber de sus familiares, de un amigo, de los que se interesaban en conseguir un trabajo o de los que simplemente querían reunirse para "verse las caras," para cambiar impresiones sobre la situación cubana y el futuro en aquel entonces incierto de la estancia en Miami.

(The Círculo [Social Circle] arose from a necessity very logical in those days: a place was needed which would serve as a place of reunion for those who had arrived from Cuba—for those who wanted to inquire about their relatives, or about a friend; for those seeking a job opportu-nity or those who simply wanted to get together to see each other "face to face," to exchange impressions of the Cuban situation and the future, in those uncertain times, of the stay in Miami.) (Kelton 1981: 5)

Because the Cuban-Jews were unable to meet in American synagogues in Miami, these *reencuentros* (reunions) served as important forums where they could discuss political, financial, and emotional matters, as well as simply relax among old friends. Before they started El Círculo, there were only two places to which they could turn for religious and community support: Temple Menorah, which provided free reli-gious and social support; and the Greater Miami Section of the National Council of Jewish Women (NCJW), which provided broad-based assistance through its New Americans Program.[3] This program provided a broad range of services to the Jewish (and Gentile) Cuban émigrés, as it had done for émigrés of many nationalities throughout the century. These included meeting trains and planes; acting as interpreters; locating housing; providing citizenship tutoring; providing technical assistance with immigration and naturalization problems, indemnification claims, and searches for relatives and friends; attending Naturalization Court proceedings; conducting English classes and individual instruction; and providing free clothing through NCJW's thrift shops (NCJW Oct. 1960 and May 1962: 2, 4). Through the New Americans Program, the NCJW Greater Miami Section "became the headquarters for registration of Jewish Cubans who had come to the United States seeking asylum," assisting five hundred Cubans to enter the United States from January to May 1962 alone (NCJW May 1961: 4; May 1962: 7).[4]

Additionally, NCJW became involved in educating the public about the Cuban exodus through its monthly Council Division Meeting lectures, such as "The Cuban Explosion" (NCJW January 1961), "Cuban Confidential: First-Hand Reports of Conditions in Cuba" (Mar. 1961), "Cuban Refugee Art Show" (Dec. 1961), "Adjusting to a New Way of Life: Panel Discussion Featuring Four Cuban Refugees" (Mar. 1962), and "Where Do We Go From Here? A Panel Discussion Featuring Four Recently Released Cuban Prisoners of the Bay of Pigs Invasion" (Mar. 1963). The organization reached out to the community socially, hosting Hanukah parties for Cuban children in 1962 and 1963 which also served as *reencuentros* for their parents (NCJW Jan. 1962: 5; Feb. 1963: 4). On one occasion, NCJW invited "several Cuban ladies living here who belong to the Cuban Jewish Social Club" [El Círculo] to its general meeting. "At the end of the afternoon," the bulletin notes, "we wished each other 'Hasta luego' and not 'Adios,' for we were most 'sympatico' [*sic*]" (NCJW Mar. 1963: 7).[5]

NCJW also worked with the Cuban Refugee Center, sponsored by the United States government. In cooperation with this program, HIAS, and the more familiar Catholic-based "Operation Peter Pan," NCJW provided homes and transportation to children en route to relatives elsewhere in the United States (NCJW May 1961: 3; May 1962: 4). The Cuban Children's Program, which subsumed these projects, brought fourteen thousand unaccompanied children to the United States between 1961 and 1963 (Masud-Piloto 1996: 40; García 1996: 23). Cristina García writes of the "Peter Pan" children: "Many parents in Cuba, unable to emigrate, sent their children ahead to the United States, hoping to be reunited at a later date. Some parents worried about political indoctrination in Cuban schools; others hoped to save their boys from military conscription; and others were motivated by rumors that the government was going to send Cuban children to the Soviet Union and the Eastern Bloc for training. Consequently, more than half the children who arrived in Miami unaccompanied were between the ages of thirteen and seventeen, and over two-thirds were boys" (García 1996: 23). Masud-Piloto (1996: 40), using statistics provided by the United States Department of Health, Education and Welfare, estimates that 7,041 children arrived in the United States through the efforts of the Catholic Welfare Bureau (i.e., Operation Peter Pan); 117 arrived through Jewish Family and Children's Services; and 28 through United HIAS Service (which NCJW represented in Miami).

Marcos Kerbel was one of these children. In 1961, he arrived alone in Los Angeles at the age of fourteen, through the HIAS-sponsored children's project. As an adult, he moved to Miami and became an active member of the Cuban-Hebrew Congregation. Below, Kerbel describes the development of the Cuban-Jewish community in Miami Beach and, specifically, where it placed its emphasis.

> *Kerbel:* The Cuban-Jewish community is not orthodox in their
> religious practices. And when people tell me, and when I continuously hear
> about it, I point out—I'll show you where it is. Look at this book [opening
> *Círculo Cubano-Hebreo de Miami, 1961–1981: 20 Aniversario*, the booklet
> marking the twentieth anniversary of the Cuban-Hebrew Congregation,
> which I had brought to his office]. First you see this historic role with
> Article Number One.[6] Article Four: the objectives. Let's see, Article
> Number Three: here, it's a non-profit organization, right? The character.
> And look at the words—very important here because of who wrote it: Dr.
> Félix Reyler. He wrote "social, fraternal, charitable, philanthropic, civic,
> educational," and then "religious" comes last. . . . [Turns to back cover
> photo of Félix Reyler, a founding member and the second president of the
> congregation, from 1963 through 1965.] Having been an attorney and a
> judge in Cuba and a prominent international banker in Miami, he was very
> precise in what he wrote. And I kept asking him why.
>
> *Bettinger-López:* Why, then?
>
> *Kerbel:* Well, because first of all the Cuban-Hebrew Congregation
> was founded as the Cuban-Hebrew Social Circle, primarily for the other
> purposes I mentioned before. But it was founded with the expectation
> that the other shuls in town would give the religious services to the
> arriving destitute Cuban Jews. However, they found out that most Miami
> congregations were not very hospitable, open, or warm to the Cuban Jews,
> in general, with the exception of Rabbi Mayer Abramowitz of Temple
> Menorah. For one, it was hard for [American Jews] to understand that
> you could be Jewish coming from Cuba. And second, due to the
> Cuban Jews' financial condition, their membership would cause a strain

to the temple budgets, since most of them could not afford the yearly dues or make donations upon their arrival, and their children required educational services. I think the founders of the Cuban-Hebrew Congregation realized that they needed an exempt number to accept tax-deductible donations. This is why the name was changed to include the word "congregation." Because you see, the founding name was not Cuban-Hebrew Congregation; the founding name was Cuban-Hebrew Social Circle of Miami. If you go into the book—here [points to photo in booklet: "Cuban-Hebrew Social Circle of Miami"].

Kerbel's discussion of the ideological premises upon which the Cuban-Jewish community of Miami formed reflects our previous discussion of the arrival of the Jewish Cubans in Miami Beach in 1959 and the early 1960s. Upon rejection by most of the preexisting American Jewish community in this area, these *Cuban* Jews, acutely aware of their controversial identity, set out to create an institution which could simultaneously function as a social, cultural, and religious establishment: where friendships from Cuba could be carried into a new time and place; where the particularities of Jewish culture, as it had developed in Cuba, could be reestablished and carried forward; and where a group of people experiencing a common rejection could take solace in religious and social solidarity.

The Círculo's primary objectives thus focused on making a better life for the Cuban Jews in Miami. They aimed "to restore the social activities of the Cuban Jews in Miami, through an active society and in a secure or permanent place" (objective two) and "to provide social assistance to people [presumably congregation members] lacking sufficient economic resources" (objective three). The objectives also were oriented toward the larger Jewish community of Greater Miami, indicating that the Cuban Jews still sought to forge ties between their own "Cuban" congregation and the other local "American" ones. Finally, El Círculo sought to forge ties with secular organizations throughout the city of Miami, as stated in objective four, "to establish relations with diverse Organizations with social, charitable, philanthropic, beneficial, educational, civic and Jewish religious character situated in Greater Miami" and in objective eight, "[To have] Commercial, Industrial, and Social orientation in Greater Miami."

Indeed, as Kerbel discusses, Jewish religion was a secondary community objective: although briefly mentioned in objective four, religion is only emphasized in objective six: "to facilitate religious services to the Cuban Jews and to the Latin Americans." Particularly telling in this objective is the focus on linking religion with Cuban and Latino Jews, a reaction presumably due in large part to the Cuban-Jewish community's negative experiences with American congregations.

The list of Círculo objectives also reveals the Cuban-Jewish community's efforts to emphasize its ties to the democratic ideals of the United States and its rejection

**REGLAMENTO**
**CAPITULO I**
**DISPOSICIONES GENERALES**

Art. 1.- La Sociedad se constituyó al amparo de las Leyes del Estado de la Florida bajo la denominación social de "Círculo Cubano Hebreo de Miami", en Inglés, "Cuban Hebrew Social Circle of Miami, Inc.", pudiendo designarse abreviadamente como "El Círculo".

Art. 2. - Su domicilio radicará provisionalmente en 1534 Washington Avenue, Miami Beach, Florida. La Junta Directiva está facultada para cambiar su domicilio cuantas veces estime sea conveniente a los intereses sociales.

Art. 3. - El Círculo es una Organización No Lucrativa de carácter social, fraternal, caritativa, filantrópica, cívica, educacional y religiosa; sus actividades estarán regidas por la más absoluta independencia de criterio y respeto por la pureza y el derecho de la libertad individual.

**CAPITULO II**
**OBJETIVOS DEL CIRCULO**

Art. 4. - El Círculo tendrá por finalidad, entre otros, los siguientes objetivos:

1)—Defender los ideales democráticos de nuestra civilización occidental.

2)—Restaurar las actividades sociales de los Hebreos Cubanos en Miami, por medio de una sociedad activa y en local fijo o permanente.

3)—Facilitar asistencia social a personas carentes de recursos económicos suficientes.

4)—Establecer relaciones con las diversas Organizaciones de carácter social, caritativa, filantrópica, benéfica, educacional, cívica y religiosa hebreas radicadas en la Gran Miami.

5)—Establecer relaciones con los Hebreos radicados en los Países de la América Latina.

6)—Facilitar servicios religiosos a los Hebreos Cubanos y Latino Americanos.

7)—Realizar el Censo de los Cubano-Hebreos que viven fuera de Cuba.

8)—Orientación Comercial, Industrial y Social en la Gran Miami.

9)—Creación de un Buró de Empleos para los miembros del Círculo.

10)—Conseguir Becas para estudiantes de distintas enseñanzas.

11)—Cooperar con las actividades locales relacionadas con el Estado de Israel.

12)—Divulgación y orientación de las Leyes de los Estados Unidos y del Estado de la Florida en particular.

13)—Información y cambio de impresiones sobre acontecimientos internacionales.

14)—Lograr descuentos en distintos servicios médicos, dentales, farmacéuticos y demás de utilidad común para los Socios.

*General Provisions and Objectives, Círculo Cubano-Hebreo de Miami, written in 1961. Source: Félix Reyler, "Los Primeros Años del Círculo," in Círculo Cubano-Hebreo de Miami, 1961–1981: 20 Aniversario (Miami: Cuban-Hebrew Congregation of Miami, 1981), 8.*

*Translation:*

*By-Laws*

*Chapter 1*

*General Provisions*

*Article 1: The Society set itself up under the protection of the Laws of the State of Florida under the social designation of "Círculo Cubano Hebreo de Miami", in English, "Cuban Hebrew Social Circle of Miami, Inc.," enabling it to call itself "El Círculo" as an abbreviation.*

*Article 2: Its head office is provisionally situated at 1534 Washington Avenue, Miami Beach, Florida. The Board of Management is authorized to change its head office as many times as is seen fit for social interests.*

*Article 3: The Círculo is a Non-Profit Organization of a social, fraternal, charitable, philanthropic, civic, educational and religious character; its activities will be ruled by the most absolute independence of criteria and respect for purity and the law of individual liberty.*

*Chapter 2*

*Objectives of the Círculo*

*Article 4: The Círculo will have for its purpose, amongst others, the following objectives:*

*1)- To defend the democratic ideals of our Western civilization.*

*2)- To restore the social activities of the Cuban Jews in Miami, through an active society and in a secure or permanent place.*

*3)- To provide social assistance to people lacking sufficient economic resources.*

*4)- To establish relations with the diverse Organizations of social, charitable, philanthropic, beneficial, educational, civic and Jewish religious character situated in Greater Miami.*

*5)- To establish relations with Jews situated in Latin American countries.*

*6)- To provide religious services to the Cuban Jews and the Latin Americans.*

*7)- To learn the census of Cuban-Jews who live outside of Cuba.*

*8)- Commercial, Industrial, and Social orientation in Greater Miami.*

*9)- Creation of an Employee Bureau for the members of the Círculo.*

*10)- To obtain scholarships for students for different types of education.*

*11)- To cooperate with local activities connected to the State of Israel.*

*12)- The popularization and orientation of the Laws of the United States and of the State of Florida in particular.*

*13)- Information and exchange of impressions on international events.*

*14)- To receive discounts on different medical, dental, pharmaceutical and other services of public benefit for our Members.*

Early documents of El Círculo. Source: Félix Reyler, "Los Primeros Años del Círculo," in Círculo Cubano-Hebreo de Miami, 1961–1981: 20 Aniversario (Miami: Cuban-Hebrew Congregation of Miami, 1981), 9.
Translation:

> The undersigned accept and take possession of the duties of this society, designated under the names, for those who were previously elected unanimously, whose duties we hold during the initial social year of this organization called "Círculo Cubano Hebreo de Miami", in English, "Cuban Hebrew Social Circle of Miami, Inc.".

### ENRIQUE KALUSIN
President

DR. ENRIQUE EIBER
Vice-President

JAMES S. KNOPKE
Vice-President

JACOBO CARIDI
Vice-President

OSCAR NETTER
Vice-President

ALBERTO BEHAR
Treasurer

JOSEPH SOBIE
Vice-Treasurer

DR. BERNARDO BENES
Correspondence Secretary

JULIO KLEPACH
Correspondence Vice-Secretary

EZRA MENDA
Records Secretary

MAX GARAZI
Records Vice-Secretary

DR. FELIX H. REYLER
Executive Director

JULIO D'GABRIEL
Executive Vice-Director

OSCAR A. WHITE
Legal Advisor Secretary

Translation:

FACSIMILE OF THE
FIRST CARD SENT
ON SEPTEMBER 10, 1961

CUBAN-JEWISH COMMUNITY IN MIAMI

**INITIAL MEETING** in the Lucerne Hotel,
41st Street and Collins Avenue; Friday,
**September 22, 1961** – 8:30 p.m.

**AIM:** Constitution of the Association –
"Cuban-Jewish Community in Miami" and
other themes to discuss.

This is a special invitation, your
presence is **important**.
Félix Reyler, Oscar A. White
Enrique Kalusin

of Castro's communist orientation. The wording of objective one makes this abundantly clear: "to defend the democratic ideals of our Western civilization." This ideology is again reflected in objective twelve: "The popularization and the orientation of the laws of the United States and of the State of Florida in particular." From the beginning, community members clearly sought to identify themselves as Cuban-Jewish exiles who enthusiastically supported their new American home. Although theirs was a Cuban synagogue, the founders emphasized, that did not mean that its members were the "foreigners" Miami Beach's preexisting Jewish community had treated them as. They sought to use the Cuban-Jewish community not to distance or separate themselves from the United States, but rather to reinforce a spirit of nationalism and patriotism toward their new home and to promote its political ideology.

Before the Círculo's founding, Reyler writes, the Cuban-Jewish community was far from a unified group; rather, it was loosely defined by the many groups of Jewish Cubans who met regularly in different places to discuss current events—particularly the Cuba situation—and to take comfort in each other's presence. Without a specified meeting place, these groups met wherever space was available:

> Como nadie tenía una casa grande, las reuniones de grupos se hacían con cierta regularidad en la calle, unas veces en el kiosko de Lincoln Road y Washington Avenue y otras veces en la oficina cercana de René Portero, Corredor de Bolsa de Valores, buen cubano y hebreo de corazón, quien nos recibía con amabilidad, y con suficientes sillas para reunir a más de docena de nosotros. Otros grupos, sobre todo los que tenían niños, se reunían en los parques, siendo el más popular el Parque de Flamingo, en Meridian Avenue y Calle 12.

> (Since no one had a large house, group meetings were often held in the street, sometimes in the small office on Lincoln Road and Washington Avenue and other times in the office nearby to René Portero: stockbroker, good Cuban and a Jew at heart, who received us with kindness, and with enough chairs for more than a dozen of us to meet. Other groups, especially those which had children, met in the parks, the most popular being Flamingo Park on Meridian Avenue and Twelfth Street.) (Reyler 1981: 7)[7]

Although it was disorganized, this group was at least freed from the burden of the American Jews' rejections. Its Ashkenazic and Sephardic members were reshaping, in Miami Beach, what they had worked so hard to build in Havana before Castro's rise to power. Indeed, as Reyler discusses in *Los Primeros Años del Círculo*, this was a difficult process: not only were many Cuban-Jewish émigrés strained economically, but they were also geographically, socially, and religiously unfamiliar with Miami and Miami Beach.

Even those who had previously vacationed in South Florida during the annual "Cuban invasions" felt lost in the area in which they were now forced to live as residents.

According to Reyler, soon after the framing of the Constitución de la Asociación–"Comunidad Cubana-Hebrea en Miami" (Constitution of the "Cuban-Hebrew Community of Miami" Association) in September 1961 in a small apartment on Michigan Avenue, the community moved its base to a conference room in the Mercantile National Bank on Lincoln Road. Immediately, the community began sending letters, written in English, to local Jewish businesses and social groups, informing them of the Círculo's formation and its fourteen objectives, and asking for assistance in finding a site where community members could meet socially. Only Washington Federal, a bank with which Círculo founder Bernardo Benes was affiliated, responded positively, inviting the group to use its auditorium. Benes notes: "I was the vice-president of the bank then. We used the auditorium of the bank—it was the first auditorium for the Cuban-Hebrew Congregation—free of charge. We used it for many years. Later we rented a store next to the bank." Furthermore, Félix Reyler (1981: 8–9) recalls nostalgically, "En dichos lugares celebramos muchos actos, unos recordando fechas religiosas y otros de carácter patriótico cubano y la estancia siempre era numerosa." ("In these places [i.e., the auditorium and other rented spaces], we celebrated many ceremonies, some recognizing religious dates and others of a patriotic Cuban character, and attendance was always high.")

Although religious functions took place in the auditorium of Washington Federal, by 1963 the social locus of the Círculo had become a small apartment at 1534 Washington Avenue (Reyler 1981: 9). Containing six tables and thirty chairs, this was the headquarters of Grupo Juvenil, the community's first youth group. During this time, the Círculo began to organize religious activities, celebrating the religious holidays of Rosh Hashana and Yom Kippur. As Reyler (1981: 9) notes, however, this was always done "bajo los auspicios del Círculo" (under the auspices of the Social Circle). Since the Cuban-Jewish community's social needs were being given top priority at this nascent stage of the Círculo's development, religious components had to be subsumed under a more general "social" label.

This emphasis on social needs reflects the leaders' attempts to maintain historical continuity. In Cuba in the 1950s, the Patronato de la Casa de la Comunidad Hebrea de Cuba had been the central Jewish establishment in Havana, and it had functioned primarily as a social institution. This synagogue and social center, located in the wealthy Vedado suburb of Havana and erected at a cost of nearly a million dollars, was nominally an Ashkenazic synagogue. Nevertheless, many Sephardim joined for its social aspects, while maintaining their membership at a Sephardic synagogue (usually Chevet Ahim) for purposes of religious worship.[8] The Círculo, whose membership included both Sephardim and Ashkenazim, was developed in accord with formal objectives nearly identical to those of the Patronato. Thus it was viewed by many as the "new" Patronato, formed in exile.

> Nuestra institución reviste características especiales, completamente distintas a los restantes templos locales. Las costumbres de Cuba se han trasladado a Miami, y es precisamente ese factor lo que da a todos nuestros actos, tanto sociales como religiosas, ese sabor especial que tanto nos gusta.

> (Our institution has special characteristics, completely distinct from the rest of the local [American] temples. Customs from Cuba have been brought to Miami, and it is precisely that factor which gives all of our functions, social as much as religious ones, that special flavor which pleases us so greatly.) (Cuban-Hebrew Congregation of Miami 1981: 18)

The Círculo soon grew too large for the space of the Washington Federal, and its High Holiday services were moved to a nearby South Beach hotel. For many congregants, these meeting rooms were special spaces. According to the Committee for Religious Activities, as "converted shuls," they conjured up memories of religious services in Cuba:

> [U]na vez . . . los salones del Washington Federal resultaron pequeños para albergar a nuestros socios durante los High Holidays, comenzamos a alquilar los de Hotel Di Lido y estamos seguros de que el espectáculo de nuestros jóvenes llenando el lobby del Hotel les hacía recordar los años del Centro Israelita de Cuba con sus amplios salones y del Patronato en épocas más recientes.

> (Once . . . the meeting rooms of Washington Federal became too small to accommodate our members during the High Holidays, we began to rent those of the Hotel Di Lido; we are sure that the spectacle of our young people filling the lobby of the hotel made them remember the years of the Centro Israelita of Cuba with its grand assembly halls, and those of the Patronato in more recent times.) (Cuban-Hebrew Congregation of Miami 1981: 18)

With over two hundred members and a growing budget, the Círculo urgently needed a meeting place larger than its modest apartment. In 1964, as Reyler (1981: 9) notes, the Círculo relocated down the street, to 1519 Washington

Avenue. While the group would continue to hold its most important events in the meeting rooms of Washington Federal, the new location would give its activities a firm foundation.

Perhaps the most important factor in consolidating the community was the addition that same year of Rabbi Dow Rozencwaig as the Círculo's spiritual leader. Born in Poland, Rozencwaig had been held in the Auschwitz concentration camp during World War II. In 1946, after the war had ended, he fled to Cuba. There, as general secretary of the Jewish community, he participated actively in its development (Cuban-Hebrew Congregation of Miami 1981: 17).[9] Like so many other Cuban-Jews, Rozencwaig and his family fled Cuba in the first years of the revolution, arriving in Miami as exiles once again.

While Rozencwaig began conducting Saturday morning services at the new location in South Beach, he also continued to strengthen the Grupo Juvenil, serving as advisor to over one hundred young men and women. That year, over four hundred people attended Rosh Hashana and Yom Kippur services under Rozencwaig's direction; a similar number celebrated the third anniversary of the Círculo, held in another local synagogue, Temple Ner Tamid (Cuban-Hebrew Congregation of Miami 1981: 9).[10]

As the booklet, *Círculo Cubano-Hebreo de Miami, 1961–1981: 20 Aniversario*, notes in an article paying special tribute to Rozencwaig, the rabbi emphasized Círculo involvement in local as well as international Jewish life:

> [Es] difícil encontrar algún aspecto, alguna faceta de la vida social o religiosa de nuestra comunidad en que el Rabino no haya participado en una u otra forma. Su total dedicación no se ha limitado al Círculo, ya que siempre ha dicho presente tanto en las campañas del Jewish Federation como las del State of Israel Bonds Drive, además de cooperar activamente en campañas para ayudar distintos yeshivas y hospitales, tanto en los Estados Unidos como en Israel.

> ([It is] difficult to find any aspect, any facet of the social or religious life of our community in which the rabbi did not participate in one form or another. His utter dedication has not been limited to the Círculo, for he has always been active in the campaigns of the Jewish Federation, as well as the State of Israel Bonds Drive; furthermore, he has actively cooperated in campaigns to help several yeshivas and hospitals, in the United States as well as in Israel.) (Cuban-Hebrew Congregation of Miami 1981: 17)

Rozencwaig's extra-community commitments, the booklet makes clear, encouraged Círculo members to look beyond their immediate social group into unfamiliar and even intimidating territory. Restoring the Jewish community of Cuba in Miami Beach, Rozencwaig emphasized, could not be accomplished simply by organizing a socioreligious group (the Círculo), in which Cuban-Jews would interact only among themselves. Instead, the continuation of this community meant restoring the functions of the Jewish community in Cuba and reinforcing the Círculo's stated objectives. The most important function, in Rozencwaig's view, was *tzedakah*, a Hebrew word meaning "righteous action" and referring to involvement in charitable activities.[11] Some of these organizations in Miami, including the Anti-Tuberculosis Society, WIZO (Women's International Zionist Organization), and B'nai B'rith, were familiar to the Cuban-Jews, since chapters had existed in pre-revolutionary Havana. The American Jewish community of Miami Beach had a long-standing involvement with these and other local and national organizations, such as the Greater Miami Jewish Federation, United Jewish Appeal, the Israel Bonds Drive, and Hebrew Immigrant Aid Society. It seemed logical to Rozencwaig, as it did to many in the Cuban-Jewish community, to de-emphasize initial tensions that had existed between American and Cuban Jews, and to attempt to join the two communities together in pursuit of their common interests, socioreligious commitments, and *tzedakah.*

In describing the Círculo's fourth year (1964), Felix Reyler (1981: 9) refers to the Círculo's relationship to its larger community: "En el cuarto año nuestro Círculo adquirió caracteres de Sociedad importante con actividades constantes durante todo el año." ("In its fourth year, our Círculo took on the characteristics of an important organization, with constant activities occurring throughout the year.")

Beneath the Círculo's push to establish itself as a unique and historical Jewish community lay a fundamental insecurity about its status in Jewish Miami Beach. Once the Círculo had the means, membership, and organizational capacity to establish itself as a viable Jewish community in Miami Beach, it expected to enter the ranks of those who originally had shunned their Cuban coreligionists. Rather than posing a contradiction for the Cuban-Jews, this push toward integration into Miami's older Jewish society worked to legitimize the re-formation of the Cuban-Jewish community and aid its survival in a new land.[12]

The community changed locations again in 1965, moving three blocks south to a larger space at 1242 Washington Avenue. In this new location, the Círculo expanded its religious and social functions. Rabbi Rozencwaig now conducted daily religious services, and the Círculo hired a permanent secretary and administrator and broadened its social activities. Additionally, Rozencwaig and the Comité Educacional (Educational Committee) opened the Círculo's first Sunday School here. Formed the year before under the direction of Círculo President Sholem Eppelbaum with support from the Bureau of Jewish Education, the Sunday School

*Bernardo Benes (left) and Rabbi Dow Rozencwaig in Círculo's small synagogue at 1242 Washington Avenue, Miami Beach. Cuban and American flags hang by the ark. November 6, 1969. Photo courtesy of Ziff Jewish Museum of Florida.*

was to be the first of a series of formal educational initiatives. As the school grew, the Círculo again confronted a familiar predicament: with the available space proving too small for its activities, it was forced to utilize assembly halls once used by the Young Men's Hebrew Association on West Avenue (Cuban-Hebrew Congregation of Miami 1981: 47).[13] As Oscar White, Círculo president, commented:

> In the last five years, I saw this Organization grow from a dozen members to 500 members, all with one common desire: to pray, live, and work together. Of course, our first desire and goal is to be back in our "sweet and lovely Cuba" where our life was milk and honey; but, while we wait, we must go on; we must conform and try to better ourselves wherever we are, most of all for our children, who have the greatest opportunities in these United States, [more] than in any other place in the world. (White 1965: 4)

By 1966, Cuban-Jews were increasingly accepted as part of the Greater Miami Jewish community. This was most evident in their dedication to the very organization that many felt had rejected them six years earlier: the Greater

Miami Jewish Federation. The community's intense devotion to Israel and its increasing involvement with local Jewish issues through the federation, however, often were expressed within a Cuban context. For example, during this time Bernardo Benes founded the first inter-American Hadassah—the Cuban Hadassah—in order to raise money for the federation. Furthermore, in the mid-1960s, Cuban-Jews increasingly formed part of the federation's Board of Directors. In 1966, the federation formed its Cuban Division, through which the Cuban-Jews both assisted the organization in reaching its overall goals and brought to federation projects new ideas and initiatives from a decidedly Cuban perspective. This new Cuban Division also allowed the Cuban-Jews to concentrate on pressing issues facing their community, including migration from Cuba and community development.

## The New Patronato: Birth of the Cuban-Hebrew Congregation

The Círculo headquarters remained at 1242 Washington Avenue until 1976, when the group purchased land and built a synagogue on the corner of Michigan Avenue and Seventeenth Street. After this move, the Círculo's leaders officially renamed it "Cuban-Hebrew Congregation of Miami—Beth Kneseth Szmuel Szechter." The second part of this new name was designated in honor of the father of one of the community's leaders, Jack Chester. This site has remained the hub of Cuban-Jewish life in South Beach for the past two decades. Today the latter half of the name is abbreviated "Temple Beth Shmuel," but many members from its early days still refer to it as El Círculo.

The Cuban-Hebrew Congregation's booklet, *Círculo Cubano-Hebreo de Miami, 1961–1981: 20 Aniversario*, skips the eleven-year period between 1965 and 1976. The decision to construct the Cuban-Hebrew Congregation, it says,

> fue tomada por la Directiva pocos años después de constituído el Círculo. Necesitábamos un edificio que albergara no sólo nuestro Templo, razón de ser y espina dorsal de nuestra institución, sino que además nos permitiera desarrollar asimismo actividades de carácter social, educacionales, culturales y filantrópicas.

> (was made by the Board of Directors a few years after the formation of the Círculo. We needed a building which not only would house our Temple—our reason for being and the backbone of our institution—but also would permit us to develop activities that were social, educational, cultural, and philanthropic in nature.) (Cuban-Hebrew Congregation of Miami 1981: 49-50)

The congregation, to be sure, sought to expand its religious functions, especially since now it would have its own sanctuary in which to hold religious services. Clearly, however, it also intended to maintain its highly social character. As Marcos Kerbel emphasizes, this social emphasis always had distinguished the Cuban-Jewish community. To maintain this emphasis now from a building of its own was a source of pride to the previously itinerant group. The *edificio* (building) constructed between 1972 and 1976 indeed had a "Cuban-Jewish" character. In addition to being constructed to accommodate the specific needs and objectives of the community, it was built by one of the community's own: the Cuban-Jewish architect Oscar Sklar.

Perhaps most important, as is documented in *Círculo Cubano-Hebreo de Miami, 1961–1981: 20 Aniversario*, the Cuban-Hebrew Congregation's new building was erected to continue the legacy of the Patronato, undeniably the center of Jewish life in Havana throughout the 1950s. Like the Círculo, the Patronato had functioned primarily as an apolitical social entity, with religious affairs taking second priority.[14] With a membership of nearly one thousand families and a leadership composed predominantly of wealthy Cuban Ashkenazim (some Cuban Sephardim and American Ashkenazim were leaders, too), the Patronato soon became the organ representative of Jews in Cuba, especially after its leaders received pressure from the World Jewish Congress to function as such (Levine 1993: 212).[15]

*Original architectural plan for Cuban-Hebrew Congregation, c. 1976. Source:* Cuban-Hebrew Congregation, Círculo Cubano-Hebreo de Miami, 1961–1981: 20 Aniversario *(Miami: Cuban Hebrew Congregation of Miami, 1981), front cover.*

Leaders of the Círculo hoped that the new Cuban-Hebrew Congregation could carry the Patronato's legacy forward in time and space. The 1970 yearbook of the Círculo's publication, *El Nuevo Jewban*, makes this clear: "Our front page signifies the history of continuity of our ethnic and religious origin through the years, using as a symbol the Patronato of the Cuban Jewish community of Cuba woven together with a romantic and religious project which we hope will be our future Temple in Miami" (qtd. and trans. in Bejarano 1994: 134).[16] The commemorative booklet, *Círculo Cubano-Hebreo de Miami, 1961–1981: 20 Aniversario*, similarly reflects upon the construction of the Cuban-Hebrew Congregation:

> En ese sentido, no hacíamos más que seguir las huellas de aquellos activistas que en Cuba construyeron no sólo varias sinagogas, sino además lo que fuera orgullo legítimo de la comunidad hebrea en Cuba, el querido 'Patronato.' Muchos de los que cooperaron a la creación del Patronato se han mantenido activos, trabajando en todo momento por el bienestar de nuestra comunidad.

*Plaque on the wall of the Cuban-Hebrew Congregation, 1999. Note the congregation's reference to itself as the "Miami branch" of El Patronato. Photo by Caroline Bettinger-López.*

(In that sense, we did nothing more than follow the footsteps of those
activists who, in Cuba, constructed not only various synagogues, but
that which was the legitimate pride of the Jewish community in Cuba,
the beloved Patronato. Many of those who cooperated in the creation
of the Patronato have remained active, working constantly for the well-
being of our community [in Miami].) (Cuban-Hebrew Congregation
of Miami 1981: 50)

The leadership of the Cuban-Hebrew Congregation, which in 1976 was
primarily Ashkenazic, resembled that of the Patronato; indeed, many Patronato
leaders themselves were active in creating the new community. This continuity
enabled the Cuban-Jewish community to transplant some of its most cherished
customs and celebrations to its new homeland.

One of the best-known aspects of the Jewish community in Havana was the
active role women played in extra-community affairs. Since the 1920s, the task of
reaching out to the larger community had been largely in the hands of women who
were financially secure. The Ashkenazic *Froien Farein*, later renamed the Asociación
Feminina Hebrea de Cuba (Jewish Women's Association of Cuba), provided needy
immigrants with food, medicine, clothing, furniture, and other assistance, and
established an orphanage in Havana. During the late 1920s, the Sephardim maintained a social service group called Buena Voluntad (Good Will), which provided
similar services (Levine 1993: 45).

By 1962, the Círculo in Miami had restored these committees through the
establishment of the Comité de Damas (Women's Committee). As Tete Wenguer,
Comité president in 1981, notes,

> Ayudamos a Israel con ambulancias, conseguidas éstas gracias a la ayuda
> de bellas jóvenes que participaron en los concursos de Reina Esther. Con
> el dinero, recogido con nuestro trabajo en flea markets, conciertos, y
> campañas. Ayudamos a compatriotas que llegaban a Miami con un
> kiosco que mantuvimos en el Aeropuerto de Opa-Locka.
>
> Hemos recaudado fondos para ayudar a hospitales, y también colegios
> de niños retardados mentales a los que aún ayudamos a través del Dade
> Mental Health Association.

> (We helped Israel with ambulances, obtained with the help of our
> beautiful young people who participated in the Queen Esther contests
> [see below]. With money raised through our work in flea markets,
> concerts, and campaigns [*sic*]. We helped our compatriots who arrived in

*Estella Egozi, Esther Egozi (Garazi), Alegre Barrocas (Frances), and Raquel Egozi Silverstein maintain the Círculo's "courtesy kiosk" welcome station in the Opa Locka Airport for Cuban refugees coming on "Freedom Flights." 1965. Photo courtesy of Ziff Jewish Museum of Florida.*

Miami with a stand [kiosk] that we maintained in the Opa-Locka Airport [for Cuban exiles in the 1960s].

We have collected funds to help hospitals, and also schools for mentally retarded children, whom we still help through the Dade Mental Health Association.) (Cuban-Hebrew Congregation of Miami 1981: 21)

Continuing to carry out these social and charitable functions, the Comité de Damas served both as an important link to the former Jewish community of Havana and as a means of realizing, in the group's new home, many of the Círculo's extra-community objectives. Even so, as Wenguer emphasizes, the committee's main function was to help unite the Cuban-Jews of Miami: "Sobre todo, el Comité de Damas, a través de sus actos y bailes [actividades], lo mismo para jóvenes que para mayores, quiere unir a los hebreos cubanos, para poder así ayudar a mantener a través de los años, esa llama de amistad y confraternidad que siempre ha caracterizado al judío cubano." (Above all, the Women's Committee, through its actions and dances [activities], as much for young people as for adults, wants to unite Cuban Jews so as to be able to help maintain through the years that

flame of friendship and fraternity that always has characterized the Cuban Jew)
(Cuban-Hebrew Congregation of Miami 1981: 21).

One of the social events most instrumental in bringing the community together
was the Concurso de Reina Esther (the Queen Esther Beauty Pageant). Sponsored
originally by the Comité de Actividades Sociales and later by the Comité de Damas,
this pageant took place during the congregation's Purim festival each year. Commemorating the biblical passage in which beautiful Queen Esther offers her life to
save the Jewish village persecuted by the Persian Empire and subsequently convinces
the king to halt these plans, the Concurso each year named one young woman its
"Queen Esther." In 1976, 1979, and 1980, the contest itself took place at the Baile
de las Debutantes (Dance of the Debutantes) in the Cuban-Hebrew Congregation's
social reception area—just one of many examples of how the new building's ample
space was used to further the original Círculo objectives.

In addition to their social function, the beauty pageants served as fundraising
events for local charities and pro-Israel campaigns. On a page commemorating nine
of its "Queen Esthers," the Círculo booklet describes these *tzedakah* functions:

> Los fondos recaudados durante los concursos para eligir a nuestras
> Reinas Esther fueron dedicados a la realización de obras benéficas y de
> estancia social de carácter local, y a la adquisición de 9 ambulancias y
> bloodmobiles que fueron donados a nuestros hermanos de Israel, 5 de
> ellas en 1970, en uno de los concursos más reñidos que registra la
> historia de nuestra institución y los 4 restantes en años posteriores.

> (The funds collected during the pageants to choose our Queen Esther
> were dedicated to beneficent works and social assistance of a local
> character, and to the acquisition of nine ambulances and bloodmobiles,
> which were donated to our brothers in Israel, five of them in 1970—in
> one of the most competitive pageants in the history of our institution—
> and the remaining four in later years.) (Cuban-Hebrew Congregation of
> Miami 1981: 73)

Another continuation of the women's tradition of *tzedakah*, begun many decades
before in Cuba, can be seen in the pages commemorating the congregation's new "Sisterhood." These pages also document an attempt to couple charitable functions with the
community's efforts to emulate aspects of the surrounding American Jewish community:

> Surgió la idea de crear un comité que existía en casi todas las sinagogas
> americanas, pero que para nosotros resultaba ser algo nuevo, un "Sisterhood,"

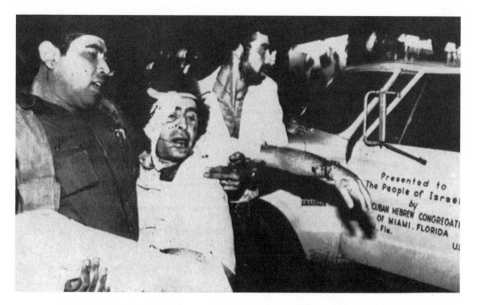

*Bloodmobile donated to Israel by the Cuban-Hebrew Congregation. Source:* Cuban-Hebrew Congregation, Círculo Cubano-Hebreo de Miami, 1961–1981: 20 Aniversario (*Miami: Cuban Hebrew Congregation of Miami, 1981*), 42.

> ya que en Cuba estábamos acostumbrados a otros tipos de comités femininos tales como el "Froeinfareim" [*sic*] de caráter comunitario local, la "Wizo" y distintos comités de ayuda a Israel y otras instituciones de aspecto benéfico.
>
> (The idea arose to create a committee which existed in almost all American synagogues, but which was something new for us, a "Sisterhood," since in Cuba we were accustomed to other types of women's committees, such as the "Froeinfareim" with a local community character, WIZO [Women's International Zionist Organization] and various committees for helping Israel, and other institutions serving charitable functions.) (Cuban-Hebrew Congregation of Miami 1981: 22)

In 1968, the Círculo's "American" Sisterhood formed as a committee separate and distinct from the larger "Cuban" Comité de Damas, which was made up of much younger women. Unlike the Comité, which was composed entirely of women, the Sisterhood included Rabbi Rozencwaig on its Board of Directors, and a 1981 photograph shows Arón Kelton, president of the Cuban-Hebrew Congregation, serving this board as well. The idea of the Sisterhood, according to *Círculo Cubano-Hebreo de Miami, 1961–1981: 20 Aniversario*, the Cuban-Hebrew Congregation's twentieth-anniversary booklet, was supported enthusiastically by both Rabbi

Rozencwaig and his wife Ana, who is warmly referred to as "nuestra querida 'Rebezzen' Jane" ("our beloved 'Rebezzen' Jane")[17] (Cuban-Hebrew Congregation of Miami 1981: 22). The Sisterhood initially directed its efforts toward the Cuban-Hebrew Congregation's Sunday School, and by the early 1980s it took an active role in supporting the Beyit Lepletot orphanage in Jerusalem. In February 1981, the Sisterhood donated a fully equipped "bloodmobile" to the American Red Magen David for Israel and substantial funds to the Kupat-Holim clinic in Jerusalem. Within the congregation itself, the Sisterhood was responsible for hosting celebrations of the traditional holidays of Mother's Day, Father's Day, Purim, Hanukah, and others. And in 1981, the organization was a vital participant in the campaign to construct yet another *edificio*, adjacent to the original building (23).

The establishment of the Círculo's Sisterhood marked another milestone in the congregation's "Americanization" process. Now the Cuban-Jews had their own chapter of a national Jewish organization.[18] Rabbi Rozencwaig's involvement with the Sisterhood suggests a new effort to associate the Círculo with the American congregations and thus with American Jewry in general. By 1968, he and other congregation members saw the Círculo as more than a social circle. As a vital Jewish social, charitable, and religious center, its next tasks were to improve community relations and try once more to build alliances with other Miami Beach congregations. At the same time, the Círculo also must remember its roots, its leaders emphasized, for on that foundation would its future be constructed.

## Guanabacoa Cemetery and the Casino Deportivo

In pre-revolutionary Havana, the cemetery and the beach club occupied important roles in Jewish life. More than two generations of Jewish Cubans had been laid in the Guanabacoa Cemetery by 1959, and all generations had spent countless hours at the Casino Deportivo, the social Beach Club of Havana's Jews. In an interview, Bernardo Benes recalls:

> The first mistake we made [in Miami] was not buying enough plots in Mount Sinai Cemetery. Rabbi Rozencwaig, in 1969, wanted to buy a big chunk of plots. Now we're burying our loved ones in different cemeteries. We should have bought the whole cemetery. . . .
>
> The second mistake we made was not building a beach club. 3,500 people came to the [one-day] "beach club" we had in Miami on July fourth, 1969 . . . It would've been a wonderful thing. In fact, the Beach Club in Cuba was run by a for-profit group, because we weren't allowed in high-society clubs.

Benes's disappointment at the community's failure to fully reestablish in Miami these important aspects of Jewish life is shared by much of Miami's Cuban-Jewish community today. Eva Simazi, an active member of Torat Moshe, nostalgically recalls the Casino, lamenting its absence in Miami:

> *Simazi:* We [Cuban Jews] had a great life in Cuba, really. We used to go to a club which was called the Casino Deportivo de Habana. It was like a bath club with more—like a country club and a bath club at the same time. And it was great.
>
> *Bettinger-López:* For both Sephardim and Ashkenazim?
>
> *Simazi:* It was for everyone. And the *goyims* were there because it was something from Havana, it was a country club.[19] Like if you say, we go to the Turnberry Country Club [a premiere country club in Northeast Miami-Dade County], an ocean club. And we used to [figuratively] live there, because they had bowling alleys and they had billiards and they had squash courts and tennis courts, and we had two pools and we had the ocean, and we had everything there, and we were always going there for social events. It was great. I mean, it's what I miss most.

Benes's and Simazi's sentiments are mirrored in a short article in *Círculo Cubano-Hebreo de Miami, 1961–1981: 20 Aniversario,* the Cuban-Hebrew Congregation's twentieth-anniversary booklet, recalling the Cuban-Jewish community's *balneario* ("spa" or "health resort") days. As in most descriptions in the rest of the booklet, the description of this important aspect of community life is preceded by a reference to its predecessor in pre-revolutionary Havana. Entitled "Balnearios," the article begins by asking, "Quién no recuerda el Casino Deportivo de Cuba?" ("Who does not remember the Beach Club of Cuba?"). It then describes the beach club in Havana which Benes and Simazi—and, indeed, most Cuban-Jews over the age of fifty—remember so fondly today. The article continues: "En el mismo se daba cita alrededor de los años 50 gran parte de la comunidad cubana hebrea, los mayores a disfrutar de un día de playa y del dominó, y los más jóvenes a disfrutar de sus deportes veraniegos, la natación y el 'volleyball' y de los añorados 'Té Bailables' de tan grata recordación." ("In the 1950s, a great portion of the Jewish Cuban community would arrange to be in that place, the adults to enjoy a day at the beach, playing dominoes, and the younger generation to enjoy the summer sports of swimming and volleyball, and those afternoon dances remembered so fondly") (Cuban-Hebrew Congregation of Miami 1981: 30).

From 1969 through 1971, the article documents, "el Círculo tuvo su pequeño 'Casino Deportivo' aquí, en Miami Beach" ("the Círculo had its own small 'Casino Deportivo' here, in Miami Beach") (30). This social event was held during the summer,

The balnearios. *1969–71. Source: Cuban-Hebrew Congregation,* Círculo Cubano-Hebreo de Miami, 1961– 1981: 20 Aniversario *(Miami: Cuban Hebrew Congregation of Miami, 1981), 30.* Translation of captions: *(right) Partial view of the pool at the Hotel Coronet; (bottom) Group of Círculo members enjoying a game of dominoes; (opposite) Inauguration of the Balneario season at the Hotel Coronet.*

the off-season for tourism, at the Hotel Coronet (1969 and 1971) and the Hotel Allison (1970). Since many Miami Beach hotels closed to tourists during this time, their poolside spaces were available for large local group gatherings. In these mini-Casinos,

> las familias y amigos se reunían bajo el gran toldo cercano a la piscina, los "ya no tan jóvenes" volvieron a ejercitar sus músculos en los reñidos partidos de "volley ball," y los jóvenes organizaron competencias de natación y sus bailes, a la luz de la luna. Como olvidar, "el Rincón de Blanco" con su cafetería, su arroz con pollo, su café criollo, los tranques en el parqueo.

> (families and friends met together under the huge sunshade near the pool, those "no longer so young" once again exercised their muscles in hard-fought games of volleyball, and the young people organized swimming competitions and moonlight dances. How can we forget "Blanco's Corner," with its cafeteria, its chicken with rice, Cuban coffee, getting stuck in traffic in the parking lot.) (Cuban-Hebrew Congregation of Miami 1981: 30)

The Círculo's paramount social commitment was expressed in such gatherings. The *balnearios* allowed the Cuban-Jews simultaneously to remember their history, to carry forward their social commitments, and to involve the younger generation in the Círculo in an exciting way. As Yosele Gilfarb notes, for the younger generation these were perhaps the most memorable community events. It was here that youngsters "were able to take advantage of sharing with friends and family a unique 'Jew-Ban' atmosphere" within a relaxed beach environment (Cuban-Hebrew Congregation of Miami 1981: 29). These events had a peculiar character: those present at the *balnearios* assembled not under the banner of religion, but rather as a Cuban-Jewish social group, eating unkosher *arroz con pollo* (chicken and rice) and drinking *café criollo* (Cuban coffee).

The *balnearios* lasted only three years. The Círculo's disappointment at the termination of the "nuevo Casino" (new Beach Club) era is reflected in the final paragraphs describing the *balnearios*.

> Desafortunadamente, fue éste, el de 1971, el último Balneario que se pudo organizar. Cada vez resultaba más difícil encontrar un Hotel que cerrara durante el verano y que nos permitiera tener el área de la playa y piscina a nuestra entera y exclusiva disposición, los costos se fueron haciendo prohibitivos y el entusiasmo fue decayendo.
>
> Los tres años del Balneario fueron tres años que siempre recordaremos con mucho cariño.
>
> (Unfortunately, the last Balneario that was able to be organized was in 1971. Each time, it became more difficult to find a hotel which closed during the summer and would allow us to have the beach and pool area all to ourselves. Consequently, costs became prohibitive and [community] enthusiasm was declining.
>
> The three Balneario years were three years that we will always remember with much fondness.) (Cuban-Hebrew Congregation of Miami 1981: 30)

The "second" Casino Deportivo thus was even shorter-lived than its 1950s Havana predecessor. The community was left without an outdoor social facility and was forced to confine its social activities to the Washington Federal meeting rooms and, after 1976, the Cuban-Hebrew Congregation's reception areas.

## "We Must Continue": Cuban-Jewish Youth and the Círculo

While community leaders sought to "transplant" Jewish Havana to Miami Beach, they also recognized the need to acknowledge the inevitable changes resulting from the abrupt move. Undoubtedly, one of the greatest community concerns had to do with transmitting the "Cuban-Jewish spirit" to the "one-and-a-half" generation (those who came to the United States at a very young age) and the second generation (those born on American soil) (Pérez Firmat 1995: 1). Rabbi Rozencwaig's establishment of the Grupo Juvenil in 1963 was an initial effort to give Cuban-Jewish young people a sense of pride in their unique identity. The group's sixth president, Yosele Gilfarb, describes it as hosting "meetings, dances, and other various activities" (Gilfarb 1981: 29). Another youth group, Club Hatikvah, formed in 1978, with similar goals.

A short article, "Actividades Juveniles," describes these groups, revealing community leaders' disappointment at the younger generation's low level of interest and participation in these youth-oriented organizations and activities.[20] An unnamed author writes:

> Uno de los aspectos que más atención ha recibido por parte del Círculo desde su fundación lo ha sido el de los jóvenes. Una y otra directiva señalaba en su plataforma de trabajo como una de sus metas más importantes la de organizar a los jóvenes, y esos esfuerzos se vieron recompensados en cierta forma, no completamente como hubieran sido nuestros deseos, pero nos queda la satisfacción de haber realizado nuestro mejor esfuerzo.

> (One of the issues that has received most attention from the Círculo since its founding has been its youth. One Board of Directors after another cited as one of the most important features of its work program to organize the young people, and those efforts were realized to some extent—not as completely as we would have wished, but still we have the satisfaction of having done our best.) (Cuban-Hebrew Congregation of Miami 1981: 28)

As a grown man and a father, Gilfarb in 1981 reflected on the community's youth activities over the preceding twenty years. His article, "We Must Continue," is the only English-language article in Círculo Cubano-Hebreo de Miami, 1961–1981: 20 Aniversario, the Cuban-Hebrew Congregation's twentieth-anniversary booklet. In contrast to the author of the above passage, Gilfarb recalls an enthusiastic, community-oriented youth group, although he too expresses concern about the level (or lack) of youth involvement in community activities in 1981, the year his article was published. His portrayal of the younger generation's perspective on the community's beginning years indicates a strong link between the generations which is reinforced by common aims and a common organizing structure. It also allows us to follow the community's history in a way which generally is impossible to do using "official" community histories written by members of the older generation:

When we started meeting, our gathering place was so small that it readily picked up the nickname "The Cave." Notwithstanding the size of the locale, the Cuban-Jewish youth made it the "in place" to be.

Meetings, dances, and various other activities helped forge a strong leadership that would last for years to come. Early presidents of the group realized its potential and attempted to keep the young people together.

As the Cuban-Hebrew Congregation grew and moved to better facilities, we found new guidelines to meet and follow. Whereas the burden of the early years was to forge strong ties between us and the Cuban-Hebrew Congregation, now we had to keep the young people interested in the roles we would play in the continuing development of the Cuban-Hebrew Congregation.

During the "balneario" years, we were able to take advantage of sharing with friends and family a unique "Jew-Ban" atmosphere.

The Cuban-Hebrew Congregation kept its attention on us with the organization of the famous "balnearios." These summer meeting places offered a new dimension to the youth—the outdoor environment.

Whereas in previous years we were confined to indoor meetings, with the exception of occasional field trips, now we were able to share the relaxed atmosphere of a beach area between ourselves and our families.

Twenty years [1961–1981] is a long time, and we, the youth movement of those early years, have become part of the "older" group.

In the same manner that we and the Cuban-Hebrew Congregation have grown, the youth movement must continue to grow.

If it should become stagnant, it would truly be a crime. Not only a crime against all of the effort and well wishes of the Cuban-Hebrew Congregation, but a crime against ourselves.

For we remember what it meant to have a place to call our own. A place to discuss topics ranging from politics to movies, to dance, to play, to just plain enjoy being together. . . .

[The members of the Cuban-Hebrew Congregation] still have the youth in mind, giving them free reign to increase the activities that help in maturing socially and religiously.

The *old* youth must depend on the current youth to build on the foundation started in 1961. The youth of today will have [at] its disposal facilities and funding never before offered.

We the "old youth" know how good being together can be. All we ask the youth of today, is to experience it.

We've come a long way from the "Cave," we must continue (Gilfarb 1981: 29; emphasis in original).

Gilfarb's nostalgic piece brings home an overarching message conveyed by the Círculo's twentieth-anniversary booklet: the need for increasing emphasis on intergenerational continuity in community affairs. As an "in-betweener," positioned between younger and older generations, this author presents a compelling reason why the younger generation in 1981 should extend the previous generation's efforts and goals into the future. Cuban-Jewish youth must not abandon their own community, he stresses: apathy leads to stagnation, which is a "crime" against the very community that allowed Gilfarb's generation to grow up and have "a place to call our own," and that maintained an energetic "Jew-Ban" atmosphere. Gilfarb's overall message is clear: youth are the future of the community. As proof, the "old youth" now fill influential positions in the Cuban-Hebrew Congregation and aspire to carry the Cuban-Jewish community forward.

Gilfarb, however, defines Miami Beach's Cuban-Jewish community in a way that differs markedly from the older generation's definition. Whereas community leaders continually evoke the "original" Cuban Jewish community of pre-1959 Havana, Gilfarb dates the community's origins—its "foundation"—back to 1961, the first year of the Círculo. While sharing the older generation's hopes for the community's future, Gilfarb, representing the younger generation, has a very different understanding of the community's history and thus of its *raison d'être*.

Certainly Gilfarb shares with the older generation a perception of the original Círculo, at its founding in Miami Beach, as an undeveloped, disorganized, even "primitive" Jewish organization. The nickname "The Cave" appears to signify much more than the small size of the Grupo Juvenil's—and the larger congregation's—meeting place at 1534 Washington Avenue. When the Cuban-Jewish community acquired a larger and thus more prestigious facility (at 1519 Washington Avenue), it could implement more ambitious goals and activities, in effect moving from the Stone Age of the Cave to the Modern Age of the Meeting Room. A new and more "refined" Cuban-Jewish community thus could emerge, in turn giving rise to a more organized and developed form of "Cuban-Jewishness."

This updated and more modern version of Cuban-Jewishness was recognized throughout the community during the late 1960s and early 1970s. Having emerged in 1964 from "The Cave" at 1534 Washington Avenue, the Círculo tried to capture the essence of the new and developing community through the annual publication of a bulletin, *El Nuevo Jewban (The New Jewban)*, beginning in the early 1970s. Through this medium, the members of the community forged a unique and exclusive space for themselves. As Jewbans/Jew-Bans (different spellings were used by the Cuban-Jews to stand for "JEWish-CuBANS"), these people combined and reconfigured, in Eva Simazi's words, "the best of both worlds—the Jewish and the Cuban." This new notion of community selfhood took the hyphenated Cuban-Jewish identity assumed early in the 1960s one step further; in effect, it loosened the community's explicit ties to both "Cubans" and "Jews," forging a separate, emancipated group identity.

This Jew-Ban identity, Gilfarb thinks, made possible the creation of a "unique Jew-Ban atmosphere" which suffused community events such as the *balnearios, Concursos de Reina Esther, and Bailes de las Debutantes.* This is what enabled the three generations to coexist happily throughout the 1960s and 1970s. That was no small feat: members of these generations often had been born or raised in different countries, with the oldest born in the Mediterranean or Eastern Europe, the middle in Cuba, and the youngest in the United States.

With the establishment of the Cuban-Jewish community, the Jewish Cubans' arrival in Miami in 1959 and the early 1960s had come full circle. By the late 1960s and early 1970s, the Círculo was moving in a new direction, increasingly looking toward the future rather than the past. The designation "Jew-Ban" marked this shift in focus and identity, as *judaísmo* and *cubanidad* now became inextricably linked, both to each other and to Miami Beach. Indeed, South Florida now was home to a large proportion of Cuba's Jews, who chose to look ahead toward their community's growth and development. In this future, they envisioned a Jew-Ban community which would continue to grow and prosper.

## Vandalism or Terrorism?

The year 1981 was both an exciting and a horrific one for the Cuban-Hebrew Congregation. Two days after the congregation's twentieth-anniversary celebration at Miami Beach's luxurious Fontainebleau Hotel, the synagogue's walls and windows facing Michigan Avenue were riddled with bullets in a drive-by shooting, only hours before the congregation was scheduled to gather for evening services for Shavuot, the Jewish Harvest Festival which celebrates God's giving Moses the Ten Commandments. In an article entitled "Vandalismo o Terrorismo?" ("Vandalism or Terrorism?"), the Círculo describes the confusion surrounding possible reasons for the shooting: "Muchos lo consideraron como un ataque de elementos extremistas en represalia al bombardeo y destrucción de la planta nuclear de Iraq, en las afueras de Bagdad, realizado el día anterior por la aviación israelí. Otros lo consideraron como un acto de anti-semitismo, otros aún, como un simple acto más de vandalismo" ("Many considered it an attack by extremists in retaliation for the Israeli Air Force's bombing and destruction of a nuclear plant in Iraq, on the outskirts of Baghdad, the day before. Others

considered it an act of anti-Semitism; others still, a sheer act of vandalism")
(Cuban-Hebrew Congregation of Miami 1981: 76).

The shooting focused the attention of many local groups—including the
Anti-Defamation League, the Miami Beach Police, the Rabbinical Association of
Greater Miami, the Greater Miami Jewish Federation, and the Jewish Defense
League—on the generally low-key and apolitical Cuban-Jewish community, in an
effort to solve and understand the crime. Arón Kelton, president of the congregation, told the *Miami Herald,* "This came as a complete shock. We haven't had an
argument with anyone. No one has ever threatened us or vandalized us and we're
not involved in political issues" (qtd. in Cuban-Hebrew Congregation of Miami
1981: 76). The congregation never learned who committed the crime or the
reasons behind it. It was, however, an event unprecedented in Cuban-Jewish history,
and it reminded the Cuban-Jews of the precarious space occupied by Jews in
American society and around the world. Some also interpreted it as a warning
against becoming involved in Cuban political affairs, as Bernardo Benes, a founder
of the community, had done through his involvement in the 1978 *El Diálogo* with
Castro (discussed below). Others maintained that this was a random act of
vandalism, possibly related to the rampant drug dealing and drug use on the streets
bordering the Cuban-Hebrew Congregation. In any event, the shooting shook the
community to its foundations and forced it to reconsider its role as a social,
religious, and possibly political entity.

## The Cuban Sephardic Experience in Miami Beach

The historical narrative presented in the preceding section is based (with some
exceptions) on the "official" history of the Círculo Cubano-Hebreo that is presented
in the Cuban-Hebrew Congregation's 1981 booklet, *Círculo Cubano-Hebreo de Miami,
1961–1981: 20 Aniversario.* It is presented in this way to preserve the specific character and content of this material and to show how a group of people, linked by a
shared interest, chooses to remember its history textually. What becomes increasingly
visible through this process of historical reconstruction, and through the analysis of
alternative histories, however, is the selective process by which any historical narrative
(including, of course, my own) is constructed. Therefore I wish to present yet
another historical perspective on the development of the Cuban-Jewish community
in Miami Beach—one which will function as an ongoing ethnographic narrative and
will analyze the history of the community presented in *Círculo Cubano-Hebreo de Miami,
1961–1981: 20 Aniversario,* which concluded when the booklet was published in 1981.

## Chevet Ahim and the Cuban Sephardic Hebrew Congregation

The Círculo's twentieth-anniversary booklet, *Círculo Cubano-Hebreo de Miami, 1961– 1981: 20 Aniversario,* celebrates the development and vitality of the Cuban-Jewish community of Miami Beach. Its focus, though, is one particular group of Cuban-Jews: the members of El Círculo Cubano-Hebreo de Miami, the Cuban-Hebrew Congregation of Miami. At the same time that the predominantly Ashkenazic Círculo developed in the heart of South Beach throughout the 1960s and 1970s, a Cuban Sephardic community sprouted from and subsequently grew alongside this original community. Established in 1968, the Cuban Sephardic Hebrew Congregation quickly became the religious and social locus for much of the Cuban Sephardic community, although many Sephardim retained multiple memberships in the Círculo, the Cuban Sephardic Congregation, and, to a lesser extent, Temple Menorah (many Cuban Ashkenazim maintained dual memberships in the Círculo and Temple Menorah).[21]

Today a bronze plaque outside Torat Moshe, the Sephardic Cuban congregation, reads:

> The Sephardic Congregation of Florida, originally known as Cuban Sephardic Hebrew Congregation, was founded in 1968 by Cuban Jewish refugees forced into exile during the early 1960s.
>
> The commitment to perpetuate our heritage and tradition combined with tireless efforts helped us create Temple Moses as a living monument to our plight. We will never forget what we left behind on the island of Cuba.
>
> It is our hope that this building will serve all future generations of Jews arriving in Florida as a house of prayer, refuge and friendship.
> Temple Moses, City of Miami Beach
> Board of Directors
> December 2, 1980
> 25 Kislev 5741µµ

The Cuban Sephardim, like the Ashkenazim who founded the Círculo, saw the development of their congregation in Miami Beach as a way to reestablish the congregations and Jewish community centers they had maintained in pre-revolutionary Cuba. While most Sephardim did not have as explicit an attachment to one particular synagogue as the Ashkenazim had to the Patronato, most congregation members came from Havana, where the largest Sephardic synagogue in Cuba, Unión Hebrea Chevet Ahim, was located. Thus, the group vision which emerged for the Sephardic community in 1968 took shape largely within the framework of the remembered Chevet Ahim.[22]

Founded in 1914, Chevet Ahim initially had developed as a religious and social establishment, although, as Rabbi Melarmed notes below, its social functions could not be realized until the congregation acquired a locale suitable for social events.[23] Chevet Ahim's establishment in Havana, he writes, coincided with the arrival of thousands of Sephardim in Cuba in the first two decades of this century:

> La primera institución hebrea que se conoce en Cuba fue la "United Jewish Congregation" [Congregación Judía Unida], fundada en 1906, del rito Ashkenazí, la que también poseía un cementario en el pueblo de Guanabacoa, cercano a la Habana. Este cementario antes perteneció a los pocos Sephardim existentes en la capital cubana. Según la *Enciclopedia Judía*, la "United Jewish Congregation" se componía de unas mil personas, pero sin embargo, los primeros Sefaraditas que emigraron a Cuba en 1904, teniendo un número aproximadamente igual al de los Ashkenazim, no pudieron formar una comunidad hasta que occurió la inmigración en gran escala de 1907, proviente en su mayoría de Turquía y de Siria; y no fue hasta 1914 que lograron constituir la sociedad religiosa y de beneficencia Shevet-Ajim.
>
> . . . La Comunidad Sefaradí poseía una sinagoga en la Calle Inquisidor 407, donde existía también la escuela Teodoro Hertzl; sepultaban sus fallecidos en el cementerio de la Sociedad Ashkenazí, situado en Guanabacoa. Sin embargo, no tenían un Club Social, debiendo reunirse en lugares provisorios hasta que adquirieron el local de la Avenida del Prado 557, donde realizaban sus actividades sociales y conducían sus oraciones durante las grandes fiestas religiosas.
>
> (The first Jewish institution in Cuba was the "United Jewish Congregation," founded in 1906 by an Ashkenazi group that also owned a cemetery in the town of Guanabacoa, near Havana.[24] Previously, this cemetery had belonged to the few Sephardim present in the Cuban capital. According to the *Jewish Encyclopedia*, the "United Jewish Congregation" was composed of some one thousand people. Nevertheless, the first Sephardim who emigrated to Cuba in 1904, who were approximately equal in number to these Ashkenazim, were unable to form a community until the great immigration of 1907 occurred, primarily from Turkey and Syria; and it was not until 1914 that they were able to build the religious and charitable society of Shevet-Ajim.[25]
>
> . . . The Sephardic Community had a synagogue at 407 Inquisitor Street, where also was located the Theodore Hertzl School; they buried their dead in the Ashkenazi Society's cemetery in Guanabacoa. However, they did not have a Social Club, so they met in temporary locations until they acquired a space at 557 Prado Avenue, where they began their social activities and conducted prayers during the major religious holidays.)
> (Melarmed 198?: 2–3)

The separation of the predominantly Turkish and Syrian Sephardim from the American Ashkenazim residing in Cuba in the beginning of this century was not due only to cultural and linguistic differences. In contrast to the wealthy and sophisticated American Jews whose settlement in Cuba was motivated primarily by business interests, Turkish and Syrian Sephardim arrived in Cuba as poor immigrants with uncertain futures. These Sephardim tended to become peddlers and street vendors, struggling to earn enough money to buy food, clothing, and other basic necessities for their families. Particularly in the early years of their settlement, the Sephardim had little interaction with the American Jews of the United Hebrew Congregation, who considered them "plebeians." In 1911, the American Ashkenazim went so far as to refuse six Sephardic immigrants entry to the hotel where they were conducting services (Epstein 1981: 27; Levine 1993: 21).

Furthermore, the two groups had different long-term plans. The American Jews saw Cuba as a site of temporary settlement and intended to return home to the United States after setting up small factories, retail stores, and import-export firms on the island, which they then would oversee as absentee owners (Levine 1993: 5). The Turkish and Syrian Jews, on the other hand, viewed their migration to Cuba as permanent and sought to establish roots in their new home as quickly as possible. When they were not "accepted" by the United Hebrew Congregation, they founded their own congregation, Chevet Ahim, complete with a religious school and community outreach efforts to help the poor (Epstein 1981: 27).

Although the Sephardim never established lasting relations with the American Ashkenazim in Cuba, they did blend to some extent with the developing Eastern European Ashkenazic community of the 1920s, when thousands of Eastern European Jews arrived in Cuba. According to Sapir (1948) and Levine (1993), however, the two communities remained largely separate, both institutionally and socially. In fact, the grand Patronato de la Casa de la Comunidad Hebrea de Cuba was built in 1953 in hopes of linking the Ashkenazim and Sephardim socially, while allowing separate spaces for worship services.

Marcos Kerbel discusses the success of the Patronato's centralized arrangement for both Sephardim and Ashkenazim in pre-revolutionary Havana, and laments the change in community structure in Miami. He begins his discussion with the establishment of the Círculo in Miami in 1961:

> Enrique Kalusin and Dr. Félix H. Reyler had the idea of "Cuban." Along
> with Bernardo Benes and Oscar White, the latter who was already a
> practicing attorney in Miami, they conceptualized the Cuban Jewish
> community here in Miami. So they were the four that were behind the

founding of the Cuban-Jewish community in Miami Beach, because they were very active in the youth groups in the forties and fifties in Cuba, Benes being the youngest one.

You see the other names in the first Board of Directors? For example, Alberto Behar? He's Sephardic. You see Ezra Menda? He's also Sephardic, as well as Salomón Garazi. So this community was organized as one united group with both Ashkenazic and Sephardic Jews together. But one situation arose. Once you got into the religious aspects—and I always say that the institutions of religion and politics were created for the purpose of uniting people, but unfortunately many of their leaders are the first that create divisions. The moment that the rabbi was hired, Rabbi Dow Rozencwaig— he is a darling of a man, but his primary language is Yiddish. And the older group which started the congregation was the Ashkenazi group who had experienced two exoduses in their lifetimes, having immigrated from Eastern Europe (Poland/Russia/Lithuania) to Cuba and then to Miami, and [so] whose primary language was also Yiddish. Of course the Sephardim didn't speak Yiddish—they spoke Ladino and Spanish. So that also created a barrier after awhile. Also, the religious rites of the Ashkenazim and Sephardim are different. The Sephardim later realized that they needed their own organization to continue their religious traditions, so the Cuban Sephardic Congregation was founded. While we were socially one group, religiously we were separated, due to a difference in religious approach.

. . . I've always said over the years, why did we have to build a second temple [Temple Moses/Torat Moshe]? Why did we have to build two different temples in two different buildings to house the Cuban Jews? What I thought we should've done was to have one temple building with two chapels and a school, and following the concept of what was known in Havana as the "twin-cinema" approach, you would have two shuls side by side: one for Ashkenazim, one for Sephardim, and the members would move for religious services to one side or the other, but everyone would be together under one roof.

The "twin-cinema" approach was never realized in Miami Beach. Instead, the "separate congregation" approach moved most Cuban Sephardim five blocks away from their Ashkenazic compatriots, to an old store at 715 Washington Avenue. They nicknamed it *La Cueva* (*The Cave*), Susana Hamla told me, "because you had to get through a hallway. It was very dark and very depressing [laughs], and that's why they called it La Cueva. Because it was almost like a cave. Terrible. On Washington and Seventh. But you know, when we started, [we took] whatever we could get. We couldn't afford a nice place, so we got that. But you know, that was the beginning."[26]

Immediately, 150 families joined the new Cuban Sephardic Congregation/La Cueva, led by Rabbi Nissim Maya, the son of Chevet Ahim's chief rabbi, Gershon Maya. Nissim Maya's experience with Jewish communities throughout Cuba placed him in an important position for the Cuban Sephardic community's development in Miami Beach. His experience as a professor of Hebrew, a cantor, and a *mohel* in the Camagüey province of Cuba, and his familiarity with Havana's Jewish community through his father's involvement with Chevet Ahim, gave him a broad base from which to relate to diverse members of the Cuban Sephardic community in their new Miami Beach home. Rabbi Maya's familiarity with provincial life was particularly important to the many Cuban Sephardim who had settled in Cuba's provinces rather than its capital. A rabbi who was not "Havana-centric," as was most of Miami Beach's Cuban-Jewish community, was reassuring to these people who practiced a style of Judaism different from that of their urban coreligionists.[27]

As Kerbel suggests, the Sephardic members of the Círculo's Board of Directors were among the founders of the new Sephardic community; Alberto Behar, in fact, served as the first president of the Cuban Sephardic Congregation. This group, Susan Epstein writes, primarily sought "to meet for prayer and reminiscence"—to congregate together in a way reminiscent of the Sephardic community of Cuba (1981: 49). The Cuban Sephardic Congregation hosted both religious services and social activities in its storefront synagogue, much as its "parent" congregations had done in Cuba.

Unlike Kerbel, Susana Hamla attributes the development of the Cuban Sephardic Hebrew Congregation neither to linguistic differences between the Ashkenazim and Sephardim nor to friction surrounding the selection of an Ashkenazic rabbi for the Círculo, but to the fundamental need for Sephardim to have their own Sephardic place of worship: "They built La Cueva because they wanted a house of worship. We came from our country—we lost everything. We didn't have a place to worship. . . . The Sephardim needed their own Sephardic shul. And we couldn't belong to the other Sephardim [Sephardic Jewish Center] because we couldn't afford it. They didn't open the door—if they'd opened the door for us, we'd have a shul. So we didn't have a place to worship, and they didn't want us. . . . And the Círculo—they were Ashkenazic. We wanted Sephardi."

Before the development of the Cuban Sephardic Congregation, most Cuban Sephardim belonged to the Círculo or Temple Menorah, sometimes both. Hamla's discussion of her family's movement between synagogues upon arrival in Miami in the mid-1960s is reflective of the experience of many Cuban Sephardim during this time:

> In the beginning, we didn't have a shul, so there was only one [Cuban-Jewish] community, and I was a member of the Cuban-Hebrew Congregation. For my kids to go to [Hebrew] school, I joined Temple

Menorah—they went two days a week and Sunday. I used to live across from Temple Menorah. And I liked Temple Menorah because I couldn't afford a yeshiva. After they had Bar Mitzvahs, I dropped my membership at Menorah, and we [Cuban Sephardim] had this congregation on Washington and Seventh, called La Cueva—The Cave. So I dropped my enrollment with Cuban-Hebrew [Congregation], because I couldn't afford at that time to belong to so many congregations, and besides, we had our own.

Hamla, an active member of Torat Moshe today, clearly identifies most strongly with the Cuban Sephardim, as her statement indicates ("We had our own [congregation]"). Her affiliation with Temple Menorah was motivated by religious concerns: she wanted her children to receive a substantial religious education, something they could not receive through the Cuban-Hebrew Congregation's Sunday School in those years (1966–68). Her affiliation with the Círculo was based on the fact that, for seven years (1961–68), this group was *the* locus of Cuban-Jewish life in Miami, for both *polacos* and *turcos.*

The establishment of the Cuban Sephardic Congregation changed these circumstances entirely. Not only was membership at more than one synagogue expensive; more importantly, the development of this new congregation allowed Miami Beach's Cuban Sephardim an unprecedented expression of ethnic loyalty and identification.

The new Cuban Sephardic Congregation quickly assumed social functions similar to those of the Círculo: within a few years, its leaders had created a Sunday School for children; a *Macabi,* a primarily Sephardic social group for high school students which had originated in Cuba; and a *Hebra Kedusha,* a Jewish burial society composed of volunteers who wash and take care of the body after death, and, most importantly, make sure that every Jewish body has a burial, even if there is no family or the family cannot afford it. The existence of a Hebra Kedusha often signals a large or active Jewish community.[28] The congregation also purchased adjacent plots of land in the Mount Sinai Cemetery during this time (Temple Moses/Florida Sephardic Congregation 1979: 5). In 1969, Victoria Adouth, a Zionist leader in Cuba, organized the Sisterhood Damas de Buena Voluntad (Sisterhood of Women of Good Will), an "Americanized" version of the Sephardic women's group in Cuba, Buena Voluntad. The Sisterhood's tasks, Adouth wrote in the congregation's 1979 retrospective *Libro de Oro* (*Book of Gold*), were "trabajar, unir, reunir, cooperar, contribuir, tolerar, armonizar y superar. Este es nuestro lema. Es el secreto que conduce al éxito" ("to work, to unite, to get together, to cooperate, to contribute, to tolerate, to harmonize, and to overcome. This is our motto. It is the secret that drives success") (Temple Moses/Florida Sephardic Congregation 1979: 11). In 1972, Adouth

*Original architectural plan for Cuban Sephardic Hebrew Congregation—Temple Moses, c. 1978. Source:* Bulletin,
*Sephardic Congregation of Florida, January–February 1995, front cover.*

organized another women's group, Comité de Recreo y Cultura (Recreational and Cultural
Committee) (11). These two groups bore a close resemblance, in both structure and
function, to the Círculo's Comité de Damas and Sisterhood. They reflected the Sephardic
community's desire to reach out to the larger community of South Florida through service
activities, just as it had in Cuba.

Indeed, the community surrounding the Cuban Sephardic Hebrew Congregation
developed quite rapidly, in large part because, by 1968, most of its members were
already familiar with the environmental, social, and religious landscape of Greater
Miami, and they had the experience of the Círculo as a guide in the development of
their own Sephardic Cuban-Jewish community. By the early 1970s, the congregation
boasted a membership of over 350 families and thus urgently needed a new facility—one which would be larger and brighter than La Cueva and could accommodate
the swelling congregation (Epstein 1981: 49–50; Temple Moses/Florida Sephardic
Congregation 1979: 5).

Two options presented themselves: either the community could relocate to a larger
pre-existing building in Miami Beach, or it could purchase land and construct its own
synagogue (Temple Moses/Florida Sephardic Congregation 1979: 5; Epstein 1981:
49–50). The latter option gained immediate support from much of the community;
and, by 1973, the Comité Pro-Edificio (Pro-Building Committee) formed. Working in
conjunction with the Comité de Recreo y Cultura, the Sisterhood, and a new central
Board of Directors for the community, the Comité Pro-Edificio raised funds for the
future synagogue. The congregation laid the cornerstone for the Cuban Sephardic
Hebrew Congregation—Temple Moses at 1200 Normandy Drive in July 1978, and
held official dedication services in December 1980 (Temple Moses/Florida
Sephardic Congregation 1979: 5; Epstein 1981: 49–50).

The establishment of the new congregation changed the Cuban-Jewish community in numerous ways. With a social and physical space the Cuban Sephardic community could claim as its own, increasing numbers of Sephardim— not only Cubans, but other nationalities as well—flocked to the new synagogue in the early 1980s. Hamla describes this development: "We grew, little by little, because more people were coming from Cuba, and besides, Sephardics were coming from other countries: Venezuela; we had Moroccans also . . . But usually this community is Cuban Sephardic. Most of us are [originally] from Turkey, some from Greece, some from Syria." As Hamla indicates, the Cuban Sephardim in Miami sought to maintain their links not only to Cuba, but also to their ancestral homes in present-day Asia, Europe, and the Middle East. As a community grounded in a specific location, they could accomplish this task more effectively than as a "homeless" group renting La Cueva in South Beach.

The Cuban Sephardic community changed in another crucial way as a result of the move to Normandy Drive (Seventy-first Street), which was over sixty streets north and a few avenues west of its previous location, and over fifty streets north of the four-year-old Cuban-Hebrew Congregation. This relocation took the Sephardic community to Normandy Isle, connected only by bridge to Miami Beach. In the wake of this institutional shift came a migration of the congregation's members to

*Woman prays in rear of Orthodox synagogue. Photo by Gary Monroe.*

Normandy Isle and the surrounding North Beach area. Within a few years, the Cuban Sephardim had carved a religious and social niche north of the established Cuban-Jewish hub in South Beach. For many Cuban Sephardim, this enclave grew to encompass the most important aspects of life, for it included their places of residence, worship, and social life.

Although the Cuban Sephardim performed social and charitable functions as a community, their emphasis on preserving Traditional (Halachic) Sephardic religious practice distanced them ideologically from the Orthodox/Conservative Cuban-Hebrew Congregation.[29] The Cuban-Hebrew Congregation (*Círculo Cubano-Hebreo*) began in 1961 as a Conservative congregation, without a gender separation in its sanctuaries. With Rabbi Rozenecwaig's arrival in 1964, it became an Orthodox congregation and thus separated men and women in its sanctuaries. With Rabbi Konovitch's arrival in the mid–1980s, the congregation switched back to Conservatism and thus dismantled the gender separation in its sanctuaries. In 1998, it reintroduced the gender separation in its small prayer room.

With the establishment of Temple Moses came an official decision to deem it a Traditional congregation. Hence, the 180-seat sanctuary, which opened into a social hall capable of accommodating 450 people, was divided in half by a curtain (Epstein 1981: 50–51). Women and men sat on opposite sides of this barrier, so that, as nineteen-year-old Albert Ralvey told me, "no one would be distracted by members of the opposite sex, and everyone could focus on the religion." Unlike the Cuban-Hebrew Congregation, Temple Moses/Torat Moshe has always maintained the traditional gender barrier in both of its sanctuaries.

Temple Moses's new rabbi, Amram Amselem, focused primarily on family participation and education. Within one year of Temple Moses's construction, he established the Instituto de Educación Para Adultos (Institute for Adult Education), a joint effort of the Cuban Sephardic Hebrew Congregation and the Cuban-Hebrew Congregation to teach Miami's Cuban-Jews more about their heritage, traditions, ethics, and the Bible (Epstein 1981: 50). Efforts to link the separate (or separating) Sephardic and Ashkenazic Cuban communities of Miami Beach thus bore fruit as early as 1981. The education of community members of all ages became a "paramount goal of the community's leaders" (92), an unnamed fifty-nine-year-old Sephardic man explained to Susan Epstein:

> Hay una generación que no ha aprendido nada de la religión, nada del judaísmo. Y se han estado perdiendo los valores. Hay asimilación, hay falta del concepto del judaísmo. Y eso queremos recuperarlo. Y estamos haciendo este esfuerzo . . . este edificio, esta sinagoga, esta biblioteca, este Instituto. La actividad que hay es para salvar a los remanentes del judaísmo cubano.

(There is a generation that has learned nothing about religion, nothing about Judaism. And they have been losing their values. There is assimilation, there is a lack of the concept of Judaism. And that is what we want to recover. And we are making this effort . . . [through] this building, this synagogue, this library, this Institute. The activity that exists is designed to save the remnants of Cuban Judaism.) (92)[30]

In this man's comments, we see a fundamental push toward preserving, in exile, that which is uniquely *Cuban Jewish*. Even so, he notes, we can no longer think of "Cuban Judaism" as a whole; rather, from where we stand today, we can save only its scattered (and tattered) remnants. To recover the "concept of Judaism," and specifically "Cuban Judaism," he says, Cuban-Jews must make a concerted effort to "recover" in Miami Beach those institutions through which they define themselves and learn their traditions and history.

What is particularly interesting in this man's account is his understanding of the larger notion of "Judaism" as what someone outside the Cuban-Jewish community might think of as a very specific "form" of Judaism: that which developed in Cuba in the first half of this century and (re)established itself in Miami throughout the 1960s, 1970s, and early 1980s, which this man calls "Cuban Judaism."[31] For him, "recovering Judaism" is encompassed within the reconstruction of the Jewish community he knew in Cuba and the teaching of Jewish heritage and traditions. Thus, the *edificio* of Temple Moses, like that of the Cuban-Hebrew Congregation for its founders, symbolizes the recovery of Cuban-Judaism. And within this building lies the heart of this unique form of Judaism: the "synagogue" and the "library." By attending classes at the Instituto, this man learns more about the value of Judaism. In this way, he can assist in the recovery process, saving the "remnants" of Cuban Judaism and, by extension, Judaism itself.

If, for this Sephardic man, "Cuban Judaism" encompasses "Judaism," what does this tell us about relations between Cuban Sephardim and Ashkenazim in Miami Beach in the late 1970s and early 1980s (when Epstein conducted these interviews)? Initially it appears that his conception of "Cuban Judaism" is confined to the Sephardic sphere—the building, synagogue, and library of Temple Moses. However, he also includes the Instituto, a joint initiative between the Cuban-Hebrew Congregation and Temple Moses, in his list of community "efforts" to recover Cuban Judaism. This points to his inclusion of the Cuban Ashkenazim in his conception of Cuban Judaism. The initiative proposed by the Instituto—to join the two communities in an effort to learn about Jewish religion, heritage, and traditions—thus points to an attempt to unify the *turcos* and *polacos* in community objectives and activities, much as Havana's Patronato tried to do three decades earlier.

## Temple Moses: A Growing "Sister" Congregation

Although efforts such as the Instituto attempted to draw the two congregations closer together, different visions and goals sometimes took them in separate directions. Some friction also remained over the "breakup" of the Sephardim and Ashkenazim in 1968. Yet these feelings generally gave way to friendly interactions and good will, such as a 1981 letter from the Executive Members of Temple Moses to leaders of the Cuban-Hebrew Congregation, congratulating the latter on its twentieth anniversary. Even within the letter, however, are expressions of ambivalence concerning the relationship between the two groups, as the letter's authors repeatedly alternate between referring to the Cuban-Hebrew Congregation as Temple Moses's "sister" and addressing it in a more distanced manner:

> De nuestra mas alta consideración. Expresamos el sentir de esta Congregación hermanada a vosotros en un común destino.
>
> Reconocemos, y así expresamos, de la gran labor, dedicación y sentido de judeidad [judaísmo] y sionismo llevados a cabo por vuestros dirigentes en veinte años de util actividad.
>
> Declaramos y agradecemos de la ayuda recibida de Uds. en todos los momentos, para constituirnos en la Sephardic Congregation of Florida que hoy representamos.
>
> Aprovechamos para extender nuestras felicitaciones a todas las directivas pasadas y presentes, por estos primeros veinte años de actuación.
>
> Rogamos a D–os para que esta celebración se repita en muchos otros periodos similares de años para bien de todo el Aham Israel.
>
> Shalom.

> (With our deepest regards, we express the feeling of this congregation linked in sisterhood with you in a common destiny.
>
> We recognize the hard work, dedication, and sense of Jewishness and Zionism brought to fruition by your leaders in twenty years of useful service.
>
> We are grateful for the help we received from you at all times, in forming the Sephardic Congregation of Florida we now represent.
>
> We take this opportunity to extend our congratulations to all past and present Boards of Directors, for these first twenty years of existence.
>
> We pray to G–d that this celebration may be repeated following many similar time periods, for the good of all of Aham Israel.
>
> Peace.) (Cuban-Hebrew Congregation 1981: 64)[32]

Ambivalence is evident in the use of the pronouns *vosotros* and *ustedes* in the original Spanish text, when addressing the Cuban-Hebrew Congregation leaders. The authors begin by addressing these leaders with the more familiar and informal *vosotros* ("you" plural, informal) and continue by emphasizing the bonds of sisterhood shared by the Cuban-Hebrew Congregation and the Sephardic Congregation of Florida/Temple Moses, who share a common destiny. The *vosotros* form is also used in the next paragraph to refer admiringly to the community service activities and vital religious functions of the Sephardic Congregation's "sister Congregation." However, when the discussion of community outreach narrows to refer specifically to the assistance given by the Cuban-Hebrew Congregation to its "sister" in the latter's initial stages of development, the tone of the letter immediately becomes more formal. As if expressing gratitude to a "big sister," the authors use the formal *ustedes* (*Uds.*) ("you" plural, formal). At the same time, they distance their own congregation from its "sister" by identifying themselves specifically as representatives of the Sephardic Congregation of Florida—Temple Moses—not the Cuban-Jewish community at large.[33] In this sense, Temple Moses seems to be exerting its independence, like a "little sister" who has grown up and left the "nest" but still seeks to maintain family ties.

## Collective Memory

While Temple Moses continued its efforts to unite Cuban Sephardim and Ashkenazim in a social and educational setting, it maintained an inward focus. Of utmost importance to the Cuban Sephardim was (re)construction of a strong youth program which could serve as "preventive medicine" for the predicament addressed by the Instituto. The Sunday School and the Macabi encouraged Cuban Sephardic youth to learn about their heritage and religion, as illustrated in the Macabi's introductory page in the *Libro de Oro:*

> Las raíces de nuestra Comunidad Sefaradita se encuentran en Cuba. Allí también, durante muchos años, existió un grupo juvenil que se denominó Macabi.
>
> Al comenzar el éxodo de los cubanos hebreos, muchos de aquellos jóvenes que tomaban parte activa en la Macabi de Cuba, tenían hijos que se encontraban ya en edad de formar sus propias organizaciones juveniles.
>
> . . . La Macabi del presente no difiere mucho de la del pasado. Compuesta de jóvenes de Enseñanza Secundaria, es un grupo que toma parte muy activa en los actos sociales y religiosos de nuestra comunidad . . . [como] la campaña Pro-Israel.

(The roots of our Sephardic Community are found in Cuba. There also, for many years, existed a youth group called Macabi.

When the exodus of Jewish Cubans began, many of those young people who took an active part in the Macabi of Cuba had children who were of the right age to form their own youth organizations.

The Macabi of today does not differ much from that of the past. Composed of Secondary School youth, it is a group that takes a very active role in social and religious functions in our community . . . [like] the Pro-Israel campaign.) (Temple Moses/Florida Sephardic Congregation 1979: 20)

Through such groups, children participated in a variety of religious, social, and charitable activities not directly associated with their congregation (Epstein 1981: 51). Parents also sent their children outside the Cuban Sephardic community to Jewish day school—most notably to the Hebrew Academy, located midway between the congregation's old South Beach Cueva and its new Normandy Isle synagogue. Many who could not afford the academy's tuition enrolled their children in an after-school Hebrew School three days a week, generally through either the Sephardic Jewish Center or Temple Menorah (Epstein 1981: 91). This association with the once-hostile Sephardic Jewish Center marked a turning point for the Cuban Sephardim, as their children entered a domain previously inaccessible to the community.

Even before Temple Moses was built, a group of university students formed *El Club*, a social club oriented toward not only college-age Cuban Sephardim living in Miami, but also those attending out-of-town universities. Its social functions thus continued through school vacation periods, to accommodate those who were back home only for weeks at a time. El Club, in fact, grew out of the Cuban Sephardic Congregation's yearly Reina Esther Beauty Pageant. While the congregation elected its *reina* and *madrinas* (queen and her court) at a get-together in 1977, this group of students decided to make social activities available on a continuing basis and thus formed El Club (Temple Moses/ Florida Sephardic Congregation 1979: 21).

Such activities became essential as means for the Cuban Sephardim collectively to remember their history. The past of Cuba could be recreated in such events as the Reina Esther Beauty Pageant and the festivities surrounding it. It is no coincidence that both *polacos* and *turcos* chose to transplant these events to Miami, continuing traditions that identified them as Cuban-Jews. Eva Simazi views the Purim Festival in pre-revolutionary Havana, for example, as the predecessor of Temple Moses's annual Purim Festival in Miami: "[In Havana] we were always at the Macabi, and we were always at the Betar, and we were always together. Yeah, we had field trips, and we had dances, and during Purim time, we had the Queen Esther contest. So every girl was a debutante type of thing. Every girl wanted to be Queen Esther, and we used to sell tickets for benefiting the temple. See, everything was centered to temple. And here [in Miami], we try to do the same thing. Our temple: we have a Purim picnic every year. We get together like maybe seven hundred people. The young people come, and they play, and they swim, and they eat, and they all get together. But that all comes out of temple." As Simazi's comments indicate, community traditions may change: although Temple Moses continues its Purim festivities, the Queen Esther Beauty Pageant has been eliminated from the Purim program. What is important is community adherence to tradition. The past can be recreated through the addition or subtraction of any given traditional event, but this must be done in a way that triggers the collective memory and binds the past with the present.

Another factor in "continuing" the Cuban Sephardic community in Miami Beach was the community's association with Jewish groups apart from the synagogue. Both La Cueva and its successor, Temple Moses (which, by 1981, had a membership of over 450 families), emphasized the importance of reaching beyond the community for charitable, religious, and social purposes (Epstein 1981: 40–41). As previously discussed, the congregation—and particularly its Sisterhood—encouraged its members to join outside groups. Susan Epstein notes the numerous connections, in 1981, between Cuban Sephardim in Miami and local, national, and international Jewish groups: "Virtually all of the subjects, even those who are not official members of Temple Moses or other synagogues, belong to one or more of the following groups: WIZO, Sisterhood de Damas Buena Voluntad, Macabi, Hadassah, HIAS, Jewish National Fund, as well as other groups contributing to fund-raising campaigns for the state of Israel" (Epstein 1981: 92).

Historian Margalit Bejarano also discusses the Cuban Sephardic community's involvement in issues surrounding Sephardim from other Latin American countries:[34] "The Sephardic Community extends its services to all the Sephardim coming from Latin America. After inaugurating Temple Moses, in 1980, the president [I. Bichachi] wrote: 'Latin America and its Sephardic Congregations are looking at us. We give them security in front of possible political uncertainties.' With the main office of the Sephardic Federation of Latin America [FESELA] in Temple Moses, the Sephardic Cuban Community of Miami has taken a leading role among Latin American Sephardim" (Bejarano 1994: 135).

Indeed, from its beginning, Temple Moses identified itself as a synagogue for all Sephardim, particularly the thousands of Latin American Sephardim who have settled in South Florida in the past two decades. Moisés Jrade, a former president and active member of the synagogue, notes, "We saw Latins coming to Miami and felt it would be nice if everybody felt at home." As the founding congregation of the Florida chapter of the American Sephardic Federation (ASF) in 1985 and of the Miami chapter of FESELA a few years later (efforts spearheaded by Salomón Garazi, an active community member and benefactor), it was ideally positioned to serve as a link between Sephardim in the United States and Latin America.

The confusion surrounding the synagogue's official name highlights this universalist tendency. While Epstein, in her master's thesis, refers to it both as Chevet Ahim and as the Cuban Sephardic Hebrew Congregation/Temple Moses, the congregation's leaders often refer to it as the Sephardic Congregation of Florida, opting not to characterize their synagogue along national lines. The aforementioned letter to the Cuban-Hebrew Congregation is written on letterhead reading "Sephardic Congregation of Florida, Inc./Temple Moses," with no mention of Cuba. Susana Hamla cites the arrival of numerous Latin American Sephardim in the late 1970s and 1980s as the reason behind the name change to "Sephardic Congregation of Florida": "We changed the name because we didn't want to sound like we were only Cuban. [Our congregation] was built by Cubans. But we didn't want to be the only ones, since we had people from some other countries."

By the early 1980s, the membership of Sephardic Congregation of Florida/ Temple Moses increasingly represented Sephardic communities from Central and South America. While the congregation's leadership was still predominantly Cuban, it truly was becoming a pan-American congregation. Following the establishment of its Florida ASF chapter, the congregation hosted the ASF's 1985 annual convention in Miami. Many topics were discussed, including the subject of the Jews of Cuba. In 1990, Salomón Garazi became president of FESELA, leading to increased Cuban-Jewish involvement in the organization.

In conjunction with ASF's establishment in South Florida in 1985, Garazi instituted *Semana Sefaradí*, a week-long event celebrating Sephardic culture. Over the years, the event, commemorating the Jewish expulsion from Spain in March 1492, has grown and now lasts for several months each spring. In 1992, Temple Moses hosted a major quincentenary (five-hundred-year) commemoration of the expulsion, while Spain's king read a proclamation in a Spanish synagogue welcoming the Jews and asking for forgiveness. Garazi arranged for a reenactment of the expulsion and a reading of the king's speech immediately after it had been delivered in Spain. Dressed in fifteenth-century costumes borrowed from the Miami Opera, several University of Miami theater students reenacted the expulsion in the Spanish language to a packed house of approximately eight hundred people. While the event received some support from Cuban Ashkenazim who felt a sense of solidarity with their Sephardic coreligionists, it served primarily to create a bridge between the Cuban Sephardic community and other Sephardim both in South

Florida and throughout the world. Through the reenactment and the king's proclamation, the Sephardim experienced a heightened sense of social acceptance, self-esteem, and self-determination (Henry Green to CB-L, July 12 and 23, 1999).[35]

In its international and pre-Cuba historical focus, Temple Moses differed from the Cuban-Hebrew Congregation, which gave its national ties to Cuba and the United States a higher priority than other international commitments. By its twentieth anniversary in 1981, the Círculo, through its community outreach projects and the remarkable financial success of many of its members, had gained acceptance by much of Miami Beach's older Jewish community. Even while seeking to strengthen these ties to Jewish Miami Beach, however, the Cuban Ashkenazim focused equally on maintaining, in the words of the Committee for Religious Activities, "that special [Cuban] flavor which we love so much" (Cuban-Hebrew Congregation of Miami 1981: 18; translation mine).

## At Home in Miami Beach

With the Círculo's entry into the larger Jewish community of Miami in the mid-1960s, its local commitments increased. Before this, in the wake of the American Jewish community's rejection of its Sephardic and Ashkenazic Cuban coreligionists, this group of émigrés—who, in a sense, belonged nowhere—of necessity associated with each other. The Cuban-Jews focused on building their own community where they could feel Jewish—something denied them by Miami's Jewish community—and recreate to the greatest extent possible the life they had known in Cuba. Out of this experience emerged the Círculo Cubano-Hebreo de Miami.

The Cuban Sephardic Hebrew Congregation arose under markedly different circumstances. As Círculo members in the early 1960s, most Cuban Sephardim encountered the American Jews' rejection to the same extent as the Cuban Ashkenazim, if not to a greater extent. As Félix Reyler, a former Círculo president, notes, however, much of this tension lifted by the mid-1960s, as *polacos* and *turcos* alike (though especially the former) prospered socioeconomically in Miami and achieved fuller acceptance by American Jews. By 1968, as the Cuban Sephardim developed a new "Jewban" congregation in La Cueva, a different set of concerns arose: Would their new congregation cause a rift between Cuban Ashkenazim and Sephardim in South Florida? Was there enough support for another Cuban congregation in South Beach? How would this move affect assimilation and/or integration of Cuban-Jews with American Jews and Gentiles? How would this affect future generations?

By 1980, when Temple Moses began functioning as the locus of the Cuban Sephardic community, the pressing question for its leaders concerned the extent to which the Cuban Sephardic community would *choose* to involve itself in its larger community—

not whether it would be rejected in such efforts, as in the early 1960s. At this time, both the Cuban-Hebrew Congregation and Temple Moses decided to focus primarily on their respective synagogues, while maintaining a connection with both the larger Cuban-Jewish community of Miami and Miami's overall Jewish community. Nearly two decades had elapsed since their arrival in Miami as Cuban émigrés, and the Cuban-Jews no longer felt in a liminal position where they were denied, by the very people whom they considered religious brethren, the identity they claimed. By the late 1970s and early 1980s, the Jewbans finally felt at home in Miami Beach.

## History and Memory

The written accounts of Susan Epstein, the Cuban Hebrew Congregation, and Temple Moses consider the history of the Cuban-Jews in Miami in a very bounded way. With few exceptions, they fail to place these communities within any larger historical framework. A discussion of the international political, social, and economic events occurring as these communities developed (among them, the Camarioca boatlift and airlift from 1965 to 1973, El Diálogo in 1978, and the Mariel boatlift in 1980–81) is absent from these accounts. Perhaps this is because most Cuban Sephardim and Ashkenazim did not consider these events to be linked directly to their community histories; or perhaps they are moments remembered vividly by individuals but forgotten in text, since the written word signifies that which is chosen to be remembered collectively and passed on through the generations. Indeed, it is often easier to exclude controversial stories from such community histories than to "soil" history, as it were. The effect of such exclusion, however, is to leave the Cuban-Jewish communities trapped in an isolated world of their own—a world which actually never existed.

In my conversations with individuals from South Florida's Cuban-Jewish community, a sharp contrast emerged between my interlocutors' memories as South Floridians and their memories as Cuban-Jews, or Jewbans. As members of the Cuban-Jewish community, they recalled many of the events described in the community's "official" histories listed above (many, in fact, referenced these written histories as they told their stories), focusing specifically on the Jewish Cubans' arrival in the United States, the community's formation, and its structure today. As we spoke about larger issues (including anti-Semitism, Cuban migration, the Jewish Diasporic experience, and Cuban-American politics), however, new stories emerged which were cradled in a larger historical context. It was within this context that new perspectives on the development of the Cuban-Jewish community emerged. And these perspectives challenged, or at least recontextualized, the "official" histories of the community.

## Bernardo Benes and *El Diálogo*

The mid-1970s saw a heightened call for normalization of relations between the United States and Cuba by groups of young (often second-generation) Cuban-Americans.[36] With the election of Jimmy Carter as president of the United States in 1976, the first steps in this direction materialized. As part of his human rights agenda, Carter met secretly with Cuban officials in New York and Havana throughout 1978 to discuss the release of political prisoners and other topics. By August 1978, the two governments had reached an agreement for the release of thousands of prisoners. When the Carter administration refused publicly to acknowledge its role in these talks, the Castro government decided to use the scheduled prisoner release program as a public-relations campaign to improve its relations with Cuban exiles (García 1996: 48).

In September 1978, Castro invited émigrés to Cuba to participate in a dialogue with the government, focusing on the release of political prisoners in Cuba and possible émigré travel back to the island for purposes of family reunification. A successful *diálogo*, he announced, would effect the release of up to three thousand political prisoners. The *diálogo* offer came as a shock to the émigré community. Never before had Castro addressed the *gusanos* (worms) in such a reconciliatory and accommodating tone. During his press conference, Castro carefully referred to the émigrés as "'the Cuban community abroad' rather than the usual *gusanos, escoria* [scum], and *apatriadas* (people without a country) and publicly stated that perhaps he had 'misjudged' the community" (García 1996: 47).

The Cuban émigré community, unaware that Castro's interest in reestablishing relations with the United States first had been expressed in negotiations between the United States and Cuban governments months earlier, believed that the release of these political prisoners rested in its hands. Opinion on the issue was sharply divided. Hard-line, anti-Castro conservatives, who composed the most powerful constituency in Miami's Cuban exile community, suspiciously rejected any such offer. The Castro regime, they argued, could carry out its gesture of good will without the advice of Cuban émigrés, and they saw the *diálogo* as nothing more than a ploy to divide the émigré community and reduce its lobbying power in Washington (García 1996: 48). On the other hand, a significant number of émigrés, including those associated with groups such as Areíto, the Antonio Maceo Brigade, the Cuban-American Committee for the Normalization of Relations with Cuba, Casa de las Américas, and the Cuban Resource Center, embraced Castro's offer of dialogue (Masud-Piloto 1996: 73). It was time, they argued, to normalize relations between two estranged governments and reunite thousands of separated families.

Prior to the *diálogo* offer, the Cuban-Jewish community of Miami generally avoided involving itself in political issues, especially those concerning Cuba. In 1978, however, it suddenly found itself in the political spotlight. One of its founders, Bernardo Benes, became, in his own words, "one of the most active members of the Dade County [Cuban] community." As leader of the Comité de los 75, the committee of seventy-five Cuban émigrés chosen by the Cuban government to participate in *El Diálogo*, Benes called attention not only to himself, but also to the very community with which he was most closely associated.

"One moment, Bernardo Benes was the highly respected 'Cuban Henry Kissinger,'" begins a 1994 *Miami Herald* article on Benes, referring to his success as a banker; "[t]he next, he was a social leper, forced to wear a bulletproof vest" (Laughlin 1994: 2). Benes found himself in imminent, life-threatening danger after hard-line Cuban exiles accused him of collaborating with the Castro regime. Cuban radio, a powerful political and social force in Miami, launched virulent attacks on the *dialogueros*, targeting their leader as a Castro sympathizer. Protesters picketed his bank with signs reading "Bernardo Benes is a traitor" (2), and local television stations broadcast these images on the evening news. Benes received numerous death threats, many of which were transmitted to him by the Federal Bureau of Investigation. In May 1983, militant extremists bombed Miami's Continental Bank, of which Benes was president.[37]

Although the Cuban-Jewish community always had avoided political issues, the aftermath of the *Diálogo*, which saw the arrival in the United States of 3,600 political prisoners from Cuban jails and an easing of travel restrictions between the United States and Cuba, brought the controversy into its sphere. As Eva Simazi notes, Benes, "[perhaps more than any other Cuban-Jew,] contributed to Cuban-Jewish history in his involvement in Cuban politics." Reaction from within the community varied; an overwhelming ambivalence surrounded Benes's involvement in this monumental political event. Marcos Kerbel, a past president of the Cuban-Hebrew Congregation, describes the complications created through Benes's personal agenda and his Cuban-Jewish identity:

> *Kerbel:* Very few of the Cuban-Jews were involved in politics in Cuba or are involved here in Florida. . . . We were taught by our elders to stay away from politics. Politics becomes even more controversial when you're Jewish.
> *Bettinger-López:* Why?
> *Kerbel:* Uh, it created a lot of problems, in Cuban affairs. For example, somebody who played a very active role in Cuban politics in Miami is Bernardo Benes. And unfortunately he and his family paid a very big price, even though most of his ideas were correct. Although the

timing was correct from the prisoners' point of view, it was off from a
Miami exile mentality to have a dialogue with Castro. Even though 75
Miami Cubans went on the mission to have this dialogue, Benes was
singled out as the leading figure in the negotiations with Castro for the
release of thirty-five hundred Cuban non-Jewish political prisoners. I
believe it was jealousy and because he was Jewish.

Rafael Losger, also an active member of the Cuban-Hebrew Congregation,
explained the situation along strikingly similar lines:

> In the Cuban [exile] community, you have many different opinions—pro
> and con [concerning relations with Cuba]. You as a Jew are an outsider.
> Individually a few of us—like Bernardo—are involved. As a [Jewish]
> community, once you get involved, they will accuse you of something. Like
> in Russia right now: Jews were the ones who implanted Communism
> because Jews were all Communists. Now Jews did away with Communism
> because all Jews are capitalists. Always the Jew is the scapegoat. So we have
> to watch—when it comes to politics, we identify Jews as a religion; we try
> to stay away from political situations where we can *never win* and we will
> *always lose* by expressing our views. No, politically we [the Cuban-Hebrew
> Congregation and the Cuban-Jewish community] usually don't get involved
> as an organization. And I'm all together with that thought—that we, as a
> community—as a *religious* community—we should stay out of politics.

While Benes earned a certain level of respect as a successful diplomat, the
Cuban-Jewish community viewed him ambivalently. As Kerbel and Losger note, the
issue of religion could not be separated from that of politics; and the community, as
a *Jewish* community, bore some of the brunt of Benes's individual actions. Anti-
Semitism, Kerbel and Losger feel, fueled the hostility of many Gentile hard-liners
toward Benes. Indeed, many suspect that the unsolved 1981 shooting at the Cuban-
Hebrew Congregation to be linked to Benes's role in the *Diálogo* and his frequent
travel to Cuba, totaling seventy-five visits between 1978 and 1986 (Benes's own
estimate, cited in Levine 1993: 264).

The way in which the Cuban-Hebrew Congregation has chosen to remember
this shooting in its twentieth-anniversary booklet, *Círculo Cubano-Hebreo de Miami,
1961–1981: 20 Aniversario,* sheds light on our consideration of Benes's involvement in
the *Diálogo.* The title of the article discussing the shooting, "Vandalismo o
Terrorismo?" ("Vandalism or Terrorism?"), and the text which follows it, present the

shooting as an event which can be interpreted in one of two ways: either vandals randomly shot at the Cuban-Hebrew Congregation without any religious motivations, or anti-Semites deliberately chose to deface a sacred place of worship. No mention is made of an eminent synagogue member's involvement in the 1978 *Diálogo* and the controversy this engendered within Miami's Cuban-Jewish community.

Marcos Kerbel remembers the event differently. He still questions, as do many others, whether the shooting was linked directly to Benes's involvement with *El Diálogo*. In his discussion, Kerbel underscores Losger's concern over involving a socioreligious community of Cuban-Jews in a political debate over Cuba: "We'd like to think that it was some other unrelated incident, because at that time there were a lot of drug dealings in Miami Beach. The shots that were fired penetrated the sanctuary through the glass. Fortunately services had just ended.[38] It's unknown if it was a reprisal by anti-Castro Cuban militants for Benes being involved in dealings in the dialogue with Castro, or if it was an unrelated drug-related crime. We are very careful not to get involved in anything that's controversial, especially in anything related to Cuban politics, because it tends to affect the entire Cuban-Jewish community."

Benes's role in United States–Cuba relations did not end with the *Diálogo*. The year 1979 proved to be a monumental one for Cuban-Jews on both sides of the Florida Straits. That year, Benes drew his community into the spotlight again by taking Rabbi Abramowitz—who had been such an important figure in the development of the Cuban-Jewish community in Miami Beach—with him on a return trip to Cuba. Benes told me, "I don't know if Rabbi Abramowitz told you, but I took him to Cuba with me in 1979—he was the first rabbi to set foot in Cuba since 1959.[39] We went to the cemetery and the synagogues. He performed Jewish rituals." Through this move and others, Benes reestablished relations with the Jews remaining in Cuba, who in 1980 numbered approximately eight hundred (Volsky 1980: 6).

Based on this connection, and fearing a complete disintegration of the dwindling Jewish community on the island, Benes requested that the Patronato's leaders transfer three religious objects—a Torah, a yarmulke, and a talis—to the Cuban-Hebrew Congregation. In September 1980, Benes discussed this move with a *New York Times* reporter: "The elders [of the Patronato] can plainly see that the days of Judaism in Cuba are numbered. This is why we agreed that it was important to continue our traditions here [in Miami]" (qtd. in Volsky 1980: 6). Indeed, the arrival of these sacred items in the Cuban-Hebrew Congregation marked a momentous event for Miami's Jewbans. Volsky describes the atmosphere as both joyous and sad, for, through this event, the reporter writes, "the congregation had symbolically cut the sentimental cord that bound it to Cuba" (6).

The Torah from Cuba is mentioned only twice in the Círculo's 1981 booklet. Part of Volsky's *New York Times* article is reprinted alongside other clips of news articles concerning the Cuban-Jewish community in Miami, in an "Ecos de Prensa" ("Echoes of the Press") layout placed toward the end of the booklet (Cuban-Hebrew Congregation of Miami 1981: 70). In the collage layout reviewing the shooting at the synagogue, news articles are reprinted; in one, brief mention is made of the Torah, although in a narrow historical context: "One bullet grazed the velvet cover of a century-old Torah, but did not damage the sacred scroll" (qtd. on 77).

Benes had warned me, "Many other Cuban-Jews will tell you that I am controversial." This assertion was confirmed in a roundabout way: while many interviewees mentioned his political involvement and its effect on the Cuban-Jewish community, the official publication of the Cuban-Hebrew Congregation, which I had assumed would include a discussion of the effects on the community of such important events as the *Diálogo* or the transfer of the Patronato's Torah scroll, gave (at best) a superficial treatment of such matters. The Cuban-Hebrew Congregation, thus chose to leave the controversial Benes out of its collective memory, casting him instead as a "founding father" of the community.[40]

## The Mariel Boatlift

Another event absent from the aforementioned community histories, and mentioned only in passing in Melarmed's *Breve Historia*, is the Mariel boatlift.[41] In April 1980, Castro announced that all Cubans wishing to leave the island could do so. Thousands of boats belonging to Cuban exiles soon crowded the port of Mariel, designated the new emigration center. These Cuban-Americans came in hopes of rescuing family and friends who remained on the island. This would be permitted, Castro stipulated, only if the exiles also agreed to transport strangers to Miami.

From April 1980 to September 1981, over 125,000 Cubans arrived in South Florida through the Mariel boatlift. *Marielitos*, as these émigrés came to be called disparagingly, differed significantly from the elite and middle-class Cubans who had emigrated before them. Many were dark-skinned, and most were from poor and working-class backgrounds. Additionally, to spite the United States and its Cuban exile communities and to cleanse Cuba of "anti-Revolutionaries," Castro sent several thousand "undesirables"— mentally ill, homosexuals, and criminals imprisoned in Cuba's jails for crimes against the state—on exile boats to Miami. While the "undesirables" comprised a small percentage of the Mariel émigrés, they received an abundance of negative media attention. To the further dismay of many anti-Castro Cuban-Americans, many Marielitos claimed no political agenda in Miami, maintaining that their exit from Cuba was spurred by economic decline and not political persecution. These émigrés thus resembled economic

"immigrants" rather than political "exiles," a distinction that many of the 1960s generation had gone to great lengths to articulate.[42]

By November 1980, "only 1,769 Cubans—approximately 1.4 percent of the
boatlift population—were being detained in federal correctional institutions to await
exclusionary hearings." Even so, most Americans viewed all Marielitos as "exclud-
able," the label used to designate Mariel immigrants who committed crimes in the
United States (García 1996: 71). Many Marielitos thus avoided associating themselves with the boatlift. Rosa Levy, a Cuban-Jewish Mariel émigré, told me that she
forbade her young children to disclose to others in Miami that they had arrived in
the United States through Mariel. Revealing this, she said, amounted to condemning
oneself to persecution and discrimination. Even the repatriation of many
"excludables" throughout the 1980s, through bilateral agreements between the
Cuban and United States governments, did little to redeem the reputations of the
tens of thousands of noncriminal Marielitos remaining in the United States.

This profound ambivalence toward the Marielitos came from nearly all sides in
the Miami community. While Anglo-Americans and American blacks living in
Miami resented the generous concessions made to many of the émigrés by the
United States government, much of the established Cuban exile community—
especially by mid-1981—also attempted to distance itself from the situation. In
their eyes, the Marielitos had tarnished the golden reputation Cuban exiles had
earned in the preceding twenty years.

With the Mariel exodus to Miami came an estimated 400 Jews, a significant
number considering that only 807 observant Jews remained on the island (Levine
1996: 802).[43] By this time, over 90 percent of the 1958 Jewish population of Cuba
was living abroad—primarily in the United States and Israel, and to a lesser extent
throughout Latin America.

In 1980, the Cuban-Jewish community in Miami was focusing on its own
development and other events transpiring in Miami and Israel. Mariel did not hit the
community in the same way it did Miami's larger Cuban exile community, since most
Cuban-Jews, unlike many Cuban Gentiles in Miami, no longer had relatives on the
island. Ironically, the principal organization providing assistance to the Jewish arrivals
was the Resettlement Task Force of the Greater Miami Jewish Federation, which
many Cuban-Jews of the 1960s exile generation felt had turned its back on them
twenty years before (Levine 1993: 265).

Although most Cuban-Jews lacked this personal connection, Mariel still became a
concern for the community. Arón Kelton, a former president of the Cuban-Hebrew
Congregation, discusses the synagogue's involvement in the Mariel crisis: "The United
HIAS Service had delegates coming south, working with the Jewish Federation [GMJF].

During Mariel, they approached us at the Cuban-Hebrew Congregation and we formed a committee. There were very few Cuban Jews coming through Mariel. The place where we met them—it was very hard to identify them. We volunteers wrote down information about the refugees, and HIAS processed the Jewish refugees. Every Jew that came in we helped. We gave them clothing, tickets, hospital care, whatever they needed. We did as much as we could do, under the circumstances."

Rafael Losger, another former Cuban-Hebrew Congregation president, also described the assistance provided to the Mariel refugees by the community: "As the President of the Congregation, always we made certain stands, always with the Cuban community; with the Mariel boatlift, we were there to help. We help Cuban causes."[44] These "stands," however, are absent from most histories of the community.

Melarmed's account mentions Mariel only in the context of his focus on the dwindling Jewish community in Cuba:

> Recientemente, en Abril de 1980, cuando el gobierno cubano decidió permitir la salida de decenas de miles de cubanos por la llamada "Flotilla de la Liberdad," desde el puerto de Mariel, se calcula que ya no quedan más judíos en Cuba, salvo algunos pocos a los que les fue negada la salida, o algunos padres de familia que no quisieron separarse de sus hijos o algunas personas viejas que no tienen familia en los Estados Unidos y no quieren salir porque no quieren dejar sus casas, o el retiro que reciben el gobierno cubano.

> (Recently, in April 1980, when the Cuban government decided to allow the emigration of tens of thousands of Cubans through the so-called "Freedom Flotilla," from the port of Mariel, it was calculated that now no Jews remain in Cuba other than some few who were denied permission to leave, or some parents who do not want to be separated from their children, or older people who do not have family in the United States and do not want to leave because they do not want to leave their houses or the pension they receive from the Cuban government.) (198?: 8)

Perhaps the failure to include the Mariel crisis in official histories reflects the Cuban-Jewish community's effort to distance itself from the Marielitos, much like that of the larger 1960s-era Cuban exile community in Miami. Rosa Levy's story of the Cuban-Jewish community's reaction to her Sephardic family's arrival portrays a community quite ambivalent about Mariel. When I asked her how her family was received by the Cuban-Jewish community after she arrived through Mariel, Levy replied, "I have been mentioned [within the community as a possible Communist], while I was arriving here—the moment that I arrived. They—the first ones [1960s émigrés]—mentioned that to me. . . . It's like, they have a pattern. It's like, 'You came late, because you were Communist.'" Nevertheless, Levy emphasized, once she denounced Communism and the Castro government and explained her reasons for staying in Communist Cuba, she was welcomed into the community and feels comfortable there today.[45]

## Rabbi Rozencwaig's Resignation

The year 1984 proved momentous for the Cuban-Hebrew Congregation, as Rabbi Dow Rozencwaig, among the most important figures in the congregation, resigned from his post. Controversy surrounded Rozencwaig's departure. The congregation recently had made key changes in its traditions—most visibly, a shift from Orthodox to Conservative Judaism, and the substitution of English and Spanish for Yiddish, the principal language previously used to conduct synagogue services. Rozencwaig quickly became disenchanted. As Andrés S. Viglucci writes in his *El Nuevo Herald* article, entitled "Judíos Cubanos Se Amoldan a Nuevos Tiempos" ("Cuban Jews Adjust to New Times"), "Rozencwaig, líder espiritual del templo durante 22 años, afirma que renunció porque los dirigentes de la congregación querían abandonar la ortodoxia" ("Rozencwaig, the spiritual leader of the temple for twenty-two years, affirms that he resigned because the congregation's leaders wanted to abandon Orthodoxy") (Viglucci 1984: 5).

The congregation, nine hundred families strong by 1984, replaced Rozencwaig with a Conservative American rabbi, Barry Konovitch, who spoke only English and Hebrew. This shift in the synagogue's level of orthodoxy, primary language used, and rabbi (and the resulting shift in the rabbi's role in the congregation, since Konovitch did not speak Spanish), was geared most directly toward the younger generation of Jewbans, who Congregation leaders feared were losing interest in both Judaism and their Cuban-Jewish heritage. The three-congregation Instituto, discussed previously, was just one of the efforts made to attract Cuban-Jewish youth to their religious and cultural roots. As Konovitch told Viglucci (in English), "Queremos que la generación más joven regrese. Estamos tratando de crear una nueva imagen. Nos hemos esforzado en garantizar un atractivo más amplio" ("We want the younger generation to return. We are trying to create a new image. We have made an effort to guarantee a broader appeal") (Viglucci 1984: 5).

As a 1986 *Miami Herald* article reveals, Konovitch's linguistic limitations, in a congregation with a majority of first-language Spanish speakers, proved difficult for the older generation (Fernández 1986a). The administrator of the congregation, Arón Kelton, explained, "Para nuestros miembros de más edad, eso ha sido un sacrificio, pero lo hemos aceptado porque sabemos que será lo mejor para nuestra gente joven" ("For our older members, that [language barrier] has been a sacrifice, but we have accepted it because we know that it will be best for our young people") (Fernández 1986a: 9). These changes, as Kelton emphasized, were only part of a natural "proceso de la vida en este país" ("process of life in this country"). "Es completamente normal. Es imposible de detener, y no queremos detenerlo." ("It's completely normal. It's impossible to stop, and we don't want to stop it") (Viglucci 1984: 5).

This "Americanization" of synagogue services and other events took place fairly rapidly after Konovitch's arrival. Many worried that this was proceeding too rapidly—after all, young people should not forget their roots as Cuban-Jews/Jewbans. The congregation's leaders maintained, however, that Konovitch was the most suitable rabbi for their community.[46]

Many members of the Cuban-Jewish community felt that Konovitch regarded the Cuban-Jews as foreigners, much as the American Jewish community in Miami Beach had done in the 1960s. Throughout my research, many people suggested that Konovitch had hurt the community through discriminatory behavior, but no one would comment further on this. One woman told me, "He did some very bad things to us Cuban-Jews, but I don't want to talk about it." Only one woman, Miriam Shalper, discussed the situation with me: "When my fiancé and I met with Rabbi Konovitch about getting married, he asked us why we wanted to get married in the Cuban-Hebrew Congregation. 'Because it's the Cuban-Hebrew Congregation,' we said. 'Well,' he said, 'I hope you know that we don't dance the rumba in this shul,' he said. We couldn't believe he said that!"[47] Throughout the late 1980s and early 1990s, much of the congregation was discontented with Konovitch. By 1994, the congregation was searching for a new rabbi.[48]

Perhaps the negative attitude toward Konovitch was influenced by the simple fact that, unlike his predecessor, Rabbi Rozencwaig, he was a Conservative rabbi and did not speak Spanish or know much about "Cuban-Jewish" culture. Konovitch's writings in congregation bulletins often describe the changing face of Miami Beach's Jewish community since the arrival of Cuban and other Hispanic Jews. These writings emphasize the impact of the Cuban-Jews on Miami Beach culture and place utmost importance on Miami Beach remaining Jewish: "Clearly the cultural center of gravity of the Jewish population [in Miami Beach] has shifted somewhat from New York to Havana. . . . Our vision of the future appears radically different from the past; but we expect that Miami Beach will remain vibrant, creative, and most assuredly Jewish" (Konovitch 1990: 2–3). In 1999, Konovitch was the rabbi at Aventura-Turnberry Jewish Center in Northeast Miami–Dade County.

## Cubanidad and the Synagogue

By 1990, Henry Green estimates, ten thousand Cuban-Jews were living in Dade County (in Chardy 1990: 4B). The community indeed had gained in strength and size and increasingly was able to focus on its development within South Florida. With rare

Interiors, Torat Moshe and Cuban-Hebrew Congregation. Note the barrier between men and women in the main sanctuary of Torat Moshe (above). The Cuban-Hebrew Congregation recently put up a barrier in its small prayer room (below) but allows men and women to sit together in the main sanctuary (opposite). 1999. Photos by Caroline Bettinger-López.

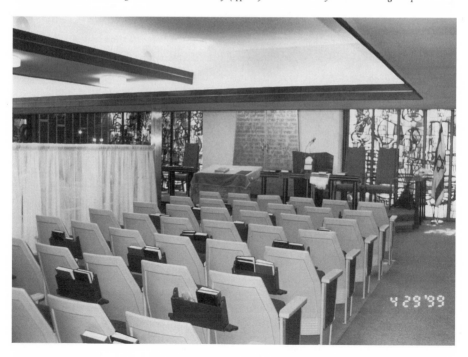

exceptions, it no longer needed to turn its attention toward Jewish migration from Cuba, since nearly all of the 1950s Jewish population now was living outside the island. "While their religious life remains divided," Margalit Bejarano noted in 1994, "Ashkenazi and Sephardi Cubans closely collaborate on behalf of the State of Israel. Through their generous donations to the UJA [United Jewish Appeal] and the [Israeli] Bond Drive, which proportionately exceed those of the rest of Miami's community, they started to be accepted by the American Jews" (Bejarano 1994: 135). Over the preceding three decades, the Cuban-Jews had worked their way into South Florida's larger Jewish community, becoming some of its most active members. They had proven to their American coreligionists that they were indeed "real" Jews and deserved to be treated as such.

While the community enjoyed improved relations with the American Jewish community, it sought to retain its "Cuban-Jewish" character through religious and social events. As Eva Simazi notes, the community's high level of social involvement set it apart from the surrounding American Jewish community: "It's a difference, I think, between the American Jewish community and the Cuban-Jewish community. We are always trying to get more involved in that social type of activity than the Americans. Because they belong to this country club or that country club—temple is just for praying. They don't see it as a social gathering place. We get more involved. For us, temple is the center of everything. For the American Jewish community, temple is just for praying."

# Noche Cubana

Noche Cubana *at Temple Moses. Source:* Newsletter, *Sephardic Congregation of Florida—Templo Moses, January-February, 1995, p. 11.*

Synagogue bulletins in recent years reflect the synagogue's centrality for Cuban-Jews. While Temple Moses has reached out to Latin American Sephardim and the Cuban-Hebrew Congregation has adopted a more "Americanized" approach, both have sought to maintain their unique Cuban identity through social events.

Temple Moses/Torat Moshe bulletins often feature a "Rincón del Recuerdo" ("Corner of Remembrance") section featuring photos and narratives of Sephardic life in pre-revolutionary Cuba. Each year, Cuban Sephardim nostalgically "return" to Cuba by attending a night of "Cuban" festivities at Temple Moses's Noche Cubana (Cuban Night) and a day of "Cuban" family fun at its Canasta Cubana (Cuban Picnic).

Cuban Sephardim also participate in broader Sephardic activities, such as the American Sephardic Federation's 1995 Miami convention, hosted by the region's Sephardic congregations and the University of Miami's Sephardic Studies Program. During this three-day event, four hundred delegates from Sephardic communities in the United States and throughout the world congregated to discuss such issues as cultural reconciliation between Jews and Arabs, Sephardic demographics, Ladino, Kaballah, the Torah, Jews of Syria and Yemen, Judeo-Arab music, Israeli dances, and the Jews from Cuba (Sephardic Congregation of Florida 1995b : 5). This last element, discussion of Jews from Cuba, reflected the international interest in the history of the "Cuban" congregation which now represented Florida's Sephardim. According to Henry Green, however, Temple Moses played much less of a role in the 1995 convention than it had in a similar convention it hosted in 1985; accordingly, the subject of Cuba was less prominent in the 1995 convention (Henry Green to CB-L, July 12, 1999).

Later in 1995, the Sephardic Congregation of Florida celebrated an even more momentous occasion, when it was asked to host a convention for Sephardic rabbis from around the world. Leading this convention was the chief Sephardic rabbi from Israel, Bakshi Doron Shalita. As Susana Hamla recounts, the convention almost was called off on account of the congregation's name: "When the Chief Rabbi came to visit us, . . . he didn't want to come to our congregation because he saw *Temple*—they used it [that term] in Germany [to designate Reformed synagogues]. And he thought that we were Reformed, or Conservative. And he asked the Board of Directors to please use the same name, but change it to Torat Moshe, or Bet Moshe, and the Board of Directors decided Torat Moshe." Traditional and Orthodox Jews traditionally use either *synagogue* or *shul* to refer to the place of worship. The term *temple* was adopted mostly by the Reform movements in Europe and the United States, in order to establish a closer link to mainstream society (hence Hamla's reference to Germany). For many religious Jews, *temple* connotes a much less interactive and traditional atmosphere, removed from the Traditional or Orthodox version of prayer.[49] Thus, at the chief rabbi's request, the Traditional Temple Moses became Torat Moshe, maintaining its second designation as Sephardic Congregation of Florida.

In the past few years, Temple Moses/Torat Moshe has made a marked attempt to bring young people back into the community. Youth programs include a preschool directed by Raquel Benzaquén, the current rabbi's wife, and Talmud Torah classes for children of ages five through thirteen. Additionally, the congregation offers classes on Judaism for young couples once a month. These classes are led by Rabbi Abraham and Raquel Benzaquén and are held in the homes of various community members. Jewish Generation X (J/X) is a joint initiative of Torat Moshe, the Cuban-Hebrew Congregation, and Temple Menorah, hosting social and cultural events within the community for those between the ages of twenty-two and thirty-five.[50]

The Cuban-Hebrew Congregation, too, has been involved in perpetuating its *cubanidad* through events, meetings, social gatherings, and newsletters. Its primary concern, however, is with its "Jewish" identity, not necessarily linked to nationality. As the current rabbi, Shimon Dudai, explains, recently the Cuban-Hebrew Congregation has focused most intensely on three areas: seniors; young couples, families, and singles; and children (Dudai 1996: 1). Initiatives include forming a "Founding Committee so we can plan special events and programs to suit the tempo and taste of our Seniors" and "opening a Day-care or Pre-K facility under the auspices of the Shul" in order to attract "young Jewish working families with children who live in the neighboring area," and to "attract a group of young people to actively participate in this New Phase of our Shul's development" (1).[51]

The Cuban-Hebrew Congregation is continuing the direction of change begun with the arrival of Rabbi Konovitch. By placing more emphasis on its "Jewish" aspect, it has attempted to attract Ashkenazim from all backgrounds, not only Cuban. Rabbi Dudai articulates the congregation's new direction in his closing statement: "And finally—we will be introducing our New Siddur-Prayer Book—and new style of services. The objectives are more participation by the Congregation in the service, reading and understanding the prayers as well as chanting, resulting in a more meaningful and spiritual experience" (1). The rabbi discusses only Judaism in his article: no reference is made to the "Cuban" aspect of the Cuban-Hebrew Congregation. In this he differs from those who wrote congregation bulletins in previous decades and focused primarily on this aspect. In fact, as the bulletin's cover illustrates, the congregation now labels itself first as Temple Beth Shmuel and second as Cuban-Hebrew Congregation of Miami.

Even so, sometimes reference is made to the congregation's Cuban roots and its connection to Torat Moshe through *cubanidad*. In a 1998 issue of *El Nuevo Jewban*, for instance, the congregation promoted an upcoming "Latin Night" hosted by Fanny and Marcos Kerbel (Apr. 1998). Its thirty-sixth "double chai" anniversary booklet, *1961–1997: Celebrating Thirty-six Years*, opens with an advertisement for the Estate and Charity Funding Network, of which an active congregation member, Reinaldo Winer, is president. At the top of the advertisement is Winer's photograph and the words, "I am a JEWBAN. My heritage is rich in combining traditions from Cuba, Israel and the U.S.A. It is my responsibility to guarantee that future generations will enjoy the benefits of my legacy" (Cuban-Hebrew Congregation of Miami 1997: inside of front cover). This opening essentially frames the rest of the booklet, which celebrates the Círculo's strength and vitality by examining its past, present, and future. Winer links his "JEWBAN" identity with his past experiences and carries this powerful identity with him as he discusses his experience with estate planning. By making a planned gift to a charity, he states, "we can affirm that our strength and continuity will endure and that EL CIRCULO will be here for our children, not just for 36 years, but forever" (inside of front cover). Institutional continuity and the perpetuation of "JEWBAN" heritage through the generations thus are ensured by remembering the Círculo's past and properly planning for its future.

A 1996 Cuban-Hebrew Congregation bulletin shows photographs taken at the congregation's Canasta Party, a uniquely "Cuban" event. And in the caption, it reinforces its connection to its "sister" congregation: "Special thanks to those who came from Temple Torat Moshe" (Gorfinkel 1996: 4). By maintaining this connection, the Cuban-Hebrew Congregation and Torat Moshe support each other today as equal partners in one Cuban-Jewish community in Miami.

# El Nuevo Jewban

Since Castro's rise to power, the United States has followed a policy of economic and diplomatic isolation of Cuba, attempting to undermine the Castro regime and prevent the exportation of Communist ideology from the island. In response to the Cuban Missile Crisis, President John F. Kennedy in 1963 implemented a United States embargo on travel to Cuba, under the authorization of the Trading with the Enemy Act of 1917. Yet restrictions on travel to Cuba for United States citizens and permanent residents have not been without conciliatory elements. The late 1970s, for instance, witnessed several initiatives to establish a bridge between the two powers—particularly *El Diálogo* and President Carter's subsequent suspension of the ban on travel to Cuba by United States citizens, termination of reconnaissance flights over the island, and implementation of agreements on fishing rights and maritime boundaries.

With the Mariel crisis and electoral victories by the conservative Reagan and Bush administrations, such initiatives toward rapprochement quickly ceased. In 1982, President Reagan halted air-charter links between the United States and Cuba and declared it illegal for United States citizens to spend dollars in Cuba, effectively creating a travel ban. In 1992, President Bush signed into law the "Cuba Democracy Act"—also known as the Torricelli Bill—which prohibited United States companies operating in third countries from trading with or investing in Cuba (including the trade in many foods, medicines, and medical supplies). It also banned ships engaged

Canasta Cubana *at the Cuban-Hebrew Congregation. Source: Estelita Gorfinkel, "Women's League of Temple Beth Shmuel,"* Bulletin of Temple Beth Shmuel–Cuban Hebrew Congregation of Miami 4 *(October–December 1996): 4.*

in trade with Cuba from using United States ports within six months of their last visit to the island. Finally, the bill authorized United States presidents to withhold debt relief, economic assistance, and free trade agreements from countries providing aid to Cuba (Bernstein 1998a; Duncan 1993: 216; Pérez 1995: 384–85; U.S. Department of the Treasury, Office of Foreign Assets Control 1999: 1).

In the aftermath of the *balsero* migration from Cuba in 1994, President Clinton tightened embargo restrictions even further. For the first time, it was declared illegal for Cuban-Americans to visit family members on the island except for emergency cases. United States researchers were required to obtain specific licenses for travel to Cuba, and only "regularly employed" journalists could make the trip. In 1995, Clinton loosened the rules a bit, creating more categories under which academics and researchers could get licenses. But in February 1996, after Cuban fighter jets gunned down two unarmed planes belonging to the Miami-based nonviolent exile group Brothers to the Rescue, Clinton signed into law the Cuban Liberty and Democratic Solidarity Act—also known as the Helms-Burton Bill—which imposes, without judicial review, fines of up to $55,000 on United States citizens who violate the embargo sanctions and allows for confiscation of their property. In addition, such individuals may face up to $250,000 in fines and up to ten years in prison under the

Trading with the Enemy Act. Under these acts, mail cannot be sent from the United States to Cuba, although mail can be accepted in the United States from Cuba. After Helms-Burton, Clinton barred all direct flights between the United States and Cuba (Bernstein 1998a; Stanley 1997: 12; U.S. Department of the Treasury, Office of Foreign Assets Control 1999: 1–7).

In order to improve people-to-people contact between Americans and Cubans and to ease the hardships faced by the Cuban people, the United States government reinstated Miami-Havana charter flights in March 1998 and Los Angeles–Havana and New York–Havana charter flights in August 1999. All these continue today. The United States government insists that these measures can be carried out without supporting the Castro regime. While certain groups of people may obtain permission to visit Cuba, United States citizens and permanent residents continue to be barred from spending money in Cuba—an act which, in effect, prevents travel to the island. There are only three exceptions to the travel ban. The first is the "general license," which covers official government travelers; full-time, accredited journalists; members of international/United States organizations traveling on official business; and individuals traveling once a year to visit close relatives in circumstances of humanitarian need. These people may visit the island at any time with their general license. The second exception is a "specific license," for which individuals involved in humanitarian assistance, religious activities, professional or scholarly research or study, athletic competitions, and professional meetings and conferences must apply prior to visiting Cuba. The third exception applies to "fully hosted travelers," people whose Cuba-related expenses are covered by a person not subject to United States jurisdiction. This exception is possible because it is only a violation for United States citizens and permanent residents to spend money in Cuba; travel itself is not restricted (Bernstein 1998a; Shenon 1999: A8; U.S. Department of the Treasury, Office of Foreign Assets Control 1999: 6–7).

Many hard-line anti-Castro exiles celebrate the United States embargo as a moral victory against a Communist dictator who would not allow the Cuban people access to the sanctioned goods and services even if the embargo did not exist. The embargo thus serves, in their opinion, to foment discontent among the Cuban masses toward the Castro regime. Pressure on Cuba, they also contend, will give the United States leverage to force elections after Castro dies (Bernstein 1998a).

Those who favor rapprochement between the two countries, on the other hand, argue that the embargo is a product of the Cold War mentality and is strictly a political show of force. The embargo, they contend, serves only to intensify the hardships of the Cuban people amid the "Special Period"; if it accomplishes anything, it is to make Cubans distrust the United States, thus reinforcing Castro's mantra of the past four decades. Castro will remain economically comfortable with or without the embargo, they think, and it should be lifted so that exposure to United States goods, services,

and democratic ideology will spur the Cuban people to seek better lives for themselves
and thus develop a new sense of self-determination.

The United States embargo on trade with, and travel to, Cuba, and the various
viewpoints on the subject, are essential pieces of information when considering issues of
identity among Cubans and Cuban-Americans. Without frequent contact between these
two groups, each has evolved in accord with shifts in United States–Cuba political
relations. What does contemporary Cuba mean to a Cuban-American who has not seen
the island in four decades? How does this person identify with the United States? In
Miami's Cuban-Jewish community, how have the two countries' political relations
contributed to a sense of Jewban identity, or *jubanidad?*

## Returning to Cuba

The Jewbans, thirty-eight years after the Cuban Revolution, are no longer exiles.
Most consider themselves American-Cuban-Jews. Cuba, their now legendary homeland,
functions for most as a far-away place to which they return in memory and conversation,
although a small but significant number now visit the island and are plugged into events
there. Most émigrés' hopes of returning "home" after a temporary exile in the United
States were dashed long ago; even if given the opportunity today—that is, if Cuba were
governed democratically—most would choose to remain in their new American home.

Even in 1981, this attachment to the United States was extremely strong, as Susan
Epstein documents in her thesis on Miami's Cuban Sephardic community. In 1981, 86.6
percent of her interlocutors "stated that if Castro were killed or deposed, they would visit
Cuba, but had no intention of resettling on the island, as they now regard Miami as
home" (1981: 98). Her interlocutors' words indeed paint a picture of a Cuban Sephardic
community rooted in Miami Beach. Some, such as the woman quoted below, noted that
they had no intention of returning to Cuba ever, under any circumstances:

> Aunque yo nací en Cuba y he querido siempre a mi país, salí de allá,
> como es natural, por la presión comunista en la cual no queríamos
> nosotros vivir, y gracias a este país que nos dió albergue nos ayudó en
> todo el sentido de la palabra y lo adoramos todo. Ya somos cuidadanos
> americanos y es lógico en veinte años pues ya hemos echado raíces aquí y
> sería muy difícil volver a empezar otra vida, y además, nos gusta . . .
> queremos vivir aquí en [los] Estados Unidos.

> (Although I was born in Cuba and have always loved my country, I left
> there, as is natural, because of the Communist pressure under which we did
> not want to live, and thanks to this country that gave us refuge and helped

us in all senses of the word—we adore all of it. Now we are American citizens, and it is logical that in twenty years we have grown roots here and it would be very difficult to return to begin another life, and furthermore, we like it . . . we want to live here in the United States.) (Epstein 1981: 98)

Another man stressed his love for the island, while justifying his reasons for leaving:

No regresaría . . . para una visita sí . . . pero para volver a establecerme no. No podría porque mi vida espiritual está aquí, aunque el país donde Ud. nace Ud. debe amarlo porque yo amo a Cuba. No puedo olvidar que mi personalidad, incluso mi intelecto se formó en Cuba. Yo admiro al carácter de aquel cubano que había en Cuba, que era de una mentalidad muy democrática. Es verdad que alguna que otra vez se oyó hablar de antisemitismo. Pero no fué en una forma . . . masiva organizada. Los judíos nos sentíamos en Cuba como unos cubanos más. Salimos de Cuba porque no podíamos soportar un sistema de vigilancia, una imposición de ideas, y pensando no solo en nosotros, sino en nuestros hijos, optamos por salir del país. Hoy nos sentimos muy felices de estar en [los] Estados Unidos.

(I would not return . . . for a visit, yes . . . but return to settle, no. I would not be able to because my spiritual life is here, even though the country where you are born should be the country you love, because I love Cuba. I can't forget that my personality, including my intellect, was formed in Cuba. I admire the character of the type of Cuban of old who had a very democratic mentality. It is true that, once in awhile, anti-Semitic language was heard. But it was not in a form . . . an organized mass. The Jews in Cuba felt like any other Cubans. We left Cuba because we couldn't support a system of vigilance, an imposition of ideas; and thinking not only of ourselves, but also of our children, we chose to leave the country. Now we feel very happy to be in the United States.) (Epstein 1981: 100)

Both my Ashkenazic and Sephardic interlocutors echoed these sentiments. Eva Simazi, a Sephardic in her early fifties, discussed her aversion to the notion of her family members setting foot in Communist Cuba, much less returning to the island permanently:

*Simazi:* There was a time, when my sister in-law—being Colombian, she can travel from Columbia to Havana—her parents went there, and they brought us pictures of the places where we lived. And of course you get emotional, and whatever. And especially my son, he says, "*Tía* [Aunt], maybe I will go with you," and I say, "Over my dead body." But he wanted to go. Maybe it's my mistake, maybe I should've let him go. But now he's a man. He can do whatever. I cannot stop him anymore—if he wants to do it. But he will know that it will be against my will, or against my way of thinking. But it's his judgment. I would like to go myself, but not now. And then also I would think that I have in the back of my memory, this beautiful country. That in order to go now, and see the destruction that is there. . . . It's been thirty-seven years.

*Bettinger-López:* Do you think if Castro's overthrown, that you'd want to move back there?

*Simazi:* No, not move. What for? Sixteen years [in Cuba]—I was almost raised here. Our roots are here now. I would love to go back, but I don't think that I will move back there. Not only that—now we think more as Americans. . . . I don't think that we could adapt ourselves. It's a whole new generation that exists there now. Even if they don't have the same regime. But that generation is different. The outlook is different.

When I asked Damien Losger, a twenty-one-year-old Ashkenazic, if he thought his parents would ever return to Cuba with the intention of staying, he replied: "No, I know they wouldn't. I'm sure they'd visit. They'd try to open up a business there or something, where they could go back every once in awhile. But as far as living there, I don't think so. That part of their lives is so far away." These testimonies reveal a sense of connection with the United States, realized within Miami. They suggest a new way of looking at Cuba, as a place of nostalgia rather than return.

As the notion of the "Jewban" reveals, the Cuban-Jewish community changed during its years in exile. The Cubans' less-than-friendly reception by the American Jewish community led to the former's consolidation in 1961 into the Círculo Cubano-Hebreo de Miami. Through this organization, a new identity took shape for the émigrés. No longer *Jewish* Cubans or *Cuban* Jews, they became a fusion of the two. As hyphenated "Cuban-Jews," they had turned their original rejection into a sense of solidarity.

As the Cuban-Jewish community developed in Miami Beach throughout the 1960s, the "Cuban" and the "Jewish" aspects increasingly fused, serving not only to complement each other, but also to redefine each other. As Ofelia Ruder, the Cuban-Hebrew Congregation's office manager and unofficial historian, told me, "In Cuba we were the Jews. We became the Jewbans in Miami." "Jewban" articulated a first redefinition of identity by the Cuban-Jews in South Florida. This occurred across all generations of Cuban Sephardim and Ashkenazim, as the entire community moved into uncharted territory.

In the past decade, the Jewban community again has been transformed. As older members of the community have passed on, the middle and younger generations increasingly have taken up the reins as the community's leaders. These people were born in either Cuba or the United States, speak Spanish and/or English as first languages, and have a close connection to South Florida, where most grew up and/or raised children. For them, the community is a vital force which was born in Miami Beach and developed as a result of two forces: the memory of Cuba and the disdain of South Florida's Jewish community.

Anthropologist Ruth Behar's 1995 article, "Juban América," profoundly articulates this very identity. "Moving from Poland to Turkey to Cuba to the United States," Behar travels through time and space to locate her own connections with her family's diasporic history (1995b: 151). As a Jew who left Cuba at the age of four and a half and grew up in New York, and whose physical connection with Cuba was cemented only as an adult, Behar searches in her writing for the sources of her "Cuban connection." This connection, she emphasizes, is formed not only through physical contact with the island; it is shaped also by stories and photographs, not only of Cuba, but also of Poland, Russia, and Turkey, the places in which her grandparents were born. Behar's connection with her birthplace thus is shaped largely within the United States, from whence she is able to relate to the past and the present.

"In Cuba," Behar writes, "my mother would have remained a *polaca*, and my father a *turco*; at the very least, they would have always been the children of *polacos* and *turcos*. It is within the United States that they have settled into their Cubanness" (1995b: 161). If her parents' experience in the United States allowed them to consolidate their *cubanidad*, Behar wonders, where should she locate her own identity? How can we reconcile the gap between Behar's mother, whose thick accent and difficulty with the English language serve as "ever-present reminder[s] that she is an immigrant in an America which is not hers," and Behar herself, who, in the eyes of the "typical" American, is "white like you, english-speaking [*sic*] like you, right-thinking like you, middle-class living like you, no matter what I say?" (1995b: 162; Morales 1986: 148, quoted in Behar 1995b: 162).

Through her physical, psychological, and emotional travels, Behar arrives in a land called "Juba." This place, however, differs from Poland, Russia, Turkey, Cuba, and the United States, for it is empty. Perhaps it has waited a lifetime for her to discover it. What is so liberating for Behar about this strange and yet "home-like" land is that it is open to "construction." There are no limits on the foundations Behar may lay upon its soil. Juba is, for Behar, an "imagined homeland," a place in which the "imaginer" can "create fictions, not actual cities or villages, but invisible ones" (Rushdie 1991: 9–10, qtd. in Behar 1995b: 165). Juba simultaneously and unproblematically can be Poland, Russia, Turkey, Cuba, and the United States, all in one; or, it can be none of these. It can incorporate events which seemingly are eons from the imaginer's present. It is a mosaic of all the fragments of Behar's history, built through family stories and collective memory.

The intersection of religion, nationality, displacement, and resettlement, among all other aspects of life, occurs within Juba. And it is precisely this intersection that allows Behar to articulate a new, unhyphenated identity. As a "Juban," she shares a unique position in the United States with other American-Cuban-Jews of her generation and after, each of whom has an imagined "Juba" of her or his own. Cuba's proximity to the United States and the Cuban-Jewish community's vivid memories of life in this tropical paradise serve to reinforce for these "Jubans" their *cubanidad* and thus their *jubanidad.*

The political and economic challenges to the Jewish Cubans posed by the 1959 Cuban Revolution brought about a mass migration of this community of approximately 15,000. Ironically, as Behar notes, the Jewish Cubans were warmly embraced as "Cubans" by the very "neighbor" which three decades before had rejected them for being "Jews" (1995b: 157). The communities these émigrés developed in New York, Puerto Rico, and, most notably, Miami, were both transplanted and reconstructed. On the one hand, they were modeled upon fresh memories of Jewish life in Cuba; on the other, they developed under completely unique social, political, and economic circumstances.

The Jewish Cubans entered America and in time became the Cuban-Jews. This hyphenated identity reflects the significant changes these émigrés underwent as they attempted to reestablish their Jewish community among their unwelcoming coreligionists in Miami Beach. Their nationality thus became even more significant to their practice of Judaism, contributing to "that unique [hyphenated] Cuban-Jewish flavor" so many of my interlocutors emphasized in our conversations.

As new generations were born and raised on American soil, the Cuban-Jewish community again changed. To them, the United States was no longer a temporary refuge, but a permanent home. Their congregations had grown in size and strength and increasingly were becoming important landmarks in South Florida.[52] Cuban-Jewish identity now incorporated a new nationality and new experiences within an already diasporic past. The Cuban-Jews articulated this new identity through the consolidated (unhyphenated) "Jewban" designation, also written as the hyphenated "Jew-Ban" and expressed in its Spanish form, "*Jewbano.*" The result of consolidating the hyphenated Cuban-Jewish and Jewish-Cuban identities into a new form that spanned time and space, the Jewban identity reflected more permanent settlement in

South Florida and the United States.[53] It thus became a great source of pride for the community, for it represented the Jewish Cuban triumph over adversity. Both Sephardim and Ashkenazim used this designation, and continue to do so today, to refer to themselves in conversation and in writing, as in the Cuban-Hebrew Congregation's bulletins from the 1970s, 1980s, and 1990s, entitled *Jewbano* and *El Nuevo Jewban* (*The New Jewban*).

Ruth Behar uses a different spelling (Juban) to articulate the Jewban identity. Her discussion of constructing her own personal "Juba" is particularly interesting, for, unlike most other Jubans, she regularly returns to Cuba in order to rediscover a home she left as a young child. These visits also serve a more complicated purpose: they allow her metaphorically to visit her grandparents' European homelands across the Atlantic Ocean, as she learns more about their lives in Cuba. These journeys ultimately allow Behar "to imagine a Juba, a Juba that I want to build, salt pillar by salt pillar, from both my family stories and my own struggle to reclaim all the little forgotten villages of my *mestiza* identity" (1995b: 165).

Behar's discussion of her own Juban identity brings us to the present day, where the *patria* (homeland) exists for most *jewbanos/jubanos* as a distant memory, a reality which is forty years outdated. That does not mean, however, that its significance is diminished for them as individuals; for, as Behar illustrates, *cubanidad*—as well as *polaco/a* and *turco/a* identity—is simply understood in a different way in the United States. South Florida's Jewbans/Jubans have chosen to build a Juba together as a community, a Juba resting on the foundation of a double diaspora. Through two twists of fate, their Jewish journey landed them in tropical Cuba, and their Cuban journey brought them to the United States. Through this Jewish Cuban journey, "El Nuevo Jewban" was born.

# Part II.

# Explorations

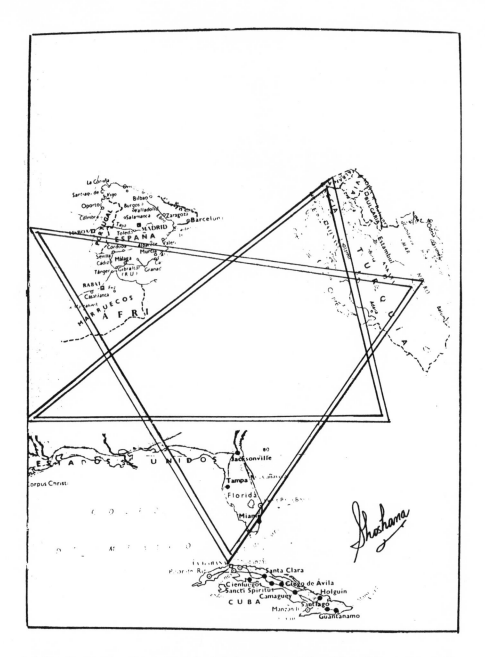

*Rabbi Meir Matzliah Melarmed's map of the Cuban Sephardic world. Source: Melarmed,* Breve Historia de los Judíos de Cuba y la Comunidad Sefaradita de Miami *[Brief History of the Jews of Cuba and the Sephardic Community of Miami] (Miami: N.p. 198[?]), cover illustration.*

# Chapter 3

## Separate Spheres: Reflections on Ethnicity and Gender

*We at our Congregation have much more than one bond. For it is not only our*
*Jewishness that binds us, but our friendship and relationship that go back over 60*
*years. My father went to Cuba in 1929 and many people in the community*
*knew him since then. I know people and have friends with whom I went to prep*
*school, high school, and college. So does my wife and the rest of [my] family. I defy*
*any other Congregation or Jewish community to be able to say the same thing.*

—*Salomon Gold, former president, Cuban-Hebrew Congregation*

For Miami's Latino—and particularly Cuban—Jewish communities, the fifty-
eighth annual meeting of the Greater Miami Jewish Federation in 1996 was
no ordinary event. Isaac Zelcer, an Ashkenazic Cuban-Jew, had broken new
ground by becoming the first Latino Jew to hold the position of incoming federation
president. This was the night for the federation to formally announce to Miami's
Jewish community this unprecedented accomplishment, and to officially welcome
Zelcer into his new position.

## Isaac Zelcer, Cuban-Jews, and the
## Greater Miami Jewish Federation

Zelcer's connection to Miami's Latino Jews gratified many people in this
community; his nomination to this position by an organization dominated by
American Jews, many thought, signaled the true integration of Latino and American
Jews. They rallied in support of the federation, as it welcomed a representative for
Latino Jews in Miami and named an "immigrant" to represent Greater Miami's
Jewish sector, traditionally headed by a member of the city's established American
Jewish community.

*Entre Nosotros*, the self-described "magazine of the Jewish communities of Latin
America," featured Zelcer on the front cover of its August-October 1996 issue.
Inside were several photographs and a brief history of the Zelcer family which
focused on Isaac's success in business and participation in South Florida's Jewish
life since he arrived there as an exile in the early 1960s.

El hecho que tengamos un presidente latino por primera vez en la historia de la Federación dice algo de la constitución de la comunidad judía de Miami. Judíos latinos forman cada vez más una parte integral e importante de nuestro ambiente e Isaac Zelcer y su familia son un ejemplo digno que refleja lo mejor de los valores que nos forman. (*Entre Nosotros* [agosto–octubre 1996]: 7)

(The fact that we have a Latino president for the first time in the history of the federation says something about the constitution of the Jewish community in Miami. Latino Jews increasingly form an integral and important part of our environment, and Isaac Zelcer and his family are a fitting example that reflects the best of the values which shape us.) (*Between Us* [Aug.–Oct. 1996]: 7)

As I conducted interviews the week before the federation's 1996 annual meeting, the subject of Zelcer's presidency was on the tips of most Cuban-Jews' tongues. Sephardim and Ashkenazim, females and males, young, middle-aged, and old (though particularly the middle-aged and older generations): all seemed to want to show their support for Miami's Cuban-Jewish community and its noble representative, Zelcer, by attending the meeting. Curiously, no one asked if I, an "outsider," would be attending the event; after all, I was an anthropology student living in Ann Arbor, a Jew on the margins of both the American and Cuban Jewish communities of Miami. Yet, when I revealed my knowledge of the event and my intention to attend, my interlocutors showed approval and appreciation. Through my attendance, I was affirming my enthusiasm for, and interest in, their cause and their community.

Eva Simazi, a past president of Torat Moshe's Women's Committee and an active member of the Cuban Sephardic community, mentioned Zelcer's nomination as she recounted the numerous contributions Cubans have made to Miami and the United States:

> *Simazi:* I think there are a lot of people in our [Cuban] community who have given not only to Miami, but to the country. You have [Jorge] Mas Canosa at the [Cuban-American National] Foundation; you have [Bernardo] Benes. Tomorrow, for example, is the installation of Isaac Zelcer.[1]
> *Bettinger-López:* Oh, are you going to that?
> *Simazi:* Of course.
> *Bettinger-López:* Great, I'll see you there.
> *Simazi:* Of course [smiling].

Simazi clearly was excited that I would be attending this event which meant so much to her as a Cuban and particularly as a Cuban-Jew. She viewed Zelcer as a representative of the Cuban community at large, as well as an excellent spokesperson for the Cuban and American Jewish communities of Miami. By participating in this event, she felt, I was expressing my support for all these communities simultaneously.

Amid this atmosphere of celebration and excitement, tension brewed. Not all Cuban-Jews felt that their community was alive with support for Zelcer and the federation. Bernardo Benes, a founder and active member of the Cuban-Hebrew Congregation, lamented what he viewed as an apathetic response to "non-community" issues on the part of Miami's Cuban-Jews: "Cuban-Jews identify with the Cuban-Jewish mentality and community, not with the larger total Jewish community. I don't mean to sound negative, but it's a ghetto mentality, [that] of Cuban-Jews. For example, next week, Isaac Zelcer will be the first Cuban-Jew being elected president of the Greater Miami Jewish Federation—the first Cuban-Jew! But we have not done much and have not merged [with the American Jewish community]." Although he celebrated the unique community which has arisen in Miami since the early 1960s, Benes regretted the "self-ghettoization" of Cuban-Jews in Miami because it had led to a disinterest in the affairs of the Greater Miami Jewish community—a disinterest expressed even when a fellow Cuban-Jew was elected president of the foremost Jewish organization in Miami. In Benes's opinion, the Cuban-Jewish community was too complacent in its inward focus and failed to acknowledge that it was part of a larger Jewish community in South Florida. As part of this larger community, he thought, Cuban-Jews must be willing to forgive the American Jewish community for its neglect of them in the 1960s. Putting the past behind, Cuban-Jews should make appropriate efforts to participate in South Florida's Jewish life as Cuban-American Jews.

Esther Ralvey, a member of Torat Moshe who had arrived in the United States in 1978, expressed similar sentiments. After she volunteered to fill a table at the federation reception welcoming Zelcer, her week had been filled with frustration. When I related Benes's sentiments to her, she replied, "I agree with Bernardo. I've been calling everyone I know to fill a table of twelve to welcome Isaac Zelcer. No Cuban-Jews are interested. These same people would've come to my birthday party! I don't [even] know Zelcer personally—I'm supporting what he represents." Ralvey, however, differed with Benes as to the reason Cuban-Jews showed so little interest in the Zelcer ceremony: "Cuban-Jewry in Miami decided to become American Jews. They've adapted to the American way and they're welcomed." According to Ralvey, Cuban-Jews had as much (or as little) reason to attend a reception celebrating Zelcer's installation as federation president as they would have had if an American Jew had been elected president. For most Cuban-Jews in Miami (as well as most of

Miami's total Jewish population of approximately 166,000 [Sheskin 1994: 4]), this thirty-dollar-a-plate event at a five-star hotel on a Tuesday night amounted to an insignificant event, a mere formality within a large bureaucratic structure. The federation was an important organ representing the Jewish community, though it had little effect on the day-to-day lives of most Jews in Miami, particularly those who did not involve themselves in synagogue events or larger Jewish community affairs. The "ghetto mentality" Benes refers to is precisely the element Ralvey found lacking among Cuban-Jews, who, in her opinion, had little to unite them, especially outside the synagogue. Cuban-Jews continued their unique traditions through synagogue participation; but in everyday life, Ralvey thought, they were fully integrated, if not assimilated, into American Jewish society.

Eva Simazi had a different take on the federation's reception. For her, it was simply an exciting event in which all Cuban-Jews had an obligation to participate. In her opinion, community enthusiasm abounded. For Simazi personally, there was no doubt about the event's significance:

> I'm always helping in Federation, and when Rachel [Lapidot, director of the Cuban-Latin Division at the federation] called me, she said, "You have to buy a table!" And I said, "For Zelcer, anything." Because he's a Cuban-Jew, because he's a hard worker, and because we have to back him up in whatever he's going to do now. . . . The temple [Torat Moshe]: we sent flyers to the whole community [about the federation's reception for Zelcer], because again, we feel that, as Cuban-Jews, we have to back him up. Sometimes support doesn't come with money, but with being there and backing him up.

When I mentioned that others I had spoken with were not as optimistic as she was about community support for Zelcer, Simazi expressed surprise: "I don't know why other people are having trouble filling tables. I've had no problems. . . . Sometimes it's approach [to getting people to attend these big events], and sometimes it's putting [in] your own money and inviting people. How many times I have bought entire tables, and then invited my friends?" Simazi thus explained Ralvey's problem filling her table in terms of approach: Ralvey had not "approached" the event properly, and it was costing her empty seats. Simazi did not elaborate on this, merely insinuating that one needs to "know people" and know how to take on the responsibility of filling tables for a large reception. That she had been in the United States seventeen years longer than Ralvey no doubt helped her, both socially and economically, to accomplish this end. Simazi saw the Zelcer reception as a major event for the entire Cuban-Jewish community, one that was receiving gracious support from both individuals and synagogues. In this particular case, she explained, she had not needed to purchase an entire table out of her own funds, because of the widespread Cuban-Jewish support for the event.

Clearly Benes, Ralvey, and Simazi all viewed the Zelcer reception as a momentous occasion. Each assessed its significance to the Cuban-Jewish community in a different way, though. Benes viewed it as a symbol of "merging" and friendship between some Cuban and American Jews, yet he stressed that the Cuban-Jewish community's apathetic response to the occasion indicated just how little this symbol resonated within this "ghettoized" community.

Ralvey, in contrast, saw the occasion as confirmation of Cuban-Jewish integration into American Jewish society—perhaps too much integration. Although most American Jews would not attend such an event (usually only attended by the most active members of Miami's Jewish community), even Cuban-Jews who had adopted American Jewish lifestyles still had an obligation to support the Zelcer reception. The community must not forget that this was a "historic occasion," Ralvey said, for "Zelcer is one of us."

For Simazi, both the reception and the relationship between today's Cuban and American Jewish communities were entirely unproblematic. For Simazi, the event symbolized unity and fraternity among all of Miami's Jews, of which Zelcer was an exemplary representative. This was evident, she thought, in the widespread support Zelcer's installation elicited from both groups.

## Uncomfortable Ethnography: Zelcer's Inauguration and the Woman on the Pedestal

I called Esther Ralvey one week before the event and asked if I could purchase a ticket and sit at her table. "Of course," she replied, "that would be wonderful." She reiterated what a difficult time she was having filling eight seats, so I was a welcome addition to her list.

"Will Albert be there?" I asked. I had interviewed the Ralvey family two weeks before and was anxious to speak with nineteen-year-old Albert again. Our initial discussion had proven extremely interesting, and I had many more questions for him about growing up in Miami as a "Jewban." Also, it would be nice to have a companion at the reception who was both my age and an "insider"; he could point things out to me which otherwise I might miss at a reception with so many interactions occurring simultaneously.

"Now that you're going, I'm sure he will," she replied. A tax-deductible check for twenty-eight dollars could be made out to the Greater Miami Jewish Federation, she told me, and I should bring this with me to the reception. It was to be Tuesday night at 7:30 P.M. The federation intentionally had avoided the weekends, she thought, because too many people socialized then and would forego the reception for a night in South Beach or Coconut Grove. According to Jewish historian Henry Green, however, the main reason the federation has avoided weekend celebrations for the past two decades has been to reach out to Orthodox and Traditional Jews, who will not participate in events falling on Shabbat, the Jewish Sabbath which begins on Friday at sundown and ends on Saturday at sundown (Green to CB-L, July 12, 1999). Ralvey's and Green's reasons both are valid in current times, which have seen significant declines in traditional Jewish observance and increased "competition" between synagogues and local night life for young and middle-aged Jews on Friday nights.

I arrived alone, fashionably a bit late, at the Omni Hotel in downtown Miami and entered the ballroom area designated for the federation's annual meeting. A self-serve buffet of hors d'oeuvres and entrees stood in the middle of the room. An attended bar was in an adjacent room. Over seven hundred people were present, dining casually—standing, eating, and *schmoozing*.[2] At this reception, I immediately noticed something different from other Jewish receptions I had attended in Miami over the years—Bar and Bat Mitzvot, synagogue events, Jewish festivals. Here the language most audible was neither English nor Hebrew, but Spanish.

Albert Ralvey met me as I walked in and immediately commented on this phenomenon: "This room is *filled* with Cuban-Jews," he said proudly. "I don't know if you'll ever see so many Cuban-Jews gathered in one place—the whole community is here!" Albert brought me to the area where his family had stationed themselves. I was fond of this family. They had been my first interviewees and had shown great enthusiasm for my research. They received me warmly; we all hugged and kissed hello. Soon, however, I began to feel uncomfortable, as Albert introduced me to his grandmother as "my friend" and the family proceeded to glance at each other with wide smiles. What I had feared after initially interviewing the family, and especially after my phone conversation with Esther, seemed to be materializing here: the Ralveys clearly sought to expand our anthropologist-interlocutor relationship to include a romantic attachment to their son.

Albert pulled out a chair for me and beckoned that I sit down. I preferred to stand, I replied, since he and his mother did not have chairs of their own. Upon the family's insistence, however, I sat down and proceeded to engage in small talk. They showed little interest in discussing their purposes in attending the reception, preferring to discuss issues such as the duration of my stay in Miami and how my research was going. Notably, an issue which did not arise was my marital engagement—

something which I had emphasized in our initial interview after Albert's father Alberto inquired about my personal life. (I had not minded this; many other families had done the same during our interviews.)

Albert and I walked to the buffet. After insisting to him that I could choose my own food—"I'm a vegetarian and a really fussy eater"—I selected some entrees. His family had eaten before I arrived, he explained. When we returned to the table, the entire family rose and, with mischievous smiles, said they would leave us alone. After they left, Albert smiled: "You think they're trying to tell us something?"

Trying to take this in good stride, I smiled back: "No, I doubt it. They know I'm engaged. Parents are so funny sometimes." I did not want this sort of relationship with my interviewees, and I certainly wanted to keep my personal life out of my fieldwork (a goal that I later learned is unrealizable).

As the night progressed, Albert made it increasingly clear that he had other goals. While waiting in line for drinks, he saw the Israeli consul, Ruhama Hermon, under whom he had interned for over a year, and beckoned her over to us. "This is Carrie," he said, and we shook hands.

> *Hermon:* [smiling widely at Albert] Oh! Very nice to meet you! Albert, where did you find her?
> *Albert:* Oh, I just found her.
> *Hermon:* Well, it's *very* nice to meet you. Have a wonderful time tonight, you two.

I wondered why Albert did not introduce me as an anthropology student from the University of Michigan who was doing research on Miami's Cuban-Jewish community. He seemed to be insinuating that I was his girlfriend and intentionally avoiding disclosing my purpose in attending the reception. What if others I had interviewed saw Albert and me together and made the same assumptions as everyone else, which Albert was affirming through his speech and actions? Furthermore, where were these others? I wanted an opportunity to chat with them as well. I had come to the reception because I thought it would be an extremely useful setting in which to explore issues of identity within the community. Albert and his family, though, seemed to view me as a potential girlfriend, and to them this role was equally important to (if not more important than) my role as a researcher of their community. For Albert, his Jewbanness, or *jubanidad*, was the key to my affections; in his eyes, the intense interest I showed in the things he said pointed to an intense interest in him personally. For a young woman interested in the Cuban-Jewish community, he must have thought, what better quality could a romantic prospect have than a Jewban identity?

The crowd began to file toward the grand ballroom, where the now-famous "tables" (famous at least for me, after I had heard them discussed so much by Eva Simazi and Esther Ralvey) stood. I wondered if Esther ever was able to fill her table, and just who the enthusiastic and supportive people at Eva's table would be. The Ralvey table indeed was filled with Esther's family and friends, all speaking a mixture of Spanish and English. When Albert and I sat down, however, they switched primarily to English so as not to alienate me, since I had forewarned them that "Hablo bastante español, pero hablen despacio, por favor" ("I speak a considerable amount of Spanish, but please speak slowly").

The room was filled with a constant bilingual drone, and people moved about to chat with those at other tables. After twenty minutes, the chairperson asked everyone to be seated so that the program could begin. His requests were fruitless—people milled about, disregarding his appeals. Finally, in an agitated voice, he resorted to threats: "Please get back to your seats now. Waiters are coming around serving coffee. You won't get any coffee if you don't sit down." After he repeated this five times, people slowly began to file back to their respective tables, rolling their eyes and commenting on this man's rigidity and lack of spirit for the occasion.

The chairperson returned to the podium and announced the official beginning of the meeting. The director of the Community Chaplaincy Service, a rabbi, began to lead the audience in performing the *Star-Spangled Banner* and *Hatikvah*, Israel's national anthem. "Watch this," Albert whispered to me, as the audience continued to *shmooz* through the *Star-Spangled Banner*. "Cuban-Jews are very Zionist-oriented. When we begin to sing *Hatikvah*, watch how many people join in."

Indeed, the announcement of Israel's national anthem brought a hush in the audience; as *Hatikvah* began, nearly the entire room ebulliently broke into song. Albert, who paid little heed to the United States anthem, sang loudly and proudly the anthem of the nation which, he felt, was "the true home of all Jews." In fact, he planned to settle in Israel after college. This was the longest period of time in the reception—until Zelcer came to the podium—that Albert and I went without speaking (in English) about issues of Zionism, the Holocaust, and Jews in America.[3] Much of the room, in fact, was filled with chatter during the entire first half of the presentation, which included greetings and opening remarks by the annual meeting's chairperson, an invocation by the president of the Rabbinical Association of Greater Miami (the organization which three decades before had exhorted Miami's Jews to assist their Cuban coreligionists), and a presentation to the outgoing president.

The crowd eagerly awaited Zelcer's turn on the podium. As the Nominating Committee's chairperson finished an extensive speech declaring how pleased the federation—and the Jewish community at large—was with the departing Board of Directors and how excited they were about installation of the new board, the room quieted. The "Program Agenda" which lay at every guest's place setting silently announced the moment it seemed everyone was waiting for: introduction of the new Board of Directors and remarks by the incoming president.

As the chairperson announced Zelcer's name, the audience broke out in thunderous applause. And when Zelcer approached the podium to speak, everyone in the room stood, continuing their applause. The Ralveys' faces expressed pride in their leader. Albert turned to me, beaming: "He is such a great man. I have so much respect for him."

Zelcer's speech lasted nearly ten minutes. It focused on his excitement about the coming year and the necessity for the Jewish community in Miami to remain strong and united. He made no specific reference to his own Cuban-Jewish heritage, nor to any ethnic group other than Jews generally. The room was silent during this time. Everyone focused on Zelcer. As he concluded, people applauded even more loudly than they had previously, and they continued to do so for an extended duration of time. Immediately after Zelcer stepped off the podium, a long line of people began to file out of the room. Suddenly, and all at once, a mass emigration occurred, leaving entire tables noticeably empty. Nearly half the room departed in less than five minutes.

"That is so rude," Esther whispered across the table. "Just because Zelcer finished speaking, that does not mean the reception is over." Alberto agreed and shook his head: "That's a bad example they [Cuban-Jews] are setting." Albert leaned toward me and gave his own interpretation: "You see, this is how the Cuban-Jewish community is. They're totally rude when it comes to this sort of thing. Once the guy they came to see finishes speaking, then they just leave. It makes us look so bad." I felt similarly and expressed my surprise over what we had just witnessed. Many of these Cuban-Jews, in my opinion, had just affirmed Bernardo Benes's accusations: they visibly demonstrated, as a group, an inward-facing mentality. Their reason for attending the meeting, they illustrated, was not to affirm their connections to Miami's larger Jewish community, but to celebrate a fellow Cuban-Jew's installation as president of this community, an event proving that "*we* Cubans" are just as good as "*they* Americans" are.

No sooner had the Ralveys confirmed for me their higher standards of etiquette than Alberto glanced at his family and announced, "*Vamos a Versailles!*" Everyone at the table nodded their heads, then glanced at me.

"Where's your family going?" I asked Albert.

"They're bored here—we're going to go to Café Versailles in Little Havana. Do you know where it is?"

"I've actually never been there."

Alberto picked up on this. "Never been there?" he asked, somewhat puzzled, though with an ever-expanding grin. "Well, you can't do research on the Cuban community until you've been to Café Versailles!"

I thought to myself:

> What should I do? I want to see the end of the reception, talk to many familiar faces around the room, say hello to my own synagogue's rabbi, and see how things wrap up with the meeting. On the other hand, this family is nice enough to invite me to social events, talk about the Cuban-Jewish community for hours, and enthusiastically support my research. And this Versailles trip could prove to be a fascinating ethnographic experience. But all in all—especially with the family's efforts to unite Albert and me—I think I'll just tough it out at the table here alone. It's getting late anyway.

"That is so nice of you to invite me. I'd love to go but—"

"No 'buts'—come on, my family wants you there. Besides, Versailles's *café cubano* is the best in the world," Albert insisted.

"See, my rabbi is here. I really want to say hello—I haven't seen him for a while. And there are so many other families here I want to say hello to. And I leave on a two day car drive to Michigan tomorrow morning."

"Come on, you can call them some other time. We won't take long at Versailles. You'll just stop by on your way home—it's on the way back to your house anyway." Alberto waited across the table patiently for his son to persuade me to follow them. Then he called to Albert—"Albert, nos vamos a ir. We'll meet you there. See you there, Carrie."

Esther, Alberto, Alberto's mother, and their friends ambled out the ballroom doors. By this time, half the room was empty. The executive vice-president of the federation was presenting an annual report. I looked toward the podium, then at Albert. "Come on," he said, "I've got to go."

I gave in. People were looking. The anthropologist was too timid to sit in isolation at the big round table, the lone representative of yet another group who had abandoned the reception after their "star" had spoken. And perhaps Versailles would be just as enriching an ethnographic experience. Hesitantly, I followed Albert out of the reception hall.

Walking across the cocktail area towards the lobby doors, Albert assured me that the *reunión* at Versailles would be brief. We walked toward a final set of doors before the parking garage. As we approached them, Albert opened the right door for me, while I instinctively opened the left one for myself.

"Jeez, you won't even let me open the doors for you!"

"[smiling] Sorry, it's not something I even think about. I'm not used to doors being opened for me. Sean [my fiancé] never has done it, and I've never wanted him to."

Albert challenged me. "You mean Sean never opens doors for you? Doesn't that bother you?"

"No, not at all." I explained to Albert that I never would have a problem with people opening doors for others as a common courtesy, but that in American society, the door-opening issue generally reinforces a traditional male-female relationship in which the man is "responsible" for the woman. To me, a seemingly well-intentioned act such as a man opening a door for a woman perpetuates gender stereotypes which portray women as powerless and dependent on their male providers and protectors. It would be a different story, I noted, if it were equally acceptable for women to open doors for men.

Albert disagreed with my objections. "Of course women have just as much capability for opening doors as men. But it's a question of respect. Women are such a beautiful thing—they're creators, and deserve to be respected by men. Opening doors for women is only giving them the respect they deserve for being creators and producers of life. You know, I think women should be put on a pedestal—just high enough so we can look up their dresses [laughs]."

"Albert, I need to thank you. That last thing you just said made my point for me better than I ever could have. You just showed how sexism and the door-opening tradition are completely tied in with each other."

He laughed and reiterated his utmost respect for women. We kept walking. I decided to take the laid-back approach—the "cultural relativist" approach. I wanted to learn more about Albert's viewpoint in order to better understand him, his family, and his culture. With this knowledge, I could reexamine the models of gender equality I supported and juxtapose these with Albert's views. As we approached my car, Albert walked toward the driver's side. I caught him before he got there: "Albert, I can open the door for myself." Smiling, he changed his path and walked toward the passenger door.

## The Miami Macho

Albert's comment had taken me by surprise. Not because I never had heard similar comments from others. On the contrary. I had grown up in Miami, a place where an emphasis on physical image and exposed flesh, as well as a prevailing *machismo* ideal, fosters an atmosphere much different from that of my small, liberal midwestern college town. In Miami, sexism, in its many shapes and forms, often is expressed on a very open and overt level. Yet my male high school friends from Miami—who tended to reside in Kendall and South Miami, come from middle- and upper-middle-class Anglo backgrounds, and attend college—were familiar with the slippery ground such comments as Albert's could land them on.[4] They challenged the image of the "Miami macho" by overtly treating female peers more or less as equals (although many continued to harbor sexist attitudes just below the surface). Without being conscious of it, I had associated the "Miami sexist *macho*" with certain age, socioeconomic, and, to a lesser extent, ethnic brackets. In my mind, such a person was older than I was, resided in "other" places with more street life than my suburban neighborhood, such as Miami Beach or Little Havana, and often spoke to his male friends in either Spanish or English with a Spanish accent as he cat-called to young women.

Albert challenged this stereotype. He was my age, spoke English without a Spanish accent, and initially appeared, in many respects, much like many of my Jewish (and Gentile) male high school friends. His very approach toward me, and his comments about women, however, moved into a territory that my male friends never would have approached seriously. As an anthropologist, theoretically assigned the job of analyzing others' life experiences and interactions, I found myself psychologically, rhetorically, and intellectually unprepared to deal with this. Albert undermined the stability and order which was "supposed" to come with doing ethnography and simultaneously challenged my narrow conception of the paradigmatic "Miami sexist" male.

I thus came to see the situation with Albert in a new light. This was not about Albert's being a "bad sexist" and I a "good feminist." No such dichotomous categories existed. Rather, this was about a conflicting set of assumptions, products of two different life experiences. While I disagreed with Albert's portrait of women, I understood that his views were a product of his religious, cultural, and social upbringing, and that these ideas allowed him to find order in the world. Furthermore, these ideas are not unique to Cubans or to Jews, but are held by most groups represented in American society. While they may be expressed in different ways—as cat-calls, respectful door openings, or even the tongue-in-cheek comments of my politically correct high school friends—they stem from a viewpoint which positions men and women in separate spheres.[5]

# Café Versailles

At Café Versailles, the Ralveys approached us as I parked my car. "Come, have some café cubano!" Café Versailles is perhaps the quintessential Cuban cafe in Miami. Located on Calle Ocho in the heart of Little Havana, it simultaneously evokes, through its design, artwork, and ambiance, the French city, the 1919 peace treaty ending World War I, and pre-revolutionary Cuba. Like many other Little

*Café Versailles, Little Havana, Miami. 1997. Photo by Caroline Bettinger-López.*

Havana restaurants, Versailles is perhaps most famous for its casual sidewalk café counter, a favorite social hangout for many Cubans in Miami.

Albert insisted on buying me coffee. We then ambled over to his parents and their friends. As we penetrated their circle, a concomitant shift occurred in both the language spoken and the topic of conversation. I was introduced to a new set of friends who had happened to be at Versailles and who had not attended the federation's reception.

"This is Carrie," the Ralveys announced, failing to mention my research or my reason for being at Versailles with their family that night. The same overly approving grin which the Israeli consulate bore swept over these unfamiliar faces. Like the consulate, they looked back and forth between Albert and myself. I felt a knot in my throat and hoped not to hear more comments about my "relationship" with Albert. Luckily, their smiles made any such overt comments unnecessary. Instead, they began a barrage of questions. Where was I from, they wanted to know. Did I attend college, and if so, where?

"Yes, I'm an anthropology student at the University of Michigan. I actually have to drive up there tomorrow morning with my fiancé and our two cats." I had dropped the bomb, and I knew the blast would reverberate throughout our bounded circle. Sure enough, the jovial atmosphere quickly sobered. The Ralveys' friends seemed perplexed by my statement. The Ralveys, I think, had told them prior to my arrival that I was a potential girlfriend for their son.

I had made my statement for the night. While I was enjoying my visit to Versailles with the Ralveys, the pressure now felt overwhelming. "Well, we leave early in the morning. I'd better be leaving. Thank you so much for inviting me here—I've had a great time tonight."

Alberto smiled at me. "Now didn't I tell you that you had to come here to Versailles?"

"Yeah, definitely. I'm glad that I decided to come."

After hugging and kissing everyone goodnight, I said good-bye and walked to my car. While driving home, I was disturbed by my pressure-filled encounter with the Ralveys that night, but I also was genuinely glad that I had followed them to Café Versailles. While I disapproved of Albert's inappropriate comments and of his family's not treating me as a professional anthropologist, I also understood the impetus behind this behavior. Placing religion above all else, the Ralveys were trying to find a "nice Jewish girl" for their son. In their culture, women were not intellectuals or public figures, but preservers of culture and tradition within the domestic sphere. Albert and I could relate to each other on many levels, including our common religious heritage and, to some extent, our common experiences growing up in South Florida. However, the striking influence in Albert's life of "macho" paradigms from much of traditional Cuban, Jewish, and Miami culture, and the striking influence in my own life of paradigms of gender equality from my own family, made it difficult for us to meet on common ground when it came to gender roles.

## "Ghettoization" or Integration?

I am interested in traveling in two different directions in my discussion of the events which transpired the night of the federation meeting. First, I want to consider the separate spheres occupied by Cuban and American Jews at the reception. Second, I want to discuss gender roles and my own position as an ethnographer that night.

The Cuban-Jewish community, through its "representatives" at the meeting, demonstrated an inward focus, much as Benes had described to me. The immediate departure of hundreds of Cuban-Jews (identified to me as such by the Ralveys) after Zelcer's speech made a powerful statement—intentional or not—that these people were there only to see Zelcer, not to demonstrate loyalty to, or support for, the federation as a whole.

When viewed from a historical perspective, this attitude is far from shocking, for it relates directly to the historical development of the Cuban-Jewish community in Miami Beach—a development which has its roots in ostracism and rejection. Miami Beach's established Sephardic and Ashkenazic communities (with the exception of certain individuals) snubbed the Jewish Cubans upon their arrival in the early 1960s. This, plus the émigrés' desire to create a social circle within which a common culture could be reestablished and pressing issues relating to *regreso* could be discussed, led to the formation of El Círculo, the Cuban-Hebrew Social Circle. As Bernardo Benes notes in chapter I, the community was "forced" to create its own institutions and turn inward. When Cuban Jews attempted to join Miami Beach's extant Jewish community, they were, in effect, slapped in the face and told to turn in the opposite direction. Havana-Gila, a progressive idea proposed by Rabbi Abramowitz, was rejected by the Miami Beach Jewish community, and so were the Cuban Jews.

As the Cuban-Jewish community gained in numbers, financial resources, and prominence within Greater Miami, the relationship between the American and Cuban Jews warmed. No longer alien refugees, these Jews, who spoke Hebrew with Spanish accents and hung Cuban flags in their synagogues, also spoke English fluently; involved themselves in neighborhood groups, inter-synagogue affairs, and local pro-Israel causes; and (as a community) made considerable economic gains in a brief period of time. The creation of the Cuban Division of the Greater Miami Jewish Federation in 1966 symbolized the beginning of this "alliance," and subsequent Cuban-Jewish involvement in local Jewish affairs, such as involvement with the federation and a long-standing commitment to the Israeli Bonds Drive, has, to some extent, brought the two communities together as *Jews*. In 1996 and 1997, the Cuban-Hebrew Congregation explicitly reinforced and promoted this union in its main lobby, where a large, free-standing poster beckoned the congregation to demonstrate its partnership with the Jewish community of Greater Miami through financial contributions to, and active participation in, the Greater Miami Jewish Federation and the United Jewish Appeal, a nationwide organization.

Félix Reyler's documentation of the history of the Cuban-Jewish community in Miami (specifically, the Cuban-Hebrew Congregation) in *Círculo Cubano-Hebreo de Miami, 1961–1981: 20 Aniversario,* the Cuban-Hebrew Congregation's twentieth-anniversary booklet, reinforces this emphasis on uniting Cuban and American Jews, rather than dwelling on the painful past. As a public document of collective memory, Reyler's *Breve Historia* and *Los Primeros Años del Círculo* omit lengthy discussion of the exile issue and the underlying cause of the "ghettoization" of the Jewish Cubans when they first arrived in Miami. Reyler's vague reference in the latter article to the "small amount of cooperation we received from our neighbors" (1981: 9; translation mine) contrasts notably with many personal testimonies I have heard which place strong emphasis on this point. Likely this discrepancy reflects the fact that, by 1981, when the Círculo published this booklet, relations between Cuban and American Jews in Miami had warmed considerably. The Cuban-Jewish community's turn toward development in Miami and involvement with the larger Jewish community, and its corresponding turn away from the exile issue, indicate that, by 1981, Cuban-Jews did not consider themselves outsiders as much as before—at least not on the public record.[6]

Ralvey's, Benes's, and Simazi's discussions earlier in this chapter, as well as in the "walk-out" at the federation meeting, however, suggest that issues of assimilation, integration, and separation of the two communities remain highly controversial within the community. Clearly the Cuban-Jews have chosen to remain *Cuban-Jews*, even after an apparent reconciliation with their coreligionists who initially rejected them. In discussing the transformation of Miami and Miami Beach, Henry Green gives a chilling example of the polarization between these communities. In 1980, Citizens for Dade United spearheaded a campaign to change Miami from a bilingual to a unilingual city and to prohibit "the expenditure of any county funds for the purpose of utilizing any language other than English or any culture other than that of the United States" (Dade County Resolution, Nov. 1980, qtd. in Portes and Stepick 1993: 161). Not surprisingly, perhaps, a poll taken during this time indicated that, "among various groups, Jews gave the unilingual resolution the strongest support" (qtd. in Green 1995: 132). Indeed, many Anglos—including Jews—were increasingly resentful of the growing Latino presence and socioeconomic power in South Florida. The "English Only" movement was championed by many throughout the city, which experienced significant "white flight" throughout the decade (see Sheskin 1994: 51–52; Portes and Stepick 1993). A Miami Beach Jewish resident led the unilingual campaign, under the motto "Bring Miami Back to the Way It Used to Be" (Bayor 1990: 110–11; qtd. in Green 1995: 132)—an ironic statement, considering Miami Beach's checkered treatment of Jews earlier in the century.[7]

As *Entre Nosotros*, edited by a Cuban-Jew, Betty Heisler, reflected in 1996, Latino Jews (predominantly represented by Torat Moshe, the Cuban-Hebrew Congregation, and Temple Menorah) increasingly form an integral part of the overall Jewish community in Miami. In 1994, a Greater Miami Jewish Federation survey indicated that approximately 9,100 "Hispanic" Jews lived in Dade County alone, numbering less than 6 percent of a total Jewish population of 166,000 (Sheskin 1994: 4, 5, 54).[8] It is telling that, in the passage quoted near the beginning of this chapter, *Entre Nosotros* speaks from the perspective of Greater Miami's Jewish community and its representative organization, the Greater Miami Jewish Federation, rather than from that of the Latino Jewish community. In fact, at times it seems odd that "the magazine of the Jewish communities of Latin America" speaks from this detached position, that it notes: "*Latino Jews* increasingly form an integral and important part of *our* environment" (Entre Nosotros 1996: 7; emphasis mine). What the magazine illustrates, in terms of our discussion, is a heightened level of perceived integration of the Latino/Cuban-Jewish community with the American Jewish community in contemporary Miami—to such an extent that the magazine can switch positions, speaking from the perspective of the Latino-Jewish community one minute and the Greater Miami Jewish community the next. Although, as I observed in my interviews, it is fairly common for Cuban-Jews to speak from these two perspectives, the federation meeting demonstrated that this does not mean there is perfect harmony between these communities on political, social, and cultural levels. Nor does it signify a complete willingness on the part of the Cuban-Jews to forget how the initial pain of exile was imposed on the Cuban Jews, time and again, by the very community they thought would embrace them.

## Perspectives on Gender Roles

The other issues which explicitly arose for me in the course of the evening had to do with sexism and *machismo*. That night I was placed in a position I had never before been challenged with. I was frustrated simultaneously by what I viewed as inappropriate, sexist behavior on Albert's part and by my position as an anthropologist who was "supposed" to have everything under control. One reaction to Albert's comments was that of "the anthropologist." How interesting, I thought, that someone with whom I expect to have so many experiences in common has a perspective on women's issues so different from my own. What caused Albert to move down such a different path? Why did he seem to essentialize women to a much greater extent than my male friends from high school? How did this relate to his *cubanidad*, his Jewishness, and his *jubanidad* (an identity rooted in exile in Miami)? How does he view *el macho*, and how does he relate it to Miami and Cuba? What is his father's role in this—after all, Alberto continually talked about what a *macho cubano* he himself was, and Albert continually talked about what an influential role model his father was.

My anthropological musing quickly was pushed aside, or at least compartmentalized, as my discomfort with the situation grew. I was disturbed and surprised by the way I was being treated by the Ralvey family, and particularly by Albert himself. Didn't he know better, I initially wondered? He was not living in a vacuum, after all. A flashback to our first interview contextualized things for me, placing the immediate situation within a larger framework:

> When I arrived, Esther, Albert, and I talked for approximately an hour and a half while Esther waited for Alberto to return home from fishing that day. We introduced ourselves and engaged in small talk in the beginning . . . Esther kept apologizing to me for her husband's lateness—she wanted to "start" the interview but didn't think we could until Alberto was physically in the house. Albert, on the other hand, seemed excited to be able to speak so freely about his new discoveries: he had someone to listen to him, who would

not interrupt and "correct" his "incorrect" statements. (I say this in the context of the conversation which ensued between the family and myself, when Albert was much more careful about what he said and how he said it. His father closely monitored Albert's statements and corrected anything he thought was incorrect.) I kept trying to turn the tape recorder on, but Esther asked me to wait until Alberto got home, since he had the "best information" on Cuban and Cuban-Jewish issues. I don't think she understood that I was just as interested in her views as her husband's.

Context: Alberto walks in the door. Esther asks where he has been. He apologizes to me for his lateness. The man whose boat he was on would not come home until now. He sits down on the couch next to Albert, displacing Esther, who now takes a pillow and sits on the floor. I am sitting on a separate chair next to Albert.

"Oh, I can get up if you want to sit here, Esther," I say, as I begin to rise from my chair.

"No, dear, that's all right."

"All right, we can start now," Alberto exclaims, as he gets comfortable on the couch. This is where the taped interview begins.

In this context, I understood much better why I had been treated in a way which I considered inappropriate. The stereotypical model of the male-dominated Cuban household snugly fit the Ralvey home. Esther's anxiety over her husband's tardiness, and Albert's relief over his absence, both point to a deference to Alberto as *the* power-figure of the family. Indeed, Alberto exercised this power in my presence on several occasions. Once seated, he would rarely get up if he needed something; instead, he would delegate tasks to his daughter, wife, and son (in that order) such as getting him cigarettes, preparing him coffee, and retrieving photo albums to show me. Throughout the interview, Alberto encouraged his son's *cubanidad*; by linking this identity with that of *machismo*, he invited his son to join him in this "very tough, very macho, very 'grrrr'" identity (as Alberto himself described it). Albert's veneration of his father (as described in chapter 5) and his subsequent interactions with me all point to an attempt to imitate his father and to embrace the masculine ideal presented to him in Miami. Ironically, this ideal, which rhetorically places women on a pedestal, in fact restricts them to the floor—with a pillow.[9]

Indeed, the relegation of power and decision making to the man, and the deference paid to him by his family, were themes which arose continually throughout my fieldwork. I particularly noticed the separate spheres occupied by men and women within the Cuban Sephardic community—in male-female interactions; in the ways in which women spoke to me about their husbands, and vice-versa; and most visibly in the Traditional and Orthodox synagogue structures, where women and men sat apart from each other. With women relegated to the rear of the sanctuary, where, as Eva Simazi told me, "you're sitting in the back of it—you're not really participating in the services," this structure places men in a realm substantially different from that of women. This male realm cannot be penetrated even visually: a translucent curtain, as well as a physical configuration which forces all congregants to face forward at all times (with men in front of women), separates the sexes.[10] The men, in effect, sit "closer" to God.

As we discussed this gendered configuration in the Traditional/Orthodox chapel, Eva elaborated on the role of the Sephardic woman in Traditional Judaism:

> *Eva:* I went to a wedding at [an Ashkenazic conservative "American" temple], and there was a woman cantor. We would flip if we saw a woman up there. I mean, we have to accept that, and we go to the temple, but for us, we feel funny, because we are not used to it.
>
> *Carrie:* Do you think that the rabbi and the cantor are men's roles?
>
> *Eva:* Yeah. That's the way we were taught. It doesn't mean it has to be

*Woman saying blessing over Sabbath candles, Miami Beach. Photo by Gary Monroe.*

*Orthodox men facing east toward Jerusalem, as prescribed by Jewish law, during morning prayer. Women must pray separately from men. Photo by Gary Monroe.*

the right way, but it's a tradition. In the Orthodox world, really the only role a woman can have in an Orthodox world is to raise the children as good Jews, to light the candles—which I think is a very important role— and to keep the family united. And to teach all the rules of Kashrut.[11]

*Carrie:* It's a more at-home role, whereas a man's role is more in the synagogue.

*Eva:* That's right.

Eva expressed relative comfort with the highly essentialized gender system of the Cuban Sephardic community—a system which, she explained, reflects both Orthodox Judaism and Cuban culture. Although over thirty years separate them, Albert, too, embraced a strikingly similar gender paradigm. Eva emphasized the importance of the Orthodox mother, seeing her as occupying perhaps the most vital position in the Jewish family and thus one vital for the survival of the Jewish people. Without the mother's moral, ethical, and religious cultivation of her children, Eva implies, the Jewish people—particularly the Orthodox—could not survive, ethnically and religiously.[12] The woman thus occupies a position of utmost importance within the Orthodox world, although simultaneously she is assigned a submissive role, in which she defers to her husband in nearly all cases. Although nominally responsible for child rearing and religious customs associated with the home, the woman is, in the final analysis, guided by her husband even within these domains. The woman's is not an authoritative role; rather, her role is to perform successfully the tasks delegated by her husband.[13]

Isaac Motola, an active member of Torat Moshe who recently has become more Orthodox, explains the contradictory place of the "woman on a pedestal" in Traditional Sephardic culture: "In Orthodox Judaism, the woman plays the most important role. But there are two views on this. Some people ask: if they are so important, why can't women read from and carry the Torah?" While seeming somewhat uncomfortable with this apparent contradiction, Isaac rationalizes it in terms of qualities inherent in men and women. Looking at it in this manner, he thinks, Orthodox/Traditional gender rules make sense, including the fact that women cannot read from or carry the Torah:

> In Orthodox congregations, men read from the Torah because women
> are more intelligent than men. Women are more down-to-earth and
> can get things done better than men. One of the basic teachings of
> the Torah is to be a family person. Who would be more likely to leave
> the family: the man or the woman? The man. So why should women
> read from the Torah?
>
> In Temple Moses, women aren't allowed to read out of the Torah,
> but they are Bat Mitzvahed.[14] It's a short Bat Mitzvah; they say the prayer,
> "Baruch, Atah, Adonai," then "Blessed be He, I now solemnly promise to
> take on the role of the woman." But remember that the Bat Mitzvah only
> came into effect fifty years ago. Older women today, like my mother's age,
> were taught to just recite that prayer when they turned twelve years old,
> and that was it. And that's actually another point where women are
> regarded as higher than men: age twelve for women to be Bat Mitzvahed,
> age thirteen for men to be Bar Mitzvahed. Because women are more
> mature than men. In the Orthodox culture, women reading from the
> Torah is basically just a waste of time.

Eva Simazi, a member of Isaac's mother's generation, also recognizes the contradictory position of women in Traditional Sephardic life but accepts it as a part of her cultural and personal traditions. She continued our conversation by commenting on the differences between Sephardic and Ashkenazic women and men:

> *Eva:* It's not that we are more motherly than the Ashkenazi women,
> but I think that usually an [Ashkenazi] woman has to be as much
> mother and as much wife. I think Sephardim are a little bit more of a
> wife than a mother. Let me tell you why. We love our children, we are
> always looking after our children. But we realize that there comes a
> point in our lives when the children leave. [Points to herself] The cook.
> And if we have not treated our husbands right, what do we have left? I
> think a Yiddish mother is more [of a mother] than a Sephardic mother.
> They're a little bit more, I believe. And we have been taught to thank

foot and hand, or hand and foot, to our husbands. Like, for example, on a dinner table, we first serve the husband, and then we serve the children. I think an Ashkenazi mother will serve the children first and the husband second. I have always been told that the perfect union is a Turkish guy with an Ashkenazi woman [smiles]. Maybe there's a difference there. Not so much nowadays because all women are liberated nowadays, but we always tend to serve our husbands a little more than we serve our children. . . .

The Sephardic man is more toward the man than the Ashkenazi man. The Sephardic man is a *macho*. You know, *un turco*. I think the worst husband is a Cuban Turkish [smiling]. Mine is very—he's a wonderful husband, because José . . . With his children, he's out of this world. Especially with Lily. But usually girls go more to the father and boys go more to the mother. But José is *macho, turco*.

*Carrie:* And does that bother you or no?

*Eva:* No, because he's a good husband, he's a good provider. We still love each other. We've been married now for thirty-two years. But he doesn't go to a grocery store—he doesn't do groceries for me. And an Ashkenazi husband will.

Eva thus reinforces the model of the "woman on the pedestal." As a Traditional ("Orthodox") Cuban Sephardic woman, she has "treated her husband right" so that she will "have something left" when the children have grown up and moved away. Her husband and family, she noted later, have utmost respect for her as a wife and mother, but this respect is subsumed within a larger approval of Eva's own respect for Sephardic tradition—her willingness to stay within the boundaries pre-established for her as a (Cuban) Sephardic woman.

In Eva's opinion, her generation has begun the process of "women's liberation," and her daughter's generation is taking this to previously inconceivable lengths. When I asked Eva if she thought the role of the Cuban-Jewish woman in the United States differed from that of the American Jewish woman, she responded:

I think that the American Jewish woman has been more involved [in the outside world]. Now is when the Cubans are trying. You know why? Because it's the second generation. Because the first generation that came were the housewives and the mothers with the old ways of thinking. Second generation now—it's a completely different story. You have more professionals in this generation than you did in the generation that came in the sixties. There were very few professionals at that time. Women—I'm talking about women. Now you see more.

Before, you had to get married, and you had to have a family, and
that's enough. Now, we all want to have careers. Everybody wants to
have a degree, at least. Before, high school was good enough. Nowadays,
my generation, at least, is more: I need a degree, I need a career—my
generation. But my mom's generation wasn't like that. So now is when
you're going to start seeing more Cuban-Jewish women involved in
[things] . . . But that's why, I believe, you have not seen so many women
involved in politics, because now is when we're starting to do these
things. The second generation. And the third is going to be terrific. My
niece: an industrial engineer.

As we discussed the role of women within the synagogue, Eva immediately focused
on the Women's Committee of Torat Moshe, of which she recently was president.

Eva: [Upstairs at Torat Moshe] we have all the plaques of all the
Board of Directors and all the women, the Sisterhood. First, we called it
"Sisterhood," but then we called it "Women's Committee." See the
difference again? Because now we're not "Sisterhood." It's a "Committee."
Carrie: Right. It's not just a bunch of women getting together to
chat. It's an important organization.
Eva: Right. I'm telling you, when I was president [of the Women's
Committee], I was always with the Israeli Consulate, with Hadassah, with
WIZO, with United Jewish Appeal, with current affairs, a lot.

Eva's emphasis on her own responsibilities outside the home separates her, she
thinks, from her mother's generation of Cuban Sephardic women, "the housewives
and the mothers with the old ways of thinking." She sees herself as a part of the
"new way of thinking" generation, which has challenged traditional paradigms of
"the Jewish woman" and "the Cuban woman" while maintaining strong ties with
Jewish and Cuban traditions. Eva's challenge to these traditions is notably restricted,
however, to the domain outside the home. Her relationship with her husband has not
changed with her "new way of thinking"; he still does not buy groceries. In fact,
when the domestic sphere of the marriage was threatened, an immediate return to
the status quo—the "old way of thinking"—was inevitable:

When I came here [to Miami], I found my calling. After a year, I said to
my husband, "I am bored to death." I went to the Fontainebleau Hilton,
looking for a part-time job. It lasted ten years. I became a director of
leisure sales. I started as a secretary; a year later, I became the director. I
loved it—I really loved it. But the thing was that I was traveling all the

time, and because of my husband's business, he was always traveling, and one time we didn't see each other for five weeks. I was coming back from Mexico at three o'clock and he was going to Mexico at three-fifteen. Not even to see each other at the [airport terminal] gate! And then he stayed two weeks there, so it was five weeks! When he came back, he said, "You have to make a choice: the hotel or me."

What is perhaps most telling in this passage is the language Eva uses to tell her story. Her final sentence reveals an assumption on the part of both her husband and (to an extent not revealed in her previous discussions) herself that two discrete and often incompatible options are available to women: home or career. In this model, a fundamental tension characterizes the notion of the woman who works both at home and "outside," in the workplace—a tension that Eva had failed to mention in her previous discussion of the three generations of Cuban Sephardic women. The fairly straightforward and unproblematic picture she draws of the "second-generation woman" who easily maintains both a career and a home, and keeps them separate, is undermined here. Eva's husband, the ultimate arbiter when it comes to making key decisions for both himself and Eva, decided that her movement between these two realms had become incompatible with their previous lifestyle and, in effect, forced her to quit her job and return to the more "appropriate" space of the home. The dilemma Eva and José faced when they were both traveling professionals had only one solution. Because José was the family breadwinner (and, more importantly, because tradition assigned him the role of family provider), Eva had to quit her job and return home, so that their relations could be normalized.

It is within the synagogue that many women in Eva's position find a comfortable middle ground. As president of the Women's Committee at Torat Moshe, Eva was able to reconcile her need/desire to accommodate her husband and her need/desire to work outside the home. Volunteer work at the synagogue often is considered an "acceptable" outside "job" for observant Jewish women such as Eva, especially since it is something that their husbands, who also are members of the synagogue, can relate to. Thus Eva's challenge to tradition is restricted to a domain outside the home *but within* the synagogue, as opposed to an outside job that not only takes her away from her husband but also is entirely unfamiliar to him.[15]

For Eva, "normalized" relations between husband and wife constitute the most important part of any relationship; they take precedence over "the new way of thinking" and hence over a woman's life outside the home, separate from her husband. And this holds just as true for the third generation as it does for the first and second. For Eva, her daughter's recent marriage to a Puerto Rican Jewish man brought up the question of the wife's role once again. Lily called her mother crying a few weeks after her marriage. Her husband had secured a job in Puerto Rico, she said; and that was the last place she wanted to live. "She calls me one day: 'Mom, what do I do? I don't want to move there!' And I say, 'Lily, you have to follow your man.' Simple."

Thus, while Eva approves of women entering the workplace, moving into the "outside" realm, and hence becoming "liberated," she emphasizes the maintenance of Traditional Sephardic familial relations. Eva positions herself as bound between two generations, so she has an obligation as a mother and as a Traditional Sephardic woman to advise deference to the leader of the family, the husband.

## Traditional "New Ways of Thinking"

Eva's discussion thus sheds light upon my experiences with Albert the night of the federation's annual meeting—my confusion, dismay, and frustration. The similarities between Albert's and Eva's statements concerning women illuminate a general framework within which gender relations are understood by much of the Cuban Sephardic community. Both point to a positioning of women in a sphere separate from that of men—a sphere in which, in their view, women are "placed on a pedestal." The role of the Traditional Sephardic woman, as discussed by Eva, is confined almost entirely to the home; above all else, she must please her husband and "treat him right." Only after she has accomplished this task may she focus on raising the children and upholding her duties as a Jewish woman: preparing Shabbat dinner, lighting candles, and keeping the family united. The "new way of thinking" Traditional woman, according to Eva, must continue to embrace this paradigm. Her presence in the workplace and her personal desires are assigned a low priority in comparison with her presence in the home and her proper treatment of her husband. Thus, members of the third generation Eva refers to, such as twenty-nine-year-old Lily and Eva's young niece, the industrial engineer, also must give their husbands utmost priority. Lily, for instance, has no choice but to "follow her man."

In this respect, Albert's comments are clarified as part of a larger framework. In this context, his mother, for example, is simultaneously relegated to the floor and placed on a pedestal. As a realtor, she has created a niche for herself in the professional world, though she works out of her own home. Even so, she "follows her man"—her husband—when decisions need to be made. Esther, in Eva's terms, seems a paragon of womanhood; she exemplifies all the standards of the perfect Traditional Sephardic wife. In this way, she gains the respect of her family and particularly her husband.

My actions the night of the federation meeting placed me in direct opposition to this model. Unintentionally, I challenged the basic structure of gender relations which Albert accepted as the norm. This is not to say that he had never encountered models which challenged the traditional patriarchal family structure. I doubt, however, that he ever had been confronted on such a personal level with these unconventional perspectives. Initially, when confronted with Albert's behavior, I thought that he was sexist and narrow-minded. When I expressed my distaste for having the lobby door opened for me, I assumed that Albert's surprise was insincere. Surely he was familiar with the argument I was making. On second thought, I believe that my responses to his actions and comments were very unfamiliar to him in the context in which I presented them. Just as I was confronted with an entirely new and unfamiliar situation that night, one in which I felt uncomfortable and degraded, Albert equally was challenged to confront his most basic assumptions about gender relations. Just as I mistakenly assumed that my feminist position was widely understood as a simple, standard argument, Albert assumed that his words and actions simply demonstrated his respect for me as a woman.

Even as a member of what Eva has called the "[new way of thinking] third generation," Albert embraces very traditional notions of gender roles. These roles he continuously sees accepted and implemented, not only within the Cuban-Jewish community, but throughout Miami as well.[16] His father's emphasis on *machismo* and his mother's partial conformation to the *María* model,[17] compounded with Albert's heightened participation in his synagogue's (and the larger Miami Jewish community's) activities and his recent move toward a more Traditional form of Judaism, reinforce a hegemonic paradigm which places men in a position of power and knowledge and assigns to women the responsibilities of caring for the home and cultivating the family. While Albert and Eva both emphasized that women's roles are of utmost importance, this importance is subsumed within an understanding that it is the man who makes the final decisions in a woman's life. Women thus become actors without agency, who deserve respect for the passive role they play and, perhaps more importantly, for not challenging the paradigm which keeps them in their place.[18]

## Alternative Paradigms: The Levys

I had spoken to Rosa Levy many times on the phone before my interview with her Sephardic family, who had arrived in Miami via the Mariel boatlift. Entering the Levy house nearly two months after my initial interviews with others in the community, I felt an immediate sense of comfort. Daughters Becky and Victoria—both close to me in age—greeted me at the door. As we sat down with Rosa and her husband Raúl, I asked the family to describe relations between Sephardim and Ashkenazim in pre-revolutionary Cuba. Rosa spoke first, immediately focusing on differences between Sephardic and Ashkenazic women:

> *Rosa:* The Sephardic families were not so ambitious, in the good
> sense. In Cuba, the Sephardics used to be less businessmen and less

businesswomen. The woman would stay at home with the rest of the women—with the grandmother, taking care of the kids—but didn't go out to work or to study. And I [was a teacher], and I know that, through the years, the women in the Ashkenazi group, they were more like the businesswomen, they worked with their husbands, they wanted their kids—their sons—to go to great universities. [To Raúl] Isn't that true?

*Raúl:* Yes.

*Rosa:* My point of view is that the Sephardic women stayed at home, took care of the kids, they didn't go out to work. And the Ashkenazic families made a lot of money because they worked hard. And mostly because they came from Poland or they came from World War II, that they suffered that much. They were so eager to leave and to work and to build a position in society and that's what the women saw—that they had potential, that they could get good money and good positions, and they could send their sons to good universities. They went to visit Europe, America. And I didn't see that in my Sephardic groups.

*Raúl:* More possibilities, because they had more money.

Rosa, unlike many others I spoke with, thus saw women as a force shaping the Jewish experience in pre-revolutionary Cuba. She viewed the woman's role as a key distinction between Sephardic and Ashkenazic cultures on the island. While most narratives of Jewish life in Cuba have focused on an institutional domain dominated by men, Rosa focused on another side of life: the home. It was from this perspective that she contrasted the business-oriented *polacas* with the domestically oriented *turcas.* Rosa thus arrived at a common historical conclusion about differences between Ashkenazim and Sephardim in Cuba (see Levine 1993) through a new perspective embracing women's history.

With her first words, Rosa set the tone of this interview. It was not, I immediately saw, going to be "run" by her husband, like all my previous interviews with husbands and wives. Raúl, who was less proficient in English than his wife and who generally kept quiet unless he was "called upon," certainly did not conform to the model of the *macho cubano.* His family made a specific point of his silence:

*Becky:* My mom [is more bilingual] than my dad.

*Rosa:* But he understands.

*Victoria:* She's more outspoken than he is. He's just quiet. That's his personality. And then because of his quietness, he's a little shy. He can communicate when he has to.

*Raúl:* When I need to.

*Victoria:* But he's more of a listener in Spanish, too, anyway, so—

*Rosa:* Yes, he doesn't speak in Spanish either. So it's not a problem of being bilingual—he [just] doesn't [like to] speak! [laughter]

The relaxed atmosphere in the Levy home contrasted with the tension I felt in most other families I interviewed. Most striking was the way the family discussed issues of gender. Rosa's discussion of gender dynamics within the context of Sephardic and Ashkenazic life in pre-revolutionary Cuba immediately was taken up by Becky, in her consideration of present-day Miami. As the conversation proceeded, Rosa, Becky, and Victoria negotiated a space in which past and present could be understood along a continuum, and in which the conditions of life for Jewish women in pre-revolutionary Cuba could be compared and contrasted with those for American Jewish women today.

*Becky:* And now, it's so different, here in the United States. I don't feel that separation [between Ashkenazim and Sephardim that my mom refers to]. I remember at Hebrew School when they were talking about Ashkenazim and Sephardim and I was like, "Huh? There's a difference?" And because I went to two temples, Moses and another [Ashkenazic] one—I went to Temple Moses for my parents, I went to the other one for me. That's where my friends were. And the way they run the services at Temple Moses—I always felt more comfortable in an Ashkenazic temple.

*Carrie:* Why do you think that is?

*Becky:* Well, first of all, because the services [at Moses] are in Spanish. And it is Orthodox and the other is Conservative. I felt so weird in the Orthodox temple, whereas I felt comfortable in the Conservative temple.

*Victoria:* We would hate going there [Temple Moses].

*Becky:* Yeah, me and my sister would really dislike going there. Because we're growing up in a generation where women are equal, where we're growing, and you really don't feel that inequality. And then you go somewhere where you do feel it, and you're like, "Oh my God."

*Rosa:* And let me tell you about my generation. I didn't have the opportunity to study in Hebrew. I went to synagogues and I participated in activities and social events. But the thing is, it was Castro in Cuba: for example, we got married in a temple, but not with a religious ceremony. But it was scary, and we were terrified, that the people [would] know that we are religious. And maybe that's why, in my case—my mother was just widowed when I was a young girl. And then she was afraid to come here to the United States, she was afraid to start working alone with children, so she stayed in Cuba with her family. But she was never involved, and I didn't know what was religion. So I grew up saying that I'm Jewish, and I

felt Jewish because I grew up Jewish and my parents were Jewish, but I
didn't know about religious things, like I didn't know how to read
[Hebrew] and I didn't understand the prayers.

*Victoria:* But back then everyone was Orthodox anyway so it didn't
matter—women weren't allowed to participate anyway.[19]

*Rosa:* Right. It was terrible.

*Becky:* I got Bat Mitzvahed at the Conservative synagogue, because at
Moses, it's only the men. At Moses, they won't let women read out of
the Torah, which I think is ridiculous, and it really bothers me. So I got
Bat Mitzvahed at the other synagogue, also because that's where I went
to Hebrew School. But I had a rabbi as my teacher for HSI [High
School in Israel], and I got to ask him a lot of questions, especially
because he was Orthodox. And we got to ask his daughter, like, "How
do you deal with this whole no dating thing?" Because it's weird—
things that are so normal to us because we were American, and
Conservative. It was my opportunity to ask a lot of questions—and he
answered them as best he could, but I still wasn't satisfied.

*Carrie:* Like why women can't read out of the Torah?

*Becky:* Yeah, he said that the Jewish religion has tools for women and
for men. And women are supposed to be more spiritual than men are,
and we're supposed to have a better connection to God, in a sense. So we
don't read the Torah, to connect with Him that way. And that was his
answer to why we can't read from it. But I thought it was that we weren't
given the honor to read from it. I saw it a totally different way. They see
women up here and men down here [positions hands accordingly] and
that's why men need the Torah, to reach the women's status. But what
about if we just *wanted* to read out of it, you know? What if some of us
[women] are not as spiritual as others? I would just bother him [the
rabbi] a lot about it.

*Carrie* [to Rosa and Raúl]: And do you feel that way about Torat
Moshe, or is it different?

*Rosa:* It's different—

*Becky:* I think it's different for them because she [Rosa] grew up that way.

*Rosa:* Exactly, so I got used to it. But I still feel uncomfortable.

The Levys thus create an alternative paradigm for the Jewish woman. For them,
the "new way of thinking" woman, to use Eva's language, cannot fall back into the
Traditional or Orthodox woman's role. This woman is confident of her equality with
men, is secure in her shift in social and religious roles, and trusts in her ability to
move deftly within traditionally male spheres. Rosa stands in the borderlands
between "the old" (carried into the present by Torat Moshe and its membership) and

"the new" (created and reinforced both through Conservative Jewish synagogues such as the one to which the Levys belong, and through the younger generation of Jewish women). While Rosa feels discomfort within gender-segregated Torat Moshe, she also feels most comfortable in a synagogue where her native language is spoken and where Cuban-Jewishness—something which, ironically, she never knew in revolutionary Cuba—is perpetuated.

For Becky, issues surrounding the Jewish woman in the workplace, on the bimah,[20] and on a date become increasingly problematical. As a Jew—though not specifically an Ashkenazic or Sephardic—who identifies strongly with her religious and cultural heritage, Becky finds Conservative Judaism to be most consonant with her values and beliefs, since it allows for the maintenance of many religious customs without posing gender as a serious limitation in the continuation of Jewish tradition. While Becky continually emphasizes the unique position she occupies as a Cuban-Jew, she also stresses how her personal sense of identity diverges from traditional Jewish and Cuban gender paradigms. She thus can be a part of the Cuban-Jewish community of Miami while rejecting traditional conceptions of "separate spheres" for men and women.

## Alternative Paradigms: Benjamín Cohen

Benjamín Cohen, an Ashkenazic Cuban-Jew who lives outside South Florida, discussed with me his discomfort with the patriarchal structure of both Cuban-Jewish culture and American society generally. Benjamín's consideration of the Cuban-Jewish woman's role—both historically within the "homeland" and today in the United States—places Albert's, Eva's, and the Levys' models within multiple contexts:

> [In Cuban-Jewish culture,] I don't like a lot of the way the male-female role is defined. It's difficult to separate what's Cuban-Jewish about the way the male-female is defined versus what's generational or what's Cuban, or, for that matter, what's Jewish. But it seemed to me that, in that realm, the Cuban aspect of things dominated, in the sense that, whereas the woman was treated with utmost respect, it was expected that she had a role to play as being at least somewhat subservient to the sort-of patriarchal approach; which was true in my family—my mother was always treated with utmost respect and love and affection and all that, but it was always expected that she had a sort of responsibility to [my father], and that my father was the breadwinner. There was never any question about that. That is a sort of value that was passed on to me as something to emulate, and from a very early age, I found it disagreeable.

Benjamín's discomfort with this patriarchal structure, along with other aspects of the Cuban-Jewish lifestyle, has lead him far from San Juan's Cuban-Jewish community, where he grew up. Now, living in a northern city in the mainland United States, he says that his children are exposed to more liberal, alternative paradigms of the woman's role in the family and in society generally. Benjamín speaks of the Cuban-Jewish communities of Miami and Puerto Rico in a manner which combines a strong sense of nostalgia with an accompanying sense of relief at being freed from, in his words, the "oppressive" aspects of the community in which he grew up.

Benjamín, who describes himself as "a little bit atypical [as a Cuban-Jew]," paints a picture of a fairly homogenous Cuban-Jewish community in which women are placed on a "pedestal." He and the Levy family embrace an alternative paradigm of womanhood, one in which the woman is not relegated to a pillow on the floor of the home or to a pedestal, but rather to the *bimah* and the university.[21] Through the way in which the Levy family managed the interview, with the youngest daughter Becky serving as leader of the conversation, and the topics the family members *chose* to talk about (Rosa immediately directed the question of Sephardic-Ashkenazic relations into a consideration of women's roles within each of these groups), they exemplified a model in which the woman held authority and agency, and in which the respect she deserved derived not from inherent female qualities or social or religious customs, but rather from the way she *chose* to live her life.

## Gender Roles among Cuban Ashkenazim and Sephardim

In her book examining American Sephardic identity, Judith Mizrahi explores the dynamics of gender roles within Sephardic culture. Mizrahi discusses the relative ease with which Sephardic men, as opposed to Sephardic women, may fit into the American mainstream culture:

> The role assigned to the man in Sephardic culture is consistent with the "good provider" male sex role expectation in contemporary American culture. However, the role of the woman in Sephardic culture, which is self-actualization through meeting the needs of husband and children, may be less consistent with the female sex role expectation in mainstream, middle-class, liberal America. Thus, if the American Sephardic female is able to and wishes to go outside the Sephardic community for affirmation or to seek wider choices, there may be additional conflict for her. She may have to resolve conflicting values and ambivalence towards some of the strong sex role expectations and value system with which she has been imbued since childhood. She could value coming from an old

community that was cultured and educated for generations, but reject the
limitations inherent in prescribed sex-role behavior. Her cultural sex-role
expectation, centered around traditional home, doesn't travel as congru-
ently into middle-class, mainstream liberal American culture as does the
Sephardic male's "good provider" sex role expectation. (1993: 59)

In highlighting the highly gendered systems inherent in traditional Sephardic
culture, Mizrahi sheds light on the framework within which Albert and Eva view
the woman's role in Sephardic Cuban culture. Mizrahi poses Sephardic culture as
more "traditional, conservative, [and] family-oriented" than "middle-class,
mainstream liberal American" and "[liberal] American Ashkenaze" culture (59).
The Sephardic woman, she argues, is bound to her traditional role even more
tightly than the Sephardic man, whose more flexible "good provider" role allows
him to enter liberal institutions in mainstream and Ashkenazic Jewish American
society. Still, even if he has more public mobility than his wife, he retains his
"prescribed sex-role behavior" in the home—her domain. Thus the traditional
Sephardic domestic unit is maintained.

Conservative and Reformed American Ashkenazim, Mizrahi thinks, feel more
comfortable with the idea that a woman might have a public life. Perhaps these
Ashkenazim have less highly gendered understandings of the terms *man* and *woman*,
or perhaps they simply have different gender-role expectations. This could be
related to the closer proximity of Sephardim to Latino culture, where a stronger
emphasis is placed on keeping the woman "on a pedestal" as both a sensual and a
maternal figure.

Indeed, I found somewhat more gender equality and less identification with
"Latino culture" among the Cuban Ashkenazim. In the Conservative Cuban-Hebrew
Congregation, for example, women and men sat together in Shabbat services, as
opposed to the division of the sexes in the Traditional Sephardic Torat Moshe. The
Ashkenazic community, however, had its own set of gender inequalities, embodied in
the "patriarchal approach" discussed by Benjamín Cohen. For instance, in its
bulletins, the Cuban-Hebrew Congregation, particularly before the 1990s, listed
married couples as "[Man's Name] y Señora," thus obliterating the woman's very
identity.[22] Also, in my interviews with Ashkenazic families, women often became
reticent and turned the discussion over to their husbands, though not in as pro-
nounced a manner as I observed in Sephardic homes.[23]

Cuban-Jewish viewpoints on women's roles are by no means fixed or uniform. As
Eva Simazi emphasizes, such perspectives naturally change over time. The "new way
of thinking" woman has emerged in the United States and continues to grow and
mature. While this transition may not always be smooth, as Judith Mizrahi discusses,

its results can be found in such families as the Levys and the Cohens. These people have embraced alternative paradigms of womanhood and have adjusted their lifestyles to fit their beliefs.

More traditional paradigms of womanhood generally dominate the Cuban-Jewish community in Miami. Both the Ashkenazic and Sephardic communities maintain highly gendered social and religious structures. Thus, while attitudes toward women's roles may be changing among some members of the younger generation and within individual households, many continue to place women on a pedestal, removed from the "real world." Indeed, it is from this separate position that women can continue to perform their traditional domestic and religious responsibilities.

# Chapter 4

## Diaspora and Homeland

*The copresence of those others is not a threat, but rather the condition of our lives.*

— *Jonathan Boyarin,* **Storm from Paradise**

*My grandparents really went root searching. They went to Turkey, Spain, and Israel. It was pretty cool, 'cause it was like: "The Cuban Journey."*

— *Becky Levy, Sephardic Cuban-Jew*

*You know the MacArthur Causeway? The one that goes from Fifth Street in South Miami Beach to Miami? It's considered the longest causeway in the world. You know why? Because it takes you, culturally, from Tel Aviv, Israel, to Havana, Cuba. I feel very good on either side. Since Miami Beach has so many Jews, and Little Havana has so many Cubans, I feel I can relate well to both sides.*

—*Marcos Kerbel, Ashkenazic Cuban-Jew*

## Jewish Diaspora and Zionism

"Jewishness," Daniel and Jonathan Boyarin contend, "disrupts the very categories of identity because it is not national, not genealogical, not religious, but all of these in dialectical tension with each other" (Boyarin and Boyarin 1993: 721). Both historical and contemporary positions of the Jew, as recognized by both Gentiles and Jews themselves, are ambiguous and vague, Boyarin and Boyarin argue, for Jews defy the categories and labels within which "cultures" usually are classified. Jewish identity both incorporates and transcends any and all of these categories, for it is the product of international, intercultural, and interreligious contact.

Indeed, the Boyarins contend that, while the Bible points to "a sense of organic, 'natural' connectedness between this People [the Jews] and this Land [Israel]—a settlement in the land," Judaism and the Jewish experience simultaneously unsettle the very concept of *autochthony* (1993: 715).[1] Diaspora, an essential element in the consciousness of most Jews, deflates the idea of a "pure" Jewish culture, problematizing it both historically and ethically. The coexistence of Jews and other people throughout the world, and the subsequent cultural forms which have developed as a result of contact and exchange between "Jews" and "Gentiles," illustrate that a people need not "have a land in order to be a people," that Jews can maintain a "Jewish" identity while adapting to any social, cultural, political, and/ or economic landscape (1993: 718). In fact, it is these very landscapes which create Jewish identity, in the form of a Diasporic identity: Jews never have lived in isolation from Gentiles and so have developed, as a group, precisely in this process of contact. Boyarin and Boyarin go so far as to claim that, rather than being the birthplace of the Jews, Israel "was born in exile"—the exile, that is, of Jews from various Diasporic locations (718).

Jewish Diasporic identity also transcends genealogical and racial distinctions, these authors argue. The highly problematical notion of an "original" group of Jews is deconstructed when we consider channels of contact and conversion between Jews and others. The universalistic tendencies of the Christian religion (seen in the discourse on Paul in the New Testament), which push all peoples of the world into joining one "family of spirit," contrast sharply with the traditional rabbinical insistence on "the centrality of peoplehood" and its concomitant celebration of tribal allegiances (Boyarin and Boyarin 1993: 708). This maintenance of "peoplehood," Boyarin and Boyarin note, does not mean a social isolationism; Gentile conversion to Judaism has occurred continuously throughout history, in all parts of the world. Thus, the notion of a "Jewish race" is undermined when we consider the results of this Diasporic contact and the intermixing of people of different cultural backgrounds within a broader framework—namely, Judaism.

Boyarin and Boyarin maintain that religious identity, as traditionally defined, also is disrupted by the Jewish Diasporic experience, for it is through this experience that many Jews have come to see their Jewish identity not so much in terms of religion as in terms of ethnicity. In fact, the very notion of the "good Jew" defies the compartmentalization of Jewish identity strictly within the realm of religion, for this Jew will partake in *mitzvot*, or good deeds, in all aspects of life. In this respect, the religious establishment is deprioritized in favor of an emphasis on the application of the 613 biblical commandments to everyday "secular" life. This penetration of religion into the secular sphere (and the subsequent reverse penetration) undermines the very categories of "the religious" and "the secular," allowing an ethnic identity to emerge. Since the welfare of Jews living in the Diaspora generally has depended upon a tolerance of others and a respect for cultural and religious difference, Boyarin and Boyarin claim, Diasporic culture(s) and Diasporic identity allow Jews to participate in "the common cultural life of their surroundings," while maintaining and continuing historical memory and Jewish identity in both its ethnic and its traditional religious forms (1993: 720–21). Thus any notion of Jewish identity as a strictly religious identity is challenged by the Jewish Diasporic experience. In this experience, paradigms of cultural and religious seclusion and purity are deconstructed, as alternative models of contact and transculturation appear more representative of the actual relations between Jews and Gentiles.

Diasporic identity thus maintains diversity throughout the world and is in keeping with the teachings of "historic rabbinic Judaism," the Boyarins argue (1993: 710). In contrast, they cast Zionism as an attempt to subvert these teachings, in its attempt to identify the Jewish people with the land of Israel and in the Zionist Israeli state's hegemonic, exclusionary policies toward non-Jews. The Jewish historical experience points to a flexible Jewish identity founded upon the absence of three things: autochthony, racial boundedness, and separation of the religious from the secular. The Zionist ideology, on the other hand, is premised upon the validity of these three concepts, since it is rooted in many of the exclusivist notions of European nationalism. Thus, they think, Zionism risks subverting, rather than promoting, Jewish culture (712).

The Boyarins, then, ground Jewish identity—for both Israeli Jews and Jews throughout the Diaspora—in the very notion of Diaspora. They dismiss the idea that Zionism serves as the locus of "Jewishness" for most Jews. This juxtaposition of Zionism and Diasporic consciousness initially may appear to work in theory (after all, they argue, the Israeli state was formed upon this juxtaposition). But it does not seem to account for the complexities of individual Jewish identities, especially Jews in the Diaspora.

How does the Boyarins' model work when we consider the case of the Cuban-Jews, a (largely) self-proclaimed Zionist group which intentionally merges "the

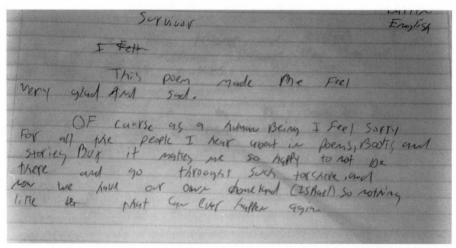

*A composition written by a young member of the Cuban-Hebrew Congregation. It illustrates the profound attachment of many Diasporic Jews to Israel as homeland. 1997. Photo by Caroline Bettinger-López.*

Cuban" with "the Jewish"? This group goes so far as to dehyphenate this hybrid, the hyphenated "Cuban-Jew" or the "Jewish-Cuban," naturalizing the *Jewban* or *Juban* within a single word, a single identity.[2] The very notions of autochthony and nationalism immediately are complicated by such a group, for, although their religion tells them to view one land as "home," they have chosen, through their collective identification as Cuban-Jews—through their named identity, in and of itself—to represent Cuba as home.[3] This is not to say that the "homelike" qualities of Cuba mirror those

*Reception area of Torat Moshe. The three homelands of the Cuban-Jews are represented through their respective flags. 1999. Photo by Caroline Bettinger-López.*

of Israel. The former often is presented as a (pre-revolutionary) "home" for *brises*, Bar Mitzvot, marriages, births, and deaths; while the latter generally is thought to function as a religious and spiritual home—a place for visits (for some, *aliyah*) and for deep spiritual awakening; a place of refuge for persecuted Diasporic Jews; and a place which serves to prevent the Holocaust (and other such atrocities against the Jewish people) from ever recurring.[4] Hayim Greenberg, director of the Culture and Education Department of the World Zionist Organization in 1951, reflects on this "double/multiple-homeness" in his discussion of the relationship between the Jewish Diaspora and Zionism: "Any country outside the dreamed land of Israel was Exile for the Jew, yet over a period of generations Jews came to regard some of the lands of their dispersion with a sort of 'at-home-ness' in an alien environment. If it is a paradox, it is not one I have invented" (1951: 11).

While the Boyarins' model depicts a "Diasporic home" *in contrast to* an "Israeli home" or "Zionist home," many, if not most, Diasporic Jews—including Cuban-Jews—fail to make this distinction, which presupposes a choice of loyalty to one ideology or the other. As Jews living in the Diaspora, these people often feel comfortable claiming, on the one hand, a national identity which reflects their place of birth and their cultural upbringing, and, on the other, a Zionist identity supporting the State of Israel morally and monetarily, even if from thousands of miles away. For many Diasporic Jews, this dual identity, far from a contradiction, is a fact of life; they cannot imagine Judaism existing within any other framework.

\*

Indeed, as I spoke with Cuban-Jews of all ages, genders, and backgrounds, I continually was reminded of this community's emphatic commitment to Israel and to Zionist causes. "We are a very Zionist-oriented community," many Cuban-Jews constantly reminded me, often adding, "much more so than the American Jewish community." Indeed, through the two Cuban synagogues in Miami Beach and the Cuban and Latin division of the Greater Miami Jewish Federation, Cuban-Jews have contributed abundantly to pro-Israel causes. Surprisingly high proportions of Cuban-Jews (compared with American Jews) have visited Israel. Unlike many other issues I explored, this connection to Israel is shared by the three (sometimes four) generations of Cuban-Jews, often appearing to function as a link between parents and children. For these people, Zionism complements, rather than conflicts with, their Cuban, American, and Cuban-American identities. Pro-Israel fundraising activities sponsored by the Cuban-Hebrew Congregation and Torat Moshe, for instance, serve to maintain the Cuban-Jewish community's connections with, and support of, Israel; simultaneously, they

*Israeli, Cuban, and American Flags inside the larger chapel of the Cuban-Hebrew Congregation. Photo by Caroline Bettinger-López.*

function as causes through which outsiders can identify the community and its allegiances. For these people, then, Zionism becomes intimately linked not only with Jewishness, but also with Cuban-Jewishness, or *jubanidad*. Although they see their devotion to Israel as a result of their duty as Jews to support the biblical homeland, this becomes inseparable from their identity as Cuban-Jews, since this devotion is demonstrated through the efforts of the *Cuban*-Sephardic (as Torat Moshe continues to be called) and *Cuban*-Hebrew congregations. Furthermore, while many aspects of *jubanidad* are rooted within a Cuba of forty years ago and thus are physically inaccessible to most of the younger generation, Zionism serves as one of the links connecting that "Juba" of old—created and recreated through memories, stories, and photographs—with the "Juba" which has grown up in Miami since the early 1960s (Behar 1995b: 165).

Celebrations of Israeli independence by
the Cuban-Hebrew Congregation.
Cuban and American flags are vital
elements of these celebrations; they allow
the younger generation to make a visual
link among Zionism, cubanidad, and
Americanness. Source: Cuban-Hebrew
Congregation, Círculo Cubano-
Hebreo de Miami, 1961–1981:
20 Aniversario (Miami: Cuban
Hebrew Congregation of Miami, 1981),
72. Translations: (top) The Círculo
participates in the parade commemorating
Israel's 25th Anniversary in 1973;
(bottom) Our children celebrate the
Anniversary of Israel's Independence.

The concept of Diaspora, in the more general sense in which the Boyarins refer
to it, enters into Cuban-Jewish identity in yet another way—as an idea with which all
Jews can connect. Cuban-Jews are not Diasporic solely in their Cuban connection;
Cuba merely served as one "stop" on their Diasporic journey. Likewise, connections
with the Mediterranean and Eastern Europe (pre-Cuba Diasporic locales) do not
form the basis of Diasporic identity, for these, too, were merely sites of (re)settle-
ment for Jews. Thus, while many Cuban-Jews in Miami see Cuba and the United
States as examples of Diasporic locales and identify with them as such, they also
identify more broadly with the notion that, as Jews, they are a Diasporic people. For
many Jews, in fact, identification with the concept of the Jewish Diaspora forms the
backdrop for identification with a particular nation or culture. Thus, many Diasporic
populations today, including the Cuban-Jews, find themselves multiply rooted: in the
culture and nationality of their (re)settlement, in the culture and nationality of their
birth, in the culture(s) and nationality(nationalities) of their parents' and grandparents'
births, in the Zionist cause, and in a notion that, as Jews, they are a Diasporic people.
The next section deals with the first two aspects.

## Cuban Diaspora and Memory: "No Es Fácil"

Diaspora does not signify only Jewish migration and dispersion throughout the world;
lower-cased, the term diaspora refers generally to the scattering of any people with common
beliefs or origins. Thus, as we consider the Cuban-Jewish community in Miami, another

diaspora comes into focus: the Cuban diaspora.[5] Commonly associated with the communities of Cuban émigrés which emerged throughout the world in the wake of the 1959 revolution, this diaspora shares many characteristics with the Jewish Diaspora—so many, in fact, that many Gentile Cuban émigrés compare themselves and their exiled compatriots to the Jewish people.[6]

In fact, diaspora, displacement, and migration were concepts familiar to many Cubans even before 1959. Lacking an indigenous population (which was decimated during the Spanish conquest of Cuba in the sixteenth century), Cuba is a land of immigrants, in the most literal sense of the term. As Ruth Behar notes, the island's prominent geographical position at the entrance to the New World allowed it to become a site where diverse people and goods crossed paths and formed new social spaces. "Like an *ajaico*, a hearty stew of heterogeneous ingredients," she writes, "Cuban culture has been concocted from diverse migrant displacements and resettlements" (1995b: 164).

Alberto Ralvey, too, emphasized pre-revolutionary Cuba's importance as a center of immigration: "Cuba, after the [Spanish-American] War, was not a country of emigrants. Nobody left Cuba—nobody wanted to leave Cuba. There were people going to Cuba all the time, and everybody was living happily in Cuba. So it was not a country of emigrants."

*Community leaders posing next to a statue of José Martí in Bayfront Park. As part of a booklet commemorating the Cuban-Hebrew Congregation's twentieth anniversary, this photo is a visual reminder of the community's attachment to its patria. 1963–64. Source: Cuban-Hebrew Congregation, Círculo Cubano-Hebreo de Miami, 1961–1981: 20 Aniversario (Miami: Cuban Hebrew Congregation of Miami, 1981), 72. Translation: Honoring the Apostle José Martí, in Bayfront Park, on January 28th. The year? Probably 1963 or 1964.*

With the large-scale migration from Cuba immediately after the revolution, however, the recipe for *ajaico* changed. No longer a stew into which diverse ingredients were added, *ajaico*, as it existed in Cuba, had essential ingredients strained out of it. While immigration to Cuba halted, emigration from the island proceeded *en masse*. Representing Cuba's elite, these émigrés fled their homeland in fear of political and economic persecution by the revolutionary regime. Establishing "exile centers" in Miami, New York, and Puerto Rico, they set the stage for succeeding generations of émigrés, most of whom would arrive in three distinct waves of subsequent migration (Camarioca, Mariel, and the *balsero* migration). Four waves of migration certainly subtracted many ingredients from the Cuban *ajaico*. The unidirectionality of the migration, which effectively prevented diasporic Cubans from returning to the island, diluted it further.[7] The result, four decades and over one million émigrés later, is a heterogeneous Cuban diaspora with a profound attachment to the *patria* (homeland) and nostalgia for an idealized, pre-revolutionary Cuba. Many diasporic Cubans harbor equally affectionate feelings for their second "diasporic" home (the third home for those who themselves were immigrants in Cuba, as many older Cuban-Jews were).

Two authors, Román de la Campa and Carmelita Tropicana, demonstrate that the distinction between the "real" Cuba and the Cuban diaspora is not clear-cut. De la Campa discusses his "nomadic tendencies," his discomfort in "both Cubas"—the territory governed by the Castro regime, and Miami's Cuban exile community (1994: 312). He seeks to forge a new, though decidedly "Cuban," space, separate from that created by the (spoken and unspoken) rules, often strictly enforced, which define relations between Cuban émigrés and the Cuban nation-state.

In a different vein, Carmelita Tropicana similarly wrestles with the pain of exile, experienced through a loss of memory of her native Cuba, which she left in the early 1960s at the age of seven. Tropicana is the alter ego of Alina Troyano, a Cuban-American lesbian playwright and performer who, focusing on *cubanidad* and the humorous aspects of exile, made her debut within feminist and queer performance spaces in New York City's East Village (Muñoz 1995: 77). Her performance piece, *Milk of Amnesia*, premiered in New York at Public School 122 in the fall of 1994 as a benefit for Las Amigas Buenas, a support group for Latina lesbians in New York City, and Lesbian Avengers, a direct action group. The autobiographical piece was based on Troyano's/Tropicana's 1993 visit to Cuba, and her purpose in writing it was "to bring to life . . . Cuban culture" for people of all backgrounds, "to offer them Cuba, *my* Cuba" (in Román 1995: 92–93; emphasis in original).

*Milk of Amnesia* begins with a voice-over of Troyano ironically recounting her loss of memory and consequent loss of identity. As a young exile in the United States, she never drank the "American" milk served in cartons at her Christian school. Then, one day, her milk carton fell, and milk spilled all over the floor. A nun came over, she remembers: "Her beady eyes screamed: You didn't drink your milk, Grade A pasteurized, homogenized, you Cuban refugee" (Tropicana 1995: 95). From that day on, Troyano learned to embrace America by drinking her milk with eyes closed, holding her breath in order to avoid tasting the flavor. This was her reality check, when she finally accepted that *el exilio* could be permanent, for this American milk finally had replaced the sweet condensed milk of Cuba. In confronting reality with closed eyes and a held breath, however, Troyano chose to exclude important sensory experiences from her adjustment to her new home. At this point, she writes, her amnesia began (Tropicana 1995: 95).[8]

The play continues as a former bus conductor, Pingalito, tries to stimulate Tropicana's memory with sensory input reminiscent of Cuba: the smoke of a cigar, a jolting motion much like the bumpy rides in her grandfather's 1950s Chevrolet in Havana, fifteen interesting facts about Cuba. Tropicana is in the hospital. Hoping to cure her amnesia, a doctor performs a battery of tests, as well as hypnosis. He asks her to count backwards, but she refuses (perhaps because she is unable to). Nothing works—not even stepping onto Cuban soil and touring Havana. Only when she returns to the house in which she was born does she regain her memory. "I remember," she exclaims, celebrating her newfound connection with her homeland. "We are all connected, not through AT&T, E-mail, Internet, or the information superhighway, but through memory, history, herstory, horsestory" (Tropicana 1995: 108).[9] Tropicana finally can drink the milk of both Cuba and America.

A reading of *Milk of Amnesia* leaves one wondering whether Tropicana's memory loss is literal, figurative, or (most likely) both. "No es fácil," several characters living in Cuba repeat throughout the piece. This phrase refers explicitly to the difficulties the Cuban people currently face during the "Special Period" (Castro's euphemism for Cuba's present economic plight). It also points to the pains and complications, for Tropicana, of remembering, rethinking, and reconnecting with Cuba and, more broadly, of understanding "who we are" (Román 1995: 92).

"Two overdetermined options or paths," José Muñoz writes, "seem available to Cuban Americans: joining the ranks of white Marxists [in the United States] who fetishize the island in an uncritical fashion as a utopian site, or following the path of reactionary right-wing Cubans" (1995: 80). These two political paths have "smothered" Tropicana's memory in exile. She rejects them, choosing to return to Cuba without a political project, seeking merely to regain her memory and thus her identity. Once she surmounts this blockage, though, she is able to (re)formulate her political position regarding the island; unsurprisingly, this position does not fall along either of the two "overdetermined paths" described above.

Tropicana's discussion of the politics of identity cuts through debates over the authenticity of the current Cuban nation-state and the resulting discourse over who can lay claim to "Cuban" identity and where this can (or should) be done. Rather than defining herself along an axis of nationality, she prefers to identify with the underdog, a position which changes as she moves across geographical boundaries and social spaces. "In New York, I am a woman of color [and] in Cuba, I was labeled white," Tropicana says (in Román 1995: 90). As a result, when "I'm in the U.S. I'm [intentionally] more Cuban and [when] I'm in Cuba I'm [intentionally] more American" (Tropicana 1995: 109). Tropicana's visit to Cuba allows her better to understand her position as a lesbian Cuban-American (or Cuban–New Yorker), to savor the taste of both "the sweet condensed milk of Cuba and the pasteurized homo milk from America" (Tropicana 1995: 110). At the end of the play, she recites a poem:

REMEMBER

QUE SOY DE ALLÁ [That I am from there]

QUE SOY DE AQUÍ [That I am from here]

UN PIE EN NEW YORK (A FOOT IN NEW YORK)

UN PIE EN LA HABANA (A FOOT IN HAVANA). (Tropicana 1995: 108–9)

Allying herself with any one political position, identifying with any one home, and drawing any singular distinction between a diasporic Cuba and a "real" one—for Tropicana, these are impossibilities. In recognizing the inevitable intersection of memory, identity, and politics, she makes a conscious attempt to subvert the essentialized products which generally arise from the two "overdetermined paths" of Cuban-American left-wing Communist sympathizers and right-wing anti-Castro conservatives. While the politics of Cuban-American memory for the first group encompass an idealized reverence for the current socialist Cuban state, the politics of Cuban-American memory for the second group center on nostalgia for an idealized pre-revolutionary Cuba as a lost homeland. For Tropicana, however, the politics of Cuban-American memory are underlaid by the impossibility of ever "returning" to the homeland—a fact that, paradoxically, she understands only through her return trip there. Rife with the contradictions of exile, Milk of Amnesia challenges the finite and bounded paradigms set up in the "two Cubas" discussed by de la Campa.

While Tropicana's political message differs widely from the prevailing (generally right-wing conservative) attitude toward Cuban affairs found in the Cuban-Jewish community in Miami, her emotional message resonates strongly within any discussion of identity for Cuban-Jews—and more generally, all Cubans—in the diaspora. For many Diasporic/diasporic Cuban-Jews, the feeling of connection with the "homeland" serves to maintain a sense of Cuban identity, whether this connection is reclaimed through a return to Cuba many years after leaving, as it is for Tropicana, or simply through nostalgia for the island or involvement in current Cuban-American affairs. The questions Tropicana raises about how any diasporic Cuban can connect with a land which is foreign and intangible, yet simultaneously familiar and proximate, are salient in any context. Tropicana highlights how Cuban-Americans of all generations, religions, races, and creeds share this predicament; it cannot be localized along any one axis.

Tropicana's discussion of her double connection with the United States (New York) and Cuba (Havana) does not reflect the sentiments of most Cuban-Jews living in the United States.[10] Tropicana is claiming Cuba not merely as a lost *patria*, but rather as a "home" in which she has one foot *now*. In fact, because her memory of the "old" Cuba has failed her, the Cuba she knows, the Cuba with which she feels intimacy, is the "Special Period," Castro-governed, *no-es-fácil* Cuba of the 1990s—in short, the Cuba that is deplored by much of the Cuban diaspora. This is one of the salient differences between Tropicana and Miami's Cuban-Jewish community (and much of the city's Cuban community). For the latter two groups, nostalgia generally is reserved for the past, for the "Cuba of yesterday." For Tropicana, in contrast, nostalgia can be found only in the liminal space between past and present, in the space of "return" (in the present) to a place called Cuba.[11]

## Geographic Place and Historical Space in Diasporic Identity

Traditionally, James Clifford writes, *diaspora* has been defined by specific features: "A history of dispersal, myths/memories of the homeland, alienation in the host (bad host?) country, desire for eventual return, ongoing support for the homeland, and a collective identity importantly defined by this relationship" (1994: 305). This definition, he continues, does not adequately account for the complexities of migration and displacement, especially those which have transpired throughout this century in the wake of decolonization, modernization, and the redefinition of geopolitical and social boundaries. A more nuanced approach to defining diaspora, he argues, includes a consideration of preexisting assumptions about what composes a "homeland" or "host country" and how identity may be linked to the forms and shapes an individual or "diasporic" community perceives these national bodies to assume.

In her article, "Encuentros y Encontronazos [Encounters and Clashes]: Homeland in the Politics and Identity of the Cuban Diaspora," María de los Angeles Torres localizes many of Clifford's ideas within Cuba and its diaspora. How can we characterize the political and ideological relationships, she asks, between Cuban émigrés who left the island at various times following the Cuban Revolution—who may have as little in common as a claim to Cuba as a homeland—and the Cuban government, which continually changes its official policies regarding these very relationships? Torres documents the (connected) evolution of United States and Cuban governmental policies toward Cuban émigrés since 1959, and the effects this evolution has had on the émigré communities. Furthermore, she shows how these communities, in turn, have influenced these two governments' reactions to each other, to Cubans living on the island, and to Cuban émigrés in the diaspora.

The effects of undulating and often unstable relations between the United States and Cuban governments since 1959, Torres argues, are visible in the changing perceptions of Cuba in the minds of diasporic Cubans. At times a yearned-for homeland and at times a foreign enemy, Cuba is shaped politically and psychologically, for many émigrés, in the complex interactions among two governments and one powerful right-wing exile community. Perhaps more important, Cuba is shaped on an individual basis, influenced by the year of an individual's emigration from Cuba, her/his age at this time, her/his family's place of resettlement, and external social and cultural factors. Torres also discusses the limitations of attempting to classify Cuban émigrés politically along the aforementioned axes. The "bridge" generation, for instance, strongly resembles the "one-and-a-half" generation in one respect: both were "born in Cuba and raised abroad" (1995: 215). Politically, however, they could not differ more; while the more radicalized "bridgers" desire a return to the homeland, the more conservative "one-and-a-halfers" have no desire to reconnect (215, 234). The subtleties involved here, Torres thinks, demonstrate that more than one "Cuban community" exists in the diaspora and that many Cuban émigrés' relationships to their "homeland" are constructed through alternative avenues—alternative, that is, to the perceived representative of the Cuban establishment in the United States: the Cuban American National Foundation.

The present period, Torres writes, has seen a shift in the way Cuban émigrés are portrayed by the Cuban government: no longer deemed "counterrevolutionaries," these émigrés now are labeled as "anti-Cuban" (233). Indeed, this seemingly subtle distinction resonates profoundly in a discussion of the relationship between the Cuban diaspora and the island nation-state, since, "today, those who continue to leave are no longer betraying the revolution, but rather the nation" (233). Through this distinction, the Cuban government emphatically denies the possibility that culture outside its geographical boundaries can be "Cuban" (233). This stance functions as a "slap in the face" for Miami's right-wing Cuban exile community, which intentionally depicts itself as "the successful Cuba"—formed through a love for, and dedication to, the nation—ninety miles away from its ideologically, politically, and economically poorer counterpart.

According to the Cuban government, this is not a counterrevolutionary Cuban community but rather something else, intentionally undefined though decidedly unrelated to the Cuban nation, state, *and* nation-state. The distinction here is essential to the Cuban government's aims: while most diasporic Cubans claim a Cuban *national* identity, positioning it in direct opposition to any identification with the revolutionary state, the Cuban government denies this identity, refusing to concede "that the nation has grown larger than the state boundaries permit" (Torres 1995: 233). Countless Cuban émigrés view the Cuban nation and the Cuban state as separate entities—the first representing a geographical place and spiritual space which serves as home, the second representing a more transitory entity, characterized by a governmental body with a specific political ideology. The Cuban government denies this distinction, conflating a government, a geographical territory, and a country's denizens (but not a country's emigrants) with a notion of *being Cuban*.[12]

The theoretical dilemmas discussed by Clifford crystallize our consideration of new models of the Cuban nation. Claiming Cuba as a homeland, for instance, is not a privilege recognized equally on both sides of the Florida Straits, but rather is highly contested and highly politicized. Further, if the seemingly straightforward question of who can claim a geographical territory as a homeland is so controversial, how should we consider issues of support for, and return to, a homeland—issues which often are subsumed within an overall identification with, or claim to, that very homeland? Torres elaborates upon the dilemmas which arise in trying to define Cuban identity—both for those on the island and those in the diaspora—based solely on a notion of allegiance to the nation-state. The very function of the nation-state as "the singular [organizer] of national identity, which demand[s] either political or cultural homogeneity," is fundamentally challenged by the competing claims of diverse political and cultural factions to a Cuban identity (Torres 1995: 233). An émigré's national identity, Torres contends, develops in multifaceted ways, many of which are completely unrelated to the geopolitical body of the nation-state. The process of mass border crossings and the concomitant transformation of both home and host countries have given rise to multiple identities and new identities, such as *jubanidad,* formed in the process of displacement and migration.

"The empowering paradox of diaspora," Clifford writes, "is that dwelling *here* assumes a solidarity and connection *there.* But *there* is not necessarily a single place or an exclusivist nation" (1994: 322; emphasis in original). Indeed, Clifford's model— or lack thereof—certainly holds in the case of the Cuban diaspora. The *there* for any individual Cuban (and especially Jewish-Cuban) émigré may represent a variety of places and spaces which have become inseparable in her/his memory, which have

contributed to an overall sense of belonging somewhere(s). Certainly this view undermines more traditional notions of Diasporic/diasporic identity existing within the
dimensions of "Here" *versus* "There," each location being isolated and singular.

## Locations, Homes, and Myths

At times of estrangement and alienation, bell hooks writes, "home is no longer
just one place. It is locations. Home is that place which enables and promotes varied
and ever-changing perspectives, a place where one discovers new ways of seeing reality, frontiers of difference. One confronts and accepts dispersal and fragmentation as
part of the constructions of a new world order that reveals more fully where we are,
who we can become" (hooks 1991: 149, cited in Massey 1992: 15).[13] Hooks's emphasis on the plural—on *locations*—and on the notion of *home* itself as both plural
and a process, fits well within a discussion of the plurality and fluidity of identity,
both individual and collective. It also resonates strongly in a discussion of diaspora,
characterized by movement, instability, and change. As discussed by Boyarin and
Boyarin (1993), Clifford (1994), de la Campa (1994), Torres (1995), and Tropicana
(1995), many of the complexities of the notion of diaspora are intertwined with
confusion over the notion of home. What is the difference, if any, between *home* and
*homeland?* What geographical territory/territories should any given diasporic people
consider as *home* and *homeland?* Who can—both theoretically and practically—lay
claim to each? When does a *home* become a *homeland?* Like Clifford, hooks avoids turning her discussion into a debate over "Here" versus "There," or "Identity A" versus
"Identity B." *Home*, she emphasizes, needs to be understood outside its traditional,
unidimensional context. Without doing so, I would add, we cannot begin to assimi-
late the aforementioned authors' reformulations of the concept of diaspora.

It is in relation to hooks's concept of *home* that I wish to consider the concept of
*myth*, as discussed by Jean Luc Nancy (1991) and Jonathan and Daniel Boyarin
(1993). In his discussion of the tense relationship between myth and community,
Nancy argues that, as "that necessary fiction that grounds the inconsistent
specialness of the existent communal group," the myth necessarily poses a direct
threat to change within, and reconfiguration of, the community; for it is rooted in
stability, tradition, and monotony. Its very point, in fact, is to commemorate a
specific event which occurred in the *past* (Nancy 1991: 57, cited in Boyarin and
Boyarin 1993: 698).[14] In one reading of Nancy, the Boyarins elaborate upon this
issue: it is incumbent upon all people—both Jews and Gentiles—"to assume the
challenge of the myth of freedom from myth, to let come a community that is free

from myth," the Boyarins argue. Diasporic Jews may have a particular contribution to make to this effort, "especially in the experience of Diaspora that has constrained Jews to create forms of community that do not rely on one of the most potent and dangerous myths—the myth of autochthony" (Boyarin and Boyarin 1993: 699).[15]

While this approach proposes Diasporic Jews as models for the "new," uncommitted community in a seemingly plausible and potentially liberating way, it does not adequately account for the experiences of the Cuban-Jews in Miami. Unlike the model community depicted by Nancy and the Boyarins, today's Cuban-Jewish community in Miami remembers and carries forward traditions and myths, though it does so within the context of building a new, Diasporic/diasporic community. As mentioned previously, the Cuban-Jewish community's identification with a specific nation necessarily invokes mythical narratives: the myth of the Caribbean (specifically Cuban) Jew, the myth of the "Cuban exile" in Miami, and many more. These myths show just as much, if not more, connection to the intimate relationship between these Jews and a nation (Cuba) as they do to the Jewish Diasporic legacy, which, according to the Boyarins, is marked by an absence of autochthony. This is not to say that Cuban-Jews refute or subvert the Jewish myth of the absence of autochthony through their identification with Cuba; for them, there is no contradiction between holding a Diasporic Jewish identity *and* a Cuban Jewish identity, or a Diasporic Jewish identity *and* a Cuban exile identity. For many Cuban-Jews, in fact, these complement each other.

In many respects, then, Cuban-Jews fail to "assume the challenge . . . to let come a community that is free from myth" (Boyarin and Boyarin 1993: 699). In my interviews, it was frequently noted that the power structure of the Cuban-Jewish community did not change much in the move from Havana to Miami. Community leaders, in fact, have worked to perpetuate community myths. Since it is so young—having solidified in Cuba only in the 1930s, 1940s, and (mostly) 1950s—the community has a limited pool of "myth-making" resources; religion, institutions, and people make up the fundamental components. With this set of tools, however, the community is able to move forward largely by remembering and recreating memories of its past. It is no coincidence, for instance, that the Cuban-Hebrew Congregation was founded to function as "El Patronato in Miami"; in one sense, the congregation writes in its *Historia de la Casa de la Comunidad Hebrea de Cuba*, "We did nothing more than follow the footsteps of those activists who, in Cuba, constructed not only various synagogues, but that which was the legitimate pride of the Jewish community in Cuba, the beloved Patronato" (Cuban-Hebrew Congregation of Miami 1981: 50; translation mine). Equally intentional was the founding of the Cuban Sephardic Hebrew Congregation, following the model of its Cuban predecessor, Chevet Ahim.[16]

The list of original general provisions and objectives of the Cuban-Hebrew Congregation (as published in *Círculo Cubano-Hebreo de Miami, 1961–1981: 20 Aniversario,* its twentieth-anniversary booklet), far from focusing on the Jewish people's rootlessness, grounds the Cuban-Jewish community in Miami in both its Cuban (historical) component and its new American home.[17] The Cuban-Jewish community, in these respects, challenges the Boyarins' portrait of a Diasporic Jewish identity freed from myths and thus from national allegiances.

Despite this reliance on myths, the Cuban-Jewish community does not fall into the dilemma of stasis to which Nancy and the Boyarins refer, largely because of the presence of Jewbans of the one-and-a-half and second generations. Raised in Miami, the members of these generations have a relationship to Cuba fundamentally different from that of their parents and grandparents, who spent significant portions of their lives on the island. Yet in helping to maintain the Cuban-Jewish community in Miami, largely through activities in the two Cuban synagogues, members of the younger generations carry the community and its tie to Cuba forward, though often with a set of aims and within a framework entirely different from those of their first-generation elders. In fact, the "Cuba" which these younger people choose to include in their Jewban community structure directly reflects the "Cuba" they have come to know through their parents and the greater Cuban-Jewish community. In many ways, then, they serve to propagate myths of "Juba" in a more concentrated form than do their parents. They lack the benefit of direct experience, so they know only the most important—"legendary"— aspects of Jewish life in Cuba, which translate into much of their understanding of what life in Cuba was like for their parents, as well as what Judaism was in Cuba.

The myth, as discussed by Nancy and the Boyarins, celebrates an event prior in time and uses this event to locate a specific group in a specific place. Thus, they argue, the myth is a component essential to any claim of autochthony made by any group. As bell hooks demonstrates, however, myths and the "homes" they create are multiple for any given group. Furthermore, they are a characteristic inherent in all groups. The specific place which a myth evokes is not *the* singular home of a particular group; instead, it is one of many locations, which can range from geographical places to social spaces, with which a group identifies. hooks refuses to compartmentalize "home" in opposition to "other places," and thus "*the* myth of a group" in opposition to "other stories." If "home is that place which enables and promotes varied and ever-changing perspectives" for estranged and alienated peoples, then it cannot be singular or bounded, as Nancy and the Boyarins suggest it is (hooks 1991: 149). We cannot consider myths to be unchanging or interpreted in a universal way. As the Cuban-Jewish community demonstrates, a group simultaneously can evoke multiple myths, claim multiple homes, *and* identify with the Diasporic/diasporic experience. Furthermore, these three components are often understood in markedly different ways by those of different ages, genders, and sub-ethnic groups, and those who arrived in Miami at different times after the 1959 revolution. No ethnic group lives entirely in the present. The very fact that it has formed as a *group* signifies at least one common link among group members—a link that necessarily connects these people in both the present and the past. As hooks points out, myths and links shared among group members (such as Jewish, Cuban, and Cuban-American connections) create many homes for each individual. These homes cannot necessarily be separated from each other; these homes allow an individual to confront from a new perspective what has been passed on as "history"; these homes function, in hooks's words, as "frontiers of difference."

## The Cuban-Jews: A Double Diaspora

The Diaspora experience, as the Boyarins highlight, is essential for understanding Jewish identity today. Cuban Jews pose an exemplary case of this; they are, in a sense, in a "double diaspora," as their two diasporic components ("Jewish" and "Cuban") are understood by many Cuban-Jews to work in conjunction with each other. In fact, many Cuban-Jews emphasize that the Cuban diasporic experience which landed them in Miami was, in a way, a continuation of their Jewish Diasporic experience. This was true in two senses. First, as Eva Simazi discusses, the Cuban diasporic experience is part of the general notion of the "Diasporic Jew." Simazi emphasizes that the Jewish people's familiarity with uprootedness and movement permeates their views of nationality and homeland and so eases the migration experience for Jews: "I would say there is a difference between the Jewish people and the rest of the world. We are more able to detach ourselves from where we are and move on. . . . I mean, we are Cubans, but we were able to detach ourselves, and now we're here. And if we have to move from the States to someplace else, we [unlike Gentile Cubans] will do it. Because, again, it's our idiosyncrasy: the Wandering Jew."[18]

In a second sense, the Cuban-Jews' *Cuban* diasporic experience functioned, for many, as the (delayed) second part of the "fairy-tale" Jewish exodus from Eastern Europe and the Mediterranean earlier in this century. As Levine and Szuchman note in their documentary film, *Hotel Cuba*, the Caribbean island originally had been seen by most Jewish immigrants as a "stepping point to the United States." While thousands of Jews indeed did use Cuba as a "hotel" in the earlier part of this century, the film writers note, many remained there and contributed to the developing Jewish community centered in Havana. For these people, Cuba no longer was a "hotel"; it had become a "home" (Levine and Szuchman 1985). When the opportunity arose for these Jews to migrate to the United States, decades after they had settled in Cuba, many nevertheless saw this as a continuation of the larger story of Jewish migration to the United States. Esther Ralvey reflects on this diasporic experience: "I feel more connected to the idea that my children are going to be American—happier with that than the idea that they'd be Cuban. Not because of Cuba, but because I've been happier here, and this is a better environment, and I see this as a—many years ago, my family wanted to come here, and my grandparents wanted to come here, and like, I achieved that. . . . in my case, I feel more closer to being in America than being in Cuba."

For Ralvey, her nuclear family's arrival in the United States represents the realization of her grandparents' dream. Cuba, she emphasizes, certainly was "home" to her; but as life became increasingly difficult for her family under the Castro regime and as emigration to the United States became a viable option, her grandparents' original desire to come to the United States and call it "home" served to support her decision to leave.

In an essay reflecting on diasporic identities, Purnima Mankekar stresses the importance of attempting "a redefinition of *homeland* that challenges prevailing uses of the term either as a place of origin or authentic selfhood or, on the other hand, as a telos or point of return" (1994: 368; emphasis in original). This redefinition, Mankekar argues, should account for the fact "that diasporic subjects might build alliances within the homeland *as well as* the diaspora" (368; emphasis mine). These alliances are perhaps *the* marked feature of the Cuban-Jewish community in Miami today. Just as the community shows a double loyalty to both its diasporic roots and to the state of Israel, it feels equally connected with its diasporic home, Miami, and its "original," spiritual home, Cuba. The parallels between the two diasporas are striking. Unlike the nationalistic rhetoric of both Israeli and Cuban nation-states, the Cuban-Jewish community does not recognize that any rift actually exists between "Diasporic Jew" and "Zionist," "Cuban" and "Cuban-American." As Arón Kelton, a former president of the Cuban-Hebrew Congregation, emphasized to me: "I love Cuba. Cuba was very good to me and my parents. I also love the U.S. . . . I'm almost half-Yankee now. And I love Israel."

# Chapter 5

## History, Memory, and Identity:
## Reflections of a Cuban-Jewish Family

*If I ever write my life story, I'm going to title it "Hebrew with a Cuban Accent."*
*Wouldn't that be a great title?*

—*Albert Ralvey, age 19*

Leaders of the Cuban-Jewish community in Miami have attempted continually to preserve Cuban-Jewish/Jewban identity through synagogue publications, bulletins, and newsletters published in four languages: Spanish, English, Hebrew, and Yiddish.[1] This identity is most effectively transmitted throughout the community, however, through inter-synagogue events, occasional calls for Cuban-Jewish unity (as when Isaac Zelcer was elected as president of the Greater Miami Jewish Federation), and, perhaps most importantly, through the social, and especially familial, domain.

A pointed example occurred in an interview with the Ralveys:

> *Albert* [age 19]: It's funny, most Jews, when I tell them I'm Cuban—even some who are from Miami, but especially those who aren't from Miami—they're shocked, they're literally shocked. Argentina they know; they know there's Jews in Argentina. And South America, they're not so shocked about the Jews. But Cuban Jews? Because when they think of Cuba, they think Castro, they think—
>
> *Alberto* [age 43]: They think rumba! They don't think Jewish people to start with. The community was not a huge community to start with. The community at its peak was thirty-five or forty thousand altogether, for the whole country, when the whole population of the whole country was six million. So forty thousand was less than one percent of the population, same as here.[2]

## Remembering Cuba

As my interlocutors continually emphasized, most first-generation Cuban-Jewish émigrés in Miami tended to retain the friendships they established in Cuba. As such, their social circles tend to consist of other Cuban-Jews, often from similar backgrounds, who become surrogate-like parents to friends' children. As their parents reminisce about Cuba in a social setting, these parents construct a dialogue—a dialogue nearly always in

Spanish—which is uniquely Cuban-Jewish and through which their children learn about Judaism, Jewishness, and Cuba. It is precisely through this dialogue that the second generation is able to construct the "Juba" described by Ruth Behar (1995b).

Institutionally and socially, this "Juba" is constructed through *reencuentros* (reunions) sponsored by the Cuban Hebrew Congregation and individual members of the Cuban-Jewish community. These include reunions of groups from grade school, Hebrew school, and Jewish organizations in Cuba, among others. In November 1986, for instance, the congregation hosted a *reencuentro* for the pre-revolutionary Havana chapter of Hashomer Hatzair (Young Guardian), a worldwide Zionist youth organization founded to support the creation of the state of Israel and the implementation of a socialist regime there (Pincho Papir to CB-L, Apr. 30, 1999). In June 1999, the congregation participated in a *reencuentro* celebrating the fiftieth anniversary of the Centro Israelita's graduating class of 1949. This event was organized by Moreno Habif, who founded the school's alumni organization in 1952. Twenty members of the 1949 graduating class, along with two of their former teachers, attended the three-day celebration. They received a blessing from Rabbi Dudai during Shabbat services, ate lunch on Lincoln Road, and danced to Klezmer music at Habif's dinner party.[3] The next day they relaxed on a chartered boat while wearing

*Commemorative flag from 1986 reencuentro sponsored by the Cuban Chapter of Hashomer Hatzir. Photo taken in 1999 by Caroline Bettinger-López..*

T-shirts designed by Habif and carrying the legend "50 Years After" (Moreno Habif to CB-L, July 28, 1999).[4]

In the familial setting, the process of constructing "Juba" often is reinforced when parents recount stories of their own parents' and grandparents' immigrations to Cuba, their settlement on the island, the growth of the family on Cuban soil, and the family's subsequent migration to the United States. The Cuban-Jewish/Jewban identity that their children learn is channeled primarily through this oral narrative.

As the second-generation Jewbans experience a vicarious anamnesis, or reminiscence, of Cuba and other pre-Cuban Diasporic locales through their parents' narratives, they incorporate these "memories" into their own identities. Their own "Cuban" and "Jewish" experience in Miami becomes difficult to separate from their understanding of what these experiences meant to their parents, growing up a generation before them on an island only ninety miles away, though worlds apart from Miami. They know and remember Cuba through their contact with Cubans in Miami, through their Cuban synagogues' emphasis on "Cuban-Jewish" identity, and, most importantly, through the stories of their parents and "surrogate" parents.[5] Cuba becomes, for many, a sort of homeland, though one which, paradoxically, is anything but home. The seemingly insurmountable distance—political, social, and temporal—between these Jewbans (as well as many second-generation Cuban-Americans) and Cuba historicizes the island for them in a way that neither their parents nor most other Americans their age can quite relate to. Their Cuban identity develops and manifests itself in Miami, in the "Cuba" which has developed there.

The Jewish component of the Jewban identity plays out much differently in the lives of many Jewbans of the one-and-a-half and second generations. As previously discussed, many Cuban émigrés compare themselves, as exiled and diasporic people, to the Jewish people, whose fundamental characteristics, many claim, are uprootedness, movement, and adaptation. While second-generation Jewbans often point to the similarities between Jewish and post-revolutionary Cuban experiences, they continually emphasize the peculiarity of the Jewish experience. Their understanding of this experience differs radically from their understanding of the Cuban experience, for, while they are actors in their Jewish experience, they have no direct participation in their "Cuban" (that is, the Cuba across the Florida Straits) experience. Their Cuban experience is, in a way, an "unlived" one: images they transform, images they take from the stories of their parents and others who once lived on the island, images from various cultural and political institutions with connections to Cuba. This is a process of imagining history through "knowing" unfamiliar and distant experiences; second-generation Jewbans (and, more generally, second-generation Cuban-Americans) incorporate these "unlived" experiences into their individual identities, making them "real" memories.

## Jewish Life for Young Jewbans

Judaism, as both a religion and an ethnicity, is widely practiced throughout South Florida (see Boyarin and Boyarin 1993). A telephone survey conducted by the Greater Miami Jewish Federation in 1994 determined that approximately 166,000 Jews live in Miami–Dade County, comprising 8 percent of the county's population. This is the sixth largest Jewish community in the United States (Sheskin 1994: 4). Throughout the county, Jewish institutions and cultural life abound, ranging in scope from religious services and youth groups to community sports, social centers, and dating services. Hence, the ways in which young Jewbans come to know Judaism fundamentally differs from the ways in which they come to know Cuba. Since first-generation Cuban-Jews have become active in organizations such as the Greater Miami Jewish Federation and with pro-Israel causes, second-generation Jewbans have frequent contact with "Jewish" issues. Furthermore, since many parents send their children to Hebrew school (either day school or after-school programs), many second-generation Jewbans are in frequent contact not only with their religion, but also with Jews of different nationalities and levels of religious observance. The experiences of their families in Cuba surely contribute to their Jewish identities, but this experience is augmented by their personal experiences as *Jew*bans, growing up in Miami.

## A "Miamero" from Cuba

For second-generation Jewbans, history, memory, and experience often are indistinguishable. Where does their "Jewish" or "Cuban"—or "Jewban"—lived experience in Miami meet their unlived, "remembered" experience? How does the meaning of "Cuba" or "Judaism" differ for Cuban-Jews of different generations? These are issues I wish to explore in further detail, through a consideration of the ways in which the Ralvey family discussed issues of Cuban-Jewish identity.[6]

Because of political restrictions on travel to the island, second-generation Jewbans can know Cuba only through their parents' stories and through their experiences in the "Cuba" on this side of the Florida Straits, in Miami.[7] On a breezy summer night in Miami Beach, nineteen-year-old Albert, whose family left Cuba when he was three years old, discussed his "Cuban" experience with his parents and me.

> *Albert:* My memories of Cuba are—
> *Esther:* —those of a three-year-old.
> *Albert:* —instances of dreams, nothing. Absolutely nothing. I don't remember. So the Cuban community that I've seen here is the people in Hialeah, people in Sagüesera, which, um—[8]

*Alberto:* —You don't relate to them.

*Albert:* I don't relate to them. But at the same time, I kind of do. I can see where they're coming from and I'm very steeped in their heritage. I can understand everything they're talking about, and I can talk to them as a Cuban. But I don't . . . understand much of that, possibly because I'm a Jew. . . . I was born in Cuba, but even though I consider myself Cuban, it's more difficult—

*Alberto:* Let me put it to you this way: he can say whatever he wants. He defined himself one day when I put a picture, a movie, about Cuba, and he started crying. . . . He can consciously say whatever he wants—subconsciously, he's as Cuban as I am.

*Albert:* I won't deny that, even consciously, I'm as Cuban as he is. But for me, the hatred I have towards the totalitarian system and my feelings toward Cuba—it's more difficult for me to separate [these two things] because I don't have the memories that he has to base it on.

Albert explains that he was brought up talking about politics "from day one"—especially Cuban politics. In 1966, Alberto was imprisoned for one year after participating with other family members in the first hijacking of a large passenger plane from Cuba, in an effort to escape the island; he spent the following year in a forced labor camp. Alberto's father spent five years in political prison for the same offense. After serving the required twelve years of military service in the Cuban army, twenty-seven-year-old Alberto went to Venezuela and subsequently, in 1979, to the United States with twenty-six-year-old Esther and three-year-old Albert. As he grew up, Albert continuously was reminded of the history of his family's exile in Miami. When I asked him whether he felt pride in his Cuban heritage, he replied: "Of being Cuban? You know what I'm proud of? I'm proud of my father—more than anything. I'm proud to be related to my father. Because his story has always followed me wherever I go. Whenever I've gone through difficult times in my life, I've thought about what he went through. And I've thought about the dignity and the pride that he's always had."

Albert experiences his Cuban identity through his parents' memories and through the Cuban history he is confronted with on a daily basis in Miami. In particular, he remembers his father's struggles against the Castro regime. The pride he takes in his father's heroic actions gives him a Cuban identity. Although, as he told me, he can "walk around [the streets of Little Havana], speak Spanish, order Cuban coffee, sit down, and talk to anyone as a Cuban," Albert's *cubanidad* is based largely on a vicarious participation in his father's *cubanidad*. Furthermore, the anti-Castro, anti-Communist ideology of most Miami Cubans supports his vision of *cubanidad* and supports his father's *contrarevolucionario* (counterrevolutionary) acts thirty years ago. His parents' stories link him to the reality of many Cubans living in Miami and thus give him a Cuban identity. Albert does not identify with Cubans remaining on the island, however; his *cubanidad* is rooted and experienced in Miami. He explains:

> A newspaper columnist who writes for the *Herald*—he was talking to young Cuban immigrants a few years after the Mariel boatlift, and he talked to me, and he said, "Are you a *Marielito?*" which means from Mariel, and I said, "No, I'm a *Miamero,*" which is like a Cubanism of being a Miamian. And that's really the way many Cubans, many young people who came here very young and people who were born here to Cuban parents—that's the way they feel about themselves. They don't consider themselves completely Cuban, per se. They don't relate to Castro, and they don't relate to the current method in which Cuba is run. But they have a sense of culture and a sense of relation—they look at the Cuban flag and consider it their own, even though that Cuban flag today represents a totalitarianist government. They see in that flag what their parents talk to them about.

"What their parents talk to them about," which makes them proud of their Cuban heritage, is not the Cuba of today; rather, it is the Cuba-of-memory, the pre-Communist state. The *idea* of Cuba—the "nation," as Torres (1995) calls it—they consider their own: the Cuba their parents glorify and the Cuba they see in Miami.

As a *Miamero,* Albert can lay claim to the Cuban flag without ever again laying foot on Cuban soil: his own *cubanidad* is neatly contained within his identity as a Miamian. What is not contained within this *cubanidad* is an empathy for, or a sense of connection with, those Cubans remaining on the island.

> *Alberto:* I separate totally Cuba and the Cuban people from the government.
>
> *Albert:* I don't, because if for thirty years, Communism is still going on, it gives me a very low opinion of the people living in Cuba today, that it's still like that. . . . The way that I feel about it is like that. I'm very mad—I have an anger toward my grandparents in Cuba. I love them, 'cause they're my grandparents. And I feel bad that I haven't had the opportunity to know them. But I'm very mad at them because they don't leave. Because, for me, I can't see the point of them staying there. But they say that they'll stay there until things get better or something, and they continue to hold onto their pseudo-socialist ideals, even going through what they're going through. And that makes me—I have a lot less faith in the Cuban people than my father does.
>
> *Alberto:* You don't know them [Cubans] as a people.
>
> *Albert:* Because I'm seeing them with more of an objective point of view, I believe.
>
> *Alberto:* Out of ignorance.

*Albert:* Maybe.

*Alberto:* You didn't grow up among them. I did.

*Albert:* I know, but I can see it with an objectivity and with some amount of knowledge, because I have been brought up around Cubans, and I have been brought up speaking about politics *since day one* [said comically yet seriously; Alberto and Carrie laugh]. So I think that maybe my opinion isn't as informed as yours, but I wouldn't say my opinion comes from ignorance.

*Alberto:* No, no, no—we're not talking about total ignorance.

*Carrie:* It's just that you haven't experienced it.

*Alberto:* Right. That's what I mean.

*Albert:* And I would say that I have a degree of objectivity that you don't have, which can be extremely helpful. [To Carrie] Even though my dad is capable of extreme objectivity, I still see it a different way from him.

*Carrie:* Sure. There's something about not being involved in the situation immediately, but having some other sort of involvement in it. That gives you a totally different perspective on it.

*Albert:* Look, what I feel is the most important thing is for Cuba to become a democracy. I want Cuba to become a democracy as much—

*Alberto:* I'm working for it! [All laugh][9]

*Albert:* —as much as my father does. I feel politically—I'm one hundred percent behind my father, but, um—

*Alberto:* He uses me on top of that. Every time he wants to know something—

*Albert:* Yeah . . . sometimes I need information about what's going on in Cuban-American affairs, and I've got this fountain here. But—what I want is democracy, but honestly, I have a much less optimistic view than my father does. And for that reason, to a certain extent, I've given up on the dreams that I was brought up with. I don't think that the death of Castro would bring about that change. And I think the only time that change would happen would be when American interests were very well served by it. And right now, what Castro's [government]—in Spanish, you say *castrismo,* which is "Castroism," which is different from Stalinism—what it has achieved is to block a population of potential immigrants from surging onto American soil. And as long as that is a possibility, America will not make a move to stop that.

*Alberto:* That's another topic. America doesn't care.

*Albert:* No, they care that it doesn't happen.

*Alberto:* They don't.

*Albert:* They don't care if Castro lives or dies?

*Alberto:* They don't care. But that's a different topic.

Albert maintains that his only connection with his grandparents in Cuba is a detached familial one—that he has no understanding of their choice to live under Castro and thus no connection with them on a physical, ideological, or intellectual level. Even so, he personalizes his grandparents' decision to remain in Cuba. Through his juxtaposition of himself and his grandparents—that is, the Cuban in exile (not by choice, but due to his parents' decision to leave) versus the Cuban in Cuba (remaining by choice)—Albert reinforces his own Cuban identity, which has been formed largely through his family's and his community's anti-Castro position and the stories he has been told of repression in Cuba under the Castro regime, particularly those stories of his father's political imprisonment in Cuba. Thus, while Albert's connection with Cuba remains geographically confined to Miami, it is reinforced and reconfigured through letters and phone conversations with his relatives who choose to remain in the "homeland." This differs significantly from most other Cuban-Jews of Albert's age, who have grown up with their grandparents and relatives living nearby in the States (especially in Miami). Most Cuban-Jews migrated to the United States with their entire families in the 1960s.

Even though Albert retains this unusual connection to Cuba, Alberto dismisses his son's disheartened views of the Cuban people living on the island today. Because Albert "does not know them," Alberto claims, he is not justified in passing the judgment that he does on the Cuban people. When Alberto disagrees with Albert's views on the position of the United States in regard to *castrismo*, however, he allows Albert an opinion on this subject because Albert does know the United States. When the situation moves closer to "home"—home in this case being the United States—Alberto loses his authority (based on direct experience) over Albert. Albert's familiarity with "America" gives him a certain legitimacy when speaking with his father about United States policies concerning Cuba; he does not have this legitimacy when speaking about relations between the Cuban people and the Cuban government. In Alberto's eyes, they are both on equal footing when they discuss the United States, which is familiar to both of them from direct experience.

After considering these points of divergence, it is interesting to consider Albert and Alberto's discussion of their similar political position on Cuba. As a founder of the political advocacy group, Concilio Cubano (Cuban Council), Alberto represents, for his son, a specific political position on Cuban affairs which Albert also has embraced. Alberto registers wholehearted support for his son's views on the present Cuban State only when Albert's views are identical to his own. In fact, as we see in their conversation, Albert allies himself politically with his father and uses his father's anti-Castro position as an authoritative scale on which to measure his own opposition to the Castro regime.

Throughout this conversation, we see a tension between Albert's and Alberto's views on contemporary Cuba, the Cuban people, and Cuban identity. Alberto's expectation that his son be as "*cubano*" as he is reveals itself frequently in this interview. Alberto measures his son's *cubanidad* against his own; Albert's emotional reaction to the movie about Cuba is evidence, in Alberto's eyes, of Albert's "subconscious" *cubanidad*, equal to that of his father. Albert, however, has a different perception of what it means to be a "Cuban." Because the "real" Cuba is intangible for Albert, he lays claim only to the Cuba he knows: the Cuba of memories and dreams, and the Cuba which has "transplanted" itself to the heart of Miami. His pride in his father's courage allows him to take pride in his own Cuban heritage, since he associates his father's political acts with "true" *cubanidad*—not the compromised, "pseudo-socialist" *cubanidad* of people living in Cuba today.

These very models of the "true Cuban" versus the "traitorous Cuban," or the "Cuban in exile" versus the "Cuban in Cuba," have their roots in Miami. They are myths, in the Boyarins' sense of the term, which were created in the wake of political exile in the 1960s and which resonate as profoundly within Miami today as they did forty years ago. These myths serve to differentiate "types" of Cubans; in doing so, they mythologize "real Cubans" (those who live outside of the current nation-state) as patriotic heroes and displaced victims of "the Communist oppressor" ninety miles away.[10]

Through his connection to his "pseudo-socialist" Cuban grandparents, Albert experiences these myths directly. For him, the people on the other end of the phone line legitimize his disapproval of those who have chosen to stay in Cuba. Indeed, Albert thinks, there are two types of Cubans: those on the island and those in the diaspora. By having this direct connection, Albert experiences the distance between these two types of Cubans and places himself in opposition to the first. Like his father, he becomes an anti-Castro *verdadero cubano* (true Cuban) through this process of identity politics.

## Roots in the "Fatherland"

As we sat in the Ralveys' living room, Esther described her feelings about "being American" versus "being Cuban," and how these contrasted with her husband's views:[11]

> *Albert:* My dad, when he was in Cuba, he suffered politically.
> *Esther:* In spite of that—in spite of being persecuted—
> *Alberto:* Oh yeah—
> *Esther:*—and pushed around in Cuba—'cause that's the interesting
> thing: I have better memories from Cuba than you [to Alberto].
> *Alberto:* Oh yeah [chuckles]—
> *Esther:* [In Cuba] I had an adolescence and some life and some memories.
> You were in prison and the army, and you know [now speaking to Carrie], he

169

had a very bad experience. And I feel more connected to the idea that my children are going to be American—happier with that than the idea that they'd be Cuban. [Alberto and Albert talking in background] Not because of Cuba, but because I've been happier here, and this is a better environment, and I see this as a—many years ago my family wanted to come here, and my grandparents wanted to come here, and like, I achieved that. Now my son wants to leave [to Israel] [smiles], but anyway—in my case, I feel closer to being in America than being in Cuba. Even though I love being Cuban and I'm very proud of it and I always acknowledge that, but he's [Alberto] more attached to Cuba.

*Alberto:* Yeah, I'm involved in political things. [To Carrie] I don't know if you've heard about Concilio Cubano?

Alberto proceeded to tell me about Concilio Cubano, an umbrella organization currently composed of "130 organizations of dissidents and human rights fighters and professional associations" in both Cuba and its diaspora. According to its Official Statement, the Concilio Cubano was formed under the premise that "only urgent and profound [but peaceful] changes will prepare them [the Cuban people] to confront, in a mature fashion, the rights and challenges demanded by civilized society . . . [and that only these changes will] open a new historical chapter with freedom, national independence, democracy, solidarity, and social justice" (Cuban Council 1995). This politically moderate human rights group, of which Alberto is a founder, advocates dialogue and compromise between Cuban exiles and dissidents within Cuba, on the one hand, and the Castro regime, on the other. Concilio Cubano functions "as a permanent forum where all participating organizations can fashion joint political proposals while still maintaining their own identity" (Cuban Council 1995). The Concilio rests upon four propositions, as quoted from the Official Statement:

> FIRST: The determination to work for a totally peaceful transition toward a democratic society under the rule of law, devoid of any vindictiveness, and equally comprising all Cubans.
>
> SECOND: Obtaining unconditional amnesty for all political prisoners.
>
> THIRD: Launching a series of legal transformations that will provide the necessary framework, within the law, to secure absolute respect for all universally recognized human rights, as well as equal participation by all Cubans in an opening process that will lead to economic independence.
>
> FOURTH: The belief that, in order to harmonize the peaceful transition we are advocating with the principle that Cuba is the fatherland and the home of each and every Cuban, it is essential to provide such conditions as will guarantee participation for all Cubans, with no exclusions whatsoever.

The fourth point is particularly compelling in a discussion of the relationship of Cubans in the diaspora to their "home." Because Cuba is the "fatherland" and "home" "of each and every Cuban," the Concilio claims, Cubans of all backgrounds, creeds, allegiances, and nationalities need to unite in the name of democracy and freedom. All Cubans have a mutual responsibility to contribute to this effort, it proposes, for all are linked in an unmistakable and undeniable way. In establishing a "brotherhood" network which spans the globe, the Concilio prioritizes Cuban national heritage over all other factors.

Alberto's narrative reveals his sincere commitment to this fourth proposition; he earnestly believes in a fundamental, though perhaps intangible, connection among *all* Cubans. For Alberto, this connection applies to all people born and raised in Cuba, and to second-generation diasporic Cubans who, in most cases, never had physical contact with the island. "Subconsciously," he feels, Albert is "as Cuban as I am." Throughout the interview, Alberto did not acknowledge diversities of Cuban communities, claiming that all Cubans in Miami belonged to "Miami's Cuban community." For Alberto, this community is wholly distinct from other Latino communities in the United States, precisely because, in his opinion, no divisions exist among Cubans of different generations. All Cubans collectively identify as *cubanos* and understand *cubanidad:*

> Cubans can understand that a tree can only grow flowers and branches if it has roots. If we don't know and respect our roots, we have no identity—we are no one. . . . And that's what leads to the breakdown of the family and the community. Cubans are so strong because we know our roots. Mexicans in East Los Angeles don't, and they're poor and live broken lives. They have no common identity—nothing to bind them together. . . . Chicanos, for example, hate to be Mexicans, even though they bring the flag, and they eat the food, and they sing the song. But they are never accepted as Americans, and they have nothing to do with Mexico. So they live in a limbo, without roots. So the Cubans are so proud that they integrate with the Americans with no problems, but they keep their Cubanity and they keep being proud of their roots, so they don't feel like other Hispanics feel.

This passage demonstrates the importance of identity in Alberto's worldview. Cuban collective identity, or "unity," is so powerful that he cites it as the foremost reason for the "Cuban success story" in Miami. It overrides other factors that typically are used to explain the plight of various ethnic groups, such as the legacy of racism in the United States.[12]

More interesting still is Alberto's comparison of Cubans who "are so strong" with "poor" and "broken" Mexican Americans living in East Los Angeles. Not only does this comparison invoke one of the most disadvantaged communities in America to symbolize Chicano culture; it also leaves out the large population of Miami Cubans and the Cubans living in Cuba who also lead "poor and broken lives." Alberto's perspective, then, shows how a prevalent Miami myth called the "Cuban success story" shapes his understanding of Cuban roots and Cuban identity and allows him to position his *cubanidad* apart from the identities of "other Hispanics."

Alberto argues that the second generation shares his *cubanidad*, but he denies them the "authority" to speak on Cuban affairs. For Alberto, such authority derives from several factors, including physical connection with the island at some point in one's life and participation in political affairs. No matter how informed Albert becomes concerning Cuban affairs through his father and the media, he always will be "ignorant" of the island. "You don't know them [Cubans] as people," Alberto told his son, "you didn't grow up among them." In María de los Angeles Torres's terms, Alberto allows second-generation Cubans to claim Cuba as a nation while denying them an understanding of the political, economic, and social complexities surrounding the current nation-state.

## Periphery versus Center: Jewbans in Miami's Cuban and Jewish Communities

While Alberto emphasizes that his children are "Cuban" in much the same way that the rest of Cuban Miami is "Cuban," Albert consistently counters this assertion, opting to locate himself on the periphery of Miami's Cuban community. While he feels a strong connection to this community, to his Cuban roots, and to movements calling for political change in Communist Cuba, Albert also feels that he has one foot outside the Cuban community. His experience growing up in Miami Beach, among American Jews and Anglo Gentiles, he feels, has connected him with something different, not completely "Cuban." That something is Judaism. Albert views Judaism as different in nature from *cubanidad*. As a Jew who has spent many months in Israel, he stresses, he now can relate to all other Jews throughout the world, of all levels of faith and cultural backgrounds. He cannot relate to all the people who claim Cuban heritage in the same way:

> If I'm in the streets of Little Havana, I can walk around, speak Spanish, order Cuban coffee, sit down, talk to anyone as a Cuban, and a lot of things will be taken for granted. They'll see me just as a Cuban. If I walk into a synagogue, immediately a lot of questions arise among people:

where are you from, where's your family from, you know, things of that
nature, that—it's harder to relate in an environment like that, where a lot
of times, you're being questioned.

But at the same time, I can relate better in general to Jews than I can to
Cubans. Before [I went to Israel], no, because before I didn't see the similarities between Jews. I saw a lot of different sections, and they were all different:
the Cuban Jews, the American Jews, the Sephardic, the Ashkenazic, the Orthodox, the Conservative, the Reformed. Everything seemed to be linked by a
thread that I could not see. Now since I've been to Israel and since I've been
working in Jewish-related things, I can see the similarities better.[13] But for a
child, it's very hard to see those similarities. With Cubans, it isn't.

The very "things" Albert once took for granted as shared among all Cubans
have come full circle; now he sees these as "things" creating an all-too-facile connection between people who share only a nationality. This issue is increasingly problematical for Albert personally, particularly because he sees Cuban nationality as something which his generation has "inherited"—unlike religion, which is chosen. The
meaningful ethnic and religious connections which Albert values most do not exist
among all Cubans, but they do among all Jews. The beauty of these connections, for
Albert, is that they are challenging to perceive; one must, he emphasizes, deeply consider the meaning of Judaism—and go to Israel—to see the spaces where all Jews
come together as one people.

For Albert, in fact, Jewish identity becomes conflated with Israeli identity, something which all Jews can realize, though only upon physical contact with the Jewish
homeland: "There's a time in your life when all of a sudden it hits you: you're Israeli.
Living in the States now, I don't feel Israeli; but I did in Israel. You know when it hit
me? When a Brazilian woman asked me for directions in Hebrew and I answered her
in Hebrew. . . . But that's one of my goals in life, and it's not just idealistic. I want to
live in Israel and feel Israeli again."[14]

"Being Israeli"—especially for non-native Israeli Jews who have made *aliyah*—
does not mean, however, that they must renounce all aspects of their prior culture
and traditions, as Boyarin and Boyarin (1993) suggest. Rather, Albert emphasizes, it
requires embracing Israeli culture, a requirement of the national policy in the Law of
Return, which allows any Jew unquestionably to enter Israel as an émigré and receive
full citizenship rights immediately upon arrival. Through this process, migrants are
restricted in the degree to which they can retain their previous culture. Albert emphasizes that, nevertheless, a process of cultural exchange naturally occurs in any migration situation: "People who come to Israel—even today—they have their own customs and traditions and everything. But bottom line: you go to Israel, you become an

Israeli. You're given full rights of citizenship upon arrival, and the price of that is that, to some degree, you'll lose your native culture. But to another degree, you're adding your culture to the Israeli culture." This process has great significance for Albert personally; after completing of college, he plans to move to Israel, join the army, and "become Israeli" again—this time, as a permanent citizen.

Albert recognizes that Israeli citizenship cannot erase his own identity as a Cuban-Jew. His connection to Israel, however distant it may appear from his connection to Miami Beach, has an intimate link with both Cuba and "Juba"— the places he knows through his parents' stories, and the places he knows from his own experience as a Cuban-Jew growing up on the periphery of the "other Cuba," Miami. The intersection of Cuba, Miami, Miami Beach, and Israel—all within a Jewish framework—is a profound reality for Albert, much more so than for any other Cuban-Jew I spoke with. While other Cuban-Jews emphasized the "Jewish" connection between South Florida and Cuba, Albert stressed the necessity, at least for him personally, of including Israel in this connection (he does not say that this connection is, or should be, shared equally by the Cuban-Jewish community). In linking the biblical homeland with the various Diasporic/diasporic locations he calls "home," Albert undermines the Boyarins' proposal that Jewish identity must exist in the absence of any such identification with specific locales. Home, for Albert, is locations, as bell hooks (1991) describes; it cannot be localized or compartmentalized.

Albert's discussion below of the intersection of his Cuban and Jewish identities, however, supports the Boyarins' argument for a diminished religious component in the concept of "Jewishness" (Boyarin and Boyarin 1993). While, *as a Jew*, he intends to become a full-fledged Israeli citizen, Albert emphasizes that this does not necessarily entail wholeheartedly embracing his religion or rejecting his *cubanidad*:

> *Carrie:* When we last talked, you said that you weren't as interested in becoming super-religious—that you were more interested in becoming Israeli. Do you think that way still?
>
> *Albert:* I was raised Cuban. I can't really escape basically twenty years of stimulus-response. So, in a lot of things, like in leisure activity and in diet, I'm a Cuban. And those are two things that are an integral part of the Jewish religion. If you want to become religious, you have to follow certain patterns for leisure activity and diet. So, in a sense, that kind of infringes on my identity. So, in a sense, I want to redefine my identity, and I'm in the process of redefining my identity, to incorporate something else into my identity. But I'm not going to change. I'll always be the

person that I was raised to be. And maybe someday, I'll end up having become kosher—after years of having lived in Israel, and it was an easy thing to do, and there weren't good Cuban sandwiches around. Just incidentally, I might become religious. But I'm not pursuing it actively.

Albert's discomfort and inconclusiveness concerning the issue of where he can best situate himself as a Cuban-Jew intending to move to Israel become salient here. Before his trip to Israel, his identity as a Cuban-Jew was unproblematic; neither component infringed upon the other. In fact, they fused to form an indistinguishable whole. The question of what it means to be Israeli—often embodied in the idea of the *Sabra*—has complicated this for Albert, challenging the comfort he once felt in linking Judaism with a "non-Jewish" nation.[15] Furthermore, while Albert dreams of "being" Israeli and "being" a Sabra, this is, by definition, impossible, since he is a native-born Cuban.

Where does "religious" Judaism intersect with "secular" Judaism, and how does each of these relate to Zionism and Israeli citizenship and identity?[16] While Albert is in the "process of redefining [his] identity, to incorporate something else into [his] identity," he vacillates between conceiving of this "something else" in religious or in secular terms. The issue remains unresolved for him; while he recognizes that his *cubanidad* does not "fit" properly with strict religious practice, he deems it, if not frankly impossible, at least unlikely that he will relinquish this identity and its essential practices. Although he plans to move to Israel as a Zionist (an ideology which is not necessarily connected with the Jewish religion), he cannot help associating Orthodox Judaism with the Israeli state.

While Albert makes this association between religious observance and nationality, he is ambivalent about the consequences of this relationship for Israeli society. Opting to locate himself as a "pro-Israel" *Sabra*, he celebrates the military lore surrounding being Israeli and frowns upon those who reject what he views as a legal and moral obligation to protect the Jewish homeland:

> See, if you want to be a citizen, if you want to be a part of society—
> the first thing that everyone in Israel asks you is, "What'd you do in the
> army?" It's universal. . . . I mean, there's some who don't [enter the Is-
> raeli army]—there's basically two different kinds of people who don't:
> there's the men—the yeshiva people who study Torah all day. What they
> do is, they say, "We're learning, so we can't go to the army now." And
> they keep putting it off until they're too old to go into the army. And a
> lot of them are not pro-Israel—they're just in their own little world . . .
> and the others are the conscientious objectors.

Albert sees his strong Zionist inclinations as subsuming his Diasporic identity. As revealed in his discussion, these elements cannot necessarily be separated from each other:

> *Carrie:* Do you feel like there are any contradictions for you between having a Diasporic identity and a Zionist identity?
>
> *Albert:* No, because—when I first came back from Israel, I was very against the whole Diaspora mentality. Especially when I would see Israelis living in the United States, I would get kind of pissed off. I would kind of think of them as traitors. But with time, I've come to realize that if you look at them as another country looks at expatriates—not in a negative light, but like if there's an American in Ghana—if you look at it like that, it's not so bad. It's only people who think that Israel still needs to prove itself: then there's a conflict. If people don't believe that Israel exists yet, and it's still struggling to exist: then there's a conflict. But if you're like me, and you think Israel is a state with all the modern problems of other states— . . .
>
> Diaspora is Jewish identity, let's face it. There's some validity to their [Boyarin and Boyarin's] argument. What makes Israel exist is Diaspora. If it weren't for Diaspora, there wouldn't be Israel. Menachem Begin was a very strong proponent of this. When he would pray, he would purposely pray in a thick Yiddish-accented Hebrew—not the Israeli Sephardic-type Hebrew. And he would say that, if it wasn't for Poland—for him, Israel was just as strong in Poland as it was in Jerusalem. . . . You see, Diaspora is the ground of Zionism; therefore, it is the ground of Zionist identity.

Albert thus affirms part of the Boyarins' argument: Israel "was born in exile," the exile of the Jews from various Diasporic locales (Boyarin and Boyarin 1993: 718).

Unlike the Boyarins, however, Albert sees Jewish commitment to the Israeli nation-state not as something which challenges the vitality of Jewish identification with the Diaspora, but rather as an addition to the well-developed Diasporic identity of Jews worldwide. By uniting Zionist and Diasporic identity, Albert highlights our discussion of the way these concepts often become indistinguishable for many Diasporic Jews, and specifically for Cuban-Jews in Miami. Zionism and Diaspora do not work in opposition to each other, he stresses; on the contrary, they are linked inextricably in a sort of "evolutionary" process by which identification with a Jewish homeland emerges through the very absence of any such autochthonic connection for Jews throughout history. While "Jewishness" for the Boyarins is "not national," it is, to the utmost degree for Albert, linked to "being Israeli" (Boyarin and Boyarin 1993: 721).

Before Albert's connection with Israel, his "Jewishness" existed (and still exists, to a lesser degree) within an undeniably "Cuban" framework. As Albert discusses, this "Cuban framework," realized within his own Jewban identity, is the product of interactions between himself and those surrounding him in Miami. Being the "Other" within this environment, he emphasizes, has always left him in a liminal position. The only place where he could ever reconcile this "Otherness" is Israel, where the difficulties of being an "Other" disappear in a common identity shared among Israelis, a common understanding of the Israeli self and its relation to an Israeli whole.

> *Albert:* From a very early age, I was made aware by other Jews that I was Cuban. And from a very early age, I was made aware by other Cubans— and other Americans—that I was Jewish. I was always very aware of my differences. And growing up, I have found it very difficult to find my niche among any group of kids because I always felt like an outsider. . . . For me, it's always been a challenge to define myself in different places. The only place I didn't have that problem was in Israel. It was the only place, the only time in my life, where I didn't really worry about what I was or where I came from. I didn't have that specter of ethnicity following me, or maybe the illusion of that specter of ethnicity following me. When I was in Israel, I was a Jew, everyone else was a Jew. That's as simple as it was. And it was a beautiful thing; it must be how Americans feel—or white, Anglo-Saxon Protestants feel. And it's an amazing feeling. But—
>
> *Alberto:* That's the way I feel here.
>
> *Albert:* That's the way he feels here because he's more at ease with himself, but also he has a lot less commitments to his heritage, as far as Judaism goes. And I don't have equal commitments to my Cuban heritage as he does, but I have a certain degree of them. So I have two commitments, and even though they're not antagonistic—
>
> [Alberto looks upset, breathes deep.]

Unlike many other Cuban-Jews I spoke with, who also emphasized a feeling of social isolation within American society due to their *Cuban-Jewish* identity, Albert chooses to look outside the established Cuban-Jewish community for social and cultural solidarity. Albert maintains his links with the Cuban-Jewish community, most notably by regular attendance of synagogue services at Torat Moshe and by attempts to involve his parents in rediscovering Judaism within this Cuban-Jewish space. However, Albert also distances himself from this community in his choice of friends ("now most of my friends are Israelis, and I've been hanging out with them a lot"), his choice of work (the Israeli Foreign Ministry in Miami), and his focus on speaking Hebrew, rather than the Spanish which is characteristic of the Sephardic Cuban community.[17]

Albert's intense Israeli nationalism differs markedly from the attitudes of most other Cuban-Jews with whom I spoke—especially those of his generation. Albert contextualizes his nationalism by reference to his father's Cuban, and to a lesser extent Israeli, nationalism. He likens his father's "real" *cubanidad* to his own dedication to the Jewish homeland. Just as his father's dedication to a homeland ("Cuba") insures a "real" *cubanidad*, Albert is assured a legitimate identity through his commitment to his own homeland of choice, Israel.

> *Albert:* Coming from the Cuban perspective, Jews are very familial people—they're very family-oriented, for the most part, and Cubans are as well. So Cuban families are very into keeping things together and keeping the family together. And you'll find that a lot of Cubans don't send their kids away to school on purpose—they won't let their kids go to— even go to University of Florida—'cause it's too far away, and they want to have them close.[18] My parents are like that. So my parents are not hot at all on the idea of me going to live in Israel. I don't know if they talked to you about this—they don't want me to go.
>
> *Carrie:* Yeah, your father mentioned that.
>
> *Albert:* But at the same time, he can't stop me. And he doesn't try to convince me not to go.
>
> *Carrie:* Does he understand, do you think, why?
>
> *Albert:* He says he doesn't—that he can't understand why I would leave my family and a very solid future. And why I would leave the relative stability of Miami to something that could end up anywhere. I could end up as anything there. I think he understands that I'm a young man and I want to experience life, and I want to create my own destiny. But he doesn't understand why I have to go so far. And at the same time, he's responsible for it, to a great degree. Because he was always very pro-Israeli. But with my father, Cuba was always much more of a topic of discussion than Israel. I mean, when I was ten years old, I was having political discussions with my father about Cuba.
>
> *Carrie:* Not about Israel?
>
> *Albert:* Not about Israel. I had no idea what was happening in Israel. He always had a relative interest in Israel, and he remains to have a relative interest, I think. But with Cuba, he knows everything. He knows all of the players, and he knows all of the moves. And that's what I'm developing, as far as Israel is concerned.
>
> *Carrie:* You think it's the same sort of nationalism?
>
> *Albert:* Yeah, it's funny. My father and I are alike in a lot of ways. Not completely alike, but he's a moderate, and I'm a moderate as well. And both of us have a very strong aversion to extremism. But at the same time, we have very strong views about our political opinions. And I feel a

connection to Israel that he doesn't feel. He feels a connection to Cuba
that I don't feel. And my mother doesn't feel connected to anything.

*Carrie:* She feels more connected to America, doesn't she?

*Albert:* Yeah, exactly. For my mom, America is really what it's about.
For her, this is the Golden Land. . . . After 1973, Cuba broke relations
with Israel, after the Yom Kippur War. And the Israeli embassy in Havana
was closed. My father—when he was a kid—he was involved with a
group called Macabi, that was like the Zionist group, and he . . . [also
dated] the daughter of the ambassador. So he had an opportunity—he
could've gone with her [to Israel]. . . . So my dad had the opportunity to
go to Israel, and he didn't go to Israel. And in a way, I'm doing what he
didn't do. And I think to a certain degree, he sees that. He sees where his
life might've led to, if he'd taken that step.[19]

While his parents have difficulty understanding his fervent Zionism, his father,
Albert thinks, can understand and participate in it vicariously, in much the same way
that Albert participates in Alberto's *cubanidad.* Albert thinks that his father sees Israel
as an alternative path not taken.[20] Israel, for Alberto, must have been an imagined
place; temporally, culturally, and geographically foreign, it existed light years away.
Still, Albert thinks, because Alberto almost "became Israeli," it holds a special
significance for him.

Albert's commitment continues a tradition of political commitments running
through his family's paternal side. Alberto's 1966 plane hijacking, which involved
Albert's father, uncle, (male) cousin, and grandfather, is the most salient example of
this. Albert's reverence for his father's political commitments does not extend to his
mother's commitments. For Albert, Esther's not feeling "connected to anything" is synonymous with her feeling connected to the United States, to her perception of America
as the "Golden Land." His perception of her as "disconnected" is appropriate to a decidedly female sphere, where connections with the "outside" world are discouraged and
where the woman is revered for her domestic genius, not her political persona. Albert's
linking a connection to America with a connection to "nothing" reveals much about his
personal relationship with the United States, too. Albert's connection to America, he
declares, is simply tactile; for him, it has no intellectual or emotional meaning. This is
clear in the following narrative, in which Albert responds to my inquiry concerning
how he defines himself and how he feels toward his dual (Jewish and Cuban) heritage:

I acknowledge that I'm Cuban. I don't know how much pride I have in
being Cuban. I speak Spanish fluently, but I was brought up on Miami
Beach, and Miami Beach during the time that I was growing up wasn't
predominantly Hispanic or Cuban. During the time that I was growing

up, it was mostly Americans and some Jews. So when I think of myself, I think of myself more as a Jew—I think of myself as a Jew first, and then I think of myself as a world citizen. I don't [really consider myself American too much]. After that, yeah, I'd say Cuban, but I think maybe it's just because the things that I've gone through personally that have made me look at myself as an international entity, than to pigeonhole myself as a Cuban, or a Cuban-American.

Albert thus situates his Jewishness in multiple, seemingly incongruous directions; directions which defy the Boyarins' juxtaposition of Zionism with Diaspora. While he takes a firm Zionist stance and insists upon his identification with Israel and Jewish Israelis, he also maintains an internationalist position and, to a lesser degree, a sense of Cuban nationalism. Within this Cuban nationalism lies a Diasporic/diasporic connection with the island, although Albert lives this connection primarily through others' memories. Unlike many other second-generation Jewbans, Albert thinks the upper- and lower-case "diasporas" can be separated. Still, Albert emphasizes, as a Cuban-Jew he has an experience which neither American Jews nor Cuban-Americans have. Furthermore, although the United States is his "official" home, he does not identify himself as an American in the way he thinks American Jews, and especially Gentile Anglo-Americans, do.

By ranking his "Cuban" identity third, Albert contradicts his internationalist position: how can one simultaneously identify with a nation and refuse to identify with one? Albert demonstrates how personal alliances and self-definitions are not always theoretically congruent, and how memory, history, and identity become fused. Although he grew up in the United States, Albert rejects an American identity. While he left Cuba as a young child, he identifies himself the way his parents identify him: as a Cuban.

Albert's understanding of his connections with both Judaism and Cuba sometimes differ from that of his Jewban peers. As I spoke with his peers, it became clear that, in their lives, Jewishness and *cubanidad* merged in a way reminiscent of Yosele Gilfarb's discussion of the "unique Jew-Ban atmosphere" of the Círculo (see chapter 2). While Albert often separates the two—at times even opposing one to the other— he sometimes fuses them into a unique *jubanidad,* as do many other first- and second-generation Cuban-Jews.

## Religious Intermarriage: "Cuban Cubans" and "Jewish Cubans"

After five hours of formal interviewing, the Ralveys and I relaxed into a more informal, bidirectional conversation. During this time, Albert and Alberto learned that I was engaged to a man from a Catholic family.

*Alberto:* So your research is for the bachelor's grade?

*Carrie:* Yeah.

*Albert:* Is your boyfriend getting his master's?

*Carrie:* No, he's getting a bachelor's, too.

*Alberto:* He's studying the same [thing as you]?

*Carrie:* No, he studies history.

*Albert:* Is he Cuban?

*Carrie:* No, he's Puerto Rican.

*Alberto:* [voice raises] Ah, he's Puerto Rican?

*Carrie:* Well, Puerto Rican and Irish.

*Alberto:* [surprised and uneasy] He's not Jewish?

*Carrie:* No, he was raised Catholic.

*Alberto:* Are you marrying him?

*Carrie:* Yeah, next May.

*Alberto:* And what do your parents say about that?

*Carrie:* They're fine with it. They love him as a son. Let me turn this [tape player] off [laugh]—

The upbeat atmosphere of the previous five hours almost immediately turned sullen with my disclosure of Sean's religion. Sensing this discomfort, I turned the tape recorder off, for this, I thought, was not part of my "ethnographic research." Instead, this was the informal small talk which I assumed would characterize the beginnings and endings of my interviews. Yet my conversation with Alberto illuminated many issues surrounding Alberto's identity as a Jew. Below is a reconstruction of that conversation, from memory:

*Alberto:* Well, [deep breath] all I can say is if you really love him—you do love him?

*Carrie:* Oh yeah.

*Alberto:* I hope you don't mind that I'm asking you these questions. It's just that you've asked us all these questions, and now we want to ask you a little, you know [all laugh]?

*Carrie:* Of course. I have no problem with this. Hey—it's only fair [all laugh]!

*Alberto:* Look, let me tell you this—not to sound like I'm telling you what to do with your life or anything. But this is just from my experience, what I think is best. You can go out with this guy—that's fine. I've gone out with Gentile girls in my life [laughs]. And you can even marry this guy. But let me give you some advice—just to keep your marriage strong—you should not have kids with a non-Jew. It only causes problems for your children. I don't care what you do with him, but be careful about having kids. It can ruin a family.

*Carrie:* Yeah. Thanks [pause]. Well, I'd better be going.

I was uncomfortable and avoided the issue of religious intermarriage, which nevertheless followed me throughout my discussions with Cuban-Jews (as well as Jews from other communities). I was also curious to explore further the disdain for intermarriage that I frequently encountered when talking to Jews. How did Cuban-Jews view marriage? Were there differences between Ashkenazim and Sephardim on this issue? What about differences between pre-revolutionary and current perceptions of intermarriage?

Two weeks later, Eva Simazi and I were discussing differences between Sephardim and Ashkenazim. Eva, a Sephardic Cuban, explained:

> *Eva:* One main difference is that when we have children, we name after the living, whereas Ashkenazis name after the dead.
> *Carrie:* Oh, I see! Do you know Alberto and Esther Ralvey?
> *Eva:* Of course.
> *Carrie:* I've been wondering about why they named their son Albert. That explains it.
> *Eva:* But there's a reason there. It's probably because Alberto's father is not Jewish.

The pieces began coming together. However, I wondered why, if Alberto's father was Christian, the family had an *apellido* (last name) that is as common among Sephardim as Smith or Jones is in the United States.[21] E-mail correspondence with Albert clarified this and more:

> Hi Albert!
> . . . I have a few questions for you. Can you explain better to me your family's history—wasn't one of your father's parents Jewish and one Christian? Because I remember meeting your grandmother at the Federation reception—and since I know your mother's parents are still in Cuba, I assume that was your father's mother and that she was Jewish. But then whose last name was Ralvey (I thought this was predominantly a Sephardic name)? Also, where did "Albert" and "Alberto" come from? Are they family names?

Albert replied:

> Greetings Motek,[22]
> . . . That was my father's mother you met at the reception. My father's father was Christian. In Cuba you have two [last] names: one for the father and one for the mother. My father knew that he wanted to be identified as what he was, so he kept his mother's maiden name. My grandfather's last name is

García. When I was born they named me Alberto after my grandfather and
father, and they gave me the middle name Diego. So I was born Alberto
Diego García. Imagine!! They might as well have named me Porky Pig.[23]
When we left Cuba to Venezuela, it was changed to Alberto Isaac Ralvey.
And in America they changed it to Albert. It's been good because, since
Ralvey is not immediately associated with Judaism [by non-Jews] and my
other names don't imply being Hispanic, it allows me a certain freedom
of movement between both worlds and [in the worlds] of non-Hispanics
and non-Jews. . . .

Alberto's discussion of relations between Ashkenazim and Sephardim in Cuba
highlights the rarity of his parents' interreligious union. Even marriages between
*turcos* and *polacos*, he emphasizes, were very uncommon in pre-revolutionary Cuba
and often caused discomfort for many Jews: "So for many years [in Cuba], when
an Ashkenazi girl married or was going out with a Sephardic Jew, it was like marrying or going out with a Gentile." Indeed, this sentiment was echoed in nearly every
interview I conducted. Jews married Jews in Cuba, and marriages between
Ashkenazim and Sephardim were a radical break from the norm. Note the language used by Rafael and Elena Losger, Cuban Ashkenazim in their early fifties, to
describe this phenomenon:

> *Rafael:* Cubans were very warm, nice, open-minded people. The Jews
> [in pre-revolutionary Cuba] were well-received. Because of circumstances,
> they maintained—it was like a ghetto—I'm using ghetto in the good
> sense of the word. We kept together as a community, in our studies and
> our prayers, in our celebrations and our sorrows . . .
> *Elena:* We would marry only other Cuban Jews, and there weren't that
> many intermarriages [between Sephardim and Ashkenazim] like we have
> now.
> *Rafael:* Many years ago, there was a cultural difference between Sephardim
> and Ashkenazim, and lately—the last thirty years—it's completely gone with
> the wind. Many of our friends are marriages of Sephardim and Ashkenazim.
> *Elena:* Many years ago in Cuba, there used to be like, the Ashkenazim
> would marry the Ashkenazim, and the Sephardim would marry the
> Sephardim.

The radical character of a marriage between Jew and Gentile in pre-revolutionary
Cuba crystallizes when we consider that "intermarriage" meant the union of Sephardim
and Ashkenazim. Alberto's admonition against my marrying and having children with a
Gentile suggests the trouble and confusion created for him personally, as a child, by his

parents' interreligious marriage. Indeed, Alberto's Jewish identity and involvement in Jewish social youth groups such as pre-revolutionary Cuba's *Macabi* often conflicted with his Christian heritage. Thus, in an effort "to be identified" as a Jew, Alberto Ralvey García chose his Jewish mother's maiden name as his *apellido*, or last name.

While Alberto describes Jewish life as separate from "Cuban" life in both Cuba and the United States, he stresses the fluid way Jews moved about in Cuban society and, to a lesser extent, in American society. In neither society were Jews an oppressed minority; there was partial "ghettoization," but it was self-chosen, since Jews were, in Alberto's words, "totally assimilated with the Cubans . . . in the cultural and economic areas."

Alberto's view that, in present-day Miami, Cuban Jews and Cuban Christians should be understood as separate groups appears to stem from his experience with the Jewish community in Cuba. This community, although well established and accepted within greater Cuban society by the 1950s (when Alberto was a small child), remained markedly separate within this larger societal experience, not only in religious functions, but also in social life. Today in Miami, these older distinctions remain salient for Alberto. The Jews, the "Other" group in Cuba, remain, in his words, "Jewish Cubans"; while Gentiles of Cuban descent, particularly white Catholics, are the "Cuban Cubans." The understanding of who is a "real" Cuban becomes linked with Catholicism, so that those of Jewish heritage must claim a qualified Cuban identity.

Alberto, however, situates himself in a position which blurs this distinction. As a Jew, he connects himself to the "Otherfied" Cubans; but his Christian heritage, he implies, allows him to travel in circles of "Cuban Cubans" that are largely inaccessible to other Cuban-Jews in Miami. For Alberto, Miami's Cuban-Jewish community exists within finite boundaries that community members avoid crossing. Alberto's position both inside and outside these boundaries is facilitated by his double identity.

"I consider myself totally Cuban, *totally* Cuban. I mean, no one's more Cuban than me [laughs]," Alberto emphasizes. He points to his involvement with Concilio Cubano as merely one avenue through which his "true" *cubanidad* is expressed. As the discussion proceeds, he continually links seemingly separate aspects of his life within a recognizably "Cuban" framework.

> *Alberto:* I'm part of the Unión Liberal Cubana, which is a political party
> that belongs to the international U.L.[24]
> *Carrie:* And this is separate from religion, right?
> *Alberto:* Has nothing to do with Judaism—it's totally Cuban. I'm the Jew
> in the group—there are no other Jews in any of the other organizations that I
> know of. I'm the only Jew involved in that, because I'm so Cuban [laughs]!

Alberto's distinction between "Cuban" Cubans and "Jewish" Cubans becomes salient in this discussion. He sees himself as a bridge between these two groups who, he thinks, generally exist separate from each other in Miami. Alberto stresses the ease with which he moves through "homogeneous" spaces where "Cuban Cubans" generally are found. This does not mean that he identifies himself, or is identified by others, consistently in varying social situations. In fact, he notes,

> Among Cubans, I identify myself as a Jew.[25] And I'm called *el judío* all the time. I play dominoes, and they call me Larry Harlow, [who] was a musician in New York, a Jewish guy, that played in the salsa bands. And he played trumpet. His nickname was *El Judío Maravilloso*, "The Marvelous Jew." They call me that—it's always *el judío, el judío, el judío*, and I don't mind, I don't care. It's like if they call me a *cubano*, I don't care, that's what I am; I don't regret it. They are not offending me by calling me *Jew*. That's what I am. Like if somebody called me *Cuban*, I don't get offended by that.
>
> *Albert:* I guess I'm just a little bit more sensitive than he is about that.
>
> *Alberto:* Well, because you have softer skin—you have not been through what I have been through.
>
> *Albert:* No, it's not that. I mean—
>
> *Alberto:* It is.
>
> *Albert:* Yeah, it is that.
>
> *Alberto:* Because before that I was called a *gusano* (worm), and before that I was called a *contrarevolucionario* (counterrevolutionary). I have been called many things in my life, never in a nice way. [I have] hardened skin.

Alberto's experiences as "un verdadero hombre cubano" ("a true Cuban man") contribute to the ease with which he crosses the apparent boundaries between groups in Miami. His distinctive, idiosyncratic identity is to be the "alternative" member of the Cuban group—different, but not completely "Other," since he shares certain fundamental characteristics with the group's members, including a Christian father.

For Alberto, Albert's discomfort with the idea of being labeled "*judío*" by Gentiles or "*cubano*" by non-Cubans (even if said in a nonoffensive tone) further establishes Alberto's authority in the realm of Cuban affairs. As a *cubano* with "hardened skin," Alberto distinguishes between the relatively benign power of words and the menacing power of "real" exile politics. Alberto again places Albert, as a second-generation Cuban-American with no first-hand "Cuban experience" that he can remember, in the "ignorant" position of taking these ethnic labels too seriously.

Albert often separates Judaism and Cuba, much like his father. Alberto's conceptions of *cubanidad* and Jewishness have been transmitted to Albert. While Albert's
"Cuban" experience has taken place largely within a Jewish framework—that of the
Cuban-Jewish community in Miami Beach—his father's "Cuban" experience shows
him that *cubanidad* is different from *jubanidad*.

## Myths, Locations, and Homes

Albert, like Carmelita Tropicana, stands multiply positioned, simultaneously occupying the positions of Miamero, Zionist, Cuban, and Jewban. (Re)occupying the position of Israeli, his ultimate goal, will place him in still another location (physical and
psychological), one in which these other positions will shift fundamentally. Although
"becoming Israeli" theoretically requires relinquishing one's previous culture, Albert
emphasizes, this ideal can never be realized fully. His identity has been shaped by numerous elements: his parents' stories of Cuba; his ambivalent connection to Cuba, the
"unknown" place of his birth; his interaction with the Cuban community in areas of
Miami such as Little Havana and Sagüesera; his lack of a similar "Cuban" interaction
within Miami Beach; and his family's membership at Torat Moshe. Such influences are
joined by his recent interest in Judaism and Zionism, and the places where these beliefs
intersect. Taken as a whole, these experiences place him in numerous *locations*—locations
which merge into *home*. bell hooks' words echo loudly in our consideration of Albert's
multiple positions; he "confronts and accepts dispersal and fragmentation as part of
the constructions of a new world order that reveals more fully where we are, who we
can become" (hooks 1991: 149, cited in Massey 1992: 15).

Dispersal and fragmentation are salient realities for Albert. As both a Cuban and
a Jew, he lives out his family's history of displacement and exile in his imagination
and, in turn, in the way he chooses to live his life. Imagination thus becomes
memory, for it is through this remembered past that Albert understands his position
*now*. Indeed, these very realities allow him to visualize his future—to construct a
model of the person he will become.

Dispersal and fragmentation reverberate in Albert's life in a figurative sense as
well. The very heritage he claims, and which others use to identify him, situates
him within certain social and psychological locales characterized by plurality and
disjuncture. Albert does not "fit" into the categories he is often presented with—
"American," "(American) Jew," "Cuban"—and thus finds himself in a site of
homelessness. He can identify to some extent with Cuban-Jews in Miami collectively, but his intense Zionism separates him even from them. While this experience of estrangement and alienation in Miami tells him he belongs nowhere, what
emerges for Albert is a sense of belonging everywhere:

I consider myself a human being—beyond anything, I think you have to look at the world as a human being; you have to look at it as one entity. You have to feel some degree of empathy for everyone. So most people—everyone draws boundaries around their worlds: they start with themselves, then they go to their families, then they go to their peer groups, and it just keeps going out until the levels are—until you get to the world level, which is like the least important for most people. So I've had a global point of view for awhile.

For Albert, home is indeed locations. Sometimes these locations even bleed into each other, forming a larger, new entity: "the world level." For Alberto as well, home takes on multiple forms. These forms are better defined and more comfortable for him than for his son. Alberto's advocacy of democratic capitalism helps him to situate himself in compatible locales: countries, ideologies, and emotions. While Albert takes a broader view, occupying the multiple and overlapping positions of world citizen, Cuban-American, Jewban, Israeli, and Miamero, his father sees himself simultaneously positioned along only three stable axes: American, Cuban, and Jew.[26] As an older man with a more consolidated sense of identity, Alberto is more comfortable switching codes, languages, and environments. For Alberto, "Cuban" and "Jewish" identities do not fuse in the same way they do for many other Cuban-Jews in Miami. This can be understood partly as a function of his dual religious heritage and partly of his "late" arrival in Miami and hence "late" incorporation into the Cuban-Jewish community.

Albert's use of myths—specifically those of Jewish life in Cuba—calls into question the framework within which Nancy and the Boyarins present the concept of myth, as well as their model of the Jews as a people "free from myth" (particularly the myth of autochthony) because of their Diasporic experience (Boyarin and Boyarin 1993: 699). Nationality and homeland myths are precisely the mediums through which Albert locates his allegiances. By his father's link to the myth of the *contrarevolucionario cubano,* so prevalent in Miami, Albert realizes his Cuban identity in "remembering" his father's brave defense of his *patria.* Furthermore, it is precisely through this myth of the brave nationalistic patriot that Albert can situate his own Israeli nationalism.

The "Cuban-Jewish" myths Albert recounts are those recounted orally and at times visually (through photos, film, and written histories) by his family and the Cuban-Jewish community. These myths allow him to imagine the past and understand the present.

> *Albert:* Among Cubans, there's much more militancy in regards to
> Zionism than among other groups. I don't know how to explain it, but,

for instance, at the awards banquet for the Friends of the Israeli Defense Forces, it was full of Cubans. Just imagine: everyone speaking Spanish. I think Cuban Jews who came here really had to prove themselves. . . . I think the reason that the militancy is there is because Cuban Jews who came to this country had a lot to prove.[27]

*Alberto:* Oh yes.

*Albert:* Not only did they have to prove themselves as new immigrants, like everyone else, but they had to prove themselves as Jews to the rest of the Jews, here.

*Alberto:* Even now.

Albert and Alberto, in effect, retold for me the myth of Cuban-Jewish Zionism within a local (Miami) context.[28] These myths allow Albert to place himself, as a Cuban-Jew, simultaneously in individual, local, and international contexts. By continually referring to the ardent Zionism of Jews in pre-revolutionary Cuba, Albert positions his own, more intense Zionism within a mythohistorical framework, claiming a personal connection with the "third" Cuban-Jewish locale, Israel.

Albert begins at a starting point similar to that of the Boyarins: Diaspora *is* the Jewish experience and thus constitutes the ground of Jewish identity. Albert's experience shows him that Zionism, though born out of Diaspora, constitutes an equally salient ground of Jewish identity. For Albert, Zionism and the Israeli nation-state have connected Jews as a group in a way actually hindered by Diaspora. The absence of a homeland or any unifying cultural traditions weakened the links that supposedly bound Jews throughout the world, he thinks. This dearth of Jewish unity was most evident in the strained relations between Sephardim and Ashkenazim. Only with the creation of Israel did these relations improve: "What I think has somehow brought both the Ashkenazim and the Sephardim together is Israel." For Albert, Israel is the realization of the Jewish Diasporic dream. It brings Jews of different backgrounds together in two major ways: physically for Israeli citizens and spiritually for Jews living in the Diaspora. Albert thus conceives of Israel in a fundamentally different way than he does Turkey, Poland, Cuba, or the United States. These places do not have the power to unite Jews like Israel does; they are Diasporic locales which hold meaning for Albert because of his family's history, but they are not places which are as wholly "Jewish" as Israel is.

As a Cuban-Jew, Albert feels that he is trying to make a place for himself in this world. As an Israeli, however, this place is already made for him, for, in this "homeland," he can link religion and nationality unproblematically. "When I was in Israel, I was a Jew, everyone else was a Jew. That's as simple as it was," Albert asserted.

While Albert favors the "simpler" notion of the Israeli Jew, he carries with him, even in Israel, a fundamental attachment to his more "complicated" Cuban-Jewishness:

> I went to school with Cuban Jews and didn't even know that they were Cuban. It wasn't an issue that came up, because I went to school with them and always assumed that they were just Jewish Americans. And then, when I went to Israel, of all places, I met some of them. And in conversation in Israel, I would always tell people that I was Cuban and people would freak out—the Israelis, they love Cuban culture—they dance merengue and salsa and everything. . . . When they found out that I was Cuban, they were so amazed, and some of the people who I'd met there, that I'd known here—I just happened to run into them—I found out that their parents were Cuban. I would never have known. So I started talking to them in Spanish, and they could hardly speak a word!

Albert's self-identification as a Cuban-Jew within Israel gives us pause when we consider his discussion of the "undifferentiated" Jew in Israel. Clearly he was proud and excited to share his "Otherness" with Israeli Jews, and to connect with other Cuban-Jews within Israel. The linguistic channel Albert chose to connect with them was not English or Hebrew; once he found that these "American Jews" were fellow Jewbans, he used Spanish to forge a link with them.[29]

Albert takes pride in his Cuban-Jewishness. Israel may be a place where all Jews can unite as Jews, but that does not mean Albert's Cuban and Cuban-Jewish identity can be erased from memory or from his sense of self. Even in the heart of the Jewish homeland, Albert automatically connects with his *jubanidad.*

# Chapter 6

## The "Other" Cuban Jews:
## Émigrés of the 1970s, 1980s, and 1990s

Miami's Cuban-Jewish community—centered around the Cuban-Hebrew Congregation and Torat Moshe—is composed overwhelmingly of 1960s émigrés. Many community leaders today, in fact, have grown up in the community and speak of it much as Benjamín Cohen speaks of the Cuban-Jewish community in San Juan, Puerto Rico, within which he grew up: "With Cuban-Jews, sometimes there's a blur between actual family and the community. It almost becomes like the community is your family. . . . So I grew up in a sense where you felt part of a very large family—and family is in quotation marks." In a similar vein, Damien Losger contrasts the Cuban-Jewish community with other Jewish communities in Miami. In it, he says, "everyone knows everyone. I think that's the whole Cuban-Jewish community. Whether we talk to them every day or not, the whole entire Cuban-Jewish community we know, and we're part of that. . . . We're all—like my pediatrician is one of my father's best friends. He's like another father to me. I was communally raised by them. . . . It's like, everyone's one big family."

As Benjamín and Damien note, the community structure which has developed in Miami over the past three decades emphasizes community solidarity, in both its social and its religious aspects. This solidarity was realized in a peculiar form; without a large inflow of Cuban-Jews since the late 1960s, the community is maintained primarily by first-generation 1960s Cuban-Jewish émigrés and their children. As Bernie Kremen remarked, the community in present-day Miami Beach resembles a "transplanted community that moved 180 miles north." Kremen highlights the Cuban-Jewish community's attempts to maintain continuity in its traditions and customs by maintaining continuity in leadership. Indeed, the well-known *apellidos* (last names) of community leaders in present-day Miami often can be traced back to those in Havana in the 1940s and 1950s.

The result, largely a product of historical circumstances, is a "familial" community composed primarily of 1960s émigrés and their American-born children. Within this structure, the position of more recent Cuban-Jewish arrivals is unclear. Torat Moshe serves as a location around which recent Sephardic (and some Ashkenazic) émigrés from Latin American countries congregate, in large part because of its use of Spanish in synagogue services. With regard to Cuban Sephardim, however, Torat Moshe's position is different, due to the infrequency with which Jews arrive in the United States from Cuba today.

The Cuban-Hebrew Congregation is not as active as Torat Moshe in Latin American Ashkenazic life, due to a combination of factors. First, the congregation conducted its services in English during the massive Latin American Jewish migration to Miami in the 1980s. Hence many of these people—both Sephardim and Ashkenazim—chose to attend Temple Moses, which conducted services in Spanish. Also, according to Marcos Kerbel, many Latin American Jews moved to North Dade and South Broward, geographically distant from the congregation's South Beach location. Finally, the relative abundance of Ashkenazic (as compared with Sephardic) synagogues in South Florida allowed Latin American Ashkenazim a wider selection of synagogues. Many I spoke with also attribute the small number of non-Cuban Latin American members of the Cuban-Hebrew Congregation to the congregation's distancing itself from the realm of Cuban, and certainly Latin American, affairs.

What happens, then, when "new" Cuban-Jews arrive in Miami? What relations, if any, do they have with the community which nominally shares their ethnoreligious identity? If relations do exist, what commonalties do they rest upon? How do recent arrivals affect community structure? Furthermore, can the community maintain its formal structure when faced with "alternative" models of what a Cuban-Jew is? Within these questions lie issues which must be considered on an individual basis—issues which cannot be generalized across an entire population of "recent arrivals." Thus, rather than constructing an argument about the community's relations with recent Cuban Jewish émigrés—a task which, after much consideration, I think impossible— I simply will present the separate stories of four families of "recent arrivals"— Cuban-Jews, that is, who arrived in Miami after 1970, after the community structure already had been established through the formation and development of the Círculo Cubano-Hebreo and the Cuban Sephardic Hebrew Congregation.

## Jacob and Luisa Lajapo

At his dining room table, within his small condominium in Sagüesera, Jacob Lajapo, a Sephardic Jew, told me about his family's experience coming to the United States from Cuba less than three years before. The Lajapos arrived in Miami in November 1993, less than eight months before the *balsero* wave of Cuban migration to Miami. Jacob (a lawyer, psychologist, psychotherapist, physician specializing in alternative medicine, and an agricultural expert for the Cuban Ministry of Agriculture) and his wife Luisa (an economist with the Cuban State Committee's Department of Statistics) decided to abandon their professional lives in Cuba when the opportunity to emigrate presented itself. With student visas to study for three years at a prominent United States university, Jacob, Luisa, and their daughter, Natalia, left Cuba for the northeastern United States, with the intention of applying for political asylum upon arrival. Because the university supplied only a tuition waiver, the family did not have money for food and housing; nor did Jacob and Luisa have the English-language skills needed for employment in most local jobs. When the United States rejected their appeal for political asylum, they needed an immediate source of income. Miami seemed to be the most viable alternative location. It offered a linguistic, physical, and, to some extent, cultural climate which was familiar to them, one in which they could work under the table to pay basic living expenses until they could obtain work permits.

> *Jacob:* We came here penniless. We had to start from zero. We were not considered refugees here—we were not granted political asylum. Immigration right now, with respect to Cuba: they grant political asylum to rafters. In our case, we said, "Okay, let's wait one year. And then apply for residency." We didn't have help from the government, we didn't have relatives—we only had one friend who could take care of us in the first days. In the second month, we started working, and with our salaries, we rented a studio. It was very hard in the beginning. Other Cubans come, they have relatives, they live with relatives, they save money, they have help for good jobs. In our case, it was very hard. But anyway, we survived. We have a very good place. Now we have everything like regular Americans. And we try to help other people—other Cubans arriving later, and to help relatives in Cuba. My parents and sisters live there. I have only one brother in Israel. But the rest of the family is in Cuba—they don't want to leave. And even if they want to come, I'd help them, but it would always be their decision, nothing to blame me about.
>
> *Carrie:* [to Luisa] And is your family also living in Cuba?
>
> *Luisa:* Yes—I call them every week. Yesterday—
>
> *Jacob:* No, her family is very small, because it's only her aunt, niece, and her former sister-in-law.
>
> *Luisa:* I have cousins, near Havana.
>
> *Jacob:* She has cousins in Matanzas, and her aunt and niece and sister-in-law in Havana. But in theory, she has more relatives here [in Miami] than in Cuba, but they don't want to know about Cubans arriving right now [laughs]. They pay little attention, it's like we are nothing.

Luisa and Jacob glanced at each other, paused, and then quickly changed the topic.

Throughout the interview, Jacob continually emphasized his family's isolation upon arrival in Miami. He painted a picture of his family as an anomalous Cuban émigré family—anomalous in the sense that neither he nor Luisa had relatives living in the United States. Without this support network, he stressed, his family was placed in a doubly disadvantaged position. Not only were they forced to subsist on their own from the moment they entered the United States, but also, because they were Cubans and even more because they were Jews, Americans assumed that they had the "know-how"—and even the financial means—to support themselves in Miami immediately and to adjust to the city and perhaps even to the United States at large. The "Cuban Success Story" and the "Jewish Success Story" certainly are pervasive myths throughout the United States, contributing to an extremely narrow vision of who "Cubans" and "Jews" are, where they live, what businesses and activities they engage in, and what the secrets of their success are.[1] As Jacob noted, the dangerous assumptions associated with such myths reverberate strongly in his interactions with Cubans and non-Cubans, Jews and non-Jews, alike:

> When we first came, we went to [the Greater Miami] Jewish Federation, to get some help. And the person who was in charge: she was Anglo-Jewish, and she couldn't understand because she saw that most Jews here are rich. And she couldn't understand that we were poor, we had nothing. And she said, "Why do you need help? Why didn't you bring your money from Cuba?" I said, "Cuban money has no change. According to top Cuban law, when you leave the country, you cannot bring anything. You cannot sell your property. When Cubans leave the country, they leave like the Jews from Egypt." She couldn't understand! For her, the only Jews needing help are the Russian Jews. The Russians now can bring money—they are in a much better situation than the Cubans. And the Federation is helping the Russians and not the Cubans. And the complaint of all the Cuban Jews coming here is that they didn't have big support from the American Jews. They [American Jews] say, "Cubans don't need any help—they have rich relatives here." It's not true. It was so traumatic to listen to that from her.

As our initial conversation revealed, the Lajapos *do*, in fact, have relatives in Miami, but they do not associate with them. The model of the "established relative" who takes "the newer arrival" under her or his wing within Miami, supporting the "less fortunate" relative until s/he has established a social and economic base in the new and unfamiliar city, does not apply to the Lajapo family. Thus, Jacob explains, it is as if they had no Miami relatives at all. Because of this, both he and his wife were in economically and socially disadvantaged positions. Upon arrival in Miami, they had no social network through which they could locate work; consequently, money was difficult to come by, and the family suffered financially until Jacob and Luisa could obtain work permits.

Jacob's and Luisa's distance from family members living in Miami is by no means an isolated instance particular to their family. In fact, it reflects a widespread tension among (non-Jewish) Cuban émigrés in Miami who have left Cuba at different times since the beginning of the revolution in 1959. A profound mistrust of more recent arrivals from Cuba exists within many sectors of the Cuban community in Miami. These people often are viewed as economic immigrants rather than as political exiles; thus, they are accused by many 1960s self-declared exiles of being sympathetic to the revolution and coming to the United States for financial security rather than political asylum. According to this argument, the newly arrived exiles have stayed so long in Cuba because they have been indoctrinated into the Communist political system there and leave only when they no longer can survive economically. They bring with them to Miami, it is claimed, Communist ideologies which run counter to fundamental American concepts of democracy and freedom.[2]

An examination of the shrinking size of Cuba's Jewish population over the years suggests how different the issues are with regard to the Cuban-Jewish community in Miami. Robert Levine estimates that Cuba's permanent Jewish population in 1959 was between 10,000 and 16,500; by late 1965, it had dwindled to 2,300; and by 1993, fewer than 1,000 Jews remained in Cuba (Levine 1993: 308). Because nearly all Cuban-Jews emigrated from Cuba in the first years of the revolution (doing so as Jewish *Cubans*), we do not often hear of tension among Cuban-Jews arriving in the United States at different times. An arrival such as Jacob Lajapo's may affect the community greatly, because, with a handful of exceptions, Cuban-Jews for over thirty years have had little contact with Jews remaining on the island; and most of this contact has been through Cuban-Jews in the United States returning for visits to Cuba.

Unfortunately, I did not pursue this topic in my initial interviews (and these are the interviews upon which I draw most heavily). At the time of my research, I was unaware of the potential impact that the arrival of people such as the Lajapos might have upon the greater community. When I review my interviews, some of these issues come to light in unexpected and often puzzling ways. As we talked about his experience in Miami, I asked Jacob if he had felt a sense of political and religious liberation since he arrived in Miami. He replied:

> Yes, despite [the fact that] Miami is a very totalitarian society. For example, I want you to see this film [*Havana Nagila*].[3] This film was made in Cuba. I spoke freely on it about human rights in Cuba, and many people in Miami say this film is Communist. Why? For example, I say in one part that there are violations in human rights, but that the conflict between the United States and Cuba has nothing to do with

human rights. . . . "Aye, Jacob—Communist—propaganda"—because they don't accept anything that's different from the radical anti-Castro position. Miami's the most extreme.

This group of Miami extremists, Jacob explains, is composed mostly of 1960s exiles. Here he makes reference to the general Cuban population of Miami. But it is important to remember that Jacob most often is associated with *Jewish* Cubans; the legacy of his important role in Cuba's Jewish communities over the past decade, chronicled in both Laura Paull's *Havana Nagila* (1995) and Robert Levine's *Tropical Diaspora: The Jewish Experience in Cuba* (1993), has followed him to Miami, as he notes above.

Jacob functioned as a spokesperson for Havana's Jewish community to the Cuban government. He was one of three Jewish leaders who participated in a meeting with the Cuban government in April 1985, which resulted in the government's granting permission for foreign rabbis to perform Jewish ceremonies in Cuba (Oppenheimer and Ynclán 1985: 7A). Additionally, he reorganized Sunday School classes at the Patronato in Havana after a ten-year hiatus. In 1975, the Cuban government suddenly had closed the school, which up to that time had functioned as a Jewish grammar school. The Castro regime subsequently outlawed all Jewish instruction in Cuba for the next ten years. In 1985, Jacob was the school's only teacher, instructing a small group of children in Jewish history and the Hebrew language. He also was vice-president of B'nai B'rith in Havana. Jacob was involved with the Cuban Communist party until shortly before he left the country, at which time he spoke out against it; his father, even after Jacob's departure, remained a loyal Communist, occupying a prominent position in the party structure throughout the 1990s.

The Cuban-Jewish community of Miami, which normally tries to stay out of the "exile political arena" (as almost every interviewee stressed), was forced to confront certain pressing political issues with the publication of *Tropical Diaspora*, the Lajapo family's arrival in Miami, and later the release of *Havana Nagila*.[4] Should "Jewish Cubans" such as Jacob not be trusted—in his particular case, in light of statements he made in *Havana Nagila*, which many people interpret as sympathetic toward the Cuban Revolution? Why did he stay in Cuba so long if he thought the system was repressive (a claim he made time and again to me)? Is he perhaps a Communist who left merely for economic reasons? If he is accepted by the community, what are the implications for relations between Cuban-Jews and Cuban Gentiles in Miami? These are pressing questions which Cuban-Jews living in Miami ask in the wake of such an uncommon event as the Lajapos' "late" arrival.[5] In turn, the couple's presence forces Cuban-Jews to reconsider their relationship to Cuba, to the Cuban community of Miami, and to their Jewish heritage.

In my interviews, Jacob Lajapo's name did not come up frequently. Interestingly, I was referred to him by a Jewish Mariel immigrant, Rosa Levy. She had met the Lajapos when they first arrived in Miami and had recommended that they ask the Greater Miami Jewish Federation for financial assistance. "They are a wonderful family," Rosa told me. When I mentioned Jacob Lajapo to Albert Ralvey, he enthusiastically interjected, "Oh yeah, Jacob is a good friend of my father's. He's an incredible man."[6] I never heard this positive feedback from Cuban-Jews of the 1960s exile generation, many of whom were familiar with the Lajapos but discussed the family only when I asked specifically about their feelings toward recent Jewish Cuban arrivals.

Why, I wondered, did I hear these positive words only from more recent émigrés? Rosa's stance on the Castro regime was as hard-line as any I heard. She made it very clear to me that her reasons for coming to the United States were political rather than economic: "We left for political reasons, because he [her husband Raúl] always dreamed of being free." Albert and Alberto also identify themselves as anti-Castro. The only reason their family left Cuba as late as 1979, they emphasize, was that Alberto was held as a political prisoner and then continually denied exit visas.

Much has been written about the marked ideological differences between the "Exile" and "Freedom Flight" generations, on the one hand, and the *Marielitos, balseros,* and other recent émigrés (i.e., within the past twenty years), on the other. In this case, a simple dichotomy is inaccurate. Rosa, Alberto, and Albert clearly were as anti-Communist as much of the Cuban-Jewish community, but they were not nearly as involved in the community's affairs as were many 1960s Cuban-Jewish émigrés with whom I spoke. Rosa, in fact, was more familiar with some of the more prominent figures of the pre-revolutionary Jewish community in Cuba than she was with their roles in the Miami community now. Rosa and the Ralveys may have had greater sympathy for Jacob than other members of the Cuban-Jewish community. Having left Cuba less than twenty years before, they perhaps identified more with the issues he raised in the video. Perhaps they understood that certain comments made by recent Cuban émigrés often are misinterpreted and taken out of context by hard-line Cuban-Americans of the 1960s generation of émigrés. Maybe these were merely unique perspectives, or Rosa and the Ralveys had more contact with the Lajapos than other Cuban-Jews, or the subject of the Lajapos simply did not arise in my other interviews. I am hesitant, however, to accept as mere coincidence Rosa's and the Ralveys' enthusiasm about the Lajapos, while other Cuban-Jews were silent about them. I explicitly informed many of my interviewees of my intention to interview Cuban-Jews who had arrived in Miami during different time periods. Although none of them mentioned that I should interview the Lajapos, many were familiar with the family (a fact they revealed after I specifically asked) and the circumstances surrounding their arrival.

## Poor Minority Jews and the Cuban-Jewish Community

When I returned to Miami six months after my interview with the Lajapo family, I wanted to press these issues further. What exactly (if anything) had transpired between Luisa's family members who lived in Miami and the Lajapos, upon their arrival in 1993? How had the Cuban-Jewish community reacted? I called Jacob at home to discuss my questions with him. Knowing this was a touchy subject, I discussed my interest in learning more about how the Cuban-Jewish community is structured and how this structure may or may not be affected by such recent Cuban Jewish arrivals as his family. When I asked specifically about Luisa's relatives, he simply replied, "We have connections now, more or less, but they [her relatives in Miami] are not helpful." Clearly avoiding any further discussion of the Lajapo family's relationship with Luisa's relatives, Jacob shifted the conversation toward the larger Cuban-Jewish community in Miami Beach:

> It's difficult to prove there's discrimination within the Jewish Cuban community [toward recent Jewish arrivals from Cuba]. It's a very sensitive topic. It's a coldness—people who came here thirty years ago are very different now. They had a bad time at the beginning, working hard. In time they made money, became rich. People who stayed there [in Cuba] became professionals. When they come here, they have trouble finding professional jobs. Some of the first arrivals make it difficult for the newer immigrants to find good jobs—they want them to scratch from the beginning. Some relatives have been more—[pause]—In fact, one can't make general conclusions; each case is different.

Jacob's ambivalence surrounding Miami's Cuban-Jewish community becomes increasingly evident through his discussion. He paints a picture of a community of exiles who are less than welcoming of their "immigrant" coreligionists, and who feel that recent arrivals should "scratch from the beginning," as these "exiles" remember doing nearly four decades earlier. Jacob's lack of involvement with the Cuban-Jewish community also is explainable in a much different set of terms, however. The combination of lower wages (at most, six dollars per hour) and the frequent necessity of working double shifts to make ends meet financially leaves Luisa and Jacob with little time to involve themselves in social or community affairs. Furthermore, it leaves them with little money for the significant amount of gasoline that is consumed in one car ride from their home to Miami Beach. However, in Jacob's view, the largest constraint on the family's connection with *any* Jewish community in Miami—be it the Cuban-Jewish community specifically or any "American" congregation—is that here, to be a Jew, you have to have money. I am the poorest Jew in Miami. And I can't afford to pay memberships, and to give big donations. . . . I'm not invited to Bar Mitzvot, to weddings, for that [economic] reason. And the temple—well, now I belong to a synagogue. [But] we don't go there—we don't have time. . . . We still have things to unpack. And the problem is, we don't know people there. And a Shabbat Sabbath is not the best place to introduce people, because people go there, they listen to the rabbi, and then they leave. And every time there are social activities, you have to pay. And we are saving money—we can't afford that. They invited us to be members for free. And in the past, we went to Temple Moses from time to time.

. . . It's an economic issue. . . . [The Jewish identity in Miami] has an economic factor. Poor Jews don't go to the parties of rich Jews. Most Cuban Jews are very rich. The poorest were minorities. They've fought to survive.

*Carrie:* Do you want to integrate with the Miami Jewish community?

*Jacob:* Yes, but I need time. Two months ago, I was working twelve, fourteen hours a day. And even all Saturdays and some Sundays. I don't have time for such a life. Now because they want to cut the work time, I have more free time. Last year it was terrible. . . . [Luisa and I] work together, for the same company. With the professional life [as it was in Cuba], it is different. We had time for other things: social activities, lecturing . . .

The connection [with other Cuban-Jews at work] is only in work. As they have been here for a long time, they belong to social establishments. My contact is with poor immigrants, people who work in the warehouse [of a clothing factory]. . . . I am anonymous here in Miami . . .

I'm living here in a neighborhood where most people are not Jewish. They are Cubans and Colombians. Most Cuban Jews live in Miami Beach.

*Carrie:* Is it difficult to be separated from the Jewish community?

*Jacob:* Yeah, we wanted to live there [Miami Beach], but it was more expensive. And we decided to buy a condo, and the most affordable was here.

Jacob draws a distinction between "poor minority" Jews and "rich majority" Jews in Miami, classifying himself as a member of the former group. In this sense, he cannot be a real participant in any congregation until he has the money necessary to establish himself in this community. As a "minority," he also is limited by time and lack of social connections with Jews in Miami. His financial situation makes it necessary for him to work double shifts to make ends meet; simultaneously, it keeps him confined to certain middle-class neighborhoods which have minimal, if any, Jewish populations. Jacob, then, sees his "minority" status as derived not from his nationality, but rather from his financial status and its resulting social ramifications.[7] This status is perpetuated and reinforced within the Cuban-Jewish community, he thinks, because of his family's decision to remain in Cuba until 1993 and because of his thoughts on the situation with regard to human rights in Cuba, as documented in *Havana Nagila*.

## Luis Tirani

Jacob's story captured my attention. Was his family's situation unique, or did other recent Cuban-Jewish arrivals experience similar difficulties within the Cuban-Jewish community and Miami's greater Jewish community? I E-mailed a journalist whom I had originally contacted after seeing his article on the Jews of Cuba on the World Wide Web. Could he put me in contact with any Cuban-Jews now living in Miami who had arrived there recently (since most of my other interlocutors did not supply me with much information concerning recent arrivals)? He gave me the phone number and E-mail address of Luis Tirani, a Cuban-Jew who arrived with his brother Enrique in Miami in the *balsero* migration in the summer of 1994. The following is an excerpt from our telephone conversation:

> *Luis:* Aquí dentro de Miami, no tenemos relaciones con muchos judíos. (Here in Miami, we don't have relations with many Jews.)
>
> *Carrie:* ¿Porque usted no quiere tener relaciones con ellos? (Because you don't want to have relations with them?)
>
> *Luis:* No, no, no, no, no! Nosotros sí quisiéramos tenerlas, pero no hemos tenido la oportunidad conocer alguna. (No, no, no, no, no! We would like to have such relations, but we have not had the opportunity to meet anyone.)
>
> *Carrie:* Sí, entiendo, porque Miami es una ciudad grande—(Yes, I understand, because Miami is a big city—)
>
> *Luis:* Sí, en Miami Beach hay una gran comunidad de judíos cubanos, pero nosotros no conocemos a nadie. . . . (Yes, in Miami Beach there's a large community of Cuban-Jews, but we don't know anyone. . . .)
>
> *Carrie:* ¿Dónde viven en Miami? (Where do you live in Miami?)
>
> *Luis:* ¿Nosotros? (Us?)
>
> *Carrie:* Sí. (Yes.)
>
> *Luis:* Vivimos en el mismo Miami, cerca del aeropuerto de Opa Locka. ¿Usted esta escribiendo acerca de los judíos? (We live in Miami, near the Opa Locka airport. Are you writing about the Jews?)
>
> *Carrie:* Sí, he escrito acerca de la comunidad. Pasé el verano pasado en Miami. Hice entrevistas con la comunidad. Pero usted había llegado por este tiempo, ¿sí? (Yes, I have written about the community. I spent last

summer in Miami. I did interviews with the community. But you had arrived by that time, right?)

*Luis:* ¿En el verano pasado? (Last summer?)

*Carrie:* Sí.

*Luis:* Sí, sí. Porque nosotros llegamos en agosto de ninety-four. (Yes, yes. Because we arrived in August of ninety-four.)

*Carrie:* Sí. ¿A balsa? (Right. On a raft?)

*Luis:* A balsa, sí. On the raft.

*Carrie:* Su cuento es muy difícil. Se rompe su corazón. (Your story is very difficult. It breaks your heart.)

*Luis:* Sí.

*Carrie:* ¿Pero ahora en Miami cosas son buenas? (But now in Miami things are good?)

*Luis:* Sí, cómo no. . . . Ah, it's very interesting to meet you when you visit Miami.

*Carrie:* Sí, yo quisiera reunir también. . . . Una pregunta más: ¿porque usted y Enrique viven acerca de Opa Locka, es muy difícil para encontrar con la comunidad judía cubana? (Yes, I would like to meet also. . . . One more question: since you and Enrique live near Opa Locka, is it very difficult to meet with the Cuban-Jewish community?)

*Luis:* Uh, I think so, sí. Sí, porque aquí en Opa Locka no hay muchos judíos. (Yes, because here in Opa Locka there aren't many Jews.)

*Carrie:* ¿Por toda su vida, fue usted un judío religioso? (Were you a religious Jew your whole life?)

*Luis:* No, en Cuba, no había mucha práctica, porque (No, in Cuba there wasn't much [Jewish] practice, because) the regime doesn't want you go to the synagogue, you know? . . . But we were always very interested to know about Jewish tradition, Jewish history, you know? And we read many books. For example, when we arrived here, we went to synagogue sometimes, but I didn't speak English very well. . . . And then my brother didn't know a good Jewish synagogue—you know?

*Carrie:* Sí. Mi familia es judía. Vamos a una sinagoga aquí en Miami. (Yes. My family is Jewish. We go to a synagogue here in Miami.)

*Luis:* OK, when you come here, we can go together.

*Carrie:* Sure.

*Luis:* Yes, of course.

*Carrie:* Si quiere, yo puedo introducir usted a la Torat Moshe y la Cuban-Hebrew Congregation. (If you want, I can introduce you to Torat Moshe and the Cuban-Hebrew Congregation.)

*Luis:* Oh, I'd like.

*Carrie:* OK. . . . Are you Ashkenazic or Sephardic?

*Luis:* Sephardi.

*Carrie:* Torat Moshe is the Cuban-Sephardic Congregation.

*Luis:* Yes, my brother, my grandparents on my father's side are from Turkey. . . . Yeah, my grandfather and my grandmother, you know? 1919 they went to Cuba—the first World War, you know?

*Carrie:* Yeah.

*Luis:* This is another history—I have many pictures—

*Carrie:* I would love to—quisiera mirar a los fotos mucho, mucho. (I would really like to see the photos.)

*Luis:* Good, OK, when you come here you will see everything, OK?

My brief conversation with Luis Tirani over the phone, many months into my research, illuminates our consideration of the relationships (or lack thereof) between Miami's Cuban-Jews of various waves of migration. As Luis discusses, the relative inaccessibility of the Cuban-Jewish community to many Cuban-Jews living on the "outside" results in a community structure composed almost wholly of 1960s émigrés. Indeed, the five Cuban-Jewish families I spoke with who had arrived in the United States since the first wave of migration in the 1960s have markedly different relations with the Cuban-Jewish community in Miami than do most 1960s émigrés. These relations are greatly affected by geography. Since four of these five families live over forty-five minutes by car away from Miami Beach, affiliation with either of the two Cuban-Jewish synagogues and the community surrounding these institutions proves difficult, especially in light of the constraints on time and finances.[8] As more recent émigrés, these families often work longer hours and are more limited financially than much of the Cuban-Jewish community.

Luis's and his brother Enrique's social detachment from the Cuban-Jewish community in Miami Beach, as discussed above, stems primarily from their geographical detachment. Living in Opa Locka, a working-class neighborhood in northern Miami-Dade County, they have no daily contact with Jewish life outside their own home, let alone any connection to Cuban-Jews. And as immigrants who arrived in Miami within the *balsero* wave of Cuban migration, less than three years before our interview (which took place in 1997), they undoubtedly are struggling economically in Miami. Unable to afford either the time or money to make the forty-five-minute drive to Miami Beach, Luis and Enrique remain in Opa Locka, secluded from the Jewish world of Miami. They would like to associate with the Cuban-Jewish community, Luis stresses, but they have not had the opportunity to meet any Cuban-Jews. The few attempts they made, upon arrival in Miami, to attend "American" synagogue services closer to their home were unsuccessful, he notes, since these were conducted entirely in English, which Luis and Enrique were still struggling to learn.

# Political versus Economic Marginalization

While speaking to Albert Ralvey one night on the phone, I raised the question of the position of recent Cuban Jewish émigrés in Miami. How did he, who himself arrived in Miami as a three-year-old in 1979, understand relations between the more established community and Cuban Jews who lived for decades under the revolutionary regime, arriving in Miami only recently?

> *Carrie:* What about other Cuban-Jews who have recently come to Miami who are anti-Castro?
>
> *Albert:* Recently come to Miami?
>
> *Carrie:* Yeah, like, I was talking to a man named Luis Tirani the other day, and he and his brother came in the *balsero* migration to Miami. . . .
>
> *Albert:* Does he go to my synagogue?
>
> *Carrie:* No, he doesn't know any Jews in Miami, and he's like, "If you could ever introduce me to other Cuban-Jews—"
>
> *Albert:* Give me his number . . . I'll give him a call. I'll invite him to the Purim picnic this Sunday.
>
> *Carrie:* I think he feels like he wants to meet the Cuban-Jewish community, but I know other recent arrivals feel that there is an established community—
>
> *Albert:* Jeez, it happened to my dad, and my dad knew most of these people in Cuba! So for someone like Luis, it could be horrible. But me being the person that I am, I'm not going to allow someone to dis [disrespect] him.

Albert points directly to a tension which exists between Cuban-Jews of different generations of migration. This tension is not necessarily permanent, as we see in the case of his father Alberto's involvement with the community today. How did Alberto become a part of the community, while Jacob Lajapo continues to feel separate from it?[9]

I called Rosa Levy, hoping that she might have answers for me. Rosa's perspective was valuable, for she was knowledgeable about the composition of the Cuban-Jewish community and about Cuban migration to Miami generally. I told Rosa part of Luis's story: he and his brother Enrique had arrived in Miami in August 1994 within the *balsero* migration. Since then, they have been trying to get other family members out of Cuba. Their parents, as well as Luis's wife and children, are "trapped" there, the Tiranis claim; they repeatedly have been denied exit visas and, Luis says, are continually harassed by the Cuban government. Luis and Enrique feel all alone in Miami; they want to associate with the Cuban-Jewish community but do not know anyone and live far from its locus on Miami Beach.

*Rosa:* And his brother is here?

*Carrie:* Yeah, his brother's name is Enrique.

*Rosa:* OK, I'm writing this. Because it's good to know this, because once in awhile, we can call them or keep in touch with them, because there is no reason to be apart.

*Carrie:* Yeah, I told Albert Ralvey about them, and he said he would call them and invite them to the Purim picnic.

*Rosa:* I can ask Alberto [Ralvey] to introduce these two brothers to the community—to be in touch with them, to invite them to dinner or something, to meet once in awhile.

*Carrie:* From your experience with Jewish Cubans who have arrived since you've been here, do you think there are any political issues which cause tension between later arrivals and the people already in the community? Because you know how Jacob Lajapo has had all these problems, and he thinks it's because a lot of people call him a Communist, which he admits to having been in the past; but he denies having any Communist sympathies now.

*Rosa:* Yeah, that's the main issue. And it's happening among all Cubans. Not just Jews. Each Cuban. There's a big difference, a big barrier, between the first ones and the latest immigration. And they [those who arrived in the United States in the 1960s and 1970s] say that, during those years, they [the more recent arrivals] could have done something to come earlier. But you have to think that these people were born in Cuba during the Revolution, and after Fidel took his powerful hand over Cuba, so they didn't have the opportunity to . . . escape, or to forge their papers sometimes. And maybe their parents: they couldn't do it, because [of] their age.

But the people here, that came earlier, in the sixties and the seventies—they made that issue like it's something so big. And they still think they have the truth. And I know, for fact, that in some ways, they are right. But these people [the most recent arrivals]—yes, yes, they have been Communists. And they have been involved in the Revolution, and in the Communist Party, and in the Comité Central, and everything. Because they have to get involved. Some people [Communist leaders] have been very bad with the other people and they have said that this person is a dissident, and they have to be punished for that, but God only knows what is in their minds.

But Lajapo—he has some—he's right, but he's also wrong, because they—or he, himself—because his father is a very, very bad Communist. A very bad one. And they [members of the Cuban Communist Party] hate the people that left earlier, in the sixties and seventies, and his father has been active in the Communist Party, and also Lajapo himself—he has been very involved. And this is a very particular issue, because he has been involved. So maybe at the last minute, the last years he spent in

Cuba, he noticed that something was going wrong. And he decided to be a dissident or something. But yes, they have been involved. Because at the latest—let's say: my immigration was in the eighties, and he was late in the nineties. In that decade—ten years the difference. Yes, those people in those last ten years—they get more involved [to support Communism in Cuba]. And I don't know if they've been forced to do that—because I cannot be a judge, from here—while I was here, very safe. And I wouldn't be so hard with them. Because I can't be in their skin. You have to live there to know what that inferno is. But nobody—only God—has the truth.

Because the big issue is that. Because there's no other one, like "You're rich" or "I'm not rich enough." There's nothing economical, but [only] political.

Rosa's discussion challenges Jacob's proposal that economic discrimination is a chief characteristic of Miami's Jewish community. Jacob categorizes himself and his family in a doubly disadvantaged position. Not only are they called Communists by Miami's Cuban community, but they are also kept out of the mainstream Jewish community because of their economic status. Since these political and economic issues apply to their relationship with Cuban-Jews, they feel separate and unwelcome in the Cuban-Jewish community. Rosa, on the other hand, sees the marginalization of a family such as the Lajapos stemming entirely from political issues surrounding Jacob's and his father's affiliation with the Cuban government. In fact, she contends, recent Jewish Cuban émigrés have an easier time adjusting to Miami socially and economically than their Gentile counterparts. As long as they do not have Communist leanings, they are wholly accepted by the Cuban-Jewish community, she stresses; many, in fact, are employed by Cuban-Jews who have established successful businesses in Miami. Through this connection, the recent arrivals are able to develop a social network through their jobs, Rosa thinks:

[Generally recent Cuban-Jewish émigrés] get adjusted in the short term, and they start working hard, and they get involved faster than the rest of the Cubans. . . . Today, for example, I heard about a factory, and the owners are Cuban Sephardics, and they hired three refugees from a government agency for refugees. And it was just today. But there were a lot of Jews, Sephardics from Miami Beach, working there [in the same positions as] the rest of the Cuban workers. So you know, every Jew is not always in the high levels.

. . . The rafters—whether they're Jews or not—they have more difficulty adapting to Miami than earlier arrivals. But they get involved in the end—in the shorter term or not. They get involved as normal residents. . . .

*Carrie:* And there's not tension between them and the Jewish-Cuban community?

*Rosa:* No, not at all. Not at all. Maybe it's my point of view, but it's mostly what I have noticed of these years, being here, that we [the Cuban-Jews] are adapted well, we don't have differences.

Jacob and Luisa partially fit Rosa's model. As Cuban-Jews, they found jobs within one year after arriving in the United States at a company specializing in clothing import and export. Owned by Cuban-Jews who arrived in Miami in the early 1960s, the company is filled with Cuban-Jews at all levels, from the Board of Directors to the warehouse positions, where Jacob loads and unloads boxes every day.

When Jacob initially revealed this information about his job in our interview, I became excited; it appeared that he and Luisa had found a niche within Miami, where perhaps they could take comfort from a sense of the cultural, ethnic, and religious solidarity surrounding them.

*Jacob:* We work for Cuban-Jews at a huge Hispanic corporation in Miami. And it's owned by Cuban-Jews. They make clothing and garments.

*Carrie:* Wow. So do they have a large Cuban-Jewish constituency working for them?

*Jacob:* Yes.

*Carrie:* That's so great. You must feel really comfortable there.

*Jacob:* Yes.

Later Jacob revealed, however, that the sense of solidarity I assumed existed at the company for him and Luisa, as Cuban-Jews, never became a full reality for them: "I have a job, thanks to the Cuban-Jews. [But] they gave me the most oppressing jobs. I didn't have an advantage, compared to other Cubans. No, I don't see any advantage in being Jewish in Miami. Maybe for other people, coming before, there was an advantage. . . . I prefer in the future, if I make money, to visit Israel. I will always be welcome there."

In a subsequent conversation, Jacob again commented on his strained relations with other Cuban-Jews at work: "One of the directors of the company where I work, he came to Miami in the early 1960s. He called me a Communist for remarks I made about the situation of human rights in some countries, including Cuba. In general, he tries to keep me very, very down. Things are improving a little, but—"

Indeed, as Rosa indicated, the fact that Jacob had had strong (previous) affiliations with Cuba's Communist party, both through his father and through his own activity, appeared to be the outstanding reason for his marginalization by Miami's Cuban-Jewish community. Did Rosa think that other recent émigrés integrated perfectly well into this community, as long as they took the "correct" political stance regarding the Castro government? The process did not seem to be so facile, something that Rosa confirmed for me later in our discussion, as she reflected on the community's immediate reaction to her own family's arrival in the Mariel boatlift in 1980:

> *Carrie:* So have you ever felt tension between your family, as Mariel émigrés, and the established Cuban-Jewish community of Miami Beach?
> *Rosa:* I have been mentioned [within the community as a possible Communist]. While I was arriving here—the moment that I arrived. They—the first ones [1960s émigrés]—mentioned that to me. As Jacob told you, it was the exact pattern. They have a pattern. It's like, "You came late, because you were Communist."

Rosa, however, was quick to qualify her statement. The Cuban-Jewish community's suspicion of her Communist leanings, she said, lasted only a brief time, for she and her family immediately "proved" themselves by effectively demonstrating their hatred of the Castro regime and justifying their "late" arrival in Miami:

> But let's say that they [the 1960s Cuban-Jewish émigrés in Miami] have a second [perspective], because in the case of my husband, he had to stay there [Cuba] because he was in the military. So they [her husband Raúl and others] were the [military] age. You couldn't move a finger if you were like twenty-one or twenty-two years old, and you had to serve in the military: you had to be there, whether you liked it or not. So maybe because my husband was young when we came—he was in his thirties—the community in Miami saw why we had stayed in Cuba. . . . He always— [my husband's] family, my husband—they always wanted to come here. So from the sixties, they couldn't move because of one reason or the other. But they were prepared to come. Maybe they [the 1960s émigrés] noticed that they weren't right [to assume that we were Communists]. We wanted to come to Miami all along.

## Berta Samopla

Jacob Lajapo recommended that I call a friend of his, Berta Samopla, to get another perspective on the situation of recent Cuban-Jewish émigrés in Miami. Berta, a Sephardic Jew who arrived in Miami in 1995, now lives in the Kendall section of Miami. One night, in broken English (the language she preferred to converse in), she told me of her dispiriting attempts to join the Cuban-Jewish community of Miami Beach, in both the Ashkenazic and the Sephardic realms.

*Carrie:* What is your relationship now with the Cuban-Jewish community in Miami, if any?

*Berta:* Now my relationship is nothing. Because once I went to the Miami Beach community—first the Ashkenazi, and afterwards the Sephardic—and I didn't have the opportunity to speak with the rabbi, because I came on a day that he wasn't there. I visited the [Torat Moshe] community asking for information, asking for some person to see, to meet, and to try to get to know other members of the community, because I was looking forward to meeting new Jewish friends. And in that opportunity, I asked for another person in the Sephardi community [Torat Moshe], I didn't have any opportunity to meet another person. I only saw a woman there, and she spoke with me, and said that they celebrate some festivities, but not all the time. And she explained that during the day, the other people are working. And in conclusion, I didn't meet with any person— I explained to her, "I need to see one person here," to explain what would I want. Because I don't live near Miami Beach, I don't have now any car, and I have to [get a ride] with another person. And I wanted for them to tell me another [Jewish] community that would be easier for me [to get to] from here [my home in Kendall]. But I couldn't obtain that information. And I gave her my phone number, and I'm still waiting for them to call me back. I didn't go again, because in that moment I felt very sad. That's the problem. Because I couldn't find any person to help me. I thought that maybe they thought that I wanted money, I don't know. Because when every person [from Cuba] came here, another family or another person thought that the person would ask for money.

Or maybe they supposed that—you know, in Cuba, we have many problems—political problems. I'm not political, I don't have any relations with that, but here—they have maybe another idea about the problems. In general, when I think about these problems, I think that maybe they think that we stayed in Cuba for another reason, I don't know. Exactly I don't know what is the problem, but what we feel is that they don't want to relate, to maintain a relation with us [recent arrivals], in general. That is my impression. I don't know what is the problem really.

When I went to the Ashkenazi [Cuban-Hebrew Congregation], I met three or four persons—I felt better, a little better there. Because they have a secretary, and she gave me the address of the other synagogue [in my neighborhood in Kendall]. She said, "And if you have time, whenever you want, maybe one Saturday or Shabbat you can come here." It was different. It was better.

These were the two moments here in my life, since I came, that I tried to meet with the Jewish community. Afterwards I decided to maintain

here—maybe in the future, when I have the opportunity to talk with
Jacob Lajapo—sometimes he visits another synagogue, and maybe in the
future we will go to that synagogue. I don't know exactly where is that
synagogue, but it's not in Miami Beach.

I know here another [Jewish] person. And it was better for me, too;
she called me, and I called back to her. She lives far away from here. But
[when] she called me, [I felt] better. Some [Jewish] people that I know,
we have the opportunity to talk and other things. But exactly with the
Cuban-Jewish community it's not the same. Well, it's not good to gener-
alize, because it was one time. But in that moment [at Torat Moshe], I
didn't meet another person. I felt different, because here it is not easy
for us to establish, or to begin—to walk. And there are many things
that I'm very sad and upset about. We had a different life in Cuba; in
the [Jewish] community, it was better. We learned to know each other,
um, *compartido* [shared]—I don't remember the name. *Compartíamos* [we
shared], in different ways. It was different. And when I came here, I felt
that many people like me [i.e., recent Cuban-Jewish émigrés] think that
same idea, that maybe we [would] meet the same persons here [i.e., have
the same feeling of togetherness with the Cuban-Jewish community in
Miami that we shared in the Jewish community in Havana]. But I don't
feel that now. I feel that it is a different society, but I don't know. I
don't know what happened. But I hope that maybe in the future, things
will change. I don't know. In the moment, I don't have any time to dedicate, to look for another synagogue now. But I am planning to visit near
from here, to look for a community of [Jewish] Americans. Maybe it
will be better, I don't know.

. . . [The more established Cuban-Jews, who have lived in the United
States for decades] must know that not all of the [Cuban] people have
the same opportunity to go away at the same time. For example, I had a
different problem than the other ones. Maybe if the situation was different twenty years before, when my father was alive, maybe things
would be different. But we had many problems in the family, especially
with the health of my own father. He had three heart attacks. And
many situations with his health. And this is one of the problems. And
another one with the family: you know, one person wants to move, and
another doesn't want it; or at one moment, the person can't do it. And
it's difficult that all the persons that moved at the same time [i.e., all the
1960s émigrés] had the same opportunity. My case was different. . . . I
had other things: when the Revolution came in January, my grandfather,
he decided not to eat until he died. And the people [1960s émigrés]
think that all the people that stayed in Cuba were Communists. I don't

know. We have another problem, because maybe here [in Miami], some people think differently [than the "exile mentality"]. And they [right-wing hard-liners] have to [be] reminded that here, it's a free country. Many people have a choice to think what they want. It's not my case [i.e., I'm not Communist], but I think that they don't have the power to give any opinion. Because each case has—or had—a specific problem. Every person has to listen to, or to know, what happened with that person. Not all the people are the same.

## Ethnic Labels and Family (Re)Unification

What can be concluded from reviewing the stories of Jacob and Luisa, Luis, Albert, Rosa, and Berta? Clearly, no consensus emerged regarding the relationship of recent Cuban Jewish arrivals to the larger Cuban-Jewish—now Jewban—community of Miami Beach. What does emerge in all these stories—with the exception of Rosa's—is a sense of ambiguity and uncertainty for these people in understanding their positions, if any, within the larger community structure. With the members of this community they share a common ethnic label: Cuban Jew. What this designation means for individuals, though, may vary infinitely.

This discussion particularly highlights the problems inherent in general conclusions about the constituency of a community, based upon its most prominent figures or even its majority viewpoint. The identity that any given individual may assume needs to be expressed in words. Not surprisingly, the label that an individual may apply to herself may be chosen by another person, but understood in a completely different way by this person. Often a tacit assumption is made, sometimes falsely, that these individuals share core characteristics.

Judith Butler discusses these identity issues as they surround problems in understanding the categories of *women* and *feminism*, and notions of the female body, in her article, "Contingent Foundations: Feminism and the Question of 'Postmodernism.'" Butler argues that the "minute that the category of *women* is invoked as describing the constituency for which feminism speaks, an internal debate invariably begins over what the descriptive content of that term [*women*] will be" (1992: 15). While some people view the category of *women* as specifying those who are inherently childbearers and caregivers, she contends, others see this category as a social and cultural construction which can be altered. Butler continues, "I would argue that any effort to give universal or specific content to the category of women, presuming that the guarantee of solidarity is required *in advance*, will necessarily produce factionalization, and that 'identity' as a point of departure can never hold as the solidifying ground of a feminist political movement. Identity categories are never merely descriptive, but always normative, and as such, exclusionary" (1992: 15–16; emphasis in original).

Butler's argument offers a cogent model for understanding the complexities of not only the Cuban-Jewish community, but also all groups characterized by a set of shared attributes, interests, or features. In fact, we easily can substitute the labels "Cuban-Jew" or "Cuban-Jewish" for Butler's "women" or "feminine." In doing so, we begin to see the dangers inherent in constructing a "model Cuban-Jew"—and, furthermore, in expecting those who do not immediately fit into this paradigm to fall into it eventually. Just as "women's" identity "can never hold as the solidifying ground of a feminist political movement" (15–16) because of its openness to multiple interpretations, neither can a singular "Cuban-Jewish" identity hold as the solidifying ground representing all Jews from Cuba living in Miami. This does not mean that either category is useless; the terms "women" and "Cuban-Jew" should continue to be used, though with the understanding that they designate "undesignatable field[s] of differences" and thus become sites "of permanent openness and resignifiability" (16). In this way, these terms allow for the inclusion of multiple positions and experiences within a common framework. They suggest, for instance, the points of intersection and the places of divergence in the experiences of recent Cuban Jewish arrivals and 1960s Cuban Jewish émigrés.

The Jewish community in Cuba today, which numbers less than one thousand, shares little with the present-day Cuban-Jewish community of Miami, which numbers approximately ten thousand (Chardy 1990: 4B). More than four decades separates the communities—geographically, physically, and, in a more complicated way, emotionally. The most recent Cuban-Jewish émigrés in Miami occupy a liminal position between these now-foreign groups, although by no means do they serve as a bridge between the two. Furthermore, their status *as Cuban-Jews*—or perhaps *Jewish Cubans*—does not serve as an immediate ticket into the established community in Miami Beach.

The Cuban-Jewish "extended family" discussed by Benjamín Cohen and Damien Losger in the beginning of this chapter needs to be reconsidered in these terms. A family, as it traditionally has been understood, is a social unit which generally shares a (family) name and is characterized by both unity/harmony *and* division/disagreement. Perhaps the most salient mark of the family is the explicit and consensual agreement among all family members that each indeed forms part of a larger whole.

This model of the family often is applied to a given community in the context of "extended family"—a larger group which encompasses many smaller, nuclear families. What the "extended family" does not include are those who in theory may be "relatives" but who have chosen to separate themselves from the larger family structure. Indeed, this is the way much of the Cuban-Jewish community—and much of the larger Cuban exile community in Miami—understands the situation of recent Cuban émigrés. As discussed earlier, much of the exile community points to these émigrés as economic immigrants rather than political refugees: these people willingly *chose* to remain in Cuba, and they migrate to the United States only in the hope of finding economic security. Thus, older exiles feel, these recent arrivals must not be allowed to join the extended family/families whose foundations are erected precisely upon the basis of political exile from the *patria*.

As Jacob Lajapo, Rosa Levy, and Berta Samopla emphasize, the reasons behind migration at a specific point in time are multifaceted and complex; they cannot be understood solely in terms of individual "choice." Migration involves family concerns, political and economic concerns, and ideological concerns, among others. Before emigrating, émigrés may ask themselves profound questions relating to their positions in the world. What are the effects of pre-planned migrations on migrants' political, economic, and social statuses before leaving the island? What will these statuses be upon arrival in the destination country? What will be the political, economic, social, and ideological consequences of their migrations for their family members who remain on the island? What will be the effects of their migrations on their personal or group ideology(ies)?

There is a fundamental disagreement, or perhaps misunderstanding, between many recent Cuban émigrés and much of the established Cuban exile community over who should have access to this powerful community and to the numerous organizations and institutions which have some connection with it. While recent arrivals may classify themselves as political exiles, the established, "official" exile community often refuses to view the newcomers as such.

The Cuban-Jewish community of Miami Beach has numerous ties to this larger "Cuban" structure and treads carefully on its political turf. Thus, this smaller community must confront the issue of recent arrivals, as well as the issue of relations with the island itself, both from within its own boundaries and from its position as a small group within the larger Cuban exile community. In her article, "A Revolution of Faith," Sue Fishkoff focuses on this issue as it relates to the Cuban-Jewish community's relations with the Jewish community remaining on the island:

> Communication between Cuban-Jewish exiles in Miami and their
> brethren in Havana is sporadic, carried on on an individual, rather than a
> community basis. . . . In fact, the Cuban Jews of Miami foment much of
> the secrecy themselves, torn between their desire to help their relatives
> stuck in Cuba[10] and a wish not to alienate the powerful, fervently anti-
> Castro Cuban-American National Foundation, which represents the voice
> of two million Cuban exiles in America. Many are also haunted by the
> memories of what they fled three decades ago. (1993: 10)

Our consideration of this link, and the resulting relationship, between the Cuban-Jewish community (composed primarily of self-declared political exiles of the 1960s era) and the larger "official" Cuban exile community (represented most powerfully by the Cuban American National Foundation) allows us to consider further where "family ties" lie. Indeed, it appears that, for Cuban-Jews, the "exile family" which has developed in Miami over the past thirty-nine years takes precedence over any notion of a "religious family." In theory, the Jews in Cuba and recent Jewish Cuban arrivals in Miami share a religion and a common cultural/national background with the established Cuban-Jewish community. Nevertheless, this latter community is hesitant to ratify the former two groups as "family," since they have "chosen" to live under Communism and thus to challenge the political and ideological foundations of Miami's Cuban exile community. Furthermore, in making this "choice," they have grown up in a Cuba which is foreign to the 1960s émigrés. The Cuban Revolution indeed revolutionized Cuba, and the generations who have grown up under Communist rule differ dramatically from the generations who have grown up on the other side of the Florida Straits.

Are recent Jewish Cuban émigrés, then, part of the "Cuban-Jewish family?" Based on the five testimonies presented above, it appears that arrival in the "second homeland" of Miami does not automatically guarantee these people a place in the "extended family" as "distant cousins" or even "foster children." Before they can be accepted, a mutual agreement needs to be reached, one in which both the community and the émigrés agree to exist in unity/harmony as members of the same family. Only after this can the division/disagreement aspect of family life be dealt with.

Jacob, Rosa, Albert, and Berta address this issue in their narratives. They contend that the Cuban-Jewish community is highly suspicious of recent émigrés upon their arrival in Miami; it associates these arrivals first and foremost with Castro and Communism. Rosa's and Albert's accounts demonstrate, however, that it is possible for relations between the "other" Jewish Cubans and the Cuban-Jewish/Jewban "family" to be (re)established. These two stories broaden our picture of the Cuban-Jewish "extended family" in Miami and allow us to see avenues through which those who feel excluded from the community eventually may become part of it.

Near the middle of our conversation, Berta interrupted her extensive narrative to direct a question toward me: "Excuse me. In general, when you talk with the other people, do you receive the same information about the Cuban-Jewish community in Miami Beach? For example, the people who have come here within the last five years—do they feel the same?"

To Berta, it was very important to contextualize the feelings of rejection she felt after visiting Torat Moshe and the Cuban-Hebrew Congregation, so that she could reframe the questions she had mulled over since those encounters. What had caused the community's distant and estranged reaction toward her, she wondered? Was this a personal issue or a larger one, centering on her status as a recent Cuban émigré? I related Luis Tirani's story to her; she was already familiar with Jacob's. Then I continued with Albert Ralvey's and Rosa Levy's recollections. After I chronicled Rosa's story of the Cuban-Jewish community's eventual acceptance of her own family, Berta paused. Her voice changed to a reassured and hopeful tone: "Really?"

Indeed, hearing of a Marielita's ability to resolve a situation that seemed similar to her own gave Berta hope for the future. This narrative told her that the possibility of entering "the family" might eventually be open to her. More important, it told her that perhaps the presuppositions of the Cuban exile community were not cast in stone; perhaps family relations could shift over time and the "other" Jewish Cubans eventually could connect with Miami's Cuban-Jews.

# Chapter 7

## Transformations of *Jubanidad:*
## Forecasts for the Cuban-Jewish Community

*[We are] the major tri-lingual and tri-cultural Jewish community in the area. . . . It is difficult to predict what the future will bring to the Cuban Jewish community. We are beset for the first time with the pressure of an "open society" and life in the "melting pot." As with all American Jewish communities, it will become increasingly difficult to maintain our integrity as Jews, and as Cuban-Jews. . . . We look forward to the next thirty years with an optimism born of the realization that we are the children and grandchildren of "survivors," those gigantic, near mythological men and women who survived two exiles in one lifetime but prospered against all odds, whose grand history, which spans three cultures and constitutes a microcosm of all Jewish history, will soon be written so that future generations may be encouraged and inspired.*

—*Rabbi Barry Konovitch, "Cuban American Jews"*

*Let me put something in perspective. When my grandparents and great-grandparents left Europe, the first generation spoke Polish or Russian or Hungarian or whatever, in addition to Yiddish. The next generation—miracle of miracles—was American. The same thing happened (is happening) to the Cuban-Jewish community, except it happened twice. When they left Europe, they kept Yiddish and learned Spanish in Cuba. Now, there is a second exile for the same people, and they learned English. We are witnessing today [in the Cuban-Jewish community] what happened in this country to Jewish immigrants after the 1920s. We aren't Polish-Jewish or Russian-Jewish or German-Jewish anymore, we're American Jews, and there is no natural connection in our generation between individual Jews whose grandparents came from the same country, except in unusual situations.*

—*David Hochman, first non-Cuban/non-Latino member of the Board of Directors, Cuban-Hebrew Congregation*

## Creating the Future

A community must deal with the future on two levels: individual and group. These levels intersect each other at numerous locales and determine the community structure itself—its ideology, goals, leaders, institutions, and relationship with the outside world. How is the future understood by any given community? Is it open to manipulation by social agents, or does it more closely resemble a fixed destiny which, in time, the community inevitably will confront? If the community sees itself occupying a position of agency, what means does it use to influence and manipulate the future it visualizes? If it sees itself subject to the decisions of a more powerful and incontestable force, how does it prepare for the future?

Upon closer examination of one specific community (the Cuban-Jewish community of Miami Beach), we begin to see how theoretically sound models of the future begin to break down in the face of real-life complexities. What becomes evident in such a consideration is the lack of any single agreed-upon conception of the community's future. Predictions of the future are products of individual experience. Such experience is, in part, the product of larger phenomena, such as gender, age, socioeconomic status, sub-ethnic group, time of arrival in the United States, and area of residence within South Florida. Predictions also are created through individual memories of the birth of the community in Cuba, important events in its history, the arrival of Jewish Cubans in Miami, and the development of the Cuban-Jewish/Jewban/Juban community. These memories are interactive, for they merge individual experience with oral and written history to yield an anamnestic composite.

## The Losger Family: Generational Change and Continuity

As I discussed the future of the Cuban-Jewish community with Rafael and Elena Losger, active members of the Cuban-Hebrew Congregation, I came to understand the dramatic shifts in worldview experienced by Cuban-Jews throughout this century. With the migration of Jews from the "Old World" of Eastern Europe to the "New World" of Cuba, and with the subsequent Jewish migration from this tropical paradise to the United States, they explain, Cuban-Jews' perspectives on culture and identity changed. Thus, a *polaca* born in Cuba or Miami has little, if any, connection with Eastern Europe, which she may associate primarily with the Holocaust, rather than viewing it as a "homeland."

> *Rafael:* Even our parents and grandparents, the ones that immigrated [to Cuba], they had the Cuban experience, they enjoyed it, they loved it.
> *Elena:* They became Cuban.
> *Rafael:* Cubans were very warm, nice, open-minded people. They [the Jews] were well received. Because of circumstances, they maintained—it was like a ghetto—I'm using ghetto in the good sense of the word—we kept together as a community, in our studies and our prayers, in our celebrations and our sorrows. And once we came to the United States, it didn't change. It has been changing lately. In the beginning, in the first ten or fifteen years, there was a tremendous continuity—not that we don't have it today—of what Cuba used to be. People knew each other, people knew of each other—

*Elena:* We would marry only other Cuban Jews; there weren't that many intermarriages [i.e., marriages between Sephardim and Ashkenazim, or between Jews of different nationalities] like we have now.

*Rafael:* Many years ago, there was a cultural difference [between Sephardim and Ashkenazim], and lately (the last thirty years) it's completely gone with the wind. Many of our friends are marriages of Sephardim and Ashkenazim.

*Elena:* Many years ago, there used to be, like, the Ashkenazim would marry the Ashkenazim, and the Sephardim would marry the Sephardim [in Cuba].

*Rafael:* And even here in the beginning. But still, the Sephardim maintain their own temple, and preservation of the culture. I enjoy it very much—I can go to a Sephardic temple and I feel at home, and vice-versa. So there's no major difference, . . . that bridge has been crossed. The major situation that we as a Cuban Jewish community have is the normal and natural assimilation of our children into the American culture, which dilutes that controlled structure that we had. Still you find that type of situation—you go to Panama, the community is that way, Mexico, Venezuela. [In these places] where the Jews are a very small minority, they tend to be very together, very introspective, very into themselves, and they don't go much out of the community—I don't mean with friends, or whatever, but at least for marriages and for the cultural situation and things of that order. So now what's been happening, at least in my case: my children know about Cuba, they speak a certain amount of Spanish, they like rice and beans [laughs]; but for all intents and purposes, they are Americans. I may tell them about Cuba, I may try to express my love for Cuba, the culture and its values, but it's hard for them to grasp it, because they don't have that experience. The hands-on experience is what makes you feel love, hate—something—and they just don't have it.

Some of our people in the community believe that, yes, you can pass it on. Case in point: hypothetically, we had this conversation, the Board of Directors of the Cuban-Hebrew Congregation. We are now called the "Cuban-Hebrew Congregation," rightfully so, for many years, God willing. But eventually, ten years from now, twenty years from now, it may not be anymore the "Cuban"—once our elders pass away, and our children are—quote—Americans, maybe they don't have the need to be a Cuban-Hebrew Congregation. So, instead, the Cuban-Hebrew Congregation should perhaps be "Temple Beth Shmuel": a temple for all Jews, not only Cuban-Jews, which is the main reason for the temple to exist. It started as a social, religious gathering hall—El Círculo—where also religion came to play part of it. That need for the social part of it is less and less, as we—Even our generation, we mingle more with Americans! We still go back to the Cuban-Hebrew Congregation. Basically there is no more the need that we had twenty-five years ago. It's the normal evolution of things. I would love to conserve it forever and ever as a Cuban-Hebrew Congregation; I don't know if that is going to happen. Who is to know?

*Carrie:* How do you feel that your kids don't have that love for Cuba?

*Elena:* It doesn't bother me, because I don't have that love for Poland—that's where my parents came from. To me, Poland means nothing. So I understand my kids not feeling anything for Cuba, because they have never been in Cuba. It's just that they happen to be Cuban.

*Carrie:* None of them were born in Cuba?

*Rafael:* No, none of them were born [in Cuba]. As a matter of fact—see, this is what happened. Since 1960, the last thirty-five years, 95 percent of all Cuban Jews have been born out of Cuba—in the United States, Puerto Rico, some in Israel, some in Venezuela. So how do you continue the link? It's very hard. It's not that they don't feel at all about Cuba—there's no way they can have the same warmth in the heart, the love for the culture, as the preceding generation. There is no way. And I understand it fully. And whoever doesn't want to understand it—you know, you want to maintain certain things, and sometimes it doesn't work.

*Carrie:* [to Rafael] So do you feel the same way as your wife, that this is the way things happen, that it's bound to happen?

*Rafael:* Well, I'm sure that, if Cuba would gain its liberty again—its democracy—my children would love to go back to Cuba, see the place where their parents were born, where they might have been born, and that rings a special place in their hearts for them. But when it comes to that tremendous feeling—that Cuban feeling—I don't think they have it, and I understand it totally. Once we lose— See, right now, the generation that came to Cuba in the 1930s: obviously, in the next five, ten, fifteen years, it's going to disappear. Then we're going to be left with the generation that was born in Cuba. And after that, unless things change drastically and some of us go back to Cuba, it's going to dwindle. There is a Cuban Jewish community in Cuba. One thousand newcomers, people who found Judaism again, and perhaps they'll continue the—quote—Cuban Jewish tradition. But I don't think it can be done from the United States, or from Puerto Rico.

. . . The Cuban community has . . . assimilated, integrated with the American Jewish community. As a matter of fact, a lot of our children are not getting married to Cubans—they're getting married to people from other countries: Americans, Colombians, Argentinians, and even then [in marriages to Latin Americans] they lose the Cuban feeling. It's only natural, normal that that would happen.

Rafael and Elena begin their discussion of Miami's Cuban-Jewish community in Havana in the 1920s. Quickly they shift to the community's beginnings in the United States—in both New York and Miami—and relations between Cuban Sephardim and Ashkenazim. Soon they shift again into the present and then to other Jewish communities throughout Latin America today. Only after covering the temporal spaces of past and present and the physical space of the Americas can the conversation shift to the future—the future of the Cuban-Hebrew Congregation specifically and the future of all second-generation Jewbans more generally. The future then brings us back full circle, to the now-mythical place where the community began. If given the opportunity, could the Cuban-Jewish community of Miami Beach, which now has emerged as something unique and separate from the Jewish community of Havana, ever renew itself in the *patria*?

By referring to the younger generation of Jewbans in quotation marks, as "Americans," Rafael points to an important distinction emphasized in chapter 6. The "Cuban-Jewish" and "Jewban" traditions must be understood outside their literal contexts, apart from these labels' implication that all Jews of Cuban heritage are necessarily "Cuban-Jews"/"Jewbans" and thus are equal parts of a unified whole. Rafael suggests that, even if Judaism can be maintained on the island—in and of itself a questionable assumption—this necessarily would be a different form of "Cuban Judaism" than is familiar to nearly ten thousand Cuban-Jews living in Miami today. Even if the younger generation of Jewbans returns to a democratic island at some future time, after Castro no longer is in power, Rafael maintains, it could not recreate the community which developed in Miami Beach under unique and unrepeatable circumstances.

Jacob Lajapo, an active member of Cuba's Jewish community before his emigration in 1993, agreed with Rafael. Jacob felt that those Cuban émigrés who had not had physical contact with the island since the 1960s do not know present-day Cuba. Their view of Cuba is anachronistic. They never can return to the Cuba they know: the Cuba of memory. Hopes of returning and recreating what once was there, he thinks, are mere pipe dreams: "Most exiles, people who were in [Cuban] prison, people who came here in the sixties, they don't know Cuba has changed, the population has changed. They want to come back to pre-Castro Cuba. It's impossible. . . . The Cuba they knew disappeared."

The Cuba of yesterday nevertheless lives on in the present-day Cuban-Jewish community. In Miami Beach, the Cuban-Hebrew Congregation occupies a preeminent role in the Cuban-Jewish community, through both its name and the Cuba-related activities with which it is involved.[1] Torat Moshe, although it has relinquished its appellation as the Cuban Sephardic Hebrew Congregation (so as not to exclude non-Cuban Sephardim), proudly hosts the *Noche Cubana*, a social event filled with food and music reminiscent of the *patria*. Cuban-Jews mark their uniqueness through their active role in the Greater Miami Jewish Federation's Cuban/Latin Division.[2] The Cuba of old is constantly brought up in both religious and social contexts. For example, the Cuban-Hebrew Congregation's bulletin for October–December 1996 comments on a recent art auction sponsored by the congregation's Art Auction Committee. This event, members of the congregation noted fondly, "reminded us [of] the social Tuesdays in the Patronato back in the 'good old days'" (Edelstein 1996: 5). Indeed, collective memory serves the community well, for it consolidates history and memory into a meaningful present—a present which facilitates the maintenance of Cuban-Jewish/Jewban identity.

Rafael (who is in his fifties) wonders whether this identity can be carried into the future if it remains outside the Cuban "homeland." Is it possible for the second generation to identify as "Cuban-Jews," when, as Rafael contends, "for all intents and purposes, they are Americans"? Once his own generation passes away, Rafael thinks, there will be no one to continue the unique Cuban-Jewish culture that arose through the process of displacement, resettlement, and community development. Furthermore, the primary function of the original community, embedded within the name Círculo Cubano-Hebreo (Cuban-Hebrew Social Circle), plays an ever-diminishing role in the lives of its members, particularly the younger generations. They socialize with, date, and marry Jews (and, to a lesser extent, Gentiles), from the United States and other Latin American countries, he emphasizes, in a natural process of assimilation. Rafael's comment illustrates, too, how relations between Cuban and American Jews have improved since the 1960s, when American Jews looked with disdain upon their Cuban coreligionists; in Rafael's words, when "you were foreign, you had an accent, you were not one of us." In the face of the second generation's "Americanization," the Cuban-Jewish identity that was maintained for nearly four decades through the Cuban-Hebrew Congregation, Torat Moshe, and the community surrounding these institutions may evolve or perhaps simply disappear.

The first place this identity shift will be seen, Rafael guesses, is in the name of the Cuban-Hebrew Congregation. Indeed, such a name change already has taken place with the Cuban Sephardic Hebrew Congregation–Temple Moses. As Susana Hamla told me, "We didn't want to sound like we were only Cuban, so we renamed it to 'Sephardic Congregation of Florida.'" Although the motivation behind the Sephardic congregation's name change was to allow the synagogue to welcome Sephardim of all nationalities (a much different reason for removing the "Cuban" designation than the reason Rafael proposes, which focuses on the Americanization of young Cuban-Jews), this still serves as a precedent for the Cuban-Hebrew Congregation.

Rafael's twenty-one-year-old son, Damien, chose to discuss the subject of his community's future as we ate in a small café. For the preceding hour, Damien had emphasized the community's past and present solidarity and the strong bonds between himself and other Jewbans his age with whom he grew up. Discussing the future, however, Damien contrasted the "one of a kind" bonds between his parents and other Cuban-Jews of their generation with the strong bonds between himself and his Jewban "extended family." The latter, he predicted, will "fade more and more" in the future. In discussing the importance of togetherness, Damien shifted from present to future. Mulling over his turkey sandwich, he seemed both confident and uncertain.

> I think all the Jewish-Cuban families are the same. I think that's why the kids get along so well, 'cause we've all been to do the same things, we've all experienced the same things; all of our parents are very similar. So I think that's why we've kept this group going.
>
> But I definitely think that the kind of bond that my parents' generation has is one of a kind. I don't think it will ever be like that again. For the reasons I explained earlier. They were all born in Cuba; my grandparents weren't. So as for my grandparents' group of friends, they didn't have that group of friends that were all Cuban. My parents and their friends—they're all Cuban, they just have these incredible bonds. But I think as time goes by, it's going to fade more and more. I'm meeting all my American friends, and assimilating to what's going on now. I think they needed that bond when they first came to this country, because they were alone, they were strangers, they relied on each other. And now, we don't need it so much. We're established, we're a part of the [Miami Jewish] community, we don't need to stick together as much.

By now, Damien's words were familiar to me. Not only did he seem to have the same perspective as his parents, but his words echoed throughout the community, across generations. There was no longer a pressing "need," I repeatedly heard, for a Cuban-Jewish community; its future survival therefore remained uncertain at best. Expecting Damien to shift the discussion toward the Cuban-Hebrew Congregation, I related what Rafael had told me about the Board of Directors meeting:

> *Carrie:* Your dad was talking about a Board of Directors meeting, where they discussed what would happen in ten or fifteen years to the congregation, when the younger generation has taken over. Are they going

to change the Cuban-Hebrew Congregation? Your dad seems pretty realistic, and he said, "Let's be realistic. Why should they keep the name 'Cuban-Hebrew' when they're all going to be married to American Jews, or (not even American) Jews."

 *Damien:* [surprised] I think things like the name will stay. I wouldn't even *think* about changing it. I'm actually surprised to hear that. Regardless of who I marry, I mean, that's the *Jewish-Cuban Congregation.*[3] If you want to be a part of another congregation, then fine. But if you're going to be part of that congregation, you don't have to be Jewish-Cuban; but you're not going to go in there and change its name. People that come into our country, they've got to become part of our country. Definitely they influence and change it, a little bit, but we're still America—it's not gong to become something different. I think that the traditions and undertones should always stay the same. As far as things like that. As far as everyday living, I think those things are going to change more. And the names: the name is going to stay, but what it means and what's really going on is going to change.

Changes within the Cuban-Jewish community, Damien thinks, will occur on an individual basis, but a change in the community's formal structure is unthinkable. The necessity for social and cultural solidarity no longer is a factor in Cuban-Jewish identity, he stresses; echoing his father, Damien points to the assimilation of most community members (especially the younger generations) into "American" and, even more, "American Jewish" society. For Damien, the phrase "Cuban-Jewish" no longer serves to designate the excluded or separate "Other"—Other, that is, to American, Cuban-American, and, most importantly, American Jewish society. Instead, it is a label which evokes an identity shared between generations—an identity in which, Damien says, "the Cuban part is definitely combined with the Jewish part—they're not two separate things."

This "Cuban-Jewishness" Damien sees as the crux of his own identity. Thus, the thought of altering the very symbol of this identity—the name of the Cuban-Hebrew Congregation itself—disturbs him profoundly.[4] For him, the formal structure of the community today no longer rests upon the need for social and cultural solace in the face of displacement and adversity; rather, it rests upon tradition and upon reinforcing the bonds that tie the community together.

For Damien, maintaining this formal community structure is more like a moral imperative than a casual decision. He compares the Cuban-Hebrew Congregation to the United States of America; while both may experience challenges to their founding principles, he contends, this gives no one the "right" to challenge or change the traditions, customs, and formal names which represent their most fundamental characteristics. While

Damien sees the assimilation of Cuban-Jews into American Jewish society as inevitable, he condemns attempts by "foreigners"—whether they are spouses, friends, or strangers to Cuban-Jews—to shake Cuban-Jewish unity by manipulating its representative structure. Damien's concern over another group's power and influence on an established unity strikingly recalls Albert Ralvey's discussion (in chapter 5) of the requisites for Israeli citizenship. While Jews will bring their Diasporic experiences and cultures into Israel when they make *aliyah* and become Israeli citizens, Albert contends, their primary loyalty must be to the Israeli nation-state. By no means may these newcomers even consider changing Israel's formal structure to make that nation resemble more closely their "original" homeland. Both Damien's and Albert's discussions assume that an ideal form—of the Cuban-Hebrew Congregation (and, by extension, the Cuban-Jewish community) and of the nation of Israel, respectively—indeed exists *now*. Other groups may have access to this structure, they think, but they should not be allowed to alter it by imposing upon it their own cultural traditions.

Rafael and Damien Losger, then, relate to the present Cuban-Jewish community in markedly different ways. For Rafael, the "hands-on experience" in Cuba—"what makes you feel love, hate, something"—forms the crux of the Cuban-Jewish experience in Miami. The development and reconfiguration of the community in Miami, he feels, must be understood in these terms. For Damien, however, "Cuban-Jewishness" is something which unquestionably is rooted in Miami. While it may make (obligatory) reference to the Cuba of old, this unique identity is rooted most firmly in the place where it holds contextual and personal meaning for him. Like Poland (the place to which the Losgers trace their roots), Cuba functions only as a vague and far-away reference. It holds little meaning for Damien as a Cuban-Jew: "I definitely don't feel ties to Cuba; like, I don't want to go there. It's just like any other country to me. Like Poland—what the hell am I going to do in Poland [laughs]?"

Thus, we see the roots of Rafael's and Damien's divergent forecasts for the Cuban-Hebrew Congregation. For Rafael, "Cuban" and "Hebrew" can—and must—be separated within this institutional name. Through experience, his children and other Cuban-Jews of their generation have known Judaism first hand: they have been educated in Hebrew School, had Bar/Bat Mitzvot, attended synagogue services, and visited Israel. Even so, they are not "Cubans." For the most part, they were born in the United States and know Cuba only through the first generation's stories of the island.

For Damien, on the other hand, "Cuban" and "Hebrew" are inextricably fused to form an identity which cannot be characterized by either of its two components.

The concept of Cuba alone is foreign and uninteresting to him, and it has little to do with Cuban-Jewishness as he knows it. For Damien, "Cuban" functions merely as a nominal component of an entirely different identity, one to which he does not relate. While he relates to Jewish life in Miami generally, he feels a special connection to the form of Jewishness expressed in the Cuban-Jewish community. Thus he embraces the "Jewban" identity, for it signifies the fused twin identities of "Cuban" and "Jewish" and locates this fusion within Miami.

## Jewish Generation X

The year 1996 was an important year for the Cuban-Jewish community. Faced with a continually dwindling turnout of young people at synagogue services and functions, community leaders at Torat Moshe–Sephardic Congregation of Florida, Cuban-Hebrew Congregation–Temple Beth Shmuel, and Temple Menorah met to brainstorm possibilities for future joint initiatives by the three congregations geared to the community's younger generations. The purpose was explicitly religious. What could be done, the leaders asked, to revive the second generation, to (re)awaken young people's interest in Judaism? Surrounding this concern was the larger issue of the Cuban-Jewish community's future. Where would it be in twenty years, as both a religious and a social/cultural community, if its leaders could not draw young people back to the community in which they had participated as youngsters?

These concerns were nothing new for the community. As noted in chapter 2, it had struggled with them even in the 1960s and 1970s.[5] In 1996, however, they were more pressing than ever. Much of the oldest generation already had passed on, and the younger generation—those who had grown up within the community in Miami—was not moving in to fill the empty spaces.

Hopeful that the younger generation simply needed a forum through which it could become involved in Jewish life, this group of community leaders proposed a solution: a social group that would function as a space in which a Jewish spirit could be stimulated. This group subsequently was named "Jewish Generation X (J/X)." David Hochman, its organizer and the first non-Latino member of the Cuban-Hebrew Congregation's Board of Directors, describes it in the Cuban-Hebrew Congregation's 1996 bulletin:

> "Generation X" is the popular label for the post–baby-boom generation, young people roughly in their twenties and early thirties. Why "X"? To indicate that it's the indefinable, lost generation—they don't think alike or act alike, and aren't easy to analyze or classify. And for Jews of Generation X, there isn't much that addresses their needs, or promotes their affiliation with the Jewish community.

Until now. "Jewish Generation X (J/X)" is the name of the initiative between Temple Beth Shmuel, Temple Menorah, and Congregation Torat Moshe to foster Jewish continuity in the lost generation. With a focus on ages 22 to 35, and a selection of events in and out of the synagogues, both social and cultural, many young people will find it comfortable to affiliate with a synagogue and become active in the community. . . . With the continued support of the 3 congregations, the lost generation will find a place as active members of the Jewish community. (Hochman 1996: 9)

Hochman notes that J/X is meant for both singles and married couples. J/X events have both religious and secular formats; they include Hanukkah parties and occasional Shabbat dinners, as well as bowling, horseback riding, and ice-skating.

In a letter dated April 18, 1997, Hochman stresses the *Jewish* nature of J/X: "About J/X, it's not about keeping Cuban-Jews together, but all young Jews in Miami Beach together." It is important to note that Miami Beach has the largest concentration of synagogues in the Greater Miami area, and that the Cuban-Hebrew Congregation lies nearly five miles from Torat Moshe and Temple Menorah. The choice of joining the three "Cuban" synagogues thus was not a decision based upon a scarcity of synagogues or upon geographical proximity; these three were chosen deliberately, because of their historical relationships and their common "Cuban" character. The very cultural and institutional context in which J/X was realized, then, marks it as an initiative with dual goals: to foster a sense of Jewish unity among young Jews of all ethnicities, and to revive the *Cuban-Jewish* spirit. Within the Cuban-Jewish community itself, these goals are continually reinterpreted and placed in a notably "Cuban-Jewish" context.

Within the Cuban-Jewish community during the summer of 1996, hopes for J/X were high. Those involved in community life immediately pointed to J/X when the topic of the community's future arose. A sense of revival and rejuvenation filled the community; finally, the second generation was showing an interest in returning to its roots, in socializing as Jews—and, some thought, *as Cuban-Jews*—within a specifically Jewish (and arguably Cuban-Jewish) setting. This attitude was captured potently in Torat Moshe's triannual bulletin, in the message from congregation President Moisés Jrade. Jrade focused specifically on the younger generation's renewed interest in affiliating with Torat Moshe, as demonstrated during Passover synagogue services that year:

La sinagoga estuvo llena durante los servicios de la mañana y de la noche; la asistencia fue récord y lo principal es que la mayoría eran personas jóvenes.

> La generación que nos va a relevar está respondiendo; están presentes
> en los servicios religiosas, sociales, [y] culturales, así como están
> trabajando con la junta directiva. Ya no tenemos miedo, ya no estamos
> preocupados, estamos seguros que el futuro será un éxito, como lo fue el
> pasado y como lo está siendo el presente.

> (The synagogue was filled during the morning and evening services;
> there was record attendance, and the main reason is that the majority
> consisted of young people.
>
> The generation who will succeed us is responding; they are present
> at religious services and social and cultural functions, and they are work-
> ing with the Board of Directors. Now we are not scared, now we are not
> worried, we are confident that the future will be a success, as the past was
> and as the present is.) (Jrade 1996: 2)

Eva Simazi, a past president of the Women's Committee of Torat Moshe, also focused on the future, and specifically on the efforts of J/X in reclaiming this future for the Cuban-Jewish community. Although her twenty-five-year-old son showed no interest in the group, Eva saw great potential in the initiative: "What I really like, which we are doing now, is the three temples are getting together. It's Menorah, Cuban-Hebrew, and Temple Moses. And that just started last year. Before, everybody was doing their own [thing]. If we do it like that, we would never have what we want for our children. Because if there's only ten kids here, where should I go? Well, let's get all the thirty together, under one roof. We are going in the right direction now."

By referring to "the three temples," Eva, too, framed J/X within a decidedly Cuban-Jewish context. Indeed, much of the community echoed Eva's stance: it was time to see all Cuban-Jews unite—Sephardim and Ashkenazim, Traditional and Conservative. These differences seemed trivial in the face of what many saw as an approaching cultural-religious death. Like David Hochman, most community members with whom I spoke emphasized the threat posed to the Jewish religion by modern society. This fear was associated with another fear: that of losing the very cultural context within which the Cuban-Jewish community knows Judaism.

J/X therefore was welcomed as a space in which the most vital form of community propagation could take place: selection of a spouse. It would allow those with a common background to realize their similarities in a setting which normally would not be available to them in a city as large as Miami, or even Miami Beach. Like many others, Eva explicitly linked J/X with the marital arena:

> *Carrie:* What about "Cuban-Jewish," is that very important to you,
> having your kids marry other Cuban-Jews?

*Eva:* I would prefer it. Why? Because there's so much things that we have in common. But it's not a main factor for the happiness of my children. I want my children to be happy, regardless. I would prefer it; I'm not going to be a hypocrite [and say I wouldn't]. Because again, when you get together, the traditions are the same. And we all know each other, it's like, my God! We all know each other. And then when you sit on the table and you reminisce, you are talking, "You remember this and that?" It's a lot to have in common.

J/X thus served as a medium through which a shared heritage might be continued into the future. Eva supported it every step of the way.

For some community members, however, the future proposed by J/X was not so promising. Many doubted the group's ability to reverse a process of secularization and Americanization which had begun so many years before. Susana Hamla expressed ambivalence about the group. While she supported the idea behind J/X, the way in which she spoke about it and her tone of voice indicated a skepticism concerning the possibility of its successful realization:

In the last seven months, there is a bond between [Torat Moshe and] Temple Menorah and Cuban-Hebrew Congregation, because in Temple Menorah there are a lot of Cuban Jews also, and Torat Moshe, and they make the commitment to help each other, to organize the youth, the younger generations, so they can go to parties and social functions together, so they meet each other. I know very little about that, but I've been to whatever they have done, when I can I go; but it's a good thing. I hear it's successful, I don't know what's going to happen. We try to help the young people as much as we can.

. . . We want them [the younger generation] to belong. They are by themselves—they don't belong to any community. We see their parents here, but they don't come. And we want to see young people so they don't mingle with non-Jewish people. We worry about that. It's a very difficult situation, and we look after that.

Susana, in fact, saw the future of the Cuban-Jewish community far from Miami Beach, and out of the realm of J/X:

With old people the community is going to die sooner or later. And that's why we [Torat Moshe] want to build another school in North Miami—that's one of our priorities now. Because the younger generation is moving north. We know that, in about fifteen, twenty years, this

community has to move up north, because if not, the old people will
die and the young people will be up north. They [the young people]
don't live in this area—it's too expensive here [in Miami Beach], and
there's too many old people for the young people to stay here.

Rather than attempting to salvage the remaining Cuban-Jewish community in
Miami Beach by luring the younger generations there, Susana suggests moving the entire
community—or at least that portion of the community which centers on this generation and the next—north, to the very area to which the young people are moving. In
her view, the community must reach out to the younger generations to determine what
these people want and where they want it. If the community waits for young people to
approach it, or simply attempts to reconfigure the current community structure
within Miami Beach, it risks losing its youth and thus its future.

Susana's hesitation about the prospects of J/X were not unfounded. By April
1997, the organization no longer was active; it was "dormant," in Hochman's words.
Simply not enough people had shown interest in J/X to sustain it. Moisés Jrade was
disappointed about this.

> *Moisés:* That [J/X] hasn't worked out.
> *Carrie:* Why do you think that is?
> *Moisés:* If I knew the answer, I would have corrected the problem. I
> don't know—it's a little difficult. I'm very puzzled about it. That has
> stopped completely at this point.

When we consider the forecasts for the Cuban-Jewish community given by much
of the younger generation, the apathetic response to J/X is understandable. Indeed,
many of them see the extinction of this community as inevitable. Outside Cuba, and
without their parents and grandparents, many think, the community has only a slim
chance of surviving. For these young people, efforts such as J/X are associated with
this dying community. While many are involved in Jewish groups in Greater Miami,
these do not include J/X or other groups run by the "Cuban" synagogues. Nineteen-
year-old Albert Ralvey, who works for the Israeli Consulate and is involved in Jewish
life outside his synagogue, Torat Moshe, sent me an E-mail message which makes this
point vividly: "Temple Moses is slowly dying. Although the membership hasn't
dropped off and High Holiday services are still packed, there are hardly any people
showing up on Saturdays. It is really sad."[6]

David Hochman uses equally dramatic language to emphasize the Americanization of Cuban-Jewish youth. As elderly Cuban-Jews die, he stresses, their culture
dies with them. Hochman, an Ashkenazic Jew, uses a culinary metaphor to convey the

shift in identity experienced by the younger generations: "The Cuban-Jewish community really is dying, because the people who identified themselves as Cuban-Jews are getting older. The last generation is in their forties and fifties now. Their children and grandchildren are apple pie, not flan."

Using language strikingly similar to that of Damien Losger, college-age Becky Levy discussed the future of Torat Moshe and the Cuban-Jewish community as death by "fading": "I think there is a Jewish-Cuban community, and I think my parents and grandparents are part of it, in Temple Moses and that area. Our [Cuban-Jewish] customs are fading away. And our generation moves on and on. And I think that, by the time we have kids, they're not going to identify themselves [as Cuban-Jews] at all. Or maybe their kids. So I think it's just going to fade away, the Cuban-Jews."

These narratives associate the Cuban-Jewish community with the past and the present, but not with the future. Damien, Albert, David, and Becky use images of death and disappearance to convey a message about the community's future, positing a vision diametrically opposed to the future Moisés Jrade forecasts in Torat Moshe's 1996 bulletin. Thus, while there is no consensus about the future of the community, an analysis of these narratives reveals a widespread expectation of a significant reconfiguration of the Cuban-Jewish community in Miami within the next thirty years. How this reconfiguration will actually work, and into which domains it will penetrate, are hotly contested issues.

## Rincón del Recuerdo

Nestled within the pages of Torat Moshe's May–August 1996 bulletin—pages filled with photos, stories, and anecdotes concerning the community that at present surrounds the congregation—lies the "Rincón del Recuerdo," the "Corner of Remembrance." Within this space, framed by graduation announcements, business cards, and a list of synagogue members' anniversaries, sits a faded black-and-white photograph of young men and women in dresses and suits, obviously taken in a foreign time and place. Confirming our suspicion that the photo is not "of here," the caption reads: "Apellidos en 1961." The names of thirty-six young people follow. After the names, the location and occasion are revealed. This is a photograph of the now-mythical Havana Macabi in 1961.

The placement of such a nostalgic image amid fragments reflecting the present is by no means coincidental. The effect is to evoke a sense of continuity with the past and to suggest, through this tangible image, what will be lost if the younger generation fails to take pride in its Cuban-Jewish heritage. Not only will these people soon pass away in body, but also, without the *recuerdo* (memory) of the next generation, they will be lost—as Cuban-Jews—from history. The Cuban-Jewish tradition, which originated in early-twentieth-century Cuba and "migrated" to the United States in the 1960s, and which further developed and reconfigured itself in its new Miami Beach home, rests in the hands of the next generation.

As Rafael Losger emphasizes, the Cuban-Jews mean little in the broad sweep of both Jewish and world history. Their significance lies within the community itself, in the pride Cuban-Jews derive from maintaining traditions and customs which are uniquely Cuban-Jewish and which they can pass on to their children: "We [Cuban-Jews] are a community of ten or fifteen thousand. . . . In the sense of history, it's like a grain of salt, it's nothing. And yet it's a very, very strong, very together, very focused community. Not only were they blessed with their Judaism, but they were blessed by being Cubans."

Rafael's hopes for the future ring out clearly in the community today: "It is my personal dream to see the community unite . . . we need to build strength."

## A Cuban-Jewish Marriage

It is precisely this dream of community unification that makes Estrella Behar, the editor of Torat Moshe's bulletins, take extra pride in her daughter Reyna's forthcoming wedding to David Behar, also an (unrelated) member of Miami's Cuban-Jewish community.[7] As members of families who have been friends for four generations and who now attend Torat Moshe, Reyna and David have known each other their whole lives. Their union not only promotes Cuban-Jewish culture, Estrella thinks, but also cements the bonds between two families, across four generations and two nations:

> So my husband Roberto is friends with Yoshua Sal Behar, and they've been friends since Cuba, since the early fifties, when they started Albert Einstein, which was a school there. I knew that the grandfathers, Enrique and Rafael Behar—and we have the same last name, but we are not family—I knew the grandfathers were friends, and this grandfather, Rafael Behar, taught the boys their Bar Mitzvah lessons, even though he's their age. He knew Hebrew. . . . He taught that generation, his own generation, and many other ones. And he's still very observant in Miami.
>
> What I didn't know and I learned the day of the engagement party [for Reyna and David]: I always thought the connection was three generations on the Behar side, on my husband's side. But I just learned that my grandfather, Isaac Elnecave, used to go visit Havana in the thirties and forties. And instead of staying in a hotel, which you didn't do, he would stay at Yoshua Behar's—Rafael Behar's father's—home. And Rafael, he was a boy. My grandfather Isaac would stay at their home in Cuba. So, even on my side of the family, we really go back four generations with

David's family. And for us [Estrella and Roberto Behar (Reyna's parents), and Yoshua and Lillian Behar (David's parents)], we've been best friends for twenty years, our families. But for us, the fact that it's four generations of friends—we're talking probably a hundred years here—it's so, so special. . . . The only difference with us is that we say "Behar" [with e as in "say"] and they go "Behar" [with e as in "eat"]. So David says that my daughter will become Reyna Behar Behar [pronounced both ways]. I love it. . . .

Everything in the United States is new, and this is old-time friends. Even from the bride and groom's great-grandparents. And look what this man [Rafael Behar, David's grandfather] remembers in 1999: that when my grandfather, Reyna's great-grandfather, went to Havana, what would he buy to take to Guines, the town he lived in at the time? [8] White cheese in a can. Which is probably like feta cheese or as close as you could get. And he remembers that fifty years later. Neat, huh? . . . I'm very excited about this wedding; I'm thrilled. . . .

There are definitely roots here, right? . . . I think this is so neat, that he [Isaac Elnecave] and he [Yoshua Behar] were friends, and visited in the thirties. And that he even stayed overnight.

If Estrella Behar sees this as a marriage not only of two individuals, but also of two families full of "old-time friends," I wondered, would Reyna and David define their marriage in these historical terms? Would the older generation use their marriage as a model for preserving the Cuban-Jewish community? Did Reyna and David feel a sense of connection to each other as Jewbans? Would they feel a sense of obligation to maintain Cuban-Jewish traditions?

Estrella addressed some of these questions as she discussed Reyna's and David's future together, and the future of second-generation, American-born Cuban-Jews in general:

The Cuban part alone [of Cuban-Jewish life] might change. But Reyna is treasurer of WIZO [Women's International Zionist Organization], of the Singles Chapter. Now the Latinos are still together, but now there are Cubans and Mexicans and Columbians and Guatemalans and Panamanian Jews. Young Jewish people that meet. And when they meet, they have hundreds that meet for happy hour, or a cigar bar. It's a very, very active chapter. Much more active than the Americans and much more active now than the Cubans because the Cubans have assimilated.

Estrella's discussion of the lack of "Cuban" Cuban-Jewish life for her daughter's generation strikingly resembles Damien Losger's discussion of "meeting all my

# Behar Family Tree

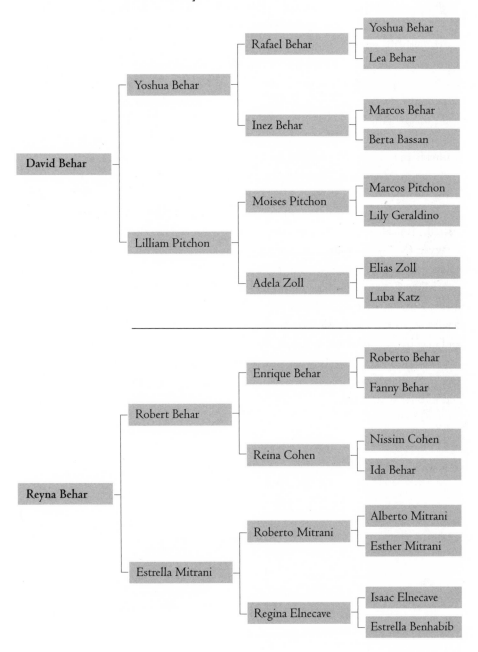

*Estrella Behar's family tree, referring to the people whose stories she recounted.*

American friends, and assimilating to what's going on now." Unlike most other Latino Jews in Miami, Cuba's Jews arrived in the United States nearly four decades ago. Time has allowed new traditions to permeate the Cuban-Jewish community—particularly the younger generation. In contrast, many young Latino Jews of other nationalities are recent arrivals in Miami; their cultural traditions are products of direct experiences in their home countries. Thus, while activity in the Cuban-Jewish community dwindles, Estrella thinks, activity in the larger Latino Jewish community gains in strength.

While it comforts Estrella to know that her daughter is interested in her own Latina heritage, it is disconcerting to know that, at age forty-nine, she (Estrella) is the youngest member of Torat Moshe's newsletter staff and one of the youngest active members of the synagogue. Yet like Rafael Losger, she understands such facts as part of the natural evolution of any ethnic group's settlement in a new country. Estrella, Rafael, and Eva Simazi celebrate the rare marriages of young Cuban-Jews, however, for these unions often bring together two families who often know each other, and they reinforce cultural tradition, continuity, and memory. Reyna's marriage to a fellow Cuban-Jew—especially a member of a family of "old-time friends"—makes Estrella particularly proud that, at least to some extent, her family has countered the trend toward assimilation. Because they will move to North Miami–Dade and may become involved in Jewish organizations there, Reyna and David Behar may not become members of Torat Moshe or participate in "Cuban-Jewish" events. Their Cuban Sephardic roots, however, remain ineradicably present in their family histories and in their shared *apellido*.

# Chapter 8

# Cuban-Jewish Identity in the Borderlands

## Denial of Identity

Isaac Motola, a Sephardic Jew in his mid-thirties, was born in New York approximately three years after his parents left Cuba in 1960 or 1961.[1] His parents and brother initially migrated to Israel on tourist visas, but they did not become Israeli citizens and his father did not achieve economic success there. They moved to New York in 1962; two years later, Isaac was born in the Canarsie section of Brooklyn.

Isaac's Cuban heritage is quite important to him personally. His great-uncle was the first cantor in the Camagüey province of Cuba, and his father was the first Hebrew teacher in the yeshiva organized by the Jewish seminary in Havana.[2] His personal Jewish experience is equally important. He studied for six years in a yeshiva and currently attends Torat Moshe every Thursday night for Torah lessons with Rabbi Abraham Benzaquén. He recounts his disbelief at a fellow Jew's denial of his Jewish identity on the basis of his nationality:

> In New York, when I got my first job, at an office, the owners were Jewish. And when I applied, and told them I was Jewish, they said it was impossible to be bilingual and Jewish. They wouldn't believe me when I told them that I was a Cuban-Jew. So Passover came and after 9:30 [A.M.], you know, you cannot eat bread, that's your cut-off time. It was about 1 P.M., and they offered me something with bread, and I said, "No, after 9:30 I don't eat bread." And they said, "You see, you're not Jewish, you should know that all Jewish holidays start at sundown." And then a religious guy from the community walks in, and they said, "Look, this Cuban guy's trying to pretend he's Jewish. He said you can't eat bread after 9:30, when we all know that you can't eat bread after sundown." And the guy answered—and I'll never forget this—"You're in disbelief that this kid is Jewish? I don't think you guys are Jewish." That was his answer. I knew that we couldn't eat after 9:30 and they didn't know that.

Like Isaac Motola, Becky Levy, a Sephardic Cuban-Jew in her late teens, experienced a denial of her Cuban-Jewish identity by American coreligionists in Miami:

When the people at my high school find out you're Jewish, they're like, "Oh, but which parent is Cuban and which one is Jewish?" They just can't grasp it. . . . No, people in Miami definitely freak out when you say you're Cuban *and* Jewish. It's not even accepted here [in Miami]! They question you, like "Oh?"

I will never forget this: when I wanted to become a member of this worldwide social organization for Jewish teenagers, I went to one meeting, and I left my name and my phone number. And they told me they'd call me back about upcoming events and whatever. Well when he called, he spoke to my grandmother, who doesn't speak English. And when I got to the phone, he said, "Oh, you're Hispanic." And I said, "Yeah, I'm Cuban." So I'm waiting for just a normal message, and he says, "Well, you know you have to be Jewish to be in this youth group." And I said, "Yeah, I know, I'm Jewish." And they were just like, very, "I don't know, uh," like all nervous. And I ended up being one of those people. But they were very—it could've just been that one person—that was just my first experience with that organization. I don't even know who that was—that was just my first impression. And it turned me off, but I ended up staying. They just freak out. I would say there is more discrimination toward the Cuban-Jews than there is toward the Jewish people, 'cause they just freak out at the mix. You can say you're Jewish, that'll be okay, but Cuban *and* Jewish?

With the stereotypes which abound in Miami (and, clearly, in New York) concerning both "Cubans" and "Jews," how do Miamians characterize Cuban-Jews? This question is complicated further when we consider the stories recounted by Becky Levy and Isaac Motola. In both cases, the issue did not surround a misrepresentation or derogatory characterization of "Cuban-Jews" by people who were not Cuban-Jews; rather, the issue was the latter's very denial of—or at least disbelief in—the former's existence. In Miami, complaints often are heard about widespread intolerance of large, well-known ethnic groups, such as "Cubans," "Jews," "blacks," "Nicaraguans," "Anglos," and "Mexicans" (see Grenier and Stepick 1992; Landers 1988; Portes and Stepick 1993). In the case of the Cuban-Jews that problem is diminished, since much of Miami's population is unfamiliar with the ethnic label "Cuban-Jew." Becky and Isaac were troubled by others' ignorance of the group with which they strongly identify. They were even more troubled by refusals to believe that such a "combination" of preestablished categories ever could exist.

## Jewban Identity and American Borderlands

When I began this project, I worked from the premise that Miami was one of many "borderlands," as Gloria Anzaldúa describes those spaces which "are physically present whenever two or more cultures edge each other, where people of different races occupy the same territory, where under, lower, middle, and upper classes touch, where the space between two individuals shrinks with intimacy" (1987: preface). Dade County's total population of 1,933,985 people is composed, according to the United States Census of 1990, of 414,000 "Anglos," 953,000 "Hispanics," 398,000 "Blacks," and 200,000 "Jews." Thus it certainly appears to fit Anzaldúa's description of a borderland.[3] Thomas Boswell and Emily Skop describe Metropolitan Miami as "America's foremost immigrant city. Forty-five percent of its population is foreign-born, the highest proportion of any major metropolitan area in the United States" (1995: 1). Miami occupies a very large area—Dade County occupies 1,944 square miles; Metropolitan Miami occupies 1,073 square miles; and the City of Miami occupies 67 square miles (Rand McNally 1997: 125). This has made possible increased spatial separation of ethnic neighborhoods. As a result, people of different backgrounds do not mix in Greater Miami as readily as one might assume. In fact, when we look at a demographic map of Miami (see Boswell 1994), we see geographical groupings frequently occurring along ethnic lines. Examples include Little Havana, associated with Cubans (although, over the past decade, the percentage of Cubans occupying this area has decreased, while the population of Central Americans has increased dramatically [Navarro 1997: 1, 12]); Little Haiti, associated with Haitians; Little Managua, associated with Nicaraguans; Homestead, associated with migrant farm laborers, especially Mexicans; and Overtown and Liberty City, two contiguous spaces which are associated with American blacks.

"Like an archipelago," geographer Ira Sheskin writes, Miami's ethnic groups "often form islands and island groups within the Miami metropolitan area. . . . These ethnic groups are not just residentially segregated in geographic space, they are segregated in social space and in economic space and political space as well" (1992: 41). Because of highly ethnicized neighborhoods which have arisen in noncontiguous geographical spaces in Miami, "borderlands" may not be as tangible and discernible in Miami as they are for Anzaldúa in her native Brownsville, Texas.

This is not to say, of course, that cultures in Miami do not "edge on each other" or that people of different races or ethnic groups do not "occupy the same territory." Much of Miami does occupy a borderlands space, in which the occupants constantly are forced to negotiate between preestablished categorical identities and face "the Other." In contemporary Miami, Cubans, Anglo Americans, and non-Cuban Latinos intermix constantly.[4] Cubans, in fact, compose over 29 percent of Miami's current population (Boswell 1994: 23). Although Cubans still compose the majority of the populations in traditionally "Cuban" areas such as Little Havana or Hialeah, many have moved into traditionally "Anglo" neighborhoods "as they climbed the social and economic ladder of success" (23). Through this movement, they have created new borderlands and drastically changed old ones.

What happens, however, when a group is not defined or recognized by the rest of the community? The case of the Cuban-Jews/Jewbans certainly seems to complicate Anzaldúa's notion of borderlands. If a group of people defines itself around the intersection of a common religion and nationality and the socioreligious institutions which have arisen at this intersection, what happens when this identification is unknown to, and thus goes unrecognized by, others? Would Cuban-Jews be classified by those unfamiliar with the "Cuban-Jewish/Jewban" identification as "Miami Beach Cubans" who "edge" on the culture of "Miami Beach Jews?" Or as "Miami Beach Jews" who "edge" on Cuban culture? Or as people who can occupy either the position of "Jew" or "Cuban?" Anzaldúa's description works on the assumption that all "cultures" and "races" are defined and generally agreed upon within a specified geographical place. What kind of space does one occupy when her/his positionality is unconventional and unknown to many of those who occupy the same geographical place as s/he does? When few outside one's immediate local (in this case, Cuban-Jewish) community identify one as a "Cuban-Jew," how does that individual identify herself/himself to others outside the community? Both Becky and Isaac faced disbelief and doubt when they referred to themselves as Cuban-Jews; Isaac even experienced hostility. To both Jews and Gentiles alike, "Cubans" were Gentiles and "Jews" were "Americans." The "edging" of "Cubans" and "Jews" on each other certainly has created—at least theoretically—a borderland in Miami; but, although Becky and Isaac identify with many elements on both sides of this borderland, they identify themselves as more than merely the overlap of its two basic elements. Their *jubanidad* exists within a separate sphere, they claim. As Cuban-Jews/Jewbans, they cannot occupy a borderland which makes no space for them.

The issue of this exclusion (or "discrimination," as Becky terms it) brings us to a more general discussion of the problems which necessarily arise in attempting to define the ethnic composition of any given area. This discussion is rooted in the inherent limitations of concepts, such as "culture" and "cultural difference" that are central to traditional anthropology (see Appadurai 1990, Foster 1991, Gupta and Ferguson 1992). Becky's and Isaac's insistence on their hyphenated "Cuban-Jewish" identity (rather than a "Jewish" or "Cuban" one) well illustrates these limitations, as does Damien Losger's understanding of his own identity: "See, I would never say that I'm Cuban. Not that I wouldn't want to be—I just would never consider myself a Cuban. I'm just a Cuban-Jew. . . . I'm not saying I'm Cuban-American; I'm saying I'm a Cuban-Jew. . . . I'm an American-Cuban-Jew."

In emphasizing his distance from a Cuban identity, Damien illustrates how the hyphen linking various labels, such as "Cuban," "American," and "Jew," creates an entirely new dimension which is more than the sum of its named parts. The notion of "culture" ("Jewish," "Cuban," or "American") is destabilized by Damien's, Becky's, and Isaac's accounts. Unwilling to concede that their cultural identities as Jewbans can be reduced to the simple equation "Jewish" + "Cuban" = "Jewban" (or "Jewish" + "Cuban" + "American" = "Jewban-American"), they assert that their Cuban-Jewish identity encompasses a new dimension, "something a little distinct, something a little different," according to Damien. The cultural identity they assume cannot be linked with any particular place or event. Instead, it is linked with the complex relations between time, space, migration, displacement, and geography, as these relate to the particular case of the Cuban-Jews. The "old certainty . . . that there is an immutable link between cultures, peoples, or identities and specific places" (Lavie and Swedenburg 1996: 1) thus is dislodged by Jewbans in Miami, as are assumptions of what composes a "culture." Damien's further discussion highlights this: "My parents and grandparents were immigrants not that long ago, and it's not like I'm American and I've been here for generations, and it's not like my parents are Cubans and they've been there for generations, and this tie to Israel is like a superficial thing, 'cause Israel has only been around for fifty years. So where's your tie? Is it to Cuba? Is it to America? Is it to Israel? Is it to Poland? Where is it?"

Although Damien claims a specific "Cuban-Jewish" identity, he does so under the assumption that this is a "homeless" identity, or at least an identity which shares multiple homes which cannot be separated from each other. Akhil Gupta and James Ferguson elaborate on this issue of homelessness in their consideration of the dimensions of cultural identity: "both the ethnological and national naturalisms present associations of people and place as solid, commonsensical, and agreed upon, when they are in fact contested, uncertain, and in flux" (1992: 12). Indeed, the citizenship oath which weds person with place contrasts markedly with the "generalized condition of homelessness" (Said 1979: 18) for so many people today—people who, like Damien, appear to be "rooted" within "American society."

How, then, should we conceptualize "American society"? If, upon closer analysis, apparent stability yields uprootedness and uncertainty, how does this affect previous conceptions of "American culture"? The "natural association of a culture ('American culture'), a people ('Americans'), and a place ('the United States of America')" (Gupta and Ferguson 1992: 12) is disrupted by the presence of the *mestizo/mestiza* in a supposedly homogeneous "America." The *mestizo* not only makes it clear that, in the contemporary world, this concept of "natural association" is a fallacious one, but also pushes us to question its viability in any place or time. If we accept this "natural association," we are accepting a model of stasis, a notion that (American) "culture" and/or "society" is (or was) inert, rigid, and definable. Both the hyphenated Cuban-Jewish and unhyphenated Jewban identities subvert this essentialized and naturalized conception of "American" identity. As a group which, because of its small numbers (in Miami, approximately 10,000; in New York and Puerto Rico, 2,000 to 3,000 each), is not even considered in discussions of America's borderlands, Cuban-Jews/Jewbans challenge notions of American culture and, more generally, the notion of culture itself.

In his discussion of his own American-Cuban-Jewishness, Damien is careful to note the flexibility of this seemingly compressed identity. Preconceived notions of what the individual components of this identity are or who they describe are problematic and limiting, he contends: "Me saying I'm an American-Cuban-Jew means something completely different from another person saying 'I'm an American-Cuban-Jew.'"

If being "American-Cuban-Jew" means two completely different things to two people, as Damien maintains, then can Cuban-Jews in Miami be viewed as members of a Cuban-Jewish "culture," or even a "cultural community"? Even after narrowing down the possibilities for cultural identification with a double hyphen, bracketing American-Cuban-Jews, or Jewbans, as a distinct culture remains problematic. There are extreme differences in opinion both within and outside the purported "Cuban-Jewish commu-nity" about who Cuban-Jews are. Susana Hamla, a former president of the Torat Moshe Women's Committee, often uses the phrase in strict reference to the members of Torat Moshe. Barry Konovitch, the former rabbi of the Cuban-Hebrew Congrega-tion, referred to his congregation as "the hub of the Cuban-Hebrew community—not only in Miami, but in the rest of the United States" (qtd. in Fernández 1986b: 12). And the Miami Herald refers repeatedly to "Miami's tiny Cuban Jewish community" (Dibble 1985: 2B) but in this context discusses only the Cuban-Hebrew Congregation and its predominantly Ashkenazic membership, ignoring the substantial Cuban Sephardic population in Miami and its representative synagogue, Torat Moshe. In each instance, the "Cuban-Jewish community" is defined in a way which excludes people who consider themselves vital elements of it. Damien's emphasis on the particularities which each person brings to the same nominal identity highlights the complexities con-tained within any ethnic, racial, gendered, class-based, or age-based label. Although all members of a group of people may claim this label for both group and individual identification, individual conceptions of the label's significance and all that it entails may differ dramatically. Common elements may be present in most of their concep-tions. If the label highlights a common nationality or race, for example, most people using that label likely will see the named element as an essential aspect of that identity. Yet the meaning of this label is, in the final analysis, entirely personal and nonspecific.

Our consideration of the complexities of identity issues has led us to focus on the active rather than the static, on particularities rather than universalities, and on disorder rather than stability. It is important to discuss this consideration—and the resulting challenges to conventional notions of "culture" and "cultural difference" which arise from it—within the context of related contemporary scholarship in anthropology. Postmodern ethnography, as discussed by Behar and Gordon (1995), Clifford and Marcus (1986), Marcus and Fischer (1986), and Tyler (1986), is characterized by fluidity and by the deconstruction of previously (or supposedly) established boundaries, reflective of both the physical and psychological dislocation and the boundarylessness of the people whom anthropologists observe (see Anzaldúa 1987). As we look at patterns of movement and migration of peoples across lands which are deemed to be "someone else's," we begin to see the complexities involved in identifying a "culture." What happens when newcomers become, over time, permanent residents? To what "culture" do they belong? These newcomers challenge conventional notions of "us" versus "them" and "ordinate" versus "subordinate."

These ideas are discussed in a somewhat more abstract form in David Harvey's *The Condition of Postmodernity*. Here Harvey discusses the "necessary relation" (1990: vii) between the rise of postmodernism, changes in the structure of the capitalist system, and a subsequent compression of time and space. The world is shrinking, Harvey argues, as technology brings us closer together than ever before. The contemporary workplace is fragmented and discordant, requiring ever-faster technological processes and flexible workers. This situation is reflected in a shift in dominant political-economic models, from Fordist-Keynesian to flexible accumulation. With this shift come changing notions of space and time, as time becomes a commodity and distances shrink. Thus we have the postmodern world, in which established models are overturned and foundations are dismantled in a chaotic and disorderly fashion.

Harvey's discussion of "time-space compression" (1990: vii) is important for a consideration of boundary deconstruction in the contemporary world, as well as in the not-so-distant past. As we experience this "compression," we are brought closer to other peoples around the globe. All this is made possible by technological advancement, new theoretical modes of thought, and the influence of these upon each other. Many consider the result to be a move toward a "global culture," where difference is minimized and connection is stressed. Others, such as Foster (1991) and Gupta and Ferguson (1992), see this characterization as dangerous. They stress that "time-space compression" does not necessarily mean a move toward a monoculture; rather, it encourages "flow" among groups, which then generates new diversities. Forces will erode the stability of national cultures, they contend; however, this erosion will cause new cultural forms to arise, rather than one global culture. Although these two arguments ("global culture" versus "flow") conflict, both depict a postmodern era characterized by the blurring of national and cultural boundaries—a blurring which challenges traditional concepts of culture and cultural difference.[5]

# Diversity within Homogeneity

Although United States census reports and much scholarly literature refer to bounded and defined ethnic groups, such as "Hispanics," "Anglos," and "Blacks," we see the problems inherent in these conceptions in our reappraisal of "Miami's Cuban community" through the case of the Cuban-Jews. If "Cubans" as an ethnic group cannot be located definitely and unproblematically, then how can we define a much larger group such as "Hispanics"?

These considerations are important for our previous discussion of Anzaldúa's "borderlands." What are the implications of theorizing such a place, where people of different "cultures," "races," and "classes" "edge each other" (Anzaldúa 1987: preface)? Although Anzaldúa's notion of "borderlands" can be a helpful concept, it makes presuppositions concerning what these elements may encompass. Moreover, in emphasizing differences between specified groups, "borderlands" may fail to highlight heterogeneity within them. In making the facile assumption that borderlands in Miami, for instance, are formed at the intersection of "Cuban culture" and "Anglo culture," we necessarily essentialize people from diverse backgrounds who hold diverse ideologies. The borderlands concept is also limiting in another respect, discussed earlier in this chapter. It can, by definition, account only for groups that are commonly recognized and defined—however problematically or unsystematically—by a larger society. The paradoxical case of Cuban-Jews in Miami illustrates this limitation. While many Cuban-Jews insist on defining themselves as "Cuban-Jews" or "Jewbans," this identity is ignored or mocked, or it simply is unfamiliar to others throughout Miami and in the United States generally. The cases of Cuban-Jews, a largely unrecognized ethnic group, and Cubans, a well-recognized ethnic group, both problematize the notion of borderlands, though from different starting points.

Certainly the concept of borderlands is a step in the right direction, as it attempts to analyze the unprecedented cultural, social, economic, and political changes which have occurred in "Late Capitalist" society. Such an effort is especially relevant with regard to issues of migration and cultural reorganization of people throughout the world. At this point, however, we must move beyond "borderlands," into territory which makes room for diversity within seemingly homogenous groups.

# Appendix

## Estampas de un Refugiado
## Por Izzy

*This is the original Spanish text of "Images of a Refugee," published in 1965, a short memoir by Izzy discussed in chapter 1.*

Hace algunos años que salimos de nuestra Cubita Bella. Primero el miedo de irnos. Si se enteran los vecinos. Si cerramos o no el negocio. Si dejamos a un empleado encargado o no. En fin, tomamos una decisión y un buen día nos aparecemos en el Aeropuerto cargados de tantas maletas como hemos podido encontrar. El avión está listo a partir. En eso oímos nuestro nombre. ¿Qué pasa? ¿Nos dejaran marchar o no? La sangre se nos congela, pero los milicianos son benignos y solo les interesa nuestra Colonia Canoe y un tubo de pasta de diente. Es natural solo el aseo les interesa. Por fin el avión levanta sus plateadas alas en raudo vuelo. Ya van quedando atrás las luces del Paseo del Malecón y el Morro. Nos sentimos tranquilos, por fin emprendemos el viaje anhelado. Nuestras vacaciones comienzan. Pero qué haremos en Miami, nos preguntamos una y otra vez. No importa. Total los días se irán rapidamente y en un abrir y cerrar de ojos estaremos de regreso. En estas meditaciones cruzamos las famosas noventa millas y ya estamos aterrizando en la ciudad de Miami, cuna del turista. Y aquí llegamos nosotros como nuevos turistas a esperar por el retorno en corto tiempo.

Buscamos donde instalarnos. ¿Difícil? Que va. Miami Beach ha sido el ensueño de todas nuestras temporadas veraniegas. Para alquilar casas nos piden contratos por un año. Están locos. ¿Quién va a alquilar casas por año si dentro de tres meses regresamos? Lo mejor es un Hotel. ¿Cuál? Cualquiera que nos deje el acomodamiento lo más barato posible. ¿Qué les parece el San Juan? Pues magnífico.

Así los dias pasan y siguen pasando. Muchos se entretienen corriendo bolas, otros sintonizando a Cuba por onda corta y oyendo los berrinches del Barbudo que arremete día tras día contra todo el que no haya sido perjudicado por su "nacionalismo." Aparecen horas radiales donde los comentaristas a diario nos alegran y confortan con la noticia de que mañana sí es el día del regreso. Otros para no aburrirse van a la Bolsa a ponerle su dinerito a alguna que otra Acción que les han indicado subirá de precio de un momento a otro. Pero, ¿y de negocios qué? ¿de trabajos qué? De eso ni se habla. Si mañana nos vamos, ¿quién va a preocuparse de pequeñeces durante sus vacaciones?

Pero así pasa un mes y otro mes. Un buen día nos despiertan de madrugada. El barrio está de fiesta. Fuerzas liberadoras han desembarcado en Cuba. Corremos a buscar noticias. Todo es confusión. La radio vocifera que estamos ganando. Pero al siguiente día el resultado es triste. Hemos sido derrotados. Nuestros hombres aprehendidos. La radio comunista se jacta del fracaso. Los jefes de la invasión enmudecen y todo aquel torbellino de alegría y de ilusiones se evapora como por obra de magia. Qué hacer ahora. La cosa ha cambiado. El regreso ya no nos parece tan fácil. Las vacaciones se están extendiendo. Los dólares se nos están agotando. Los intereses no producen lo suficiente para cubrir los gastos. Tenemos que hacer algo. Que tal si buscaramos empleo. Magnífico. Pero que pasa ahora. Aquí quieren gente con "Experience" y que no pase de 35 años. Nuevamente los empleos están limitados. Nada que como quiera que uno se ponga tiene que llorar.

Qué salida nos queda. Pues qué les parece un negocio. Si en Cuba nos levantamos, por qué [no] podemos hacerlo aquí. Empezaremos en chiquito. Buscaremos un localcito barato y nos buscaremos un socio para no pagar empleados. Así vamos tirando. Poco a poco las ventas mejoran, los locales mejoran, los sueldecitos mejoran. Ya salimos a pasear mas a menudo. Ya no gastamos los 5 ni los 6 por 1. Ahora gastamos el 1 por 1. El que sudamos aquí al estilo yanqui con el Hamburger o el Hot Dog a la hora del almuerzo. La vida es más dura pero aprendemos a vivirla. Los automóviles van mejorando. Las casas alquiladas se van sustituyendo por casas compradas.

Ya tenemos nuestro Club. Ya jugamos poker. Ya hablamos de ahorrar en Income Tax y de cuando cogeremos la Ciudadanía. Que lejos van quedando aquellos días en que pensabamos en unas cortas vacaciones y en un pronto retorno. A decir verdad, estas vacaciones ya nos van pareciendo demasiado largas, requetelargas. Como diríamos en argot beisbolero: La bola pica . . . y se extiende.

Cubita Bella
¡Volveremos!

Reprinted from *Boletín Mensual* [Cuban-Hebrew Congregation of Miami, Inc.], vol. 1, no. 1 (Nov. 1965): 14–15.

# Notes

## Introduction

1. The "faintly anti-Semitic" term polaco eventually came to refer to any foreigner in Cuba who was not American, black, Spanish, or Chinese (Levine 1993: 26, 313; Bejarano 1996b: 199). Cuban Sephardim and Ashkenazim also used the distinctions polacos and turcos to refer to each other, sometimes in pejorative contexts. For a discussion of tensions between these communities in pre-revolutionary Cuba, see Levine 1993.

2. Sephardic and Ashkenazic are, respectively, the adjective forms of the plural nouns Sephardim and Ashkenazim. The singular noun forms are Sephardi and Ashkenazi. In the United States, however, Sephardim and Ashkenazim also commonly are referred to as Sephardics/Sephardis and Ashkenazics/Ashkenazis, respectively.

3. Especially during the years surrounding World War II, however, Jews in Cuba bore the brunt of international, political, and economic insecurities. See Bejarano 1996b, Levine 1993, and Levine 1996 for further information on the effects of international anti-Semitism on Cuba during World War II.

4. Certain private clubs, however, would not allow Jewish patrons. See chapter 1 for additional information.

5. There are conflicting accounts of the number of Jewish Cubans who arrived in Miami in the early 1960s (see Bejarano 1994, Jewish Floridian 1979, Levine 1993, Liebman 1977, Rosichan 1961). Usually I will use an estimate between Levine's figure of 2,500 and Liebman's figure of 3,500, since these estimates seem most reasonable.

6. The *Círculo Cubano-Hebreo* in Miami Beach is known now as Cuban-Hebrew Congregation of Miami/Temple Beth Shmuel. The Cuban Sephardic Hebrew Congregation now is known as the Sephardic Congregation of Florida/Torat Moshe (formerly Temple Moses).

7. Fewer Sephardim of this generation were born in Greece or Syria and even fewer in other Mediterranean locales.

8. For the sake of simplicity, I sometimes refer to all members of the youngest generation (both "one-and-a-halfers" and those born in the United States) as "second-generation" Cuban-Jews, to distinguish them from their parents, first-generation émigrés who grew up in Cuba and emigrated as adults.

## Chapter 1: From Jewish Cubans to Cuban-Jews: Arriving in Miami and Establishing a Community

1. "Havana-gila" is a play on the Hebrew words of the title of the traditional Jewish song, "Hava-Nagila." According to Henry Green, "'Hava' comes from 'levoh' (to come), 'nagil' means to sing, and if you add the rest of the song—'nesmach' (happy)—you will end up with the following: 'Come and Sing and Be Happy'" (Henry Green to CB-L, July 12, 1999).

2. In her master's thesis on Miami's Cuban Sephardic community, Susan Epstein notes that the free services provided to Cuban Jews by Rabbi Abramowitz and Temple Menorah continued for five years after the Cuban Jews' arrival in Miami Beach (1981: 82).

3. The Greater Miami Jewish Federation commonly is referred to as "the federation" or simply "federation."

4. In his master's thesis on Cuban Jewish history, Jeffrey Kahn notes, "By early 1964 Cubans dominated that congregation [Menorah]" (1981: 91).

5. The Círculo's development is traced in greater detail later in the chapter.

6. In Miami in the 1960s, HIAS was run by the Greater Miami Section of the National Council of Jewish Women (NCJW).

7. "History Will Absolve Me" also calls for a more general rejection of the political, economic, and social systems of most other societies, both historically and in the present day.

8. Thanks to Zvi Gitelman for information about the Bolsheviks' relations with Russian Jews (Zvi Gitelman to CB-L, Jan. 1997).

9. This soldier sees backwardness and ignorance as characteristics of the Taino Indian population of Cuba, which was decimated by disease-carrying European conquistadors in the sixteenth century. He draws a connection between these people (who did not "make it") and those in the present day who continue to believe in any form of God.

10. Anti-Semitism probably was not a major factor in Jewish emigration from revolutionary Cuba (see discussion below). This emigration, like that of Cuban Gentiles, was stimulated by political and socioeconomic flux and a fear of religious persecution.

11. The original text is in English. This and Oscar White's article are the only English-language pieces in the 1965 bulletin.

12. No last name is given. Because of its length, I present the original Spanish text as an appendix.

13. Throughout the 1960s, the federation focused its community service efforts on poverty among American Jews in Greater Miami, many of whom were elderly (Myra Farr to CB-L, July 19, 1999).

14. Although Simazi immigrated to Brooklyn in 1961, she is speaking here about the situation experienced by her friends and family in Miami in the early 1960s. Her perception of Miami's generally positive reaction to the Cuban immigration of the 1960s contrasts starkly with García's depiction of Miami as a city boiling with resentment of the newly arrived Cuban émigrés. Perhaps Simazi's account reflects her vivid memories of, and personal sensitivity to, the negative American Jewish reaction to the Jewish Cubans, and/or her more positive experience with non-Jewish Miamians.

15. Major organizations tended to overestimate the "benevolent" services they provided to Jewish Cuban émigrés. The exception to this rule was the Greater Miami Section of NCJW, which provided extensive services under its New Americans Program. These services were delivered through HIAS, the United States government's Cuban Refugee Program, and other NCJW "hats." Thus, Jewish Cubans may recall assistance having been provided by the United States government or HIAS, when actually it was provided by NCJW.

16. Unfortunately, Kahn does not provide information concerning the relationship between the need for financial assistance and sub-ethnic group (i.e., Ashkenazic versus Sephardic) affiliation. The relative wealth of Ashkenazim (as compared with Sephardim) in Cuba has been widely documented, and it is likely that many of these 808 Cuban-Jews were Sephardim (see Bejarano 1988; Kahn 1981; Levine 1993; Sapir 1948).

17. *Meldados* is a Ladino word I translate as "meetings."

18. Over thirty years later, this distinction remains salient. Every Cuban Sephardic whom I interviewed claimed a distinct *Cuban* Jewish and *Cuban* Sephardic identity.

19. Hamla and most other Cuban Sephardim remain loyal to Rabbi Abramowitz today, emphasizing their gratitude to him and Temple Menorah for the assistance they were offered, and speaking about any negative experiences there only hesitantly.

20. Because *Yiddish* means *Jewish* in the Yiddish language, many Ashkenazic Jews use these two words interchangeably (Rosten 1968: 436).

21. The Sephardic congregation to which Peres is referring was sold, and the funds raised were used to help establish Magen David, a Sephardic congregation at 170th Street and 6th Avenue in North Miami (Henry Green to CB-L, July 12, 1999).

22. Thanks to Ruth Behar for her insight concerning issues of identity for the Jewish Cuban émigrés.

# Chapter 2: A Second Transformation: From Cuban-Jews to Jewbans

1. Temple Moses now officially is called Torat Moshe. However, most people in the community still refer to it as Temple Moses. The name change is discussed later in this chapter.

2. Ashkenazic Jews in pre-revolutionary Cuba disparagingly called the Sephardim *turcos* (Turks), while the Sephardim similarly called the Ashkenazim *polacos* (Poles). Gentile Cubans generally referred to all Jews, regardless of origin, as either *polacos* or Germans (Levine 1993: 26, 217). Ralvey's use of the term "*polaquitos*" above gives *polacos* the diminutive form; the meaning remains the same.

3. NCJW was founded in 1893 on the Jewish principle of *Tikkun Olam*, "repairing the world." Throughout the century, the progressive women involved in this national service organization have focused on four areas: community action, education, tradition, and advocacy. The Greater Miami Section was founded in 1918. At the time of the Jewish Cubans' arrival in the early 1960s, it sponsored seven major programs: New Americans (in cooperation with HIAS), Senior Citizens, Braille, Sight-Handicapped, Community Cooperation, Scholarship Grants, and International Student Hospitality (NCJW Oct. 1960). This was not the organization's first encounter with Cuba's Jews. In the 1920s, the Greater Miami section assisted Russian and Polish Jewish refugees in Cuba by sending them Passover foods, funds, and clothing (Myra Farr to CB-L, July 19, 1999; NCJW Dec. 1962: 4).

4. NCJW's May 1962 bulletin states: "We take pride in that the Council helped some 500 Cubans receive permission to enter our country this past year" (7). It is unclear if this figure refers to January 1962 through May 1962, or May 1961 through May 1962. I have chosen to interpret it as January 1962 through May 1962 because this seems to make more sense, considering that 2,500 to 3,500 Jewish Cubans arrived in Miami in the early 1960s (Levine 1993: 246–47; Liebman 1977: 300).

5. *Hasta luego* is an informal way of saying "See you later," whereas *adiós* has a more permanent connotation, meaning *farewell*. *Simpático* means *likeable* or *agreeable*, and in this context it means that the Cuban Jews and NCJW members got along well.

6. The specific passage Kerbel is referring to states the General Provisions of the Cuban-Hebrew Congregation (Cuban-Hebrew Congregation of Miami 1981: 8). See figure 7.

7. Note how Reyler's account challenges Jeffrey Kahn's portrait of the Cuban Jews as being secure financially upon arrival in Miami.

8. Estimates of the cost of constructing Patronato's vary from 750,000 to 1 million dollars (Levine 1993: 211).

9. No further information is given in the booklet as to which organization had Rozencwaig as general secretary.

10. The fact that Ner Tamid shared its facilities with the Círculo may signify increased local Jewish acceptance of the Cuban-Jews. None of my interlocutors ever mentioned this event, however.

11. Thanks to Henry Green for his valuable input on *tzedakah* (Green to CB-L, July 7, 1999).

12. In line with this portrayal of the Cuban-Jews as quickly developing into a prosperous community, the Cuban-Hebrew Congregation's twentieth-anniversary booklet, *Círculo Cubano-Hebreo de Miami, 1961–1981: 20 Aniversario*, does not discuss the economic struggles experienced by many community members upon arrival in Miami. The Cuban-Jews' increased adaptation to American society also is reflected in NCJW's 1962 and 1963 bulletins, which note that the "Cuban situation has now slowed down" and "the need of assisting Cuban Jewish refugees has lessened" (May 1962: 7; May 1963: 3).

13. By June 1968, the Sunday School had expanded to become Yavne Hebrew School, a day school attended by forty-four students. For undocumented reasons, the Círculo ended its educational efforts in 1969, and its students moved to other schools in the area. The 1981 twentieth-anniversary booklet explains tersely: "Era un proyecto sumamente ambicioso para aquellos difíciles tiempos" ("It was a very ambitious project for those difficult times") (Cuban-Hebrew Congregation of Miami 1981: 47).

14. Unlike the Cuban-Hebrew Congregation, the Patronato never had its own rabbi and instead hired a cantor to preside at religious functions (Levine 1993: 212). The Cuban-Hebrew Congregation, on the other hand, was led by Rabbi Rozencwaig from the beginning; in 1981, in fact, the congregation hired its first cantor, Moses Buryn. He is still there today.

15. The Cuban Jews never had had such a unifying institution previously. According to Levine, all efforts to unify Jewish community organizations in Cuba had failed, due to competition between Jewish institutions and personal friction among community leaders (1993: 212). The World Jewish Congress thus sought to use the construction of the Patronato as a "fresh start" for the Jewish community in Havana, and convinced the Patronato leaders to abstain from interpersonal rivalries and to organize the congregation as a place where a general assembly of fifty delegates from all the Jewish organizations in Cuba could meet and (in 1954) elect "a representative body of all Cuban Jews" (212).

16. The title *El Nuevo Jew-Ban* means *The New Jew-Ban. Jew-Ban* is a nickname for the community adopted by many of its members, since it combines their "Jewish" and "Cuban" identities. This is discussed in greater detail below.

17. Jane was Ana Rozencwaig's nickname.

18. Sisterhood does not have a national structure, although many synagogues throughout the United States have Sisterhood chapters. Each Sisterhood generally focuses its efforts and activities on its affiliated synagogue and other *tzedakah* causes.

19. *Goyim* is a Hebrew word which literally means *nations*. In colloquial use, it has come to mean *non-Jew*, or *Gentile*. It sometimes has a derogatory connotation, since it separates "us Jews" from "them Gentiles," but it is not always used in a negative fashion. Here, Simazi is nonjudgmentally referring to the secular nature of the for-profit Beach Club.

20. As discussed in chapter 7, this disappointment reverberates in the community today.

21. The Cuban Sephardic Hebrew Congregation in 1999 is known as the Sephardic Congregation of Florida–Temple Moses (name adopted in 1980) and Torat Moshe (name adopted in 1995).

22. Susan Epstein (1981) writes that, in 1968, the Cuban Sephardic Hebrew Congregation also adopted the name *Chevet Ahim*, in reference to its predecessor in Havana. This name, she thinks, served to perpetuate the link between two congregations spanning half a century and the Florida Straits. When I asked numerous Cuban Sephardim about this name, all replied that *Chevet Ahim* was the name of the Havana synagogue only, and that it was not used to designate the Cuban Sephardic Congregation in Miami. They simultaneously emphasized, however, that calling their congregation *Chevet Ahim* would have been

appropriate, because it did serve as a continuation of the Sephardic congregations in pre-revolutionary Cuba. Epstein also writes that, during its early stages, the congregation was called the Cuban Sephardic Hebrew Association, another designation unfamiliar to my interlocutors. Because Epstein does not give her sources for this name, I will continue using the designation my interlocutors used to describe the congregation: the Cuban Sephardic Hebrew Congregation, abbreviated as Cuban Sephardic Congregation.

23. Susan Epstein notes that, although the *Libro de Oro* cites 1918 as the date for the establishment of the Chevet Ahim congregation in Havana (Temple Moses/Florida Sephardic Congregation 1979: 4), "Seymour Liebman and Donna Katzin maintain that Chevet Ahim was founded in 1914. Perhaps the congregation organized informally in 1914, but did not have a specific meeting place until 1918" (Epstein 1981: 101, n. 1). Meir Melarmed, the second rabbi of the Cuban Sephardic Congregation, also dates this event to 1914 (198?: 2).

24. Robert Levine (1993), Susan Epstein (1981), the Cuban-Hebrew Congregation (1981), and all my interlocutors refer to this congregation as the *Congregación Hebrea Unida* (United Hebrew Congregation). Here I shall use "United Hebrew Congregation."

25. The congregation is called, alternatively, *Chevet Ahim, Chevet Achim, Shevet Ajim,* and *Shevet Ahim. Chevet Ahim* is most common (see Bejarano 1996a; Epstein 1981; Levine 1993).

26. When I asked Hamla if any relation existed between the Cuban Sephardim's *La Cueva* and "the Cave" described in Yosele Gilfarb (1981), she replied that she was unfamiliar with any *Círculo* reference to a "Cave."

27. See Levine's *Tropical Diaspora* (1993) for more detailed descriptions of Jewish life in Cuba's provinces.

28. Thanks to Naomi Brenner for her valuable information on the Hebra Kedusha.

29. There are two categories of Sephardic congregations: Traditional (Halachic) and Non-traditional. Ashkenazic congregations are categorized as Reform, Conservative, or Orthodox. "Orthodoxy, Reform, Conservative are not Sephardic concepts," Serge Otmezguine, president of the American Sephardi Federation (ASF), wrote in a memo to ASF members in 1998. "Sephardism is not a Denomination. Sephardim are the custodians of a *Tradition, a perspective on Judaism* which many thinkers, scholars around the world consider not only essential to our survival as Jews in The Diaspora but also *relevant to all of us Sephardim and non Sephardim alike*" (Otmezguine 1998: 3; emphasis in original). While to me many Cuban Sephardim described Temple Moses/Torat Moshe as "Orthodox," this is an Americanization and Ashkenazation of the "Traditional" Sephardic designation (Henry Green to CB-L, July 14, 1999).

30. Epstein notes how many of her interlocutors retain elements of archaic *Judezmo* (also known as *Ladino*) in their speech. The most common features include: "A word initial /n-/ is replaced by /m-/; /s/ is realized as /z/, especially intervocalically; a /g/ is imposed before /ue/; verbs ending in -*ar* are often conjugated as -*er* or -*ir* verbs in the first person singular and plural of the preterit; and *mi* is substituted for *me*" (Epstein 1981: 102). Thus, apparent misspellings and incorrect grammar in her interlocutors' speech generally are elements from Ladino.

31. Epstein's thesis was published in 1981; I do not want to extend my commentary here past the time period to which she and her interlocutors refer.

32. "*D–os*" and "*G–d*" intentionally are written with dashes in the middle of the words. According to Aaron Emert, "This is a recognition of and sacred honor to our Jewish Creator, whose holiness is such that by spelling His/Her name completely, we're taking away His/Her significance. It's an extra honor toward the belief in the existence of a Supreme Being" (Aaron Emert to CB-L, July 31, 1999). *Shalom* is a Hebrew word meaning *peace, hello,* and *goodbye.*

33. A similar, if more subtle, ambivalence on the part of the Ashkenazim is apparent in Cuban-Hebrew Congregation's 1981 twentieth-anniversary booklet, *Círculo Cubano-Hebreo de Miami, 1961–*

*1981: 20 Aniversario.* Not once does its *Historia de la Casa de la Comunidad Hebrea de Cuba en Miami* [History of the Home of the Jewish Community of Cuba in Miami] of the "Cuban-Jewish Community" mention the formation of the Cuban Sephardic Hebrew Congregation by the Sephardim in 1968 or the subsequent development of the Cuban Sephardic community on Normandy Isle. Thus, the authors of the *Historia* have written the history of the Cuban-Hebrew Congregation only, although they refer to it as the history of Cuban-Jews in Miami.

34. Bejarano contrasts the Cuban Sephardic community with the Cuban Ashkenazic community in this domain; unlike Temple Moses, she maintains, "the Cuban-Hebrew Congregation exclusively serves the Cuban public" (1994: 135). While this may have been the case several years ago, in my fieldwork since 1996, I have seen the Cuban-Hebrew Congregation serving a diverse Jewish community while maintaining its Cuban identity. Recently, for the first time, a non-Cuban Jew (David Hochman) served on its Board of Directors. The Cuban-Hebrew Congregation is not as involved in Latin American affairs as is Temple Moses, but I would not say that today it focuses exclusively on Cubans. I address this subject below.

35. The year 1992 marked a reawakening of Sephardic culture throughout the world, as many Sephardim made pilgrimages back to Spain and commemorated their unique history. Rather than dwelling on the atrocities associated with Spain's expulsion of the Jews in 1492, they celebrated the nation's Golden Age and their unique contribution to this era. In this emphasis, the commemoration differed significantly from the Jewish remembrance of the Holocaust, for two key reasons. First, Spain's Jews were forced either to convert or to leave the country, but they were not targeted on the basis of their genetic heritage, as Jews in the Holocaust were. Second, the Jewish expulsion from Spain occurred five hundred years ago, while the Holocaust took place only fifty years ago (Henry Green to CB-L, July 23, 1999). Thanks to Henry Green for his valuable historical information on Temple Moses's development and Sephardic cultural expressions (Green to Bettinger-López, July 12 and 23, 1999).

36. For a discussion of the preceding decade and a half of United States–Cuba relations, see García 1996; Masud-Piloto 1996; Pérez 1995; Portes and Stepick 1993.

37. This bombing was one of a series of bombings and assassinations of people associated with the *diálogo.* Cuban militant extremists claimed responsibility for these acts of terror. See Bernstein 1998b and García 1996 for further descriptions.

38. Most people I spoke with remember the shooting occurring in the afternoon, before evening Shavuot services. Perhaps here Kerbel is referring to morning services that had just ended, or perhaps he remembers the shooting occurring at night, after evening services. In my writing, I refer to an afternoon shooting, since that seems to be the most reliable information.

39. Levine writes, "Havana's last rabbi died in 1975 at the age of eighty-two" (1996: 802). While Rabbi Abramowitz may have been one of the only foreign rabbis to visit Cuba after the Revolution, he was not the first. See, for example, Rabbi Everett Gendler's account of his visit to Cuba in 1969. Gendler was the first rabbi from the United States to visit the island since 1961.

40. Max Lesnik, Xiomara Levy, and Eddie Levy, three other members of Miami's Cuban-Jewish community, have engaged in *diálogos* with Castro since Benes's involvement in the 1978 *diálogo.* Lesnik, a friend of Castro's from law school at the University of Havana, is editor and publisher of *Replica,* a magazine which was a major "flashpoint for controversy" (Clary 1998) in Miami in the 1970s and 1980s, when it served as an open forum in which Miami's exiles could discuss Cuban politics. Lesnik has visited Castro frequently in Cuba since his exile in 1961 and advocates an end to the United States embargo on the island. He is a highly controversial figure in Miami, both for his visits to the island and for his declaration that "I am a

socialist" (Clary 1998). Xiomara Levy and Eddie Levy, a Cuban-Jewish couple, founded Jewish Solidarity in 1993. Since then, the humanitarian aid group has delivered medicine, food, books, and other supplies to Jews in Cuba through its annual trips to the island. The Levys have visited with Castro to discuss the embargo and the current situation of Cuba's Jews. Like Lesnik, they are highly controversial figures in Miami, accused by many exiles of being Castro supporters. I never have encountered any reference to the Levys or Lesnik in any publications sponsored by the Cuban-Jewish community.

41. Although Melarmed was the second rabbi of the Cuban Sephardic Hebrew Congregation, his *Brief History of the Jews of Cuba and the Sephardic Community of Miami* focuses primarily on himself and his tumultuous relations with the Cuban Sephardic community in Miami as its rabbi. A historical context is largely missing from this account.

42. This sharp distinction between exiles and immigrants is drawn in Gustavo Pérez Firmat's memoir, *Next Year in Cuba.* Fleeing the Castro regime in 1960, Pérez Firmat's family arrived in Miami with the expectation that they would return home within weeks. As political exiles, they saw Miami as a temporary haven, a place to "wait-and-see": "Whatever we did here, good or bad, was inconsequential. Nena [his mother] proudly distinguished between immigrants and us. Time after time, she said, 'Remember, we are exiles, not immigrants.' Unlike the immigrants, we did not come to this country to start all over—we came to wait" (Pérez Firmat 1995: 120–21).

43. This estimate is taken from a religious census based upon "the total number of Jews who registered at the *Patronato* to receive packages of matzo and kosher meat from Canada, a service provided by the Canadian Jewish Congress, which became the major intermediary between Cuban Jews and the outside Jewish world because of the difficulties posed by hostilities between the United States and Cuba" (Levine 1996: 808, n. 109).

44. This statement, which seems to contradict Losger's previous discussion of the Cuban-Jewish community's general avoidance of involvement in Cuban politics, is used by Losger to support it. Losger feels that the community sometimes must take a stand on political issues, though only when doing so will not create conflict between Cuban-Jews and Miami's larger Cuban community.

45. Levy's story and those of other recent Cuban-Jewish arrivals in the United States are treated in greater detail in chapter 6.

46. As discussed in chapter 7, the complications surrounding the choice to bring an American rabbi into the Cuban-Hebrew Congregation were not easily resolved. In fact, they still loom over the congregation.

47. I was unable to contact Rabbi Konovitch when I was doing research on this issue because he was in Israel.

48. See Hochman, "Rabbi Search Committee Report" (1994), for a description of the Board of Directors' selection of its new rabbi.

49. Thanks to Naomi Brenner for her insight into this aspect of Jewish history.

50. At the time of this book's publication, J/X no longer existed. See chapter 7 for a detailed discussion of J/X's role in the community.

51. These are not translations. While Torat Moshe continues to only use Spanish in its bulletins, the Cuban-Hebrew Congregation now uses English predominantly (except for advertisements or occasional articles, usually written by community elders, in Spanish or Yiddish).

52. See, e.g., the bulletins of the Cuban-Hebrew Congregation and Temple Moses/Torat Moshe, which feature letters from United States and Israeli presidents and international leaders.

53. Thanks to Ruth Behar for her insight into the development of the "Jewban"/"Juban" identity.

# Chapter 3: Separate Spheres:
# Reflections on Ethnicity and Gender

1. Right-wing, anti-Castro exiles in the United States perhaps have been best represented by the Cuban-American National Foundation (CANF) and its founder, Jorge Mas Canosa. Mas Canosa organized the CANF in the early 1980s and maintained its close association with the Republican administrations of Ronald Reagan and George Bush and the Republican congresses of the 1990s. The CANF, particularly through its "Free Cuba" political action committee, has proven extremely effective as an anti-Castro lobbying organization. It also has been a target of controversy, being blamed by many—including the Cuban government—for contributing to widespread hunger and poverty in Cuba through its support for the United States embargo. This embargo denies the entry of American consumer goods, foods, and fuels to the island and prohibits United States citizens from spending money there. Furthermore, the United States and CANF strongly discourage other countries from engaging in trade with Cuba. This embargo has affected the Cuban people especially during the "Special Period" since the mid-1990s, when Cuba began to feel the effects of the collapse of Communism in Eastern Europe. After the 1991 collapse of the Soviet Union, the island's primary supporter and trade partner, the Castro government implemented a series of contingency plans originally conceived for use in wartime. These included a new series of austerity measures and new rationing schedules for the Cuban people (Pérez 1995: 383–84). The CANF believes that the economic pressures created by the embargo will weaken Communism in Cuba and thus lead to the eventual downfall of the Castro regime.

2. Both verb and noun, *shmooz* is a Yiddish word meaning "a friendly, gossipy, prolonged, heart-to-heart talk—or, to have such a talk" (Rosten 1968: 356). *Shmooz* stems from the Hebrew word *shmuos*, meaning "things heard" or "idle talk." As Leo Rosten says, "I have never encountered a word that conveys 'heart-to-heart chit-chat' as warmly as does *shmooz*" (356).

3. See chapter 5 for a discussion of Albert's perspective on these issues.

4. Kendall and South Miami have significantly larger populations of "Anglos"—that is, English-speaking Americans who are not first- or second-generation immigrants—than most other areas in Miami. In comparison with other public high schools, my public high school had the largest concentration of "Anglos" south of Miami Beach.

5. Although Albert's view of women is widespread throughout American society, its expressions differ among people of different cultures. I have chosen to show how sexist attitudes are revealed in one particular cultural group: the Cuban-Jews.

6. The discussion of the Jewish Cubans' arrival in Miami that is contained in the Cuban-Hebrew Congregation's 1981 bulletin differs markedly from that bulletin's 1965 discussion of the same issue.

7. For an overview of Jewish Miami Beach's historical development, see Green 1995 and Moore 1994.

8. Sheskin arrived at the figure 9,100 by asking respondents to the survey "if each person in their household 'considers him/herself' to be a member of [a Hispanic group]" (1994: 54). It is unclear how this figure relates to his previous estimate of approximately 10,000 "Jubans" living in Miami in 1992 (Sheskin 1992: 54), since, presumably, "Hispanic Jews" would include both Cuban-Jews and Jews from other Latin American countries.

9. We see a similar reversal of "the woman on the pedestal" conception in Gustavo Pérez Firmat's *Next Year in Cuba* (1995). His "beloved" wife can be found continuously in the domain of the home (and especially the bed), conceding to his wishes (demands?), whereas Pérez Firmat himself occupies multiple "outside" and "manly" spaces and has the power to make "important" decisions.

What is most (unintentionally) humorous about the book, in this respect, is its cover, which depicts Pérez Firmat sitting smugly atop a white pedestal.

10. This is the structure of Torat Moshe's small prayer room, used for Friday night services and *minyans*, quorums of at least ten adult Jews (all of whom must be male in Traditional and Orthodox synagogues) that are required for communal worship. In some Traditional and Orthodox synagogues, such as Torat Moshe's main sanctuary, women and men sit on opposite sides of a translucent curtain, both facing the *bimah*. Although this changes the physical configuration, it remains in accordance with Traditional and Orthodox Jewish law.

11. In another example of the Ashkenazation of Sephardic culture in the United States, Eva uses the term "Orthodox" to refer to Traditional (Halachic) Sephardic synagogues. *Kashrut*, or *kosher*, is a Hebrew word meaning "fit to eat, because ritually clean according to the dietary laws" (Rosten 1968: 192). Many Jews today observe the laws of *kashrut*, established by the ancient Jews for both health and religious purposes. These laws forbid the mixing of milk and meat, and restrict Jews' consumption of animals to those which are four-footed, chew their cud, and possess a cloven hoof. A *shochet*, a religious slaughterer, must examine all animals for signs of disease, infection, or abnormality and must slash the throat of the animal in one stroke. If any of these requirements is not met, the animal is no longer *kosher* (Rosten 1968: 192–93).

12. Through oral interviews (Mar. 1998) and research in Chinese- and Spanish-language secondary works, Kathy López has found similar perceptions among male and female descendants of Chinese-Cubans (a Chinese father and a Cuban mother) regarding the role of the woman as a preserver of culture. Most Chinese who immigrated to Cuba were men, which is why, many Chinese-Cubans told her, most children of Chinese-Cuban marriages do not speak Chinese (Kathy López to CB-L, July 17, 1999).

13. This is not to say, of course, that Orthodox and Traditional women in fact have no authority within the family.

14. The Bar Mitzvah and Bat Mitzvah signal the arrival of the Jewish boy and girl, respectively, at an age when adult reason and responsibility supposedly commence. At this point, the young boy or girl is committed to lifelong ethical and religious obligations. The Bar Mitzvah ceremony is not an ancient institution or sacramental ritual; it did not even exist until the fourteenth century. Only in some Orthodox and Traditional congregations are girls Bat Mitzvahed, and these ceremonies are significantly shorter than the corresponding Bar Mitzvah ceremonies for boys (Rosten 1968: 34–36).

15. Thanks to Kathy López for her insights concerning women's paid and volunteer work outside the home. Note that this discussion is not restricted to Eva's generation or to specific ethnic/religious groups, such as the Cuban-Jews. Domestic tension resulting from the woman entering the work place is a widespread phenomenon in American society (and other societies) generally.

16. As discussed in chapter 5, Albert was born in Cuba in 1976 and left when he was three years old. Thus he often is considered a "one-and-a-half" (Pérez Firmat 1995: 1) generation American Cuban-Jew. When Eva refers to the "third generation," however, she is referring to a specific age bracket.

17. "The María Syndrome" is a term used by many psychologists to describe the traditional role of the *Latina*, in which the woman is restricted to the private sphere of the home and is responsible for homemaking and childcare. As many *Latinas* currently attempt to emerge from this restricted domain into the public sphere, they often are confronted with marked resistance from their communities, which may pressure them to remain "Marías" in the home. Although this model is overly general, it does illuminate a pervasive tension surrounding the issue of the departure of women from the home and thus from that which traditionally has distinguished "woman" from "man."

18. I am using the word *agency* in the sense of self-determination, autonomy, action, instrumentality.

19. As Levine (1993) discusses, many Jews in Cuba practiced a non-Orthodox form of their religion. Thus the fact that women were not allowed to participate in religious matters in Cuba, as Victoria discusses, may have had more to do with the restrictions placed on women in traditional Cuban and Jewish cultures, regardless of their degree of religious orthodoxy.

20. The *bimah* is the raised "stage" at the front of most synagogues on which the rabbi and cantor stand. Behind it stands the holy ark containing the Torah.

21. Indeed, Becky had planned to begin college at a prestigious private university that fall; when her financial aid fell through, she was forced by economic necessity to attend an in-state university in central Florida. Still, she and Victoria commented, even going away to central Florida to school was considered a radical step in many other Cuban-Jewish families, many of whom do not permit their children to leave Miami for college. Becky noted, "They just want one big happy household. They never want to let you go. Out of my entire family, I'm the first one to get out. . . . My other family: they talk about my parents like, 'They want to send her away.' They're all mean about it. Like my aunts and uncles." Victoria, who recently graduated from a local South Florida university, stressed that she is "more old-fashioned than my sister." As the older daughter, she did not consider going away to college, something she now regrets.

22. See, e.g., Cuban-Hebrew Congregation of Miami, *Círculo Cubano-Hebreo de Miami, 1961–1981: 20 Aniversario*, pp. 54–55.

23. Most Cuban Ashkenazim with whom I spoke seemed less interested in discussing gender roles than in discussing community history. Thus the majority of my interviews on gender-role issues comes from my discussions with Cuban Sephardim. The question of gender roles, particularly within the Ashkenazic Cuban community, needs to be explored in greater depth.

# Chapter 4: Diaspora and Homeland

1. *Autochthony* is the idea of a natural connectedness or belonging of a people (i.e., aborigines) to a specific geographical place.

2. Ruth Behar examines this dehyphenation in considerable detail in "Juban América" (1995b).

3. Whether this name be *Juban, Jewban,* or *Cuban-Jew,* this same reasoning applies.

4. *Bris* means *covenant* but usually refers to the circumcision ceremony observed on the eighth day of a boy's life (in Hebrew, *Brith Milah*). In pre-1959 Cuba, young girls rarely were Bat Mitzvahed; this functioned primarily as a ceremony for thirteen-year-old boys. *Aliyah* refers to the permanent migration of Diasporic Jews to Israel and is the ultimate expression of Zionism (Rosten 1968: 50).

5. Significant Cuban communities developed in Key West and Tampa in the second half of the nineteenth century and in New York City in the first half of the twentieth century, although these communities are not commonly associated with what people today call the "Cuban diaspora." This designation generally is reserved for the communities of Cuban exiles which have developed throughout the world (particularly in the United States) in the four decades since the 1959 Cuban Revolution.

6. This is reflected in Eva Simazi's narrative:

> *Simazi:* Jews are always helping Jews, no matter where they're coming from. This is the interrelation. All Jews are brothers. They have the same blood.
>
> *Bettinger-López:* Would you say the same about Cubans, that all Cubans are brothers?
>
> *Simazi:* I don't think it's the same. That's why these guys are always telling

them that they should learn from the Jewish people. The unity that we have. No matter what we say, no matter our difference. When it comes to the nitty-gritty, we are united. When you know that there is a Jew in need, you immediately go to help. I think the Cuban population has learned that, especially here in exile. Because they have proven that, whenever there has been a crisis, they have been uniting themselves. . . .

There's a [Cuban Gentile] gentleman I know . . . and he's very pro-Jewish. And he's always putting the Jewish people as an example of what the Cuban people must do in order to obtain their freedom. But it's true. . . . Cubans could learn a lot from how Jews unite in a crisis, in order to obtain, to meet the end of whatever we need. This is a diaspora also—a Cuban diaspora! Diaspora doesn't have to be a religious thing.

Note that Simazi uses genealogical distinctions in referring to the Jewish people. By "sharing blood," she thinks, Jews are set apart from others. Her viewpoint challenges the Boyarins' argument that Jewish identity is founded upon the absence of such genealogical differentiation.

7. The issue of returning to revolutionary Cuba always has been highly politicized. However, there have been specific times when diasporic Cubans were allowed to return to the island. The most notable times were in 1979–80, when over 100,000 émigrés returned for one-week visits, and in the early 1990s. See chapter 2 for additional information.

8. In an interview with David Román, Tropicana/Troyano says that this voice-over in the play actually is Alina Troyano speaking, and that the actress in the rest of the play is both Alina Troyano and Carmelita Tropicana (Román 1995: 89).

9. The term *horsestory* refers to a horse Tropicana encounters. The stallion of a conquistador, the horse recalls Cuba's luscious beauty, as well as the Spanish colonization of the island and the decimation of its native peoples. Thus it is an important figure symbolizing Cuba's history.

10. Nor does Tropicana claim it does so.

11. A small percentage of Miami's Cuban-Jews has revisited the island, usually to see family members or to assist in humanitarian efforts. A common method of traveling to Cuba is through Jewish Solidarity, the well-known humanitarian aid group founded by Eddie Levy and Xiomara Levy, which delivers medicine, food, books, and other supplies to Jews in Cuba through its annual trips to the island.

12. Many diasporic Cubans, especially those who have lived in exile for many years and have comfortably (re)settled in new locations, have no intention of relocating to their "home" country, their *patria*, upon the (eventual) fall of the Castro regime. Their country of destination has become a "home-place," while Cuba functions more as a spiritual home, held dear in their hearts and memories.

13. The pseudonym "bell hooks" is used by Gloria Watkins. It was her great-grandmother's real name, and Watkins came to use it, in all lowercase letters, during her involvement in the feminist movement in the early 1970s. The idea behind the pseudonym, hooks said in a 1995 interview, was "to critique the idea of stardom," since "it was more important what was being said than who said it." The use of small letters was a way of saying, "It's not really me because I'm not just the book that I've written. I'm a holistic self. And it really does work to make people think about a name. What makes a name important? Those small letters that are kind of equal, that don't have that kind of hierarchical look—has an effect on people" (hooks 1995).

14. In this sense, the term *myths* refers not to *lies* or *false stories*, but rather to the legends and stories which all communities, cultures, and nations use to commemorate specific events which occurred in

their pasts. These often include the establishment of governing bodies, the connection of a group to an image or ideology, memories of war, etc.

15. I shall not elaborate upon the multiple readings which the Boyarins give to Nancy's work, since here I am interested only in discussing the relationship between myth and community.

16. Interestingly, in her history of the "Cuban Jewish Community of the Greater Miami Area," Susan Epstein writes that "the Cuban Jews who arrived in South Florida [in the early 1960s] . . . established *autochthonous* organizations"—referring to Jewish organizations previously established in Cuba (1981: 38; emphasis mine).

17. See chapter 2 for a detailed review of these provisions and objectives.

18. The concept of the "Wandering Jew," as Ruth Behar notes (Behar to CB-L, March 1997), is inherently problematical, functioning as, in Behar's words, "a trope of Jewish and sometimes anti-Jewish discourse." I have included it in the text, however, to preserve Simazi's original language.

# Chapter 5: History, Memory, and Identity: Reflections of a Cuban-Jewish Family

1. The language used depends upon the congregation. The Cuban-Hebrew Congregation, for instance, currently distributes documents primarily in English and Spanish, although documents published fifteen years ago contained primarily Spanish, with significant amounts of Hebrew and Yiddish. Torat Moshe, on the other hand, always has published its bulletin entirely in Spanish.

2. Note that Alberto's estimation of the Jewish population of Cuba is much higher than that of Levine (1993) and many others, who estimate that in the 1950s it was between 10,000 and 16,500. This is particularly interesting, since the official figures cited by these sources are based upon written records kept by Cuba's Jewish community, which often excluded Jews who left the community. Alberto's numbers, then, probably are more accurate than the official estimates, which did not consider people (including migrants) who, once they left, were detached from the community as Jewish Cubans.

3. *Shabbat* is a Hebrew word meaning *rest*. It refers to the Jewish Sabbath, which begins before sunset on Friday and ends at sundown on Saturday (Rosten 1968: 316–17).

4. Habif estimates that, between 1930 and 1960, 1,300 children attended the *Centro Israelita's* school, which emphasized *Yiddishkeit* (a Yiddish word meaning *Jewishness*)—particularly Ashkenazic culture and history (Moreno Habif to CB-L, July 28, 1999).

5. Not all Cuban-Jewish families attend either of the two Cuban synagogues; some choose to attend "American" synagogues. Furthermore, the Cuban synagogues—particularly Torat Moshe—have many non-Cuban members.

6. As I will discuss later in the chapter, the Ralveys often diverge from the "norm" for the Cuban-Jewish community, sometimes describing themselves much differently than do others in the community. This serves to emphasize further the complexities of the diaspora concept within a particular community.

7. The only exceptions to this restriction are the few second-generation Cuban-Jews who have traveled to Cuba either with a visa from the United States government, or without a visa, by means of a third country.

8. According to James Olson and Judith Olson, "the heart and soul of Cuban-American life in the United States and in Miami is the area known as 'La Sagüesera'" (1995: 95). Approximately corresponding to the space of Little Havana, *Sagüesera* is a common colloquialism used to designate any "Latinized" area in Miami.

9. Alberto is a founder of Concilio Cubano, an umbrella organization for various pro–Cuban democracy organizations. This organization is discussed in more detail below.

10. The Cuban government has created similar myths from the opposite perspective. For them, "true Cubans" are those who stayed to support the revolution; exiles, in contrast, are *gusanos*, or worms.

11. As noted in chapter 3, Esther rarely spoke during the interview.

12. It is unlikely that Cubans would have been "accepted by Americans" or could have "integrate[d] with the Americans with no problems" without the progressive political and attitudinal changes of the 1960s. These were already in place when massive Cuban migration occurred in the latter part of the twentieth century. Mexican Americans, among the first residents of the American Southwest, have a much longer and more difficult history in the United States. I strongly disagree with everything Alberto says here about "Chicano" culture, but I include the passage because it helps us understand his personal sense of being Cuban, his *cubanidad.*

13. Albert worked at the Israeli Consulate in Miami in 1996 and 1997.

14. Albert is referring specifically to the phenomenon of "feeling Israeli," as it applies to Jews.

15. The *Sabra,* according to Smadar Lavie, is the "new Israeli-born Jew" (1996: 59). The *Sabra* national identity, she writes, centers around four main themes: a simultaneous celebration of European culture and primitivization of Palestinian culture, a linking of Judaism and communalism on the kibbutz, a reinforcement of military heroism through propagation of the David-and-Goliath myth, and a remembrance of the Holocaust as an archetype of Jewish diasporic persecution (59).

16. I am using the terms "religious" and "secular" Judaism to reflect a distinction made by many Jews between a more traditional observance of the Jewish religion and a looser ethnic or cultural identification with "Jewishness." If one judiciously follows the 613 Commandments, however, no such distinction is possible, since the Commandments designate all aspects of how people should live their lives and are thus Holy (religious). Accordingly, it is human nature that makes people enter the "secular"—i.e., the profane—and then once again seek the Holy as they try to better themselves. Technically speaking, then, there can be no "secular Judaism," since Judaism is defined in part by the (Holy) Commandments (Henry Green to CB-L, July 12 and 24, 1999).

17. Although Hebrew is spoken often within this community, it is reserved primarily for religious services. Ladino is spoken even less frequently, and usually only by the older generation. Spanish is the primary language of communication (see Epstein 1981).

18. Recall Becky Levy's similar discussion in chapter 3. She discusses being the first of all her cousins to attend college outside South Florida.

19. This conversation is from a later date and is between Albert and me only.

20. Upon reading the transcript of this interview, Esther emphasized to me that Albert was wrong. Alberto, she told me, "was applying to leave Cuba for thirteen years after the 1959 Revolution. He would've gone to Israel in a minute," she said, "but there were a lot of obstacles to getting out, even when they cracked the door open." I silently wondered: was Albert simply mistaken about his father's relationship to Israel, or was there something deeper? Perhaps Albert did not want his father to have a strong claim to knowledge, experience, support, or emotion concerning Israel, so that Albert could be the expert on Israel. Albert could not possibly match his father's expertise on Cuba, so perhaps he chose to become an experienced Zionist to compensate.

21. I am describing the real family name, not "Ralvey," which is a pseudonym.

22. *Motek* is Hebrew slang for *sweetie;* when said by a man to a woman, it often has a patronizing connotation (Naomi Brenner to CB-L, Mar. 16, 1999). See chapter 3 for further contextualization of Albert's use of this term to address me.

23. In a later e-mail message, Albert explained, "My parents had no choice [but to give me the last name of García], [since] in Cuba it was very hard to change names legally . . . The Diego was my mother's Paternal Stepfather, a Spaniard who converted to Judaism and died when she was very young."

24. According to Albert, "the 'Union Liberal Cubana' was modeled after the Czech Liberal Union and other Liberal Unions that worked in Communist countries of Eastern Europe before the collapse. It was begun by people like Carlos Alberto Montaner, Cuban-born publisher and writer, in order to combat the totalitarian system in Cuba. It emphasizes its opposition on the grounds of human rights violations; yet it is small and stands as a philosophical opposition to the *Fundación Cubana Americana* [Cuban-American National Fdn. (CANF), of which Jorge Mas Canosa was founder]. My father is part of this group and we maintain a close personal friendship with Carlos Alberto. They support Concilio Cubano, which works within Cuba."

25. Note Alberto's use of the term "Cubans" to designate white Gentile Cubans, something which he emphasized throughout the interview by qualifying the Cuban identity of "other" Cubans, such as Afro-Cubans.

26. Alberto emphasized his link with the United States throughout the interview.

27. Just as many of my interlocutors and I did throughout our discussions, Albert conflates being pro-Israel with being Zionist. There is a fundamental distinction, however. A Zionist (such as Albert) makes *aliyah* to Israel, whereas a pro-Israeli American (such as Alberto) will support Israel monetarily and morally but has no intention to make *aliyah* (Henry Green to CB-L, July 23, 1999).

28. The story of Cuban-Jewish involvement with pro-Israel causes in both pre-revolutionary Cuba and Miami is one of the issues documented most widely in the sparse literature on the Cuban-Jews. See, e.g., Bejarano 1991, Bejarano 1996, Kahn 1981, Levine 1993, Sapir 1948, Cuban-Hebrew Congregation 1981, and bulletins from Temple Moses/Torat Moshe.

29. The realization that these Cuban-Jews could not speak Spanish, the language of the Cuban-Jewish community, disappointed Albert. He attributes this to the assimilation process, whereby Cuban-Jews have become increasingly "American" (see chapter 7).

# Chapter 6: The "Other" Cuban Jews: Émigrés of the 1970s, 1980s, and 1990s

1. For a portrait of Cuban and Cuban American diversity, see Ruth Behar, *Bridges to Cuba* (1995a), an eclectic collection of poems, artwork, and prose by Cubans on both sides of the Florida Straits. For a portrait of Jewish diversity throughout the United States, see Abraham D. Lavender, *A Coat of Many Colors: Jewish Subcommunities in the United Sates* (1977). This book includes descriptions of the "other Jews": small-town Jews, southern Jews, poor Jews, Cuban Jews, Hasidic Jews, black Jews, Jewish women, and Sephardic Jews.

2. For further discussion of this, see, e.g., Behar 1995a; García 1996; Grenier and Stepick 1993; Masud-Piloto 1996; and Portes and Stepick 1993.

3. *Havana Nagila* is a film produced by Laura Paull, a Jewish woman from California, who stumbled across a reference to the Jewish community of Havana in a short article on an altogether unrelated topic (the Pan-American Games in Havana) in the *San Francisco Chronicle* in 1992. A journalist with filmmaking experience, Paull traveled to Havana to document "the story of the forgotten Cuban Jews" (Paull 1996: 1). The resulting sixty-minute film, released in 1995, celebrates the revival of the Jewish community on the island since the Cuban government's loosening of its policy on religion in

October 1991, when delegates at the Fourth Cuban Congress voted to allow Communist Party members to practice their religious faiths. Jacob, an active member of the rejuvenated Jewish community, was featured prominently in the film.

4. There are notable exceptions to the Cuban-Jewish community's general avoidance of Cuban politics, such as Bernardo Benes, who organized and coordinated *El Diálogo* with the Castro government in 1978 (see chapter 2).

5. The last "major" wave of Cuban-Jews to arrive in Miami encompassed 400 Jews who came in 1980, through the Mariel Boatlift (Levine 1996: 802).

6. The Ralvey family, as noted previously, arrived in Miami in 1979, in the wake of *El Diálogo.*

7. Cuban-Jews, he notes, are found among the most prominent members of the larger Jewish community in Miami; thus, he thinks, discrimination/exclusion is not drawn along national lines.

8. Indeed, many members of the Cuban-Jewish community, especially the Sephardim and older community members, live in close proximity to their synagogues in Miami Beach.

9. Albert did not elaborate upon what actually transpired between his father and the community upon his arrival in 1979, or how this tension was resolved.

10. As mentioned previously, however, few 1960s émigrés have relatives remaining on the island today.

# Chapter 7: Transformations of *Jubanidad:* Forecasts for the Cuban-Jewish Community

1. As is discussed below, its involvement in this realm is decreasing.

2. Note how Cuban-Jews are emphasized more than other Latin American Jews in this Division. This reflects the Cuban-Jewish community's high level of involvement in the federation, as well as the simple fact that the 1960s exiles arrived in Miami earlier than most Jews from other Latin American countries.

3. Both Damien and I had been using the terms "Cuban-Jewish" and "Jewish-Cuban" interchangeably in our conversation; his use of the term should be understood in the same context as his saying "Cuban-Jewish."

4. It must be remembered that the Cuban-Hebrew Congregation is not *the* representative Cuban-Jewish institution for *all* Cuban-Jews. Torat Moshe and Temple Menorah may function as such for their respective constituencies. For Ashkenazic Damien, however, the Cuban-Hebrew Congregation is the representative institution of the Cuban-Jews.

5. See, e.g., Gilfarb 1981: 29.

6. This sentence was followed by an "Internet vocabulary" symbol, in the shape of a frown, used to express sadness or disappointment.

7. This vignette takes place in May 1999. Note that Behar is a very common last name among Sephardim.

8. Guines was a small rural town 48 kilometers southwest of Havana (Barrocas 1981: 85).

# Chapter 8: Cuban-Jewish Identity in the Borderlands

1. Isaac does not remember the exact year of his family's departure.

2. A *yeshiva* is a rabbinical college or seminary where Jews (traditionally men) meet to study and discuss the Torah and Talmud.

3. These labels are inherently problematic, as the following discussion indicates.

4. Cubans in Miami traditionally have mixed less with African Americans than with Anglo Americans. Tension between Cubans and African Americans centers around socioeconomic and political differences. While the recently arrived Cubans have enjoyed relative socioeconomic and political success, Miami's African Americans have faced tumultuous times over the past four decades, including riots, poverty, unemployment, and the lack of a strong political voice. According to the 1990 U.S. Census, 30 percent of "Non-Hispanic Blacks," compared to 16 percent of Cubans, lived below the poverty line (Boswell and Skop 1995: 37). Additionally, as Cubans arrived *en masse* throughout the 1960s and 1970s, many blacks watched in disbelief and dismay as these "temporary guests" immediately became the recipients of social and educational programs which the Civil Rights Movement had fought so long and hard to achieve. Such programs, moreover, had been implemented for blacks only half-heartedly, even after they were authorized by law (García 1996: 40). The tension arises from the opposite direction, too. Some working-class Cubans today express animosity toward blacks, who, they assert, are taking advantage of federal affirmative action and welfare programs at the expense of poor Cubans, who are ineligible for affirmative action. For a detailed discussion of this tension between the Cuban and African American communities, see Grenier and Stepick 1992; Boswell 1996; Boswell, Cruz-Báez, and Zijlstra 1996; Sheskin 1992.

5. The "time-space compression" Harvey describes is complicated by the political relationship between the United States and Cuba. Among most countries and cultures throughout the world, travel and communication are becoming increasingly easy; yet they have been increasingly difficult and complicated between these two "neighbors." This situation has allowed each culture to exclude the other from its notion of national identity, complicating questions of homeland and nationality still further.

# Works Cited

Anonymous

1990    Marti: Maestro Ejemplar, in *El Reporter de Dade* (Jan.–Feb., 1990): 5

Anzaldúa, Gloria

1987    *Borderlands/La Frontera: The New Mestiza.* San Francisco: Spinsters/Aunt Lute.

Appadurai, Arjun

1990    Disjuncture and Difference in the Global Cultural Economy. *Public Culture* 2, no. 2: 1–24.

Asís, Moisés

1989    El Judaísmo Cubano durante 30 años de revolución (1959–1989). *Coloquio* [Buenos Aires] 22: n.p.

Barrocas, Albert

1981    The Jews of Cuba. In *Sephardim and a History of Congregation Or VeShalom*, ed. Sol Benton, pp. 84–86. Atlanta, Ga. Congregation Or VeShalom.

Bayor, Ronald

1990    Models of Ethnic and Racial Politics in the Urban Sunbelt South. In *Searching for the Sunbelt*, ed. Raymond Mohl, pp. 110–11. Knoxville: Univ. of Tennessee Press.

Behar, Ruth

1995a    Bridges to Cuba. Ann Arbor: Univ. of Michigan Press.

1995b    Juban América. *Poetics Today* 16, no. 1 (Spring): 151–70.

1996    *The Vulnerable Observer: Anthropology That Breaks Your Heart.* Boston: Beacon Press.

Behar, Ruth, and Deborah Gordon, eds.

1995    *Women Writing Culture.* Berkeley: Univ. of California Press.

Bejarano, Margalit

1985    Los Sefaradíes, pioneros de la inmigración judía a Cuba. *Rumbos en el Judaísmo, el Sionismo e Israel* 14: 107–22.

1986    *Religious Repression in Cuba.* Coral Gables, Fla.: Cuban Studies Project, Institute of Interamerican Studies.

1988    *The Deproletarianization of Cuban Jews.* Judaica Latinoamericana, Estudios Histórico-Sociales. Jerusalem: Editorial Universitaria Magnes Press and Hebrew Univ.

1990a    The Cuban Jewish Community Today. *Jerusalem Letter* 117 (Dec. 19): 1–7.

1990b    Anti-Semitism in Cuba under Democratic, Military, and Revolutionary Regimes, 1944–1963. *Patterns of Prejudice* 24, no. 1: 32–46.

1991    The Jewish Community of Cuba: Between Continuity and Extinction. *Jewish Political Studies Review* 3, nos. 1–2: 115–40.

1993 [1990]*Cuba as America's Back Door: The Case of Jewish Immigration.* Judaica Latinoamericana, Estudios Histórico-Sociales. Jerusalem: Editorial Universitaria Magnes Press and Hebrew Univ.

1994     *The Jewish Community of South Florida: Proceedings of the Eleventh World Congress of Jewish Studies.* Jerusalem: World Union of Jewish Studies.

1996a    The Integration of Sephardic Jews into Hispanic America: The Cases of Buenos Aires and Havana. In *Memoires Juives d'Espagne en du Portugal,* ed. E. Benbassa. Paris: Publisud.

1996b    *La Comunidad Hebrea de Cuba: La Memoria y la Historia.* Jerusalem: Avraham Harman Institute of Contemporary Jewry, Hebrew Univ.

Benes, Bernardo, and Ofelia Ruder, eds.

1989     El Nuevo Jewban 2, no. 2 (Sept.). Miami: Cuban Hebrew Congregation of Miami.

Bernstein, Jacob

1998a    Passport to Paradox. *Miami New Times,* Aug. 6, 1998.

1998b    Twice Exiled. *Miami New Times,* Nov. 12, 1998.

Biniakonsky, Jacobo

1965     Círculo Cubano Hebreo de Miami: Continuación de 40 años de vida social Hebrea de Cuba. *Boletín Mensual* [Cuban-Hebrew Congregation of Miami], vol. I, no. I (Nov.): 12–13.

Boswell, Thomas D.

1994     *The Cubanization and Hispanicization of Metropolitan Miami.* Miami: Cuban-American National Council.

1996     *Residential Segregation by Socioeconomic Class in Metropolitan Miami.* Issue Brief 5 (Apr.). Miami: Cuban-American National Council.

Boswell, Thomas D., and Emily Skop

1995     *Hispanic National Groups in Metropolitan Miami.* Miami: Cuban-American National Council.

Boswell, Thomas; Angel David Cruz-Báez; and Pauline Zijlstra

1996     *Attitudes of Blacks Toward Housing Discrimination in Metropolitan Miami.* Issue Brief 6 (Aug.). Miami: Cuban-American National Council.

Boyarin, Daniel, and Jonathan Boyarin

1993     Diaspora: Generation and the Ground of Jewish Identity. *Critical Inquiry* 19 (Summer): 693–725.

Boyarin, Jonathan

1992     *Storm from Paradise: The Politics of Jewish Memory.* Minneapolis: Univ. of Minnesota Press.

Brenner, Philip

1989     *The Cuba Reader: The Making of a Revolutionary Society.* New York: Grove Press.

Burt, Bonnie

1994     *The Believers: Stories from Jewish Havana.* Film. Bonnie Burt Productions, 2600 Tenth Street, Berkeley, Ca., 94710.

1995     *Abraham and Eugenia: Stories from Jewish Cuba.* Film. Bonnie Burt Productions, 2600 Tenth Street, Berkeley, Ca., 94710.

Butler, Judith

1962     Contingent Foundations: Feminism and the Question of Postmodernism. In *Feminists Theorize the Political,* ed. J. Butler and J. Scott, pp. 3–22. New York: Routledge.

Campa, Román de la

1994    The Latino Diaspora in the United States: Sojourns from a Cuban Past. *Public Culture* 6: 293–317.

Castro, Fidel

1962    *History Will Absolve Me.* Havana: Editorial en Marcha.

Chardy, Alfonso

1990    As Jews Dwindle in Cuba, They Flourish in Miami. *Miami Herald,* Sept. 22, 1990, pp. 1B, 4B.

Clary, Mike

1998    Miami's Man in Havana. *Miami New Times,* Apr. 30, 1998.

Clifford, James

1994    Diasporas. *Cultural Anthropology* 9, no. 3: 302–38.

Clifford, James, and George E. Marcus, eds.

1986    *Writing Culture: The Poetics and Politics of Ethnography.* Berkeley: Univ. of California Press.

Cobian, Marina Esteva

1965    Versos Para Ti/Cuba: A Pearl in the Vast Blue Sea. In *Boletín Mensual* [Cuban-Hebrew Congregation of Miami], vol. I, no. I (Nov.): 22–23.

Cuban American National Council, Inc.

1996    Study Examines Hispanic Jews Living in Dade. *The Council Letter* II, no. 3, p.3.

Cuban Council/Concilio Cubano

1995    Official Statement by the Cuban Council. Havana: Cuban Council/Concilio Cubano, Oct. 10.

Cuban-Hebrew Congregation of Miami/Temple Beth Shmuel

1981    Balnearios. In *Círculo Cubano-Hebreo de Miami, 1961–1981: 20 Aniversario.* P. 30. Miami: Cuban-Hebrew Congregation of Miami.

1981    Comité de Actividades Religiosas. In *Círculo Cubano-Hebreo de Miami, 1961–1981: 20 Aniversario.* Pp. 18–19. Miami: Cuban-Hebrew Congregation of Miami.

1981    Actividades Juveniles. In *Círculo Cubano-Hebreo de Miami, 1961–1981: 20 Aniversario.* Pp. 28. Miami: Cuban-Hebrew Congregation of Miami.

1981    Historia de la Casa de la Comunidad Hebrea de Cuba en Miami. In *Círculo Cubano Hebreo de Miami, 1961–1981: 20 Aniversario.* Pp. 49–51. Miami: Cuban-Hebrew Congregation of Miami.

1981    ¿Vandalismo o Terrorismo? In *Círculo Cubano Hebreo de Miami, 1961–1981: 20 Aniversario.* P. 76. Miami: Cuban-Hebrew Congregation of Miami.

1981    *Círculo Cubano-Hebreo de Miami, 1961–1981: 20 Aniversario.* Miami: Cuban Hebrew Congregation of Miami.

1986    *Círculo Cubano-Hebreo de Miami, 1961–1986: 25 Aniversario,* Miami: Cuban-Hebrew Congregation of Miami.

1997    *1961–1997: Celebrating Thirty-six Years.* Miami: Cuban-Hebrew Congregation of Miami.

Dibble, Sandra

1985    Cuban Jews Suspicious of Castro for Letting Rabbis Visit. *Miami Herald,* Apr. 14, 1985, pp. 2B.

Dijour, Ilya

1962      Jewish Immigration to the United States. *American Jewish Yearbook*. Vol. 63. New York: American Jewish Committee and Jewish Publication Society of New York, p. 146–49.

Dudai, Shimon

1996      From the Rabbi's Desk. *Bulletin of Temple Beth Shmuel–Cuban Hebrew Congregation of Miami* 4 (Oct.–Dec.): I.

Duncan, W. Raymond

1993      Cuba–U.S. Relations and Political Contradictions in Cuba. In *Conflict and Change in Cuba*, ed. Enrique A. Baloyra and James A. Morris, pp. 215–41. Albuquerque: Univ. of New Mexico Press.

Edelstein, Jenny

1996      Art Auction at Temple Beth Shmuel. *Bulletin of Temple Beth Shmuel–Cuban Hebrew Congregation of Miami* 4 (Oct.–Dec.): 5.

Entre Nosotros

1996      Isaac Zelcer: Un líder en mucho más que textiles. *Entre Nosotros: La Revista de Las Comunidades Judías de Hispano-América* 4 (Aug.–Oct.): 5–7.

Epstein, Susan R.

1981      The Cuban Sephardic Community of Miami, Florida: History and Judezmo Language. Master's thesis, Univ. of Florida, Gainesville.

Fernández, Lourdes

1986a      Un hogar Cubano-Judío en el centro de Miami Beach. *Miami Herald*, Nov. 13, 1986, p. 9.

1986b      For Cuban-Jews, Congregation's a Meeting Place. *Miami Herald*, Nov. 13, 1986, p. 12.

Fishkoff, Sue

1993      A Revolution of Faith. *Jerusalem Post Magazine*, Sept. 15, 1993, pp. 6–12.

Foster, Robert

1991      Making National Cultures in the Global Ecumene. *Annual Review of Anthropology* 20: 235–60.

Gambach, Nesim

1990      Martí en lo Hebreo. *El Reporter de Dade* (Jan.–Feb.): 7.

García, María Cristina

1996      *Havana U.S.A.* Berkeley: Univ. of California Press.

Gendler, Everett

1969      Holy Days in Habana. *Conservative Judaism* 23, (Winter): 15–24.

Gilfarb, Yosele

1981      We Must Continue. In *Círculo Cubano-Hebreo de Miami, 20 Aniversario, 1961–1981*, pp. 29. Miami: Cuban-Hebrew Congregation of Miami.

Gold, Salomón

1989      Bonds that Bind. *El Nuevo Jewban* 2 (Sept.): I.

Gorfinkel, Estelita

1996        Women's League of Temple Beth Shmuel. *Bulletin of Temple Beth Shmuel–Cuban Hebrew Congregation of Miami* 4 (Oct.–Dec.): 4.

Green, Henry A.

1995        *Gesher Vakesher/Bridges and Bonds: The Life of Leon Kronish.* Atlanta, Ga.: Scholars Press.

Green, Henry A., and Marcia K. Zerivitz

1991        *Jewish Life in Florida: A Documentary Exhibit from 1763 to the Present.* Coral Gables, Fla.: Mosaic, Inc.

Greenberg, Hayim

1951        Jewish Culture and Education in the Diaspora. *Jewish Frontier* 17, no. 12: 11–19.

Grenier, Guillermo J., and Alex Stepick, eds.

1992        *Miami Now! Immigration, Ethnicity, and Social Change.* Gainesville: Univ. Press of Florida.

Gupta, Akhil, and James Ferguson

1992        Beyond 'Culture': Space, Identity, and the Politics of Difference. *Cultural Anthropology* 7, no. 1: 6–23.

Harvey, David

1990        *The Condition of Postmodernity: An Enquiry into the Origins of Cultural Change.* Oxford, England: Basil Blackwell.

Hochman, David P.

1994        Rabbi Search Committee Report. *Bulletin of Temple Beth Shmuel–Cuban Hebrew Congregation of Miami* (Feb.): 4.

1996        What Is Jewish Generation X (J/X)? *Bulletin of Temple Beth Shmuel–Cuban Hebrew Congregation of Miami* 4 (Oct.–Dec.): 9.

hooks, bell

1991        *Yearning: Race, Gender, and Cultural Politics.* London: Turnaround.

1995        Interview on C-SPAN's *Booknotes.* Nov. 19, 1995.

Izzy

1965        Estampas de un Refugiado. In *Boletín Mensual* [Cuban-Hebrew Congregation of Miami], vol. I, no. 1 (Nov.): 14–15.

Jewish Floridian

1979        Miami's Cuban Jews: 20 Years after the Revolution. *Federation Magazine of the Jewish Floridian,* Oct. 12, pp. 14–18.

Jrade, Moisés

1996        Mensaje del Presidente del Sephardic Congregation of Florida. *Sephardic Congregation of Florida–Torat Moshe* (May–Aug.): 2.

Kahn, Jeffrey A.

1981        The History of the Jewish Colony in Cuba. Ordination master's thesis, Jewish Institute of Religion, Hebrew Union College, Cincinnati, Ohio.

Kaplan, S.; R. Moncarz; and J. Steinberg

1990     Jewish Emigrants to Cuba: 1898–1960. *International Migration Review* [Geneva, Switzerland], vol. 28, no. 3: 295–310.

Kelton, Arón

1981     Mensaje de Nuestro Presidente. In *Círculo Cubano-Hebreo de Miami, 20 Aniversario, 1961–1981,* p. 5. Miami: Cuban-Hebrew Congregation of Miami.

Kochanski, Mendel

1951     The Jewish Community in Cuba. *Jewish Frontier* 18 (Sept.): 25–27.

Konovitch, Barry J.

1986     Cuban American Jews Take Pride in Rich Heritage 30 Years Later. In *Círculo Cubano-Hebreo de Miami, 1961–1986: 25 Aniversario,* p. 92. Miami: Cuban-Hebrew Congregation of Miami.

1990     To the Editor of the *New York Times. El Nuevo Jewban* 5 (Jan.): 2–3.

Landers, Peggy

1988     Growing Up in South Florida: It's a Seductive, Sunny, Rich, Dangerous, Challenging Place That Thousands of Teens Call Home. *Miami Herald,* Dec. 11, 1988, p. 1G.

Laughlin, Meg

1994     Bernardo's List. *Miami Herald* (Tropic section), Nov. 6, 1994, pp. 2, 6–18.

Lavender, Abraham, ed.

1977     *A Coat of Many Colors: Jewish Subcommunities in the United States.* Westport, Conn.: Greenwood Press.

Lavie, Smadar

1996     Blowups in the Borderzones: Third World Israeli Authors' Gropings for Home. In *Displacement, Diaspora, and Geographies of Identity,* ed. Smadar Lavie and Ted Swedenburg, pp. 55–96. Durham, N.C.: Duke Univ. Press.

Lavie, Smadar, and Ted Swedenburg

1996     Introduction to *Displacement, Diaspora, and Geographies of Identity,* ed. Smadar Lavie and Ted Swedenburg, pp. 1–25. Durham, N.C.: Duke Univ. Press.

Lerman, Isidoro

1965     Carta del Editor. In *Boletín Mensual* [Cuban-Hebrew Congregation of Miami], vol. 1, no. 1 (Nov.): 5.

Levine, Robert M.

1993     *Tropical Diaspora: The Jewish Experience in Cuba.* Gainesville: Univ. Press of Florida.

1996     Cuba. In *The World Reacts to the Holocaust,* ed. D. Wyman, pp. 782–808. Baltimore: Johns Hopkins Univ. Press.

Levine, Robert M., and Mark D. Szuchman

1985     *Hotel Cuba.* Videotape. Coral Gables, Fla.: Univ. of Miami. Distributed by Univ. of Illinois Film Service, Urbana.

Liebman, Seymour B.

1977     Cuban Jewish Community in South Florida. In *A Coat of Many Colors: Jewish Subcommunities in the United States,* ed. Abraham D. Lavender, pp. 296–304. Westport, Conn.: Greenwood Press.

Mankekar, Purnima

1994     Reflections on Diasporic Identities: A Prolegomenon to an Analysis of Political Bifocality. *Diasporas* 3, no. 3: 349–71.

Marcus, George E., and Michael M. J. Fischer

1986     *Anthropology as Cultural Critique: An Experimental Moment in the Human Sciences.* Chicago: Univ. of Chicago Press.

Massey, Doreen

1992     A Place Called Home? *New Formations* 17 (Summer): 3–15.

Masud-Piloto, Félix Roberto

1996     *From Welcomed Exiles to Illegal Immigrants.* Lanham, Md.: Rowman and Littlefield.

Matterin, Abraham Marcus

1954     Nuestro Homenaje a Martí en Yiddish. *In Colección "Martí Visto por Hebreos,"* ed. Abraham Matterin, pp. 5–8. Havana: Agrupación Cultural Hebreo-Cubana.

Medin, Lisa

1989     Zionism: The Cuban Experience. Unpublished paper. Ziff Jewish Museum of Florida or Univ. of Miami, History or Latin American Studies Departments.

Melarmed, Meir Matzliah

198(?)     *Breve Historia de los Judíos de Cuba y la Comunidad Sefaradita de Miami. [Brief History of the Jews of Cuba and the Sephardic Community of Miami.]* Miami: N.p.

Mizrahi, Judith

1993     *703 American Sephardim: Diversity Within Cohesiveness.* New York: Gemini Books.

Moore, Deborah Dash

1994     *To the Golden Cities: Pursuing the American Jewish Dream in Miami and L.A.* New York: Free Press.

Morales, Rosario

1986     "I Am the Reasonable One," in *Getting Home Alive,* ed. Aurora Levins Morales and Rosario Morales. Ithaca: Firebrand Books, 147–49.

Muñoz, José Esteban

1995     No es fácil: Notes on the Negotiation of Cubanidad and Exilic Memory in Carmelita Tropicana's *Milk of Amnesia. Drama Review* 39, no. 3: 76–82.

Nancy, Jean Luc

1991     *The Inoperative Community,* trans. Peter Connor et al., ed. Connor (Minneapolis, 1991).

National Council of Jewish Women (NCJW)

1960     *Bulletin* (Oct.).

1961     *Bulletin* (Jan., Mar., May, Dec.).

1962    *Bulletin* (Jan., Mar., May, Dec.).

1963    *Bulletin* (Feb., Mar., May).

Navarro, Mireya

1997    Inside Miami's Little Havana, a Quiet Change of Accents. *New York Times,* Apr. 6, 1997, pp. 1, 12.

El Nuevo Jewban

1970    Yearbook. Miami: Cuban-Hebrew Congregation of Miami, Inc.

1998    *Cuban-Hebrew Congregation of Miami, Inc.* 4, no. 3 (Apr.).

Olson, James S., and Judith E. Olson

1995    *Cuban Americans: From Trauma to Triumph.* New York: Twayne Publishers.

Oppenheimer, Andrés, and Nery Ynclán

1985    Cuba to Let Rabbis Lead Ceremonies. *Miami Herald,* Apr. 11, 1985, p. 7A.

Otmezguine, Serge

1998    Memo, American Sephardi Federation, South Florida Branch, Ref. "Vision Quest" Committee Agenda, June 7, 1998.

Papo, Joseph M.

1987    *Sephardim in Twentieth-Century America: In Search of Unity.* San Jose, California: Pelé Yoetz Books.

Paull, Laura

1995    *Havana Nagila.* Film. Paull Productions. San Francisco, Ca.

1996    Our Film Crew of Three: My Husband, the Internet, and Me. World Wide Web.

Pedraza, Silvia

1992    Cubans in Exile, 1959–1989: The State of the Research. In *Cuban Studies Since the Revolution,* ed. Damien Fernández, pp. 235–57. Gainesville: Univ. Press of Florida.

1996    Cuba's Refugees: Manifold Migrations. In *Origins and Destinies: Immigration, Race, and Ethnicity in America,* ed. Silvia Pedraza and Reuben Rumbaut, 1st ed., pp. 263–79. Belmont, Ca.: Wadsworth Publishing Company.

Pérez, Louis A., Jr.

1995    *Cuba: Between Reform and Revolution.* Oxford, England: Oxford Univ. Press.

Pérez Firmat, Gustavo

1995    *Next Year in Cuba.* New York: Anchor Books.

Pitchón, Marco

1953    *José Martí y la comprensión humana.* Havana.

Portes, Alejandro, and Alex Stepick

1993    *City on the Edge.* Berkeley: Univ. of California Press.

Rand McNally

1997    Metro Areas. In *Rand McNally 1997 Commercial Atlas and Marketing Guide,* 128th ed., p. 125. United States: Rand McNally.

Reyler, Félix

1965 El Perfil Fascista de Castro. In *Boletín Mensual* [Cuban-Hebrew Congregation of Miami], I, no. I (Nov.): 20–21.

1981 Los Primeros Años del Círculo. In *Círculo Cubano-Hebreo de Miami, 1961–1981: 20 Aniversario,* pp. 7–9. Miami: Cuban-Hebrew Congregation of Miami.

Rosten, Leo

1968 *The Joys of Yiddish.* New York: McGraw-Hill.

Román, David

1995 Carmelita Tropicana Unplugged. *Drama Review* 39, no. 3: 83–93.

Rosichan, Arthur S.

1961 The Cuban Refugee Situation. Paper presented at National Conference on Jewish Communal Service, Boston, May 1961.

Rushdie, Salman

1991 Imaginary Homelands. In *Imaginary Homelands: Essays and Criticism, 1981–1991,* ed. Salman Rushdie, pp. 9–21. New York: Viking Penguin.

Said, Edward

1979 Zionism from the Standpoint of Its Victims. *Social Text* I: 7–58.

Sanford L. Ziff Jewish Museum of Florida

1997 *Jewish Settlement in Florida.* Film. Sanford L. Ziff Jewish Museum of Florida/Historical Preservation Division of the Department of State.

Sapir, Boris

1948 *The Jewish Community of Cuba: Settlement and Growth.* Simon Wolin, trans. New York: JTSP Univ. Press.

Sephardic Congregation of Florida–Torat Moshe

1995a *Newsletter* (Jan.–Feb.).

1995b *Newsletter* (Mar.–Apr.).

1995c *Newsletter* (May, June, July, Aug.).

1996 *Newsletter* (May–June–July–Aug.).

Shenon, Philip

1999 U.S. to Allow Two More Cities to Set Flights to Havana. *New York Times,* Aug. 4, 1999, p. A8.

Sheskin, Ira M.

1992 The Miami Ethnic Archipelago. *Florida Geographer* 26 (Oct.): 40–57.

1994 *1994 Jewish Demographic Study of Dade County.* Miami: Greater Miami Jewish Federation.

Stanley, David

1997 *Cuba: A Lonely Planet Travel Survival Kit.* Hawthorn, Australia: Lonely Planet Publications.

Stuart, Mark A.

1973 Cuban Jews Are Alive and Well in Miami. *National Jewish Monthly* (Jan.): 44–46.

Temple Moses/Florida Sephardic Congregation

1979     *Libro de Oro*. Miami: Temple Moses/Comunidad Sefaradita de Florida.

Torres, María de los Angeles

1995     Encuentros y Encontronazos: Homeland in the Politics and Identity of the Cuban Diaspora. *Diaspora* 4, no. 2: 211–38.

Tropicana, Carmelita

1995     Milk of Amnesia/Leche de Amnesia. *Drama Review* 39, no. 3: 94–111.

Tyler, Stephen A.

1986     Post-Modern Ethnography: From Document of the Occult to Occult Document. In *Writing Culture: The Poetics and Politics of Ethnography*, ed. James Clifford and George Marcus, pp. 122–41. Berkeley: Univ. of California Press.

United States Department of the Treasury, Office of Foreign Assets Control

1999     *Cuba: What You Need to Know About the U.S. Embargo and Travel Restrictions*. Washington, D.C.: Office of Foreign Assets Control.

Vainstein, Abraham Z.

1954     De Cara al Sol. Poem. In *Colección "Martí Visto por Hebreos,"* ed. Abraham Matterin. Pp. 9–12. Havana: Agrupación Cultural Hebreo-Cubana.

Viglucci, Andrés S.

1984     Judíos cubanos se amoldan a nuevos tiempos. *Miami Herald*, Oct. 4, 1984, pp. 1, 5.

Vincent, Joan

1991     Engaging Historicism. In *Recapturing Anthropology: Working in the Present*, ed. Richard Fox, pp. 45–58. Santa Fe, New Mexico: School of American Research Press.

Volsky, George

1980     A Torah from Cuba Marks an End and a Beginning. *New York Times*, Sept. 20, 1980, pp. 1, 6.

White, Oscar A.

1965     Message from the President. In *Boletín Mensual* [Cuban-Hebrew Congregation of Miami], vol. 1, no. 1 (Nov.): 4.

# Index

Cuban Jewish Journeys was designed and typeset on a Macintosh computer system using PageMaker software. The text is set in Centaur and the chapter openings are set in Whassis ICG Calm. This book was designed by David Alcorn, typeset by Cheryl Carrington, and manufactured by Thomson-Shore, Inc. The paper used in this book is designed for an effective life of at least three hundred years.